OAKTON COMMUNITY COLLEGE

Des Plaines, Illinois

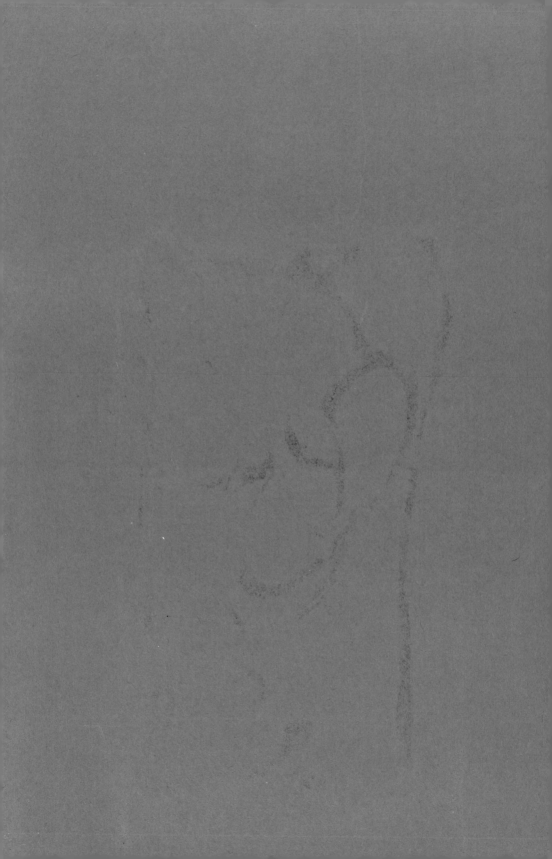

STALIN'S SUCCESSORS
Leadership, stability, and change in the Soviet Union

STALIN'S SUCCESSORS

57502

Leadership, stability, and change
in the Soviet Union

SEWERYN BIALER

Research Institute on International Change
Columbia University

CAMBRIDGE UNIVERSITY PRESS

Cambridge
London   New York   New Rochelle
Melbourne   Sydney

To J.M.A.

Published by the Press Syndicate of the University of Cambridge
The Pitt Building, Trumpington Street, Cambridge CB2 1RP
32 East 57th Street, New York, NY 10022, USA
296 Beaconsfield Parade, Middle Park, Melbourne 3206, Australia

© Cambridge University Press 1980

First published 1980

Printed in the United States of America
Typeset by Huron Valley Graphics, Ann Arbor, Michigan
Printed and bound by The Book Press, Brattleboro, Vermont

Library of Congress Cataloging in Publication Data
Bialer, Seweryn.
Stalin's successors.
Includes index.
1. Russia–Politics and government–1953–
2. Elite (Social sciences)–Russia. I. Title.
JN6581.B5   320.947   80–12037
ISBN 0 521 23518 9

CONTENTS

Preface		*page vii*
Introduction		1
Part I	Stalinism and the Soviet Political System	5
1	The Mature Stalinist System	9
2	Stalin and the Soviet Political Elite	29
3	Stalinism and the Evolution of the Soviet Polity	47
Part II	Succession and Turnover of Soviet Elites	63
4	The Approaching Succession: The Top Leader	69
5	The Approaching Succession: Leadership and Elite Turnover	81
6	The Approaching Succession: Generational Change	97
Part III	The Nature and Extent of Soviet Political Stability	127
7	Stability: Analytical Considerations	129
8	Soviet Stability and Its Sources	141
9	Soviet Political Stability and the Question of Legitimacy	183
10	Soviet Stability and the National Problem	207
Part IV	Soviet Perceptions of International Affairs and Trends in Soviet Foreign Policy	227
11	The Centrality of U.S.-Soviet Relations	233
12	The Arms Race and the Correlation of Forces	241
13	The Role of the Military Factor in International Relations	255
14	The Third World and the Translation of Power into Influence	269
Part V	Prospects for the 1980s	281
15	The Politics of Stringency	283
Index		306

PREFACE

This book was written in fifteen months, during a leave of absence from Columbia University in the academic year 1978–9; however, it has been in the making for a much longer time. The book presents a synthesis of the post-Stalinist evolution of the Soviet system. It draws on two decades of intense study of the Soviet Union; regular reading of Soviet primary materials and secondary sources; countless talks with Soviet academics and officials, dissidents and émigrés; and long discussions with colleagues in the field.

The writing of the book was supported in part by a grant from the National Council for Soviet and East European Research and in part by a research fellowship at the Lehrman Institute in New York. My deep appreciation goes to the Lehrman Institute and its Executive Director Nicholas Rizopoulos, not only for sponsoring my leave and research, but especially for providing the most stimulating intellectual environment a writer could wish for. I profited immensely from the seminars organized by the Institute to discuss separate chapters of my manuscript. I am grateful to all who participated in those sessions; in particular, I wish to thank Dr. Robert Legvold, Dr. Michael Mandelbaum, Mr. Robert Kaiser, and Dr. Myron Rush. Needless to say, I alone bear responsibility for the ideas and viewpoints expressed in the final manuscript.

The staff of the Research Institute on International Change of Columbia University provided constant support. I am very grateful to my administrative assistant, Penny Yee, and to my indefatigable research assistants, Cynthia Roberts and Michael Klecheski, who assisted me at all stages of research and writing. I thank as well Kathryn Dodgson, who assisted with proofreading, and Michael Klecheski and Richard Coffman, who prepared the Index.

My last words of thanks go to my wife Joan. Despite the heavy burden of her own professional work, she gave willingly and generously the wisdom and logic of friendly, honest criticism and meticulous attention to matters of structure and style. Without her steady and patient encouragement and without her help this book would not have been written.

Wendell, Massachusetts   S.B.
1 March 1980

If Communist systems are arrested at their present stage of development they will inevitably decay, for "not to advance is to recede." The decay of the Communist political system will make it as a phenomenon of the modernization-mobilization stage, incapable of generating from within itself the capacity to persist by changing. *Like the dinosaur, Communism may become extinct as a result of its failure to adapt to its changing environment.* While it behooves us to remember that the age of the dinosaur lasted for millions of years, we must also be aware of the fact that environments change infinitely more rapidly in the twentieth century than in the Jurassic period.

From a paper by a political scientist [italics added]

Revolutionary! It completely revises our outmoded ideas. Desmond's astonishing book demolishes our view of dinosaurs as pea-brained, cold-blooded, overgrown lizards and – using the latest palaeontological research and knowledge – reveals a quite different race of creatures: dazzlingly varied, behaviorally complex, and socially advanced.

From a review of Adrian J. Desmond,
The Hot-Blooded Dinosaurs (Dell, 1976)

INTRODUCTION

The Brezhnev period of Soviet history is ending more dramatically than it began. The invasion of Afghanistan in December 1979 will undoubtedly affect the international situation and especially American-Soviet relations more profoundly than any single event since the onset of detente in the early 1970s. Indeed, it has halted and even reversed the process of detente, while exposing the stark and dangerous implications of differing American and Soviet definitions of detente's basic rules. A brief assessment of this event (which occurred some weeks after this book was delivered to the publisher) can fittingly introduce a work which aims to provide a broader context for understanding this and other international episodes as they illuminate changes in Soviet perceptions and behavior.

The reasons behind the Soviet invasion of Afghanistan must be distinguished from the assumptions underlying the decision to undertake it. The Soviets faced the prospect of relinquishing their imperfect control over an unstable but friendly neighboring regime that might well have succumbed to militant Moslem republicanism on the Iranian model. Soviet leaders feared less the potentially dangerous repercussions of military action than the strategically significant loss of the country for Soviet Communism.

Of course one may argue that Soviet leaders took their decision precipitously, without realistic anticipation of the likely American reaction or the long-range implications for relations with the United States. All we know about the process of Soviet decision making denies us such reassurance, however. The decision could only have been taken carefully and deliberately. It signifies an important change in Soviet perceptions and behavior.[1] The decision to invade Afghanistan marks a watershed in Soviet policy, inasmuch as the Soviets have chosen to resort to new means – direct military intervention – to pursue an old goal, the extension of political power abroad.

For the first time since World War II, when the acquisition of a satel-

---

[1] Some observers contend that the invasion represents nothing new in Soviet behavior, that it marks one additional step on the Soviet route of expansionism and imperialism. What has changed as a result, they argue, is Western perceptions of Soviet policies, especially by those who did not expect this Soviet move. In my opinion, the invasion of Afghanistan signifies a major change not only in Western perceptions of Soviet policies, but also in Soviet perceptions and behavior.

1

lite empire rewarded Soviet victory, the Soviet Union has employed substantial military forces outside its recognized sphere of influence. Such a
striking departure demonstrates a new degree of confidence, self-
assertiveness, and expansionist drive that would perforce require major
reevaluation of the international situation and effective countermeasures
on the part of the Western alliance. During the past fifteen years, the
Soviet Union has achieved strategic parity with the United States and
attained the status of a global military power. Soviet international policies of the Brezhnev era have exhibited one dominant concern: How
successfully to translate the new military power into effective political
power and influence in the international arena while avoiding direct
confrontation with the other superpower, the United States. If in the last
few years Soviet behavior has become more assertive and dangerous –
witness the Soviet adventures in Angola, Ethiopia, and Yemen as well as
the use of military proxies – this behavior has nevertheless been restrained by one key priority: to balance the hunger for international
spoils with the fear of major war or dangerous conflict with the United
States. The invasion of Afghanistan clearly conveys a reordering in the
Kremlin of priorities and the assumptions that hitherto underlay them.
It clearly conveys an abandonment of certain assumptions seemingly
fixed in Soviet thinking – that the Soviet Union had much to gain from
cooperation with the West and especially the United States and much to
fear from the United States should their behavior transgress certain un-
stated but well understood bounds.

Analysts of Soviet international conduct have become accustomed to
repeat the axiom that Soviet leaders usually engage in low-risk and low-
cost operations. One could of course argue that from the Kremlin's own
perspective the action in Afghanistan also meets these criteria.[2] If so,
however, the Soviets have undertaken a major redefinition of what constitutes "low risk" and "low cost." In other words, we are witnessing the
fruits of a major Soviet reassessment of the international situation, of the
risks and costs of Soviet expansion.

To explore why at this point in international relations Soviet leaders
have chosen to redefine their assumptions and to reorder their priorities
is only marginal to the central questions raised in this work.[3] Indeed, for
many years, scholars and analysts have justifiably concentrated on just
such discrete episodes, aspects, and dimensions of Soviet policies in the
Brezhnev period. The gradual accumulation of their often distinguished
work has at the same time prepared the way and focused attention on

---

[2] A number of Western analysts regard the invasion of Afghanistan as a significant
departure from the style and behavior of the Brezhnev-Kosygin leadership.
Some argue that the decision to invade reflects loss of control in the Politburo by
men like Brezhnev, Kosygin, and Gromyko and their replacement by a group of
"young hawks." I see no evidence whatever to support this version.

[3] For my first attempt to identify the key elements affecting the reorientation of
Soviet policy, see "A Risk Carefully Taken," *Washington Post*, 18 January 1980,
Op-Ed page.

one pressing need in our study of the Soviet system: to provide a synthetic overview of just how the structure and process of Soviet politics have been transformed in the last quarter-century since Stalin's death and particularly in the years associated with Brezhnev's rule. Not only will such a comprehensive analysis deepen our understanding of current trends and decisions in Soviet internal and external policy, it will help us apply what we have learned about the working of the Soviet system in recent years to a projection of the system's likely direction in the next decade. This book attempts to meet this need; its principal task is to analyze the content and interrelationship of leadership, stability, and change in the Soviet Union. It is addressed first and foremost to students of the Soviet Union in the academy, the government, and the political and business communities; it is intended as well for the general reader who seeks the underlying sources of Soviet conduct.

The title of this book, *Stalin's Successors*, returns yet again to the essential starting point for any study of the modern Soviet political system: its founder, Stalin. The remembered force of his will and the depth of his imprint on modern Soviet life hold our minds and imaginations and tend to inhibit our understanding of what has changed fundamentally in the Soviet Union since his death. The complex of institutions perfected by him in the last decade and a half of his rule and the persons he charged to direct them at all levels account to this day for the durability of certain residual elements of what we call the Stalinist system.

Two main propositions will be argued in the book. First, the principal link between Stalin's rule and the Soviet present (and a major source of Soviet stability) is just the tenacity of that generation which entered politics during the last period of Stalin's rule and dominates the institutional structure of the Soviet Union today. The very monopoly of high office holding by this group has set the limits of change in the period since Stalin's death. Second, the rule of this favored generation is ending, and its passing will offer for the first time in decades genuine and pressing impulses for change. The departure of this group in the coming decade and the unprecedented economic challenges that its successors will face create exceptional possibilities for the further transformation of Stalin's legacy.

Part I attempts to measure how far the Soviet political system in the last quarter-century has departed from the "Stalinolithic" mold it inherited. Here I present an analysis of several important questions. To what extent have the changes in this period been shaped by initiative from above rather than effective pressure from below? To what extent have the changes in the political process taken place without fundamental alterations in the structure of administrative-executive institutions? To what extent have the changes affected not only the system of relations within the elite but also the relations between the elite and the broad social strata?

Part II examines the imminent successions of both the national leadership and the top elite of the Soviet Union. It analyzes certain unprecedented characteristics of this succession that may already be discerned at its present preparatory stage and may act to catalyze existing pressures for continued and perhaps fundamental change of the political system. It stresses generational turnover of the high and middle levels of the leadership and elite as the most significant feature of the succession process in terms of potential long-range effects. It provides a profile of this post-Stalinist generation of leaders and identifies the attributes distinguishing it from the group it will replace.

Part III concerns the pivotal matter of assessing Soviet stability and governability on the eve of the 1980s. My principal question is: To what extent is the stability displayed by the Soviet system under Brezhnev unique to the leadership dimension; does it also characterize other aspects and dimensions of the system, indeed the system as a whole? Part IV treats the trends of Soviet foreign policy in the Brezhnev period and the perceptions affecting the approach of policy makers to international issues. It focuses in particular on the centrality of U.S.-Soviet relations in Soviet policy making, the Soviet view on the use of military power in international relations, and the Soviet attitude toward the opportunities for expansion created by turmoil in the Third World. In Part V I examine the range and nature of those domestic problems in the Soviet Union that may well generate pressures for change in the 1980s beyond the systemic transformations of the last twenty-five years.

PART I
STALINISM AND
THE SOVIET POLITICAL
SYSTEM

Countless volumes by scholars and journalists relate the biography of Stalin. Yet it is surprising how little we know, how little has been systematically written, about Stalinism and the complex system of rule that Stalin created.[1] Perhaps it would be an exaggeration to suggest, as does Jerry Hough, that "indeed, if the early 1930s are excluded, it is probable that understanding of the Stalin era actually has deteriorated rather than improved over the last decade."[2] Nevertheless, our knowledge of Stalinism clearly lags behind our knowledge of the formative Soviet period and of the present Soviet system.[3] Part I of the present work will

[1] The best-known biographies of Stalin are: Boris Souvarine, *Stalin* (New York: Alliance Book Corp., 1939); Adam Ulam, *Stalin: The Man and His Era* (New York: Viking, 1973); Robert C. Tucker, *Stalin as Revolutionary, 1879–1929: A Study in History and Personality* (New York: Norton, 1973), the second volume of which, *Stalin and the Revolution from Above, 1929–1939*, should appear shortly; and Isaac Deutscher, *Stalin* (London: Oxford University Press, 1949). Of the books that deal with the Stalinist system rather than with Stalin, one should mention the still unsurpassed work by Barrington Moore, Jr., *Soviet Politics: The Dilemma of Power* (Cambridge, Mass.: Harvard University Press, 1950); Merle Fainsod, *Smolensk under Soviet Rule* (Cambridge, Mass.: Harvard University Press, 1958) and his *How Russia Is Ruled* (Cambridge, Mass.: Harvard University Press, 1953) and the posthumous edition rewritten by Jerry Hough (Harvard University Press, 1978); John A. Armstrong, *The Politics of Totalitarianism* (New York: Random House, 1961); Francis B. Randall, *Stalin's Russia* (New York: Free Press, 1965); and Robert Conquest, *Power and Policy in the USSR* (New York: St. Martin's Press, 1961). From the *samizdat* publications comes the first extensive and systematic analysis of Stalinism written in the Soviet Union by Roy A. Medvedev, *Let History Judge: The Origins and Consequences of Stalinism* (New York: Knopf, 1972).

To my knowledge the only outright apology for Stalinism published in English in recent years is Bruce Franklin's introduction to *The Essential Stalin: Major Theoretical Writings, 1905–1952* (Garden City, N.Y.: Doubleday, 1972), pp. 1–38. Of the many collections that contain excerpts and commentaries on Stalin and Stalinism from diverse vantage points, the more interesting are Julian Steinberg, ed., *Verdict of Three Decades* (New York: Duell, Sloan and Pearce, 1950); T. H. Rigby, ed., *Stalin* (Englewood Cliffs, N.J.: Prentice-Hall, 1966); Robert V. Daniels, ed., *The Stalin Revolution* (Boston: D. C. Heath, 1965). For a review of the latest "Staliniana" in *official* Soviet publications, see Michael Heller, "Stalin and the Detectives," *Survey*, 21, no. 1/2 (Winter-Spring 1975), 160–75.
[2] Jerry F. Hough and Merle Fainsod, *How the Soviet Union Is Governed* (Cambridge, Mass.: Harvard University Press, 1978), p. 147.
[3] The literature on Stalinism has been recently enriched by the very impressive collective volume, *Stalinism: Essays in Historical Interpretation*, edited by Robert C. Tucker (New York: Norton, 1977).

address one question: What was the long-range impact of Stalin on the Soviet political system?

That this question remains highly relevant today to our understanding of Soviet politics – a quarter-century after Stalin's death – provides in part an answer to it. So also does the fact that both in Western analysis of the Soviet Union and in Soviet everyday life, Stalin and Stalinism serve as key reference points for measuring change, identifying political orientations, and evaluating policies. Like the other great dictators of the 1930s, Stalin placed an indelible mark on his own society and on the world of the twentieth century. In contrast to these contemporaries, he clearly affected the nations over which he ruled more deeply and more durably. He ruled much longer than they. He was less restricted by the confining conditions of a modern authoritarian nation-state. He presided over an internally *and* externally victorious dictatorship. He changed more profoundly not only the political but also the social, economic, and cultural structures and mores of his own and succeeding generations.

To answer the principal question of Stalin's long-range impact on the Soviet political system requires in my opinion the consideration of two pertinent subordinate questions:

1. Was there such a phenomenon as Stalinism? Was there a complex of institutions and policies sufficiently different in dominant characteristics from the preceding and succeeding Soviet sociopolitical orders to be considered a distinct phenomenon of Soviet history? In other words, did Stalin create an "ism"? An answer to this question allows us to judge whether Stalin was primarily the passive agent of inexorable tendencies unleashed by the October Revolution of 1917 or the creator of a separate tradition, the practitioner of a distinctive form of Communist rule.

2. How much of Stalin was in the "ism"? What was the nature, extent, and manner of Stalin's domination of the political system of the Soviet Union?

In treating these questions, I shall not engage in psycho-history. I shall focus on Stalin's actions, not his motivations; on how he acted, not why; on his public performance, not his private personality.

1
THE MATURE
STALINIST SYSTEM

The evolution of Stalinism in Soviet postrevolutionary history went through three major stages, each of which can be associated with a different key role played by Stalin. The first stage included the period of the consolidation of Bolshevik rule, the shaping of its basic political, administrative, and economic institutions, and the formulation in practical terms of its key long-range policies and the methods of their implementation; that is to say, the NEP period of the 1920s. It was a stage in which the principal role played by Stalin was that of a *politician* who fought for power within the Communist party, adjusted his views and policies to the needs of this power struggle, and built an organizational base for it and for his future successes.[1]

The second stage encompasses the period of the revolution, or rather revolutions, "from above,"[2] roughly the years 1929–38. In this period a fundamental transformation of Soviet society took place in all areas of endeavor, and the social, economic, political, and cultural institutions of Bolshevism in power were radically reshaped. It was a stage in which the principal role played by Stalin was that of a revolutionary *transformer and restorer*.[3]

[1] This period is best treated by Robert C. Tucker in his *Stalin as Revolutionary: 1879–1929: A Study in History and Personality* (New York: Norton, 1973); Robert V. Daniels, *The Conscience of the Revolution* (Cambridge, Mass.: Harvard University Press, 1960); Stephen F. Cohen, *Bukharin and the Bolshevik Revolution* (New York: Knopf, 1973); and, in the standard history of this period, by Edward H. Carr, *A History of Soviet Russia*, vol. 4 (New York: Macmillan, 1954).

[2] The term "revolution from above" was used by Stalin himself to describe the collectivization of agriculture. It connotes a revolutionary change initiated and executed *by* and *not against* an existing political authority (*The History of the Communist Party of the Soviet Union [Bolsheviks], Short Course*, edited by Stalin himself [New York, 1939], p. 305). It is not known whether Stalin was conscious of the fact that "there is in Marxist literature a very precise meaning to 'revolution from above': it describes how Bismarck, in the absence of a vigorous bourgeoisie, carried out the modernization and unification of Germany in a counterrevolutionary fashion which, on occasion, used demagogic measures that were called 'socialist,' including the nationalization of certain industries. And Lenin himself had used the phrase in just that sense" (Michael Harrington, *Socialism* [New York: Bantam Books, 1973], p. 208).

[3] For especially noteworthy treatment of the period of revolutions from above, see Moshe Lewin, *Russian Peasants and Soviet Power* (London: George Allen & Unwin, 1968); Robert F. Miller, *One Hundred Thousand Tractors* (Cambridge, Mass.: Harvard University Press, 1970); and Sheila Fitzpatrick, ed., *Cultural Revolution in Russia, 1928–1931* (Bloomington: Indiana University Press, 1978).

9

The third stage was that of mature Stalinism, when the revolutions from above were over, the political institutions established, and the long-range social, economic, and cultural policies settled. It was a period when the key goal of the regime was the reproduction of the existing relations and the proper functioning and effectiveness of the system.[4] The principal role played by Stalin at this stage was that of a *dictator-administrator*. Only this stage of Stalinism concerns me.[5]

The mature Stalinist system displayed some key characteristics which in their interaction and combined effect made it a distinctive system, different from both the system prevailing in the early formative stage of Soviet development and the system that evolved in the post-Stalinist era. Some of its most important characteristics were:

the system of mass terror;

the extinction of the party as a movement;

the shapelessness of the macro-political organization;

an extreme mobilizational model of economic growth, tied to goals of achieving military power, and the political consequences thereof;

a heterogeneous value system which favored economic, status, and power stratification, fostered extraordinary cultural uniformity, and was tied to extreme nationalism;

the end of the revolutionary impulse to change society and the persistence of a conservative status quo attitude toward existing institutions;

the system of personal dictatorship.

Mature Stalinism rested on the foundation of an all-pervasive political terror: "the arbitrary use, by organs of political authority, of severe coercion against individuals or groups, the credible threat of such use, or the

---

[4] Despite the many valuable insights into the nature of the Stalinist system provided by the totalitarian model, in my opinion its creators make the crucial mistake of failing to distinguish between the early revolutionary and the late, highly conservative nature of the system. They suggest that the "totalitarian" impulse to reshape society is a continuous one, and they do not recognize the key characteristic of the late Stalinist *and* post-Stalinist Russia – its deeply conservative nature, domestically oriented to the status quo (see, for example, Carl J. Friedrich and Zbigniew Brzezinski, *Totalitarian Dictatorship and Autocracy* [New York: Praeger Publishers, 1961], p. 9, and especially chapter 27).

[5] Moreover, I am concerned exclusively with the domestic dimensions of Stalinism. The exclusion of Stalinist foreign policy is dictated primarily by considerations of space. I would also argue, however, that its discussion would not change the general picture. It is my view that in contrast to Nazism, which cannot be understood without an analysis of its foreign-policy aspects, these aspects are only secondary in the analysis of Stalinism. The perception of the realities of the international environment, as I shall later point out, played an immensely important role in the formation and practice of Stalinism. It provided not only a key justification of the regime but also decisively shaped the psychology of its practitioners. Yet one has to distinguish, it seems, between the contributing role of the external environment in shaping Stalinism and the imputation of the centrality of foreign policy in the overall complex of Stalinist policies (as was the case with the Nazis).

arbitrary extermination of such individuals or groups."[6] The arbitrariness of the terror system was exemplified both in the substance of the accusations and indictments which led to trials, executions, and imprisonments, and in the procedures by which this was accomplished. It was based on such "legal" principles as presumption of guilt, guilt by association, and "objective" guilt.[7] The arbitrariness made impossible the calculation of behavior which would provide a reasonable chance of survival. As Zbigniew Brzezinski has remarked, "Failure to adjust can mean extinction of life. But success in adjusting . . . does not guarantee either liberty or safety."[8] Former members of the anti-Bolshevik parties, for example, were prime and early targets of the terror, but the chief state prosecutor at the height of the terror was a prominent former Menshevik, Vyshinskii, and its most vociferous propagandist, another Menshevik, Zaslavskii. On the other hand, there perished in the terror a countless number of devoted Stalinists, who had been closely associated with Stalin throughout the struggle, who had proved their loyalty, and who were supporting him unquestionably even during the Great Purge.

The terror was all-pervasive in that no group or individual was exempt from being a target. As a matter of fact, it appears that the effectiveness of the terror "has been most telling . . . among the bureaucracy — those who most directly depend on the regime for success and status."[9] In a regime of terror, as Merle Fainsod remarked, "The insecurity of the masses must be supplemented by the insecurity of the governing elite who surround the dictator."[10] The system of terror created what Alexander Dallin and George Breslauer have called the *condition of terror* — a pervasive atmosphere of anxiety" — in the society at large, and especially among the bureaucracies and the elites.[11]

Participation in the rule of terror was not confined to its direct administrators, nor was it restricted to obeying direct commands from above. The members of the political bureaucracy were actively engaged, if not physically involved, in the terror; they were guilty en masse of initiating terroristic acts. They displayed what can be described as "preemptive obedience," the anticipation of what they considered to be their bosses' wishes and whims. It was an anticipatory obedience encouraged by their superiors and characterized favorably as "vigilance." The rule of terror led to the existence of a countless army of informers. The working assumption in the society and bureaucracy was that everybody was spying and informing on everybody else. The reality was not far removed from

---

[6] Alexander Dallin and George W. Breslauer, *Political Terror in Communist Systems* (Stanford, Calif.: Stanford University Press, 1970), p. 1.

[7] On Soviet law and legal procedures under Stalin, see Robert Sharlet, "Stalinism and Soviet Legal Culture" in Tucker, ed., *Stalinism*, pp. 155–79.

[8] Zbigniew Brzezinski, *The Permanent Purge: Politics in Soviet Totalitarianism* (Cambridge, Mass.: Harvard University Press, 1956), p. 1.

[9] Dallin and Breslauer, *Political Terror in Communist Systems*, p. 128.

[10] Merle Fainsod, *How Russia Is Ruled*, rev. ed. (Cambridge, Mass.: Harvard University Press, 1967), p. 441.

[11] Dallin and Breslauer, *Political Terror in Communist Systems*, p. 5.

this assumption.[12] Society at large, and especially its upper strata, became the victims of terror, morally if not physically. It was not an exaggeration to state, directly after Stalin's death, that "the tragedy of contemporary Russia is that the whole elite of the nation, its intelligentsia, its civil service, and all its politically minded elements share in one degree or another in Stalin's guilt. . . . Stalin made of the whole nation, at any rate of all its educated and active elements, his accomplices."[13]

Crucial to our understanding of mature Stalinism is the proposition that terror functioned principally not as a tool of social *change*, but as a normal method of rule and *governance*. The development and continuation of terror as a method of rule and governance established an enormous bureaucratic structure devoted to its administration: the police state. (It led, as Alfred Meyer ironically remarked, to the "bureaucratization of class warfare.") This bureaucracy performed tasks that went far beyond traditional police functions; it amassed direct influence over wide areas of Soviet life and participated routinely in the political process.[14]

The police commanded a major military force composed of internal

[12]In the epilogue to the Harper and Row Torchbook edition of *Soviet Politics: The Dilemma of Power* (pp. 427–8), which appeared in 1965, fifteen years after the original edition, Barrington Moore, Jr., revises his understanding of Stalinism in the original edition as follows: "The main inadequacy I now perceive concerns the pervasiveness of terror during most of the Stalinist era, perhaps at other times as well, though that is less certain. *Soviet Politics* went to the printer before a new kind of evidence became available in any quantity: that from living people who had been Soviet citizens. Printed sources, on which the book is based almost exclusively, led me to suspect that the terror was mainly confined to the upper ranks of the Communist Party and that its impact was rather light among the masses of the population, though I was, perhaps fortunately, not sufficiently certain to say so flatly. Later evidence from refugees convinced me and a good many others that the terror penetrated far deeper and that at the least the prospect of arrest was a fact of life for a huge number of quite ordinary citizens. . . . It seems to me now that the Stalinist regime, for all its material accomplishments, was one of the bloodiest and most oppressive the world has ever known."

[13]Isaac Deutscher, *Ironies of History, Essays on Contemporary Communism* (London and New York: Oxford University Press, 1966), p. 15.

[14]Our knowledge of the Soviet police state has expanded very much recently due to numerous historical accounts coming from Russia, of which, of course, the monumental three-volume work of Aleksandr Solzhenitsyn, *The Gulag Archipelago*, is a prime example. Of the accounts of former Soviet police officials who defected, I find most noteworthy the books by Aleksandr Orlov, *The Secret History of Stalin's Crimes* (New York: Random House, 1953); and Vladimir and Evdokia Petrov, *Empire of Fear* (New York: Praeger, 1956). To my knowledge, the only full-length Western study of the Soviet secret police (based largely also on the testimony of former Soviet policemen) is the book edited by Simon Wolin and Robert M. Slusser, *The Soviet Secret Police* (New York: Praeger, 1957). Of the many books on terror and the police state published by Western authors, one should mention (of the older ones) Brzezinski's *The Permanent Purge* and (of the most recent) Robert Conquest's *The Great Terror* (New York: Macmillan, 1968). See also Robert Conquest's postscript to his book, "The Great Terror Revised," *Survey*, 16, no. 1 (Winter 1971), 92–8.

security units (many divisions with their own armor and air force) and border troops.[15] It administered the entire extensive prison, camp, exile, and forced-labor systems.[16] It incorporated for all practical purposes the judiciary branch of the government, both the procuracy and the courts.[17] It controlled openly, directly, and exclusively the armed forces' counter-intelligence with detachments established down to the battalion level and plenipotentiaries at the company level. It placed official representatives in the machine-tractor stations, the key agricultural units, and small cells in major industrial enterprises. It was directly in charge of the elite communications system, the so-called VCh network, through which all high level intraparty, state, and military communications were conducted, and controlled the Ministry of Communications. It controlled directly or indirectly the ministries in charge of producing lumber, non-ferrous metals, and heavy construction.[18] It exercised powerful and direct administrative influence over a number of non-Russian republics, especially the Transcaucasian republics of Georgia, Azerbaidjan, and Armenia. In addition to control over a number of scientific research prison establishments, the so-called *sharashki*,[19] it was apparently charged with

[15]The strength of the security troops can be seen from the fact that during the critical years of the war, 1941 and 1942, nine NKVD divisions were engaged directly in front-line action; that one of the NKVD Troops' commanders, General I. I. Maslennikov, was sufficiently high in rank to command a Field Army Group; that the city commander of Moscow during its defense was an NKVD Troops' general, P. A. Artem'ev.

[16]Estimates of the labor-camp population differ widely. One of the more conservative estimates is based on the "State Plan for the Development of the National Economy of the USSR in 1941," captured by Germans and available to the Western researcher. It suggests a camp population for 1941 of just under 7 million. The total number of the civilian population employed in 1940 in industry, mining, and construction was 31.2 million. See J. Miller, "The 1941 Economic Plan," *Soviet Studies*, 3, no. 3 (January 1952), 365–86; for an estimate of the camp population, see S. Swianiewicz, *Forced Labor and Economic Development* (London: Oxford University Press, 1965), pp. 290–303; for employment in 1940, see *Narodnoe khoziaistvo SSSR v 1960 godu. Statisticheskii sbornik* (Moscow: Gosstatizdat, 1961), p. 633.

[17]During the Great Purge and even after, aside from the cases of the most prominent victims, the "normal" juridical procedures against individuals in the category of "enemies of the people" were not conducted by civilian or by military courts but by so-called "special courts" which performed the trial speedily and *in camera*. Their judges included one senior and two junior secret police officers.

[18]The extent of the police economic empire can be gleaned from the fact that the man directly in charge of it, A. P. Zaveniagin, a three-star general of the police and deputy minister of internal affairs, was one of the top Soviet economic administrators. He survived the purge of Beria after Stalin's death and became under Khrushchev the USSR deputy prime minister in charge of "medium-machine building," the post used in the Soviet Union to cover atomic research and modern weaponry.

[19]The *sharashka* is described in Aleksandr Solzhenitsyn's book *The First Circle* (New York: Harper & Row, 1968). Many top military designers, engineers, and scientists did their major work in those prison institutions at one time or another, for example, the most famous Soviet aircraft designers, Tupolev and Iliushin.

supervising atomic research. In addition to directing external intelligence, it exerted direct and strong influence on the foreign service and foreign trade establishments.[20]

Far from acting as an anonymous, discreet, and secret force, the "secret" police was an open and recognized political force, glorified and praised in the media, highly visible at all official ceremonies and political assemblies, and extolled by Soviet propaganda as a prime example for emulation. Its high officials were "elected" to the Soviet parliament and constituted in fact, from 1936 until Stalin's death, the second largest homogeneous group of deputies. The republican, provincial, and district chiefs of the police were ex officio members of the bureaus (executive boards) of the respective party organizations.

All in all, under mature Stalinism, one deals not with an outburst of terror, a "siege" of terror, but a generalized persistent regime of terror.[21] To use Hannah Arendt's expression, it was an "invasion of criminality" on an almost unprecedented scale, where terroristic "criminality as a principle" was "used as an instrument of organization of society."[22] Rule by terror as a method of governance for the foreseeable future rather than as an emergency measure received ideological underpinning and justification from Stalin's thesis on the "intensification of class struggle with the advancement and success of socialist construction."[23] This formula not only proclaimed terror a justifiable method of rule, but also, by a reverse logic, made terror the indicator of the successes of the socialist system. The reverse logic was very simple: If the enemy's pressure and activity *inevitably* become greater as the Soviet Union becomes more successful and developed, then absence of terror would either mean the denial of Soviet successes or would simply indicate a lack of vigilance in discovering enemies. This logic was an open invitation to invent plots, "unmask" enemies, and so on.

Under mature Stalinism the Communist party became extinct as a political movement.[24] The term "party" came to be used either as a legitimizing mantle for Stalin's rule, reflecting his continuing need, pub-

---

[20]To give only one example, the Soviet ambassador to Germany in the crucial years 1939–41 was Dekanozov, Deputy People's Commissar for State Security before and after his Berlin assignment.

[21]For the distinction between "siege" and "regime" of terror, see E. V. Walter, *Terror and Resistance* (New York: Oxford University Press, 1969), p. vii.

[22]See the transcript of Hannah Arendt's presentation on "Stalinism in Retrospect" at the 26 April 1972 session of the Columbia University Seminar on Communism.

[23]I. V. Stalin, *O nedostatkakh partiinoi raboty i merakh likvidatsii Trotskistskikh i inykh dvurushnikov,* speech and concluding remarks at the Plenum of the Central Committee, 3–5 March 1937, *Pravda,* 29 March 1937.

[24]The term "extinct movement" to describe the Bolshevik party under Stalin is used by Robert C. Tucker in his pioneering article "Towards a Comparative Politics of Movement–Regimes," *American Political Science Review,* 55, no. 2 (June 1961), 281–9.

lic and probably personal, to relate the roots of Soviet authority to its revolutionary origins, or as a depiction of an important part of the Stalinist administrative edifice (the party bureaucracy, the party "apparatus"). Even in its "dignified," legitimizing function, the role of the party as the carrier of ideological "truth"–while still invoked–declined visibly. It was largely replaced by the cult of Stalin and by undisguised, explicit nationalism. It is indicative of the atrophy of the party as a genuine, voluntary mass organization and "an association of people united by an ideology" that it played a secondary role as a legitimizing institution (and, incidentally, as an organization) in the only *authentic* mass mobilization effort of the mature Stalinist era, the war effort. The mobilizing impetus came from the "truths" of the state, not of the party; from patriotism and nationalism, not from ideology in a communist sense.

As a mass and an elite organization, the party ceased to perform a meaningful role in the political process.[25] It still served as a vehicle for the political education of its members, but the key role of political socialization was performed primarily by schools and mass media on the basic level, and by the various bureaucracies for their own members, including the party bureaucracy, on the higher level. All politically powerful individuals belonged to the party; party membership became an accoutrement of power.[26] But very few party members were politically powerful. Party membership did not assure participation in the political process, beyond the privilege of receiving some additional information and beyond the duty of implementing decisions adopted *at all levels* outside the party.

The ideal of mature Stalinism was to politicize all spheres of social and often even private endeavors and to depoliticize political processes. All forms of activity, whether economic, scientific, or cultural, were imbued with political meaning; but attempts were made forcibly to reduce the political process to questions of "pure" administration. The mass and the elite party became the key victim of this tendency. The

---

[25]For an imaginative discussion of the role of the Communist party under Stalinism (and in other Communist countries where a strong supreme leader is in charge), see Leonard Schapiro and John W. Lewis, "The Role of the Monolithic Party Under the Totalitarian Leader," *China Quarterly*, no. 40 (October–December 1969), pp. 39–64.

[26]Party membership, after a decline during the Great Purge, grew in the mature Stalinist period from 2,477,700 in 1939 to 6,882,100 in 1952 (see *KPSS, Spravochnik* [Moscow: Gospolitizdat, 1963], p. 4). However, the purge signified a major change in the social composition of the new enrollment. For 1929, 81.2 percent of new party members were workers, 17.1 percent peasants, and 1.7 percent white-collar workers and intelligentsia. In the November 1936–March 1939 period, workers constituted 41.0 percent of the new recruits, peasants 15.2 percent, and intelligentsia and white-collar workers 43.8 percent (see T. H. Rigby, *Communist Party Membership in the USSR, 1917–1967* [Princeton, N.J.: Princeton University Press, 1968], p. 223).

party in its "efficient" rather than "dignified" function became identical with the party bureaucracy, the paid, full-time staff of its professional "apparatus."[27]

The prime function of this apparatus was not to administer the affairs
of the mass party but to participate in the administration of the state. Its
"clients" were not the party itself, but primarily other bureaucracies. In
the pre-Stalinist period the party apparatus played a lesser role in state
affairs, but the party played a much more prominent role. Even so, it
would be wrong to conclude that mature Stalinism meant the triumph of
the party apparatus in any way other than its domination within the
party. Despite the fact that the party apparatus was expanded and more
deeply and directly involved in state-administration, it became just *one*
of the bureaucracies, albeit a very powerful one. Therefore, even in its
"efficient" function, with the "party" equated with its "apparatus," the
role of the party under mature Stalinism could hardly be described as
dominant.

The popular image of Stalinism depicts extreme rigidity of procedures
and policies and the petrification of the entire enormous bureaucratic
edifice. This image is largely valid when applied to the micro-processes
and internal procedures of each separate bureaucratic hierarchy of Stalinist Russia. The macro-dimension, however, presents, first of all, a picture of vastly overlapping lines of control, rights, and responsibilities
among the diverse bureaucratic hierarchies; and, second, of shifting lines
of responsibility and control.

The ideal of Stalinism was monocratic rule and administration.
Within separate bureaucratic hierarchies, this ideal was to a large extent
achieved by pursuing a course of extreme vertical centralization. On the
macro-level, however, the monocratic principle was applied consistently
and deliberately to only one facet of the political organization of the
society – that which concerned the relations of the various bureaucracies
with Stalin. The relations among the various enormous bureaucracies
bore scant resemblance to an organizational chart with clear lines of
authority, responsibilities, and prerogatives.

Even the picture of parallel party and state bureaucracies is misleading insofar as the parallelism was multiple not merely dual. The proper
picture would encompass a number of major and lesser bureaucracies
encroaching on each other's territory, fighting for their share of the bureaucratic empire, and duplicating each other's efforts. If the party ap-

---

[27]The size of this "apparatus" during the Stalin era is estimated around 190,000 to
220,000. See, for example, Merle Fainsod, *How Russia Is Ruled*, rev. ed., pp. 205–
7; Leonard Schapiro, *The Communist Party of the Soviet Union* (New York: Random House, 1959), pp. 524–5; and George Fischer, "The Number of Soviet Party
Executives," Cornell Soviet Studies Reprint No. 10 (n.d.). For an extensive discussion of the party apparatus, see Abdurakhman Avtorkhanov, *The Communist
Party Apparatus* (Cleveland and New York: World Publishing Co., 1966).

paratus was empowered to organize and supervise political indoctrination, it competed not only with the military's separate political department (which, while formally a branch of the party bureaucracy, was certainly run for the most part independently under Mekhlis and Shcherbakov). It also competed with the police and even the Ministry of Railroads. The prerogatives of the planners were constantly challenged by the ambitions of the police to expand their own economic empire. The rights of local party secretaries to control local enterprises were effectively countered by the managers' recourse to the influence of their respective ministries. The extent of the control by industrial ministries over their key enterprises was undermined in turn by the rights and actions of the party's Central Committee organizers (CC *partorgi*); and so on.

No existing bureaucracy was delegated the exclusive authority to serve primarily as coordinator of the competing bureaucracies. The party apparatus was best suited for this role, due to the fact that its internal structure duplicated the structure of the state administration. Instead it performed the function of external pusher-mobilizer (and controller) rather than coordinator.[28] One may associate oneself with Karl Bracher, who, in reviewing a similar phenomenon in Nazi Germany, remarked that these were not the "teething" troubles of the new system; they were the system itself.[29]

The reasons behind this shapelessness were varied, partly deliberate and partly the result of the difficulty of administering everything and everywhere in a vast country under conditions of constant emergency. As David Apter has remarked, "High coercion systems are low information systems."[30] The multiple lines of administrative responsibility reflected the center's need to compensate for the low quality and unreliability of information flowing to it through a multiplicity of sources and channels, as well as the always-suspicious dictator's need to secure validation and confirmation of routine communications. The ascendancy or decline of particular bureaucracies or their functional components partly reflected and partly determined the ascendancy or decline of their leaders at Stalin's court. The bureaucratic shapelessness reflected the dictator's need to keep the bureaucracies off balance, to prevent their and their leaders' solidification into well-established empires, to preclude any of their component parts from growing too strong without the countervailing power of competition. A secure, stable bureaucracy could only diminish the dictator's security. A divided and fluid bureaucracy provided an important margin of security for his own position.[31]

[28]For a discussion of this role of the party, see Reinhard Bendix, *Work and Authority in Industry* (New York: Harper and Row Torchbook, 1963), chaps. 6 and 7.
[29]Karl Dietrich Bracher, *The German Dictatorship* (New York: Praeger, 1970), especially pp. 340–50.
[30]David E. Apter, *The Politics of Modernization* (Chicago: University of Chicago Press, 1965), p. 40.
[31]Analyzing the type of bureaucracy found in the historical-bureaucratic societies characterized by total subservience to the king, S. N. Eisenstadt describes a pattern which is partly applicable to the Stalinist bureaucracies: "The bureau-

The chief goal of the Soviet political leadership throughout its history has been economic – especially industrial – growth at the most rapid attainable rate and regardless of the social cost. Lenin's dictum, "politics cannot but have primacy over economics," meant initially that economic growth must be correlated with and subordinated to social change, to socialist transformation of the society. In Stalinist (and post-Stalinist) Russia it came to mean basically that economic targets were too important a goal of the system to leave them to managers, technocrats, and economists. Another Soviet slogan, which viewed "politics as condensed economics," expressed rather better the dominance of economic growth among the regime's systemic goals. The issues of economic growth permeated the entire Soviet political decision-making process. Economic growth and the military power that was to proceed from it constituted the chief indicator of the success and failure of political leadership. The economic development desired and later achieved constituted the historical justification of both the social transformation decreed by the leadership and the political order established by it.

The creation and rapid expansion of Soviet industrial might was based on a particular pattern of organization, stimuli, and policies. What has come to be called the Stalinist model of economic growth exhibits the following central characteristics:[32]

> Planning for economic growth is goal-oriented. While economic growth is a decisive goal, economic criteria for deciding what, how fast, and at what cost it should develop is a tertiary consideration.
>
> The specific goals of economic development are highly selective. The aim is not an overall balanced growth but a relatively narrow range of high-priority tasks.
>
> A particularly important dimension of the unbalanced strategy of growth is the place it assigns to personal consumption,

cracy's most crucial characteristic, in such cases, was the very small extent of internal autonomy. This was manifested in the continuous shifting of officials from place to place and office to office without any fixed general rules, in the destruction by the rulers of any distinct career patterns, in the maintenance by them of strong and often arbitrary discipline not based on any general rules or criteria, in their destruction of any departmental or professional *esprit de corps* and cooperation, and in their insistence on the bureaucrats being personal servants of the ruler and of the State as personified by the ruler" (*Essays on Comparative Institutions* [New York: John Wiley & Sons, 1965], p. 223).

[32]For a discussion of those characteristics, see Egon Neuberger, "The Legacies of Central Planning," Rand Corporation (June 1968), Memorandum RM-5530-PR, pp. 5–9. An especially helpful general discussion of the Soviet economic system is Peter J. D. Wiles, *The Political Economy of Communism* (Cambridge, Mass.: Harvard University Press, 1962); John Michael Montias, "Types of Communist Economic Systems" in Chalmers Johnson, ed., *Change in Communist Systems* (Stanford, Calif.: Stanford University Press, 1970), pp. 117–34; Gregory Grossman, *Economic Systems*, 2nd ed. (Englewood Cliffs, N.J.: Prentice-Hall, 1974); Alec Nove, *The Soviet Economy*, rev. ed. (New York: Praeger, 1965).

> which, as one economic historian has observed, is treated not as "the ultimate goal . . . but as the inevitable cost to be incurred grudgingly in the process of continued growth."[33]

The setting of ambitious goals and the planning – or rather the command – that they be attained in the shortest possible (and impossible) time are calculated to bring forth the maximum expenditure of effort and energy.

A major feature has been the stress on ever-increasing quantities of output, achieved with massive infusions of inputs of labor and capital.

With the exception of the initial industrialization drive which relied heavily on imports of foreign technology, the Stalinist model of growth was designed as a closed market, virtually isolated from the outside world.

The key characteristic of the Stalinist model of economic growth was its lack of *economic* self-generating, self-regulating, and adjusting features. To run at all, let alone to perform well, it required an enormous political edifice to provide the decision making and the push, the regulation, supervision, and coordination. In fact, the Soviet political system was developed largely to run the economy and was shaped by running the economy in line with the chosen growth strategy.

The economic goals of the political elite and the strategy through which they were being pursued have forcefully influenced the Soviet political structure and process. They were either a direct primary cause of certain features of the political regime or else they reinforced or exaggerated other features to which the political elite was already committed.[34] Of these features, four are especially notable; they concern societal controls, organizational structure, the type of regulation, and the style of leadership.

The reliance of the political elite on the three major means of societal control – material, symbolic, and physical – was highly asymmetrical.[35] The achievement of the exorbitant planned targets of growth, the successful stretching of available resources, depended on the establishment of an extremely high level of discipline in the labor force, in the managerial strata, in the party. At the same time, the high rate of forced savings, the lowest priority assigned to consumer goals in the growth strategy, pre-

---

[33]Alexander Gerschenkron, "The Stability of Dictatorship" in *Continuity in History and Other Essays* (Cambridge, Mass.: Harvard University Press, 1968), p. 317.

[34]For an interpretation that places many of the political consequences of Stalinism in the Stalinist economic system, see Draginja Arsić, *Drustveno Ekonomski Koreni Staljinizma* (Belgrade: Izdanje Instituta za Medunarodnu Politiku i Privredu, 1972).

[35]On the diverse means of control and different bases of societal compliance, see Amitai Etzioni, *A Comparative Analysis of Complex Organizations* (New York: Free Press, 1961), pp. 4–16. Etzioni's major proposition is that while the different forms of power *may* reinforce each other, the excessive reliance on one base of compliance usually weakens the other bases.

cluded the reliance on material incentives, on controls through remunera-
tive power, as the primary method of achieving the required discipline.

A revolutionary regime which poses ambitious goals before society in
a situation of pronounced economic scarcity may and often does rely
heavily on normative powers to build compliance. Indeed, if one were to
judge by the extraordinary size and budget of the Stalinist propaganda
machine and its saturating activity, the stress on this form of societal
control would appear very substantial. One should point out, however,
that despite the visible stress by the Soviet leadership under Stalin (and
later) on this type of control, its importance has been secondary and its
impact limited.

The limited effectiveness of normative controls reflected in part past
costs of the party's acquisition and solidification of power (narrow social
base, alienation of peasantry, and so on). In part, however, it reflected the
dilemma of goals and means. On the one hand the revolutionary regime
adopts as its primary internal task the development of material resources
for political-military purposes as an end in itself, thereby abandoning in
practice its utopian and egalitarian goals and stressing the material, utilitarian values. On the other hand it continues in its efforts at persuasion to
rely heavily on the images, symbols, and vocabulary of its "old faith" and
only partly succeeds in investing them with new meanings more conso-
nant with reality (for example, Great Russian nationalism).

While it would be foolish to neglect the role of economic inducements,
or especially to underestimate the role of manipulation as the basis of
Soviet societal controls, nevertheless the foundation stone on which the
Stalinist leadership was able to base its economic growth strategy, the
real driving force, was coercion. Actual coercion or the threat or fear of
its application provided within all strata of Soviet society the most important source of compliance to the regime's goals. The idiosyncratic
element of Stalin's personality aside, without an inordinate reliance on
coercion, the combination contained in the Soviet economic growth
strategy – extremely unbalanced growth, scarcity of resources, and taut
planning – could hardly have been pursued for a prolonged period with
any chance of success. Of all the societal controls employed by the regime, coercion was the most instrumental, rational, and systemic; the
most institutionalized and most lasting; the most deeply implanted in
the system's fabric. To recognize the coercive base of Soviet political
controls means much more than to point to the role of its primary institutions: cyclical purges, the enormity and complexity of the Soviet police
apparatus and its large arbitrary powers, the labor-camp system and the
weight of police-directed economic and even research activity. If these
were the most visible *core* institutions of the coercive system, coercion as
an underlying driving force, a method of management, pervaded all institutions of Soviet society.

The Soviet Union under Stalin became a society of organization, to
which every social task of importance is entrusted at a much earlier

stage and to a much greater degree than in Western industrial nations. The main peculiarity of Soviet development, associated with the growth strategy adopted by its leadership, is not that formal organizations (that is, bureaucracies) constitute the basic building blocks of the socioeconomic and political structures, but that relations among those structural units are extremely centralized. The two basic features of this centralization are: first, that decision making is reserved for the system's leadership in a degree directly related to the importance of the decisions, and second, that the link between units at various levels is direct, without an intermediary, and takes the form of commands, orders, and directives.

The Soviet model of economic growth with its ideal of total mobilization and allocation of resources, with its selectivity of high growth areas, with its pressure on the tempo of growth, has infused an extreme level of hierarchical relations, a supercentralization into the macro-economic organization, and has required an equally centralized shape in the macropolitical organizations which were to mobilize resources, supervise their allocation and control, and coordinate their use. As a matter of fact, the correlation of centralized planning and centralized control with the economic growth strategy is so close that they could be considered both an *objective* of the strategy and at the same time the key *mechanism* of the strategy.

The growth strategy pursued under Stalinism not only reinforced the traditional inclination of the Communist party for tight centralization but, more importantly, infused it with an intrinsic instrumental value. That is to say, it removed the question of centralization from the field of politics alone, and beyond the rationale of preserving the power of a political elite whose claim to legitimacy was narrow, and made it into the natural modus operandi of the system, the way considered most effective in running the society.

Another closely related feature of the system delineates the degree of operational autonomy possessed by subordinate units within a sphere (e.g., within the economy) or between spheres (e.g., economic versus political). It concerns the balance between the two basic forms of managerial mechanisms employed by a supervisory authority: one, sometimes called prescriptive, which relies on straight direction, specifying in detail the required actions of subordinate units; the other, often called regulatory, which delineates the limits of accepted behavior of subordinate units, permitting autonomous choices within those limits.[36]

The economic system of planning and management was characterized by stress on detailed output targets and by proliferation of instructions not only on details of what should be done and when, but also how it should be done and according to what sequence of procedures, and following what detailed timetables. Similarly, the relations of the political

[36]For a discussion of the different specifications of control, see Amitai Etzioni, *The Active Society: A Theory of Societal and Political Processes* (New York: Free Press, 1968), pp. 114–15.

bureaucracy with the economic sector (and for that matter with other sectors) were characterized not simply by the right of the former to determine key economic decisions and by its veto power but by its attempt at detailed supervision of, and intervention in, each phase and aspect of management.

One last feature of the system, of which the Stalinist growth strategy was a major codeterminant, concerns the style of leadership. The Soviet style of leadership is most commonly referred to as bureaucratic; but this identification tells very little beyond the fact that it is a leadership exercised within and through hierarchical organizations, that it is performed on a full-time basis by professionals, and that it leads to the development of standardized, routinized procedures for dealing with everyday situations. Bureaucracies, however, exhibit different types, possess diverse functions, and, consequently, display divergent styles of leadership. The style of leadership prevalent within and displayed by Soviet bureaucracies under Stalin, and especially the way in which economic management ran the economy and was in turn run by the political elite, was geared to conditions that were rightly described as those of simulated combat. The Soviet economic and political organization in terms of its power structure, its modes of operation and means of communication, its mood, began to resemble most closely a combat army in a not-too-popular war. The simulated combat conditions and the style of leadership appropriate to it, found a fitting expression even in the terminology and language of official Russia, which was most closely based on military imagery.

In Stalinist Russia one did not solve a problem, one "attacked" it; one "retreated," "regrouped," organized a "campaign"; one was at "war" and organized one's own "camp" against the "enemy." One acted on various "fronts" – ideological, industrial, agricultural – and one had a "strategy" and "tactic" for each "sector." The most striking imagery was of the Communist party as an "army," which Stalin described thus:

> If we have in mind its leading strata, there are about 3,000 to 4,000 first rank leaders whom I would call our Party's corps of generals.
>
> Then there are about 30,000 to 40,000 middle rank leaders who are our Party corps of officers.
>
> Then there are about 100,000 to 150,000 of the lower rank Party command staff who are, so to speak, our Party's non-commissioned officers.[37]

In discussing the value system of mature Stalinism, I am primarily interested in the political culture, broadly understood. But the first thing to understand is that virtually all culture became the domain of the political in a society where all aspects of life were shaped and dominated by political power. The official value system of mature Stalinism pre-

---

[37]Joseph Stalin, *Mastering Bolshevism* (New York: Workers Library Publishers, 1937), p. 36.

sents a bizarre amalgam compounded of old Russian values, deeply rooted among the new elite and the population and deeply detested by the revolutionary Bolsheviks, and the modernizing Soviet zeal and commitment – all cloaked in Marxist-Leninist ideology or (at the very least) Marxist-Leninist terminology. The "dignified" dimension of this official value system was provided by the party in the political structure and by Marxism-Leninism in the political culture. From the old ideology came the sense of historical "inevitability," the self-righteousness, and the semireligious ardor, which were curiously blended and reinforced by the propagation of nationalism and the "Russian mission," by the cult of the leader as the carrier of ultimate truth. The new ideology chose its doctrinal references selectively, in a self-serving and mechanistic manner; it reduced them to a few slogans, incessantly repeated. Stalinism, as Isaac Deutscher remarked, was the "Marxism of the illiterate."[38] It sought to dominate a people and an elite just emerging from illiteracy.

Stalinism elevated Soviet nationalism in general and Russian nationalism in particular to a core, systemic value. It became *the* core value at least in terms of its effectiveness as a norm of compliance to the system's goals. It put at the center of attention the old conservative theme – the cult of national unity at any price – and the unreserved condemnation of individuals and groups who not only in fact, in thought, or in practice threatened to impair it, but who could potentially impair it.[39] In its last phase this nationalism degenerated into extreme chauvinism and xenophobia, closing the circle from "socialism in one country" to "imperial socialism." In an ironic twist, it proclaimed the essence of internationalism to be the willingness to defend the Soviet Union, an unconditional allegiance to the Soviet Union.

Under mature Stalinism economic stratification and inequalities of status were not simply tolerated; they were encouraged in actions and glorified in symbols. Their theoretical justification was not unlike the purest functionalist explanations of stratification in the West.[40] The mul-

---

[38]Deutscher, *Ironies of History*, p. 185.

[39]A typical example was the 1947–8 campaign against "cosmopolitanism" associated with the name of then Party Secretary Andrei Zhdanov. The brunt of this campaign was directed against Jews as the potential carriers of non-Russian values in the society. For the materials on this campaign, see A. A. Zhdanov, "Vystuplenie na diskussii po knige G. F. Aleksandrova 'Istoriia Zapadnoevropeiskoi filosofii,' " *Partiinaia zhizn'*, 1947, no. 16, 1–11, and *Decisions of the Central Committee, CPSU (B), on Literature and Art (1946–48)* (Moscow: Foreign Languages Publishing House, 1951); on the anti-Semitic aspects of this campaign, see Y. A. Gilboa, *The Black Years of Soviet Jewry* (Boston: Little, Brown, 1971); and S. Shwarts, *Evrei v Sovetskom Soiuze* (New York: Izdanie Amerikanskogo evreiskogo rabochego komiteta, 1966), pp. 198–231.

[40]Egalitarianism was declared to be an un-socialist principle in Stalin's Russia. The slogan "from each according to his ability, to each according to his work" was interpreted as a justification for extreme stratification and for the justness of such stratification. As Stanislaw Ossowski wisely remarked in his book *Class Structure in the Social Consciousness* (New York: Free Press, 1963), the precept "from everybody according to his ability, to everybody according to his work"

tiplication of ranks, titles, uniforms, and visible accoutrements of status and power was unending. The economic distance between the haves and the have-nots was ratified: One-half of the nation, the peasantry, was virtually excluded from economic and cultural citizenship.[41] The *real* urban pay-scale was differentiated to a degree similar to or higher than in developed capitalist societies (which in a country with a low standard of living hit the lower rungs of the income ladder very hard).[42] A whole series of specific measures assured the continuous advantage of the advantaged, such as the introduction of substantial payments for middle and higher education, the substitution of vocational schools for the general education of children from lower classes, the primary reliance in taxation on such nonprogressive devices as the sales tax and the taxation of basic income alone. Social services were introduced which differentiated according to rank the extent and quality of services (medicine, vacations, and the like) and generally favored the white-collar over the blue-collar employee; the same principle was extended to pensions in an even more glaring manner.[43]

Stalinism reinstated with a vengeance the principle of authority and social discipline in the workplace, the school, and even the family. The discipline that Stalinism tried to foster was to be ideally a conscious

not only rationalizes the inequalities and the elite privileges within Soviet society, but it is in substance identical with the most extreme functional theories that justify wide margins of stratification in the West. For a general discussion of the close relation of Soviet social ideology with functionalism, see Alvin Gouldner, *The Coming Crisis of Western Sociology* (New York and London: Basic Books, 1970), chap. 12.

[41] That is to say, as long as they remained in the countryside and retained their peasant status. The only opportunity open to the peasantry was to cease being peasants, to leave the countryside and join the industrialization process in the cities or the army. The young generation of peasants in this period widely utilized this opportunity, and many of them later, through the channel of general, party, or military education, attained positions in the administrative structure.

[42] Inequalities in nominal wages and salaries are not the only and the best yardstick for measuring differences in economic status. From the medium strata of officialdom upward, economic privileges of a nonmonetary character increasingly affect and determine the living standard of their recipients. These privileges are hard to measure, not only because they are rarely discussed in detail in Soviet publications, but also because they are largely qualitative rather than quantitative in nature. For a discussion of these privileges, see Seweryn Bialer, ". . . But Some Are More Equal Than Others" in Abraham Brumberg, ed., *Russia under Khrushchev* (New York: Praeger, 1962), pp. 248–51; and Mervyn Matthews, "Top Incomes in the USSR: Towards a Definition of the Soviet Elite," *Survey*, 21, no. 3 (Summer 1975), 1–27.

[43] As one sociologist has remarked: "By the end of World War II, and particularly during the last years of Stalin's life, the trend was clear: The Soviet Union was well advanced along a seemingly irreversible course toward a rigid system of social stratification, in which the upper classes would remain upper, the lower classes lower, and the twain would rarely meet" (Robert A. Feldmesser, "Equality and Inequality under Khrushchev," *Problems of Communism*, 9 [March-April 1960], 31). For a general and detailed discussion of Soviet stratification, see especially Mervyn Matthews, *Class and Society in Soviet Russia* (New York: Walker, 1972).

discipline based on the recognition and acceptance of its need. Attempts at combining the strictest discipline with its conscious acceptance found exemplary expression in the meaning with which pedagogy infused such concepts as "independence" and "initiative." A textbook for Soviet teachers colleges states: "Independence and initiative mean the display of the greatest self-denial and the readiness and ability to obey an order absolutely whatever the obstacles and dangers. . . . [Initiative] is not just blind obedience but an independent search for the best way to fulfill a command."[44] Yet in effect it was a discipline which had to rely on the fear of and the application of extreme coercive measures.

Stalinist labor laws were draconic by any standard, the Soviet Union being the only European country where absenteeism became a criminal offense, punishable by imprisonment. The broad statutory authority of the *nachal'stvo* – "the bosses" – over the urban working class was still reinforced by the internal passport system, which prescribed the domicile, and by the labor-book system, which prescribed the workplace and recorded the worker's entire labor record; thus a convenient national blacklist was compiled.[45]

The pluralism and creative freedom that existed before Stalin's revolutions from above were replaced by uniformity and conformity in the arts and social sciences. The tastes and predilections of the leader and his entourage became not only the measure of artistic achievement, but they prescribed the very scale of artistic expression. Literature, film, and theater were reduced to schematic morality plays of what should exist, should be emulated, and should be believed. A mixture of rococo and the nouveau riche taste of old commercial Russia reigned in architecture. Neoclassicism joined with folksongs and pop tunes as the principal expressions of musical taste. Victorian behavior was officially commended to Soviet citizens as the standard for everyday life. A traditionalism grounded in the Russian nineteenth century provided a confining condition for the arts and served at the same time in some measure to salvage the country's cultural life. It was a great but dead culture, propagated in the interests of national pride and patriotic mobilization, but a culture arrested in its development.[46] Sociology, political science, political economy, and even the administrative and managerial sciences became virtually extinct. History was reduced to providing changing illustrations for changing political theses to serve the here and now.

---

[44]B. P. Esipov and N. K. Goncharov, *Pedagogika*, 5th ed. (Moscow: Uchpedgiz, 1950), pp. 283–4.

[45]The most draconic labor laws began to be introduced in 1938 with the issuing of "labor books" in December. By June 1940 all workers were frozen in their jobs. For a discussion of labor discipline under Stalinism, see Solomon M. Schwartz, *Labor in the Soviet Union* (New York: Praeger, 1952), pp. 86–129.

[46]One of the most interesting attempts to analyze the nature of artistic and aesthetic expressions under mature Stalinism and to connect it with the tastes and origins of the Stalinist bureaucracy can be found in Leo Kofler, *Stalinismus und Bürokratie* (Neuwied am Rhein: Hermann Luchterhand, 1970), pp. 66–103.

What has been said about the values and culture of mature Stalinism attests to the system's conservatism in the strictest sense of the word. Its focus was not to change social relations but to preserve and enshrine those that existed. An end had come to the revolutions from above through which the system was created. Its ultimate form—the "good society"—had arrived.

The state-Communist ideology became almost entirely an "ideology" in Mannheim's sense, with the "utopia" relegated primarily to fairy-tale chapters of textbooks. Lenin once said, "Our system is socialist because it is moving to socialism." Stalin's system moved away from socialism, as it was understood by both traditional Marxists and Bolsheviks. The chief architect did not consider the emergent system a transitional phase, a temporary state of emergency, or a set of provisional arrangements imposed by circumstance. He considered it the proper model of the long-range political organization of *any* socialist society, that is to say, the only proper institutional embodiment of the idea of socialism.[47]

Stalin's last work, *Economic Problems of Socialism in the USSR*,[48] was meant as his testament. The prescriptions therein envisaged not only the system's continuation, but the reinforcement of its centralized, statist, directly regulatory features. The work was the flight of fantasy of a conservative administrator, not a revolutionary. The Soviet Union should certainly become bigger, better administered, more powerful, but it should remain essentially the same. The work proclaimed as the main law of socialism "the securing of the maximum satisfaction of the constantly rising material and cultural requirements of the whole of society through the continuous expansion and perfection of socialist production on the basis of higher techniques."[49] At the same time the Nineteenth Party Congress in 1952 proclaimed the astonishing news that the Soviet Union's grain problems had been solved once and for all.[50] Such a

---

[47]After World War II the Stalinist system was introduced almost without modification to the countries of Eastern Europe in the Soviet sphere of influence. As Wlodzimierz Brus points out: "The very fact of transplantation of Stalinism to the Peoples' Democracies proves that it has been perceived as a *model* of a socialist structure. The universality of the model has been emphasized by applying it in a practically uniform way to countries on various levels of economic, social, and political development, with different historical pasts, and of diverse 'political cultures.' Thus, a new problem is posed by the PDs' experience: Stalinism as a model, and not only as a product of concrete historical conditions" (Wlodzimierz Brus, "Stalinism and the 'Peoples' Democracies' " in Robert C. Tucker, ed., *Stalinism*, p. 239).

[48]I. Stalin, *Ekonomicheskie problemy sotsializma v SSSR* (Moscow: Gospolitizdat, 1952). This 104-page brochure consisted of three letters written by Stalin to Soviet economists, which were to serve as the basis for the first authoritative textbook on political economy to be published in the Stalinist era. The textbook, incidentally, was published only after Stalin's death.

[49]*Ibid.*, p. 45.

[50]G. Malenkov, *Report to the Nineteenth Party Congress on the Work of the Central Committee of the CPSU (B)* (Moscow: Foreign Languages Publishing House, 1952), p. 66. At the time Malenkov made his estimate, the total production of cereals in the Soviet Union was 82.4 million tons, that is lower than in 1913 (86.0 million

declaration could mean, of course, only one thing: that the achieved standard of popular welfare was considered the appropriate one for a socialist society.

One characteristic of the last, mature stage of Stalinism provides the focal point for understanding the phenomenon of Stalinism as a whole. It is personal dictatorship. This characteristic binds and conditions most of the system's other characteristics. In particular, it provides in my opinion the only feasible explanation for the mass terror which was directed against the elite and the population.[51] Neither the survival of the system twenty years after the revolution nor the effectiveness of the system in mobilizing resources after virtual completion of the revolutions from above required the unleashing and persistence of terror. However, the establishment and continuation of Stalin's absolute dictatorship would have been impossible without it. I now turn to the question of the nature and extent of Stalin's personal dictatorship.

tons) (*Sel'skoe khoziaistvo. Statisticheskii sbornik* [Moscow: Gosstatizdat, 1960], pp. 202–3).

[51]Our interpretation differs here from that of Alvin Gouldner, who in his profound article "Stalin: A Study of Internal Colonialism" (*Telos*, no. 34 [Winter 1977–8], pp. 5–48) sees in the system of terror the originating causal characteristic of Stalin's personal dictatorship. In my view the quest for personal dictatorship explains the origins of the terror in the period of mature Stalinism and its continuation

2
STALIN AND THE
SOVIET POLITICAL ELITE

To discuss a leader's domination of a system, one examines three sets of questions. One set concerns the leader's authority – the "relationship of inequality sanctioned by the legitimacy of leaders to make and enforce policy." The second concerns the leader's control – "the actual or perceived ability to provide or withhold benefits and apply sanctions." The third concerns the leader's autonomy – "the extent to which leaders are independent of environmental factors."[1] It is my contention that in the operational sphere Stalin dominated the system to an extent greater than any leader of a major nation in the twentieth century before, during, and after his rule, and that his domination in the symbolic sphere almost equaled that of such figures as Hitler or Mao Tse-tung.

Stalin's authority in the symbolic sphere was expressed in the cult of the Leader, an all-encompassing and all-pervading phenomenon of mature Stalinism. The cult created its own symbols, rituals, and language and found expression in them. It was deliberate, thoroughly planned, and institutionalized, both in the relations within the bureaucracies and between the bureaucracies and the society. It partially replaced but in the main coexisted with the cult of the Bolshevik revolution. (Symbolically, the best example of this replacement and coexistence was the conversion of the main wing of the Museum of the Revolution into a repository for gifts received by Stalin on the occasion of his seventieth birthday.)[2]

The term *vozhd'* (The Leader) entered the official and popular language. It was reserved for Stalin alone. His high associates and lesser officials were called *rukovoditeli*, leaders. (And they referred to Stalin informally as *khoziain*, boss.) Other terms were used exclusively for Stalin: The Great Teacher, The Helmsman, The Great Son of the People, The Father of the People, Our Sun, and the like. When in 1943 the Soviet anthem replaced the "International," a verse about Stalin was introduced into it. During World War II the official battle cry of the Soviet

[1] Lewis J. Edinger, ed., *Political Leadership in Industrialized Societies* (New York and London: Wiley, 1967), p. 6.

[2] With the passage of time, Stalin's cult predominated where before it had coexisted with Lenin's cult. The simplest way in which this can be appreciated is by looking at the new editions of Soviet postage stamps under mature Stalinism. In the year 1950, for example, there were issued sixty-two new stamps with Stalin alone, three with Stalin and Lenin together, and three with Lenin alone.

army was "For the Homeland, for Stalin." In honor of Stalin an entire industry wrote books, poems, and plays, composed songs, and painted pictures. The *Short Biography of Stalin* and the *Short Course of the History of the All-Union Communist Party (B)*, which Stalin himself edited, portrayed him as the demiurge of history. These works constituted the basis of political education from the high school through the university (where special departments were created for this purpose) to the higher party school. About 70 million copies of them appeared from 1938 to 1953.

When Stalin's birthday was celebrated in 1949, *Pravda*, the party daily, devoted three-quarters of its space for nine months to birthday greetings from home and abroad. The announcement of every Soviet achievement from smallest to greatest, from the opening of a provincial kindergarten to the inauguration of a gigantic dam, commenced with the standard formula: "On the initiative of Comrade Stalin. . . ." Every meeting from routine assemblies of Young Pioneers and school graduations to anniversaries and commemorative events began with Stalin's election to the honorary Presidium and ended with a standing ovation for Stalin. The press reported all details, including the precise duration of the ovation. The cult was semireligious in its character and frenzy. Even the unintended destruction of Stalin's portrait was considered a desecration and punished as a criminal offense.

The cult of Stalin, supported and nourished by an enormous organizational effort, aimed in part to circumvent the organizational base of Stalin's authority and to establish a direct relationship of authority with the bulk of officials and the masses. It is difficult to judge Stalin's success in this endeavor; evidence would indicate it was at least partial. The cult's rituals, numbing to an observer, evidently exhilarated many or even most participants. In this respect, World War II can be seen as a turning point, when the almost miraculous victory upon the brink of total disaster made credible the attribution of nearly magical powers to Stalin, and his identification with this great patriotic achievement evoked widespread, genuine admiration.

In conversations with Soviet citizens, including party members, I was repeatedly informed that any doubts they had entertained about Stalin and his cult were dispelled by the war and his performance during the war. This view emerges even in Soviet military memoirs. It explains in part why Soviet military leaders who disliked the official depiction of the war effort during Stalin's lifetime (all credit for all victories went to Stalin), were nevertheless reluctant to accept Khrushchev's attempt to denigrate Stalin's war role entirely. During the war they had considered Stalin their legitimate, authoritative, and successful leader who brought them to victory. The altered second editions of Soviet war memoirs which followed Khrushchev's ouster would appear to be more suited to the military's taste and, in fact, more objective and closer to the truth in describing Stalin's wartime leadership.

Yet the pursuit of Stalin's cult displayed certain weaknesses which evidently diminished its effectiveness, particularly its deep, lasting effects. Stalin was not the founder of the State; he had shared and did share the honor with Lenin. His lack of oratorical gifts (and his strong Georgian accent) as well as his pedantic, uninspired style of speech and writing probably impaired his success, as did his style of *mass* leadership (or rather the lack of it). In this respect Stalin and Hitler were opposites.

It was not the fact that Stalin was a distant leader. The distance was strictly enforced even with close associates, none of whom was permitted to call him by first name and patronymic, the traditional and customary means of respectful address in Russia. Indeed it may even have added a calculated air of mystery and authority.[3] Important is the fact that Stalin was an isolated leader. He rejected almost entirely the tools and methods of direct mass influence which modern means of communications, transportation, and mass movements opened to leaders in the twentieth century. He apparently feared mass contact and mass exposure. He did not attend mass rallies and meetings; he did not travel; he rarely gave media addresses; he did not even receive delegations from the populace or officialdom. He was literally a prisoner in the Kremlin. He chose to have contact with only a relatively small group of associates and officials.[4]

Another major weakness of Stalin's cult was its failure to mesh satisfactorily with the ideology of Marxism and Bolshevism, even in that emasculated form which they preserved under mature Stalinism. In contrast to the Führer principle in Nazi ideology, Stalin's practice of personal dictatorship as well as the cult of the dictator had no ideological anchoring. Entirely a matter of accepted and glorified practice, no attempt was made to provide a systematic rationalization of its virtues. In the prevailing system of ideological thought under mature Stalinism, it was alien to the schemata and terminology of even vulgarized Marxism and Leninism.

While the personal dictatorship was an overwhelming fact of life and the cult of Stalin all-pervasive, the party schools did not devote more than one lecture to the individual's role in history; they devoted numerous lectures and seminars to the role of masses and classes. The inability to reconcile the cult and doctrine probably explains why members of youth organizations and the armed forces swore the oath of allegiance to the Fatherland and the "Party of Lenin and Stalin," not to Stalin personally. This failure together with the highly bureaucratic nature of Stalin's cult goes far to explain the relative ease with which the cult was abandoned almost immediately after Stalin's death, while the regime's continuity was preserved. It also explains why it was possible to present

---

[3] This is one main thesis of the most extensive Soviet document to evaluate Stalin during the Brezhnev era, the three-volume work by Aleksandr Chakovskii, *Blokada* (Moscow: Izd. Izvestiia, 1975) (see especially vol. 2).

[4] The term "prisoner in the Kremlin" is used *solely* to convey the fact that Stalin's encounters were confined to a relatively restricted group of associates and officials. One has the impression, however, that within the Kremlin Stalin was almost never alone. It was as if he did not like or—without overdramatizing—he was afraid to be alone.

Stalinism as an excess, a temporary excrescence on the otherwise healthy body of the Soviet polity.

The mainstay of Stalin's personal dictatorship rested not in his cult but in the administrative and political arrangements he was able to establish. To understand this and to appreciate the degree of Stalin's domination of the system, one must discuss briefly some aspects of his style of leadership, his policy-making arrangements, and his policies.

Under mature Stalinism, the principle of centralized decision making was brought to its ultimate conclusion and manifested in many forms. Within each area of policy making the range of decisions declared to be the sole prerogative of the central institutions in Moscow was very broad. (In the existing atmosphere of fear and well-advised caution, even the decisions left to lower authorities were, as a form of insurance, referred to higher institutions.) The central authorities made binding decisions regarding the entire gamut of cultural, social and economic, and political endeavor. These decisions not only prescribed general outlines of behavior; they treated as well the details of implementation and the very specific expected outcomes. Once policies were established, only the issuing authority had the right to make significant changes or even to make adjustments for changing circumstances and for flaws that emerged in their implementation. The entire cycle of reference to the center would thus begin again.

Within the central institutions in Moscow, collegiality in decision making was for all practical purposes abolished. The rule that heads of bureaucratic hierarchies would take responsibility on all levels was firmly implanted. Here, too, Stalin, followed by his highly placed associates and subordinates, reinforced the tendency to push decisions, large and small, to the top. Truly astounding were the number, variety, and importance of the matters continually awaiting Stalin's decision or simply reaching his desk. Therefore, it is very important to understand the procedures by which Stalin made decisions.

Stalin's domination of the top decision-making bodies was absolute. As a matter of fact, it is difficult under mature Stalinism to speak about collective decision-making bodies at all. In contravention of existing party statutes, the Central Committee, the formal leading party organ in whose name most of Stalin's edicts were issued, was "elected" only twice, in 1939 and 1952, that is at the very beginning and end of the period. Between 1939 and 1952, only a few plenary sessions of the Central Committee took place.[5] To my knowledge, the statutory top decision-

---

[5] According to authoritative Soviet sources, six such meetings took place in the sixteen years from 1938 until Stalin's death: 21–24, 27 May 1939; 26–28 March 1940; 29–31 July 1940; 21 February 1941; 27 January 1944; 21–26 February 1947 (see *Spravochnyi tom k vosmomu izdaniiu "KPSS v rezoliutsiiakh i resheniiakh" s'ezdov, konferentsii i plenumov TsK* [Moscow: Gospolitizdat, 1973], p. 11). According to Khrushchev: "During all the years of the Patriotic War not a single

making bodies – the Politburo, the Secretariat, and the Orgburo – met quite regularly.[6] The question is not how frequently they met, however, but what was the nature of the decision-making process at those meetings. All evidence points unmistakably to the conclusion that all these institutions were nothing more than advisory bodies, very fragmented and collectively powerless.

First of all, most decisions were made in countless and almost constant meetings between Stalin and one or more selected Politburo members; these were often held informally over dinner or drinks at Stalin's suburban villa.[7] (Individual Politburo members were assigned broad and specific areas of responsibilities. These included, but were never limited to, officially designated party or government functions. At such meetings decisions concerned their particular areas of responsibility.)[8] Moreover, the Politburo and Secretariat were constantly divided into regular and ad hoc subcommittees to oversee specific tasks – the famous "triplets" *(troiki)*, "quartets" *(chetverki)*, and the like. Those fragmented bodies, it seems, had little relation to one another; they reported separately to Stalin, who was the only one to draw together the various threads of information and ultimately power.[9] Even so, toward the end of his rule, Stalin became dissatisfied with even the symbolic vestiges of collective power that were associated with the existence of these bodies. He abolished the Orgburo altogether. He changed the name of the Politburo to Presidium to underscore the functional discontinuity of its present advisory and its past decision-making role; he enlarged its membership to twenty-five, including many junior bureaucrats, and thus diluted effectively the prestige associated with membership.

Most importantly, Stalin completely dominated the decision-making process itself at large and small meetings with his associates. The numer-

---

Central Committee plenum took place. It is true that there was an attempt to call a Central Committee plenum in October 1941, when Central Committee members from the whole country were called to Moscow. They waited two days for the opening of the plenum, but in vain. Stalin did not even want to meet and talk to the Central Committee members" (Nikita S. Khrushchev, "Special Report to the 20th Congress of the CPSU," *The New Leader* [1962], pp. 19–20).

[6] According to a Soviet source (*Voprosy istorii*, 1970, no. 5 [May], pp. 13–15) quoted in Jerry F. Hough and Merle Fainsod, *How the Soviet Union is Governed* (Cambridge, Mass.: Harvard University Press, 1978), p. 178, the Politburo, Orgburo, and Secretariat met over two hundred times during the war period.

[7] For one of the best accounts of such dinner meetings at Stalin's villa from an independent observer, see Milovan Djilas, *Conversations with Stalin* (New York: Harcourt, Brace and World, 1962).

[8] For example, from 1940 and throughout the war, Zhdanov, in addition to being the CC party secretary with general responsibility for Leningrad (and later for cultural affairs), was specifically assigned to supervise naval affairs; Molotov, in addition to being the people's commissar for foreign affairs, was responsible for the tank industry; and CC Secretary Malenkov, in addition to his general responsibility for industrial management, directly supervised the aviation industry (see I. Kh. Bagramian, *Tak shli my k pobede* [Moscow: Voenizdat, 1977], p. 67).

[9] For the creation of the regular and ad hoc committees, see Khrushchev, "Special Report to the 20th Congress of the CPSU," p. 62.

ous accounts of such meetings, whether sympathetic or hostile, all agree on one point: The meetings were usually quite lively, and the clashes of opinion were frequent and bitter, as long as Stalin only listened. No sooner did Stalin ask a few pointed questions, from which participants contrived to deduce his train of thought, than the discussion began to falter. All discussion ended once Stalin expressed a definite opinion. (He usually started with the words: "It seems to me that. . . .")[10]

It is one of the most noteworthy phenomena of mature Stalinism that, to the best of our knowledge, there was throughout this period no open challenge, no "secret plot," no major gesture of defiance, no instance of criticism of Stalin from his close associates or from the elite. It is well to remember in this respect that, unlike some other contemporary dictators, Stalin did not preside over a victorious elite (though the regime was victorious), but over a crushed party, army, state bureaucracy, and even police. He effectively destroyed their spirit and their will in the Great Purge of the 1930s, and until his death they were not permitted to recover from this lesson. After 1938, Stalin's high-level purges were surgical incisions rather than massive assaults; but they were incisions that kept the memory of the Great Purge alive, should any reminder have been necessary.[11]

It is not enough to dwell on the insecurity and constant fear of a false step (and there could be no falser step than to get on the wrong side of Stalin). Stalin followed a set of principles and used a number of devices which kept the elite off balance and made the formation of an alliance within its ranks, a challenge against him, hard to conceive. The regular secret police maintained dossiers and surveillance of high officials

---

[10]For accounts of many meetings with Stalin during the 1940–5 period, see S. Bialer, ed., *Stalin and His Generals* (New York: Pegasus, 1969). Aside from the two-volume memoirs of Khrushchev, the authenticity of which is now beyond dispute (*Khrushchev Remembers*, trans. and ed. by Strobe Talbott [Boston: Little, Brown, vol. 1, 1970; vol. 2, 1974]), some of the most interesting Soviet accounts may be found in: V. S. Emelianov, *O vremeni, o tovarishchakh, o sebe* (Moscow: Izd. Sovetskaia Rossiia, 1974); S. M. Shtemenko, *General'nyi shtab v gody voiny* (Moscow: Voenizdat, 1973); G. K. Zhukov, *Vospominaniia i razmyshleniia* (Moscow: Izd. APN, 1972); A. M. Vasilevskii, *Delo vsei zhizni* (Moscow: Gospolitizdat, 1973); K. K. Rokossovskii, *Soldatskii dolg* (Moscow: Voenizdat, 1972); N. G. Kuznetsov, *Na flotakh boevaia trevoga* (Moscow: Voenizdat, 1971); N. N. Voronov, *Na sluzhbe voennoi* (Moscow: Voenizdat, 1963); A. S. Iakovlev, *Tsel' zhizni* (Moscow: Gospolitizdat, 1966).

[11]The only massive purge of the postwar period came to be known as the Leningrad Affair. It happened in 1949, after Zhdanov's death; and in its course the leadership of the Leningrad party, state, and armed forces was decimated. It also struck those leaders who were Zhdanov's protégés and associates in the Leningrad organization, such as the head of Soviet planning and Politburo member Voznesenskii, Prime Minister of the Russian Republic Rodionov, and CC Secretary Kuznetsov. Only Stalin's death, it would seem, interrupted preparations for a new purge directed against some of his closest associates and specifically the head of the secret police, Beria. The Doctors Plot of 1952 was the first step. For the Leningrad Affair and the preparations, see N. Khrushchev, "Special Report to the 20th Congress of the CPSU," pp. 45–6, 48–50, and Robert Conquest, *Power and Policy in the USSR* (New York: St. Martin's Press, 1961), pp. 95–111.

through a separate branch, the Special Department. At no time during Stalin's rule was a second-in-command appointed or a successor designated, even for a short period of time. The pecking order of Stalin's top associates changed constantly and deliberately. At all times three or four leaders of relatively similar influence watched each other and competed fiercely for influence.

Important to Stalin's arrangements were the establishment and growth of his private secretariat. Our knowledge of it is fragmentary. What we do know, however, clearly confirms its significance as a device for Stalin's control over the bureaucracies and the decision-making process. The private secretariat was an autonomous institution, distinct from other bureaucracies, with its own organization and recruitment, and subordinated exclusively to Stalin. Neither a party nor a state organ, it stood apart from both. Aside from the normal function of scheduling Stalin's work and arranging the agendas of meetings, its key function was to gather information and to control the implementation of Stalin's decisions. A large organization, it employed professional policemen, investigators, military men, and economic experts. Its head, Poskrebyshev, did not actually participate in formal decision making; only in 1952 were his efforts symbolically recognized by cooptation to membership in the Central Committee of the party.[12]

The secret police itself, the main tool but also the main danger to Stalin, was not permitted to grow too powerful *against* Stalin. It was checked by a number of administrative arrangements and policies. Besides Stalin's private secretariat, the most important of those were:

> The existence in the secretarial apparatus of the party's Central Committee of a Special Department (later named Department of Administrative Organs) which was empowered to supervise the internal affairs of the secret police;
>
> Stalin's retention of the power to appoint high police officials who were often selected from competing factions in order to minimize the possibility of a monolithic command and collusion;[13]
>
> The retention of a military intelligence apparatus (GRU), semiautonomous from the secret police, which provided an independent channel of information and an investigative body in strong competition with the police;
>
> The infrequent but significant reorganizations of the police apparatus, the most important of which consisted of dividing the

[12]For a discussion of Poskrebyshev and Stalin's Private Secretariat, see Boris Meissner, "Poskrebyschew – der Privatsekretär Stalins," *Osteuropa*, no. 1 (1951), pp. 45–6, and Boris Nicolaevsky, *Power and the Soviet Elite* (New York: Praeger, 1965), pp. 105–20.

[13]One typical example is the postwar appointment of S. N. Kruglov, who was not associated with Beria, to head the Ministry of Internal Affairs as a counterbalance to V. S. Abakumov, one of Beria's henchmen, who headed the Ministry of State Security, and the subsequent replacement of Abakumov in late 1951 by a territorial party secretary, S. D. Ignat'ev.

enormous machine into two command structures – the MVD (NKVD) and MGB (NKGB) – and the separation of the internal intelligence and counterintelligence service from control over the militarized internal security units (VVB).

It has become fashionable lately to question the extent of the personal powers of twentieth-century European dictators. The argument runs as follows: The countries over which the dictators ruled were too large, the bureaucracies too vast, the issues too complex for the dictator himself to govern effectively. His policies and preferences were continuously circumvented and shaped in practice by his subordinates, especially on the intermediate and lower levels of implementation.[14] No doubt there is validity to the view that sees the personal power of the dictator circumscribed not only by the physical conditions and capacities of his environment but also by the political circumstances of a bureaucratic empire.

With regard to Soviet Russia, the ideal of "pure" administration was of course never achieved – neither at the top nor at the lower levels. Politics did not disappear in Stalin's Russia. The divisiveness of political interests, the struggle for policy influence, the political in-fighting, and the attempts to bend existing policies to the advantage of groups and individuals were if anything more vicious than before or after Stalin. This was because they were less likely to be resolved by compromise solutions and they were often fought for no less a stake than life itself. But one can repeat after Leonard Schapiro in his review of Edward Peterson's book, *The Limits of Hitler's Power:* What does it prove? Schapiro remarks:

> Has anyone ever imagined that Hitler, or Stalin for that matter, ran a whole country alone, all the time, everywhere? If you lift the stone the crawling things appear, in the intrigues, the corruption, the local mafias – and also the occasional glimpses of decency, resistance, even heroism. None of this is surprising. . . . But what is quite clear from his [Peterson's] analysis is that the moment the Führer chose to act, or even the moment his will on any subject became indirectly known, the local chaos was galvanized into a pattern which was in accordance with his will. This was indeed the essence of totalitarianism. Not a streamlined efficient dictatorship, but a chaos of conflicting authorities – party, state, army, industry, each independent in its own sphere, but each able to act only until the moment when the Leader chooses to declare his will, either himself or through his . . . *apparat,* the all-pervading cancer which eats into the legal order of the state and the fabric of society alike.[15]

[14]With regard to Hitler and Nazi Germany, this view is most forcefully expressed by Edward N. Peterson in *The Limits of Hitler's Power* (Princeton, N.J.: Princeton University Press, 1969); with regard to Stalin and Soviet Russia, the most recent and rare revisionist attempt belongs to Jerry F. Hough in *How the Soviet Union Is Governed*, chap. 5, pp. 147–91.

[15]Leonard Schapiro, "What Is Fascism?" *New York Review of Books*, 14, no. 3 (12 February 1970), 14.

When reading the voluminous literature on Hitler and Nazi Germany, one is struck, moreover, by important differences in styles of leadership, differences which argue that Stalin achieved greater dominance and control of the everyday working of the system than did Hitler. Our most detailed knowledge of the extent and style of Stalin's leadership concerns the World War II period.[16] Even though it was a period of extreme emergency, there is strong evidence that the data of this period describe Stalin's style throughout the entire period following the Great Purge. Data for the second-best-known period, 1939–41, for example, reveal an identical pattern; and there are indications that the postwar period, if anything, only reinforced preexisting tendencies. After all, the entire Stalinist era was characterized by institutionalized emergency, by quasi-war politics and economy during a time of peace.

Art and war were said to be the only real interests of Hitler. Stalin, as the picture emerges from numerous accounts, was a leader preoccupied with the management of resources, one who concentrated tremendous attention not only on grand strategies and policies, but also on the manner and details of their implementation, on the day-by-day control of their implementation. Stalin was an administrator par excellence, by desire, by temperament and bent of mind, by his own assessment of how to set his own priorities.

Stalin's system of decision making and administration – super-centralized, ponderous, enormously complex and Byzantine, and at the same time very primitive for a vast country and an industrial society – entailed enormous waste of human and material resources. The lack of checks on the center, the fear of initiative in the bureaucracy, the inertia of decisions once taken, the suspiciousness and stubbornness of the dictator – all magnified the consequences of errors in judgment on the part of the dictator and his associates. That the system could actually work and survive depended on a number of factors.

Despite the increased complexity of the economy and of the administrative tasks assigned to the bureaucracies, the range of *real* internal priorities which the system's directors recognized, that is, priorities which in their minds really counted, was very narrow. Military power based on the growth of heavy industry and internal security was first and foremost. Together these three priorities overshadowed all other tasks, which were considered important primarily insofar as they conditioned and impinged on the attainment of these real goals. The concentration of the top decision-making process on these priorities was overwhelming; other decisions and issues could and did wait for attention, resources, and resolution; they remained suspended in a limbo of bureaucratic inertia and chronic crises. Methods employed for the attainment of the priority items were crude and primitive – unending campaigns, constant crash

[16]For a review of the literature and an evaluation of Stalin's leadership during the war, see Alexander Dallin, "Allied Leadership in the Second World War: Stalin," *Survey*, 21, no. 1/2 (Winter-Spring 1975), 11–19.

programs, pressure, threats, and inhuman effort – but because of the concentration of the effort on a relatively few items regardless of costs, they
did manage to preserve the necessary margin of achievement in the attainment of the system's goals.

It would be erroneous, however, to conclude that fear, insecurity, and
Stalin's skillful manipulation can fully explain the submission of the
elite and bureaucracy to his will and the extent of their willing support
which he was able to secure. It seems necessary to distinguish the character of elite support for Stalin on his way to dictatorial power in the
early period of his absolute rule, and in his last years.

In the formative years of Stalin's dictatorship, he achieved dominance
in the party, not only because of his superior organizational skills and
ruthless manipulation, but because he expressed the aspirations of the
dominant groups in the Soviet party and elite; he tapped their anti-intellectualism, nationalism, isolationism, modernization zeal, and anti-peas-
antism. Among the Civil War and NEP generations of party militants, and
even within the small prerevolutionary Bolshevik sect, these sentiments
were at times openly expressed and at times only thinly overlaid by the
veneer of Bolshevik ideology.[17]

The two elements important to understand in Stalin's building of
support are, first, the gradual if convulsive way in which his system was
built; and second, the rationalizations which accompanied it. The principal rationalization was that given actions served the good of the cause
and depended in each case on specific internal or external circumstances.

To illustrate the first element, let us take the case of terror. The original Bolshevism and its key spokesman, Lenin, far from repudiating terror as a tool of revolutionary government, defended it in theory and
advocated its application in practice.[18] Yet terror was regarded, and
principally applied, as a defense mechanism against real enemies, as an
instrument for consolidating the shaky, besieged, and isolated government. It was neither considered nor employed as a long-range instrument of social transformation nor as a long-range method of everyday
administration, nor certainly as even a short-term medium of control
over the movement and the elite.

The change in the pitch of terror which accompanied Stalin's ascen-

[17]A new look at Stalin's base of support on the road to absolute power is provided
in the collection of essays edited by Sheila Fitzpatrick, *Cultural Revolution in
Russia, 1928–1931* (Bloomington: Indiana University Press, 1978). See also
Sheila Fitzpatrick, "Culture and Politics under Stalin: A Reappraisal," *Slavic
Review*, 35, no. 35 (June 1976), 211–31.

[18]Lenin's views on revolutionary terror can be found particularly in the following
articles and speeches from his collected works (all references are to the fourth
Russian edition published in Moscow): "O vragakh naroda" (vol. 25, pp. 41–2);
"Kak burzhuaziia ispol'zuet renegatov" (vol. 30, pp. 8–19); "Doklad VTsIK i
Sovnarkom na VII Vserossiiskii s'ezd Sovetov" (vol. 30, pp. 185–219); "O prodo-
vol'stvennom naloge" (vol. 32, pp. 334–5).

dancy would appear to be initially quantitative in character: the build-up of the repressive apparatus, its broadened prerogatives, an increase in the scope of its activity; there was no major change in the targets and goals of persecution. Terror was directed against a specific enemy, the declared or imaginary enemy of the system from the ranks of those who traditionally would be carriers of anti-system attitudes: the old intelligentsia, the "specialists," the remnants of the bourgeois stratum, the rich peasant, the former apparently unreconstructed members of the anti-Soviet parties, and so forth.

The major leap in the qualitative nature of the terror occurred during the Civil War which Stalin declared against the countryside in the process of collectivization. It was not only the sheer magnitude of coercion which changed, but its goals: the use of mass, indiscriminate, group-oriented coercion as a tool of social transformation, and, to use Alvin Gouldner's expression, as a method of a massive transfer of property.[19] Two things should be noted here. First, at the outset, in the initial stages of collectivization, there was little or no inkling, even in the higher echelons of the party, how far the process would go, how much of this long-range campaign would quickly evolve into a virtual civil war. Second, once the process was unleashed, it found broad and willing support within the party.[20]

[19]Alvin Gouldner, "Stalin: A Study of Internal Colonialism," *Telos*, no. 34 (Winter 1977–8), p. 13. Gouldner writes: "What had been brought into being was an urban-centered power elite that had set out to dominate a largely rural society to which they related as an alien colonial power; it was an internal colonialism mobilizing its state power against colonial tributaries in rural territories.

"Here, internal colonialism refers to the use of the state power by one section of society (the Control Center) to impose unfavorable rates of exchange on another part of the same society (e.g., the Subordinate Remotes), each being ecologically differentiated from the other. The control center governs by using the state to impose unequal exchange through decisions governing capital allocations, investments, prices and price controls, access by visitors, taxes, tax exemptions and deductions, credit, loans, labor drafts, military conscription, rates of interest, wages, tariffs, customs duties, access to education, passports and visas, and electoral representation. Where these routine mechanisms fail, the control center uses force and violence against the remote subordinates." The question whether such transfer was necessary as a precondition of forced industrialization and even whether the rural sector actually played an important part as a source of resources for the industrializing effort is increasingly put in doubt by a number of revisionist writings on this subject. The latest and most comprehensive example is found in James R. Millar, "What's Wrong with the 'Standard Story,' " *Problems of Communism*, 25, no. 4 (July-August 1976), 50–5, 59–61. For a rejoinder defending the "Standard Story," see in the same issue Alec Nove, "The 'Logic' and Cost of Collectivization," pp. 55–9, 61–2.

[20]The support is best exemplified in the successful mobilization of tens of thousands of workers and party activists who were sent to the countryside during the collectivization drive. Without their efforts, collectivization would not have succeeded. For a discussion of the worker and party mobilization, see Moshe Lewin, *Russian Peasants and Soviet Power* (London: George Allen and Unwin, 1968), chap. 17. See also Thomas P. Bernstein, "Leadership and Mass Mobilization in the Soviet and Chinese Collectivization Campaigns of 1929–1930 and 1955–1956: A Comparison," *China Quarterly*, no. 31 (July-September 1967), pp. 1–47.

How could it have been otherwise when one speaks about a totally urban party, nurtured in anti-peasant attitudes, to which the peasant and peasant way of life epitomized the hated Russian backwardness; to which the attack on the peasantry was presented with substantial evidence as the party's counterattack against the peasants' attempt to sabotage grain deliveries and starve the cities; and, finally, to which the substance of the social change wrought by collectivization was in its deepest meaning a socialist reform, notwithstanding the methods used to achieve it? Yet even so, there are indications that, in the upper echelons of the party at least, the shock of the "war of collectivization" left a strong residual hope and desire that the violent base of the revolution from above was over and that the extremes of the period would subside.[21]

What must be stressed strongly is that throughout this phase of Stalin's ascendancy, the party as a whole, not to mention its elite, was exempt as a target of terror. The party had its own mechanism and institution, the Party Control Commission, for testing political loyalties and discipline, independent of the state terroristic apparatus. As recent research has shown, this mechanism constituted until 1934 a major obstacle to Stalin's attempts to introduce terrorism as a method of intra-party administration.[22]

The second qualitative change came in the 1934–6 period and culminated in the Great Purge. In this period the party and then the elite became the main target of terror. From a tool of social engineering *by* the party, terror became a medium of administration and a mechanism for the subjection *of* the party. Our knowledge of the initial period of this type of Stalinist terror is very incomplete. We know that Stalin was able at the Seventeenth Party Congress in 1934 to liquidate the Party Control Commission and the Workers' and Peasants' Inspection (RKI) and to put his henchman Yezhov in charge of the newly created State-Party Control Commission; and we know that he later purged the secret police itself to prepare it for its new task and appointed the same Yezhov to head it.

Most importantly, because of the assassination of Party Secretary Kirov (the circumstances of which are still unclear), Stalin succeeded in creating within the party a state of emergency. He skillfully built an atmosphere of hysteria, of siege, of imminent danger which clearly had

---

[21]This sentiment is expressed most strongly and described most vividly in the so-called "Letter of the Old Bolshevik" based on notes made by Boris Nicolaev-sky of conversations with Bukharin during the latter's last trip abroad in 1936 (Boris Nicolaevksy, *Power and the Soviet Elite*, pp. 3–65). The dominant tone of the Seventeenth Party Congress in 1934, the "Congress of the Victors," can also be said to express, in addition to the sense of accomplishment, the sense of relief that the worst is over, that a more moderate policy will henceforth be pursued. These hopes and sentiments found some justification in the fact that the former leaders of the "Right Opposition" were permitted to appear and address the Congress and that the Second Five-Year Plan was much more moderate and balanced in its design and goals than its predecessor.

[22]The major example of this new research is Paul Cocks, "The Party Control Commission and the Rise of Stalin" (Ph.D. dissertation, Harvard University, 1971).

no foundation in reality but which permitted him to start a general purge of the party[23] and to introduce the first steps of anti-party terror: false accusations of criminal anti-state and factional activities, forced confessions, the first show trials. One has the impression that at this stage the higher party echelons were disoriented while Stalin through his closest and unquestioning associates already controlled the party machinery and the coercive apparatus.

The party members, low and high, were used to regarding the secret police as their organ of power and Stalin as their leader. It was probably difficult to grasp at that stage the fact that the entire coercive apparatus had become independent of the party, a personal tool of Stalin, and that he himself was becoming the arbiter of life and death over the party. And when the final blow came swiftly in 1937–8, it was too late for reflection and reaction. To protest, to ask questions, or even to reflect was to condemn oneself to death. Anyway, even without suicidal attempts, the old guard was extinguished; a mere handful of Stalin's long-time associates survived thanks to unquestioning obedience; and a new elite was established to whom the need for terror at that point appeared self-evident.

For the new elite as well as the remnants of the old, what probably started with doubts and questions went through a process of rationalization and self-justification which led to an internalized acceptance of the system as it had come to be. Their behavior may have initially conformed to nothing more than what Gerth and Mills define as "rational uniformities" of social action – that is, to behavior patterns that "are only expediently oriented to norms, duties, or to felt obligations. Their stability as patterns of conduct rests on the deviator's running the risk of damaging his own interests."[24]

The growing weight of empirical evidence and theoretical generalization, however, suggests that an expedient role playing, a prolonged expression of beliefs and submission to standards of behavior which one learns are needed to advance, typically produces the internalization of these values and standards. Mills points out that the long acting out of a role will often induce a man to become what at first he merely sought to appear.[25] Similarly, Stinchcombe writes, "If a man of his own volition pursues something which requires holding some value to get, he usually comes to be quite convinced of the sacredness of that value."[26] In this

[23]Initially the purge was not a terroristic affair. It was disguised in the form of the rather well-established past practice of a party campaign to "inspect" the whole membership with regard to political loyalties, ideological preparedness, corrupt or immoral behavior, etc.

[24]Hans Gerth and C. Wright Mills, *Character and Social Structure, The Psychology of Social Institutions* (New York: Harcourt, Brace, 1953), p. 265.

[25]On this point, see C. Wright Mills, "Language, Logic and Culture," *American Sociological Review*, 4, no. 5 (October 1939), 670–80; Gerth and Mills, *Character and Social Structure*, chap. 4.

[26]Arthur L. Stinchcombe, *Constructing Social Theories* (New York: Harcourt, Brace & World, 1968), p. 110. All those propositions are based on the "balance theory" developed by Fritz Heider in his *The Psychology of Interpersonal Relations* (New York: Wiley, 1958).

sense the system of externalized institutional controls and elite recruitment tends not only to effect a shallow, ritualistic, or expedient expression of established elite values and observance of established standards
of elite behavior, but also to regenerate a rather intense commitment and
usually long-lasting adherence to these values and standards.

There were a number of straightforward and understandable rationalizations which underlay Stalin's support among the elite. A crucially
important one of these is very well known from the history of revolutionary movements or, for that matter, from the study of the psychology of
power in general. It can be called, in brief, the rationale of "the good
cause." After all, Stalin is building socialism – there is no restoration of
capitalism, private ownership is a fact, the process of production is being
planned, the profit motive has been abolished, unemployment has been
eliminated, and so forth. If it is not capitalism, it must be socialism,
because history does not move backward.[27] Not everything is all right,
mistakes are being made, some aspects of the system are unpleasant or
even bad, but they have to be suffered for the good of the cause which is
good.[28]

Closely related to this rationalization was the largely justified feeling
among the elite that it was actively participating in transforming a backward nation into a powerful industrial state. The barbarous methods
from which the elite itself suffered were felt to be a price paid for enormous, real achievements. At the same time, who could be certain
whether other methods could prove effective or even possible?

The next link in the chain of rationalization was related to the international conditions which accompanied the growth of Stalinism in the
1930s. Stalin was the beneficiary of the rise of fascism in Europe. He
profited from what can be called the "Gletkin syndrome." In Arthur
Koestler's *Darkness at Noon*, Gletkin, Rubashov's second interrogator,
eloquently expresses the justification and rationalization of Soviet behavior used by the Soviets themselves and by Western radicals in the 1930s:
"The fate of the world revolution depends on surviving the period of
world reaction and keeping alive the only existing bastion of socialism."

---

[27]The anti-Stalin writings of Leon Trotsky reveal that, even in the case of a sophisticated man, the commitment to Leninism and the adherence to Marxist-Leninist
formulas defeat his efforts to comprehend Stalinist Russia. The latest and best
attempt to evaluate Trotsky's analysis of Stalinism can be found in Robert H.
McNeal, "Trotskyist Interpretations of Stalinism," in Robert C. Tucker, ed., *Stalinism: Essays in Historical Interpretation* (New York: Norton, 1977), pp. 30–52.

[28]For a long time it was thought that this kind of rationalization underlay the false
confessions at the Moscow trials of the 1930s, as Arthur Koestler depicted them
in *Darkness at Noon*. The evidence now indicates that the explanation was less
complicated – torture and fear for the safety of families. Khrushchev recounts
that in a 1939 telegram to provincial party secretaries, republican central committees, and the heads of the secret police, Stalin reasserts, in the name of the
Central Committee, the principle of using torture "as a method both justifiable
and appropriate" against "enemies of the People," a principle which according
to the telegram had been established in 1937 (see N. S. Khrushchev, *Special
Report to the 20th Congress of the CPSU*, pp. 34–5).

Until then, says Gletkin, "we have only one duty: not to perish . . . the bulwark must be held at any price, any sacrifice."

The words of John Strachey describing the sentiments of foreign Communists in the 1930s can probably be applied as well to Soviet Communists:

> For a Communist in the nineteen-thirties who was seized of that argument, the local or temporary state of things in Russia seemed a matter of secondary importance. In front of everybody's eyes the Marxist prognosis of the development of a latter-day capitalism was apparently fulfilling itself. Outside Russia, it *was* becoming more and more impossible to use anything like the whole of the productive apparatus; unemployment *was* consequently becoming endemic; the misery of the wage-earners and peasants *was* ever-increasing; the violence, hysteria, and general irrationality of the governing classes of the main capitalisms *was* mounting; attempts at gradualist reform by social democratic methods *had* failed; finally, Fascism was being established not only in such peripheral countries as Italy and Spain, but also, and decisively, in Germany, one of the major, advanced capitalisms. It was above all this apparition of evil incarnate in the form of Fascism which gave the Communist argument power. For that argument taught that Fascism was no accidental catastrophe but the logical and inevitable consequence of "capitalism-in-decay". . . . How much did even the ugliest features of the new socialist society matter if it gave even the possibility of the re-building of civilisation upon a viable basis?[29]

[29]John Strachey, "The Strangled Cry," *Encounter*, 15, no. 5 (November 1960), 6. With regard to this way of thinking I have written in another place about Western radicals: "Studies on 'true believers' very often note that insensitivity to violence, cruelty, and suffering on one level of consciousness co-exists in them with sensitivity to the same phenomena on another level. To put it differently, what is so striking about the radical way of thinking (among others) is the extreme politicization of morality and ethics, either in its crudest form which states that what is politically right is ethical, or in its more sophisticated and sophist form which divorces moral condemnation of an act or process from its political valuation. Within this dual framework of perception and self-consciousness, the majority of radicals who took their beliefs seriously could and did excuse and accept (although not necessarily like) the cruelty, viciousness, and oppressiveness of the Soviet 'construction of socialism' as long as they believed that this represented the extreme and unique birth pangs of a better world, of a genuinely 'progressive' system. Today they cannot accept the much more limited cruelty and the dull oppressiveness of the Soviet system because very few can still believe that a birth of a better world is occurring in the Soviet Union or that the world which was born bears any relation to the vision of the good society that had inspired the revolutionaries of old. For the radical intellectual especially, the dilemma in the past was often expressed and rationalized as the value of intellectual freedom and the luxury of 'formal' democracy for the relatively few versus the value for the many of abolishing hunger and exploitation. Today, hunger in the Soviet Union has been abolished but intellectual freedom has not been restored even to the levels of the 1920s, when it coexisted with deprivation and economic hardships. The rationalization of a necessary exchange of one

All these rationalizations were of course based on the solid foundation of advantages and gains which Stalin offered to lower, middle, and upper elite echelons whatever their field of activity. This is especially true with regard to the tens and hundreds of thousands of new elite members from predominantly low-class origins who acquired positions of power during and as a result of the Great Purge of 1936–8. (I will discuss this group later in a different context.) It is sufficient to say here that they owed to Stalin, directly or indirectly, their meteoric rise into the middle and upper levels of the power structure from almost total obscurity, whether advanced from the lowest ranks of bureaucracies or recruited directly upon graduation from institutions of higher learning.

An anti-Stalinist Polish Communist essayist and literary critic wrote very perceptively in 1937 that Stalin's base of support went far beyond the upper echelons of the elite:

> The eve of collectivization and five year plans was being described as a "second revolution" [as contrasted to the October revolution]. Whatever it was, this revolution became possible because of the utilization of social reserves until then untouched. To activate them meant to undermine for a while the *social* base of all and sundry workers' oppositions, after they had already been destroyed in the *political* sense. The workers were striving for the development of industry, were demanding a fight against bourgeois elements and a systematic growth in their standard of living. Instead they got the superindustrialization, the mad tempo of construction, the decline in the standard of living, the forced collectivization, etc. The dissatisfaction was suppressed not so much by force as by the gigantic campaign to draw the proletariat into the administrative apparatus. Tens of thousands of workers were then as now transferred into the European and Asian provinces. The bright locksmith of today or the foundry worker of the Putilov factory, instead of being involved in criticism of Soviet policy, in debates over violations of Soviet democracy, and over demands to have his rights carried out in practice, was becoming tomorrow a chairman of a collective farm, a director of a state farm, or the organizer of the national existence of some remote nationality, about the very presence of which he learned only from his traveling orders. In this manner the political disarmament of the proletarian masses was being accomplished.[30]

valued item for another no longer makes sense. What does make sense is the conclusion of Edgar Morin that 'if there is a loss of freedom that must be considered formal, there is no progress in freedoms that can be considered real.' " (Seweryn Bialer, "The Resurgence and Changing Nature of the Left in Industrialized Democracies" in S. Bialer and S. Sluzar, eds., *Radicalism in the Contemporary Age, 3: Strategies and Impact of Contemporary Radicalism* [Boulder, Colo.: Westview Press, 1977], 12–13).

[30] Andrzej Stawar, *Wybrane Artykuly o Marksizmie* (Paris: Instytut Literacki, 1962), p. 190.

The regimental army commanders who found themselves in command of corps and military districts, the party district instructors who became secretaries of provinces, the factory directors who became ministers of state, the obscure propagandists who became rectors of universities – their advance was the rule rather than the exception in this period of extraordinary elite turnover. Brought suddenly into power, they were awed by Stalin's authority; they basked in the reflected glory of the adulation of Stalin; they considered the style of Soviet leadership established by then to be the natural order of things. Their hard work, however strenuous and insecure, however full of pitfalls and constant fear of mistakes and downfall, had equally staggering rewards, so unexpected but a short time before: the power of command, the pleasure of adulation, and, last but not least, the material perquisites, pitiful by Western standards, but enormous in the context of their environment.[31]

Toward the end of Stalin's rule, however, the system which he created, and especially its terroristic aspects, came to be felt by his associates and the elites more and more as a burden, as an unnecessary, irrational impediment to their enjoyment of the good life which they felt was their due, to their satisfaction over the status which their country had achieved, and to the further internal development and external security of the system itself.

The elites and leadership grew accustomed to their power and privileges. For the generation which advanced during and through the Great Purge, status was no more an unexpected gift to be enjoyed at the price of constant fear and insecurity, but something earned by hard work, sacrifices, and loyalty. Their country had survived the terrible test of total war and achieved a total victory – its prize a major empire. The great power status achieved by the Soviet Union opened new vistas for Soviet foreign policy. The industrial and educational foundations achieved under Stalin created the need and preconditions for a different kind of economic growth and development.

---

[31]In an original book based on analysis of middle-brow Stalinist fiction, Vera Dunham posits that mature Stalinism, especially in the postwar period, developed what she calls the "Big Deal": an alliance with the new Soviet middle class, functionaries, managers, technical intelligentsia, etc. She remarks: "One can see this rapprochement in part as a calculated policy of the stalinist dictatorship. But the policy grew out of spontaneous, cumulative processes where the development of the new Soviet middle class was paralleled by the transformation of the Soviet political regime from a revolutionary bolshevik force into an essentially conservative establishment, intent on preserving the status quo. This dual process brought closer together the preferences and aspirations of the political establishment and those of the middle class. It made the establishment's appeal to middleclass hopes and sensitivities a reflection not only of the manipulative policies of the regime but also of its own preferences and values. Given the staggering size of the job to be done, the old mystique of the collective lost its popular appeal and its economic usefulness. What was now urgently needed was a wide range of individually committed citizens" (Vera Dunham, *In Stalin's Time: Middleclass Values in Soviet Fiction* [Cambridge: University Press, 1976], p. 14).

The elite yearned for normalcy – for preserving the fruits of Stalinism, personal and public, without having to pay the price of insecurity in life and position. They had been brought up in the midst of Stalin's barbarism; they were its willing participants; but now they yearned for a different, what they would consider a deserved and more stable, political lifestyle, for material progress, respectability, enjoyment.[32] This in the deepest sense was the key reason why the system of mature Stalinism could not survive its creator. The leadership *as a whole*, and the elites *as a whole*, wanted a new deal.

[32]The desire for stability and the growing revulsion against terror among upper echelons of the elite were probably reinforced in the last years of Stalin's rule by growing indications that he was actively preparing another major purge. The Mingrelian Affair in Georgia and the Doctors Plot were the opening salvos of an intensification of terror which threatened again to sweep away the established leadership. For a vivid description of the mood of this period, see N. S. Khrushchev, *Khrushchev Remembers*, vol. 1, pp. 245–320.

3
STALINISM
AND THE EVOLUTION
OF THE SOVIET POLITY

Stalin's reign occupies a central place in the history of the Soviet Union. It colors strongly our understanding of the formative revolutionary period preceding it, and it affects forcefully our evaluation of the quarter-century following his death. The ongoing scholarly discussion about Stalinism concentrates largely on the question of continuity and change in the pre-Stalinist and Stalinist periods of Soviet history. Much of this discussion is artificial and unfocused and often slides into the unrewarding surrealistic exercise of "if" history.

The question is not whether such a continuity existed. How can one expect it not to have existed? The continuing elements from which Stalinism grew and established itself as the dominant state ideology and practice were, to mention a few: the principle of one-party rule and its monopoly of political power and political organization; the reigning attitude that laws and legal procedures are subordinated to political expediency; the moral relativism; the dominant belief in the efficacy of political power in effecting long-range social changes; the measures against the formation of lasting factional grouping within the party; the commitment to centralization of political and economic command; the belief in an all-embracing ideological truth that unlocks the doors to understanding historical development.[1] That all those and other characteristics of pre-Stalinist Russia were propitious and maybe even indispensable to the formation and victory of Stalinism, that they prepared the way for Stalinism, cannot be disputed. Sometimes it is ideological blindness, sometimes it is analytical confusion, and often it is a lack of factual knowledge which leads, however, to equating the incubatory preconditions of Stalinism with the developed Stalinist system itself.

Stalinism grew from preexisting conditions but created its own conditions; it built on the preexisting system but created its own system. The mature Stalinist system was not a simple, logical extension of the preexisting system. Nor was it formed in an evolutionary expansion of the old system. In a violent and convulsive social, economic, cultural, and political transition of unprecedented magnitude, which lasted for over a decade, a new system of rule and government was established in the Soviet Union under Stalin. The peculiarity of this transition and of the newly-

[1] For a fresh and informative discussion of the original Leninism and Bolshevism, see Marcel Liebman, *Leninism under Lenin*, trans. Brian Pearce (London: Jonathan Cape, 1975), especially part 3.

created system itself, which mutes and hides its separate identity, is that it occurred within the basic continuity of the authority structure, with a conscious attempt to establish a continuous legitimacy base, with the preservation of most of the symbols, rituals, and even the terminology of the preceding era. *It was a revolution in the guise of continuity.*

One could make a long list of specific aspects and items which differentiated mature Stalinism from the preexisting system of Soviet Russia. It is not those items taken separately, however, but their combination and their mutually reinforcing effect which provide the distinctiveness of Stalinism and make of Stalin the architect of an original system of Soviet government. Bolshevism in power, in theory and practice, and among *all* its factions, was strongly authoritarian; but to equate it with mature Stalinism is similar to the equation of authoritarian tendencies in the American polity with fascism. The extremes of Stalinism were not a momentary exaggeration of the authoritarian impulse and practice of Bolshevism in power, but a full-blown system of institutionalized extremes; excessive (one should not be afraid of the word) to the point of sheer criminality by any standards, including those of the Bolsheviks.[2]

One must speak here about differences of degree because it is exactly the degree that makes the difference. Social sciences, after all, deal primarily with differences of degree which make the difference; otherwise they become purely a conglomeration of reified concepts divorced from reality, analytical scaffoldings without a building behind them.

The distinctiveness of Stalin's creation is equally pronounced when one looks at the development in the Soviet Union after his death. According to Khrushchev, Stalin in his last years, wondering about the future, said to his associates: "What will you do without me? You are as blind as young kittens."[3] If Stalin had no confidence in the ability of his successors to survive, the overwhelming majority of Western analysts after Stalin's death proved too confident that the future held for the Soviet Union no change at all.[4] Both expectations were unfounded.

[2] The views expressed here are very much in accord with the position of Stephen F. Cohen in his pioneering work *Bukharin and the Bolshevik Revolution* (New York: Knopf, 1973) and especially his excellent article, "Bolshevism and Stalinism" (in Robert C. Tucker, ed., *Stalinism: Essays in Historical Interpretation* [New York: Norton, 1977], pp. 3–29). Where we differ is in the extent to which I see Bolshevism as homogeneous, the extent to which I see Leninism as highly authoritarian, and the extent to which I see a broad base of support within the party for the initial Stalinist revolutions from above – differences which have little relevance from the point of view of the purpose of this chapter.

[3] N. S. Khrushchev, "Special Report to the 20th Congress of the CPSU," *The New Leader* (1962), p. 49.

[4] Among the rather rare exceptions to the expectation of unilinear continuity in Soviet development after Stalin, one should especially mention Robert C. Tucker's articles in *World Politics* (1954–7), some of which were included later in his *The Soviet Political Mind* (New York: Praeger, 1963), part 1. A major analysis of the options for post-Stalinist development was written shortly after Stalin's death by Barrington Moore, Jr.: *Terror and Progress USSR* (Cambridge, Mass.: Harvard University Press, 1954). It still remains important in the discussion. Isaac Deutscher's expectations of major changes in Soviet post-Stalinist de-

In 1953 the dean of American sovietologists, Merle Fainsod, wrote in the closing paragraph of his major work: "The governing formula of Soviet totalitarianism rests on a moving equilibrium of alternating phases of repression and relaxation, but its essential contours remain unchanged. The totalitarian regime does not shed its police-state characteristics; it dies when power is wrenched from its hands."[5] An editorial in a major West German scholarly journal devoted to the study of the Soviet Union and Eastern Europe argued in August 1953:

> It would be a mistake to draw far-reaching conclusions from individual steps [of the new leadership] which contradict preceding Stalinist practice. One should not overestimate the relaxation of the totalitarian regime and the changes in the methods of leadership. Most of the measures which Stalin's successors undertook in the last months, concern most of all the consolidation of their rule. Some of them have been even undertaken primarily for propaganda purposes to influence people abroad.[6]

In January 1955 Bertram Wolfe concluded an article in *Foreign Affairs* with an enviable certainty:

> To sum up. The "new men" who have succeeded to Stalin's power are not so new as they look to the uninquisitive eye, for they are Stalin's men. And a good look at the "new look" suggests that it is not so new either, for more than Stalin would admit or they dared to claim, while he was alive, they worked out the Stalinist policies with him. Now that he is dead they have been able to cut the losses of some of the minor errors with which his stubbornness or prestige had become involved, but all their major policies from "peaceful coexistence" to the sensational plowing up of the virgin lands are in accord with plans elaborated and drives initiated while Stalin was alive. They do but give "arithmetical values" to "algebraic formulae" already worked out in the decisions of the Nineteenth Congress and in Stalin's so-called testament: "Economic Problems of Socialism in the U.S.S.R." What the "new" men bring to their drives is the fresh vigor of younger men and a fresh flexibility in manoeuver. But they are manifestly continuing the war on their own people – "the revolution from above" – and the war for the control of the world.[7]

velopment were closer to the mark than those of most other observers. They were, however, based on wrong premises in my view, namely, that the Soviet working class "will wake up from its stupor" and will by active pressure effect changes in the direction of restoring genuine socialism in the USSR (Isaac Deutscher, *Russia What Next?* [New York: Oxford University Press, 1953] and *Ironies of History, Essays on Contemporary Communism* [London and New York: Oxford University Press, 1966]).

[5] Merle Fainsod, *How Russia Is Ruled* (Cambridge, Mass.: Harvard University Press, 1953), p. 500.

[6] *Osteuropa* (August 1953), p. 278.

[7] Bertram D. Wolfe, "A New Look at the Soviet 'New Look,'" *Foreign Affairs*, 33, no. 2 (January 1955), 198.

While all these and countless other statements wrongly predicted the trends of Soviet development after Stalin, in a certain sense they were right. They were right in their underlying assumption that the Stalinist system could not survive without an emergence of a new dictator, without a new cult of The Leader, without mass terror, without insecurity of elites, without a continuous war on the nation (and especially on the "internal colony," the peasantry), and without extreme mobilization. In fact, in the twenty-five years since Stalin's death the Stalinist system has not survived. The Soviet Union today differs in marked respects from its mature Stalinist predecessor. With a stability surprising to the Soviet leaders themselves, the Soviet system withstood the crucial test of transition from personal dictatorship and despotism, and in the process it acquired some new, dominant characteristics.

I shall not engage in a detailed examination of the Soviet polity as it has emerged in the quarter-century after Stalin's death. Let me note, however, some of the most important characteristics of the present Soviet political system:[8]

> From a personal dictatorship the Soviet leadership was transformed into a stable oligarchy;[9]
>
> The bureaucratic hierarchies and the elite structure became highly institutionalized with stable representation in the leadership, with relatively clearly delineated lines of authority, and with a party apparatus providing the coordinating function;[10]
>
> There evolved a complex and regularized domestic decision-making process based on bargaining and compromise among major elite and bureaucratic groups which cut across organizational and functional lines;[11]

---

[8] For a general discussion of changes in the political system in the post-Stalinist era, and especially in the Brezhnev period, see Seweryn Bialer, "The Soviet Political Elite and Internal Developments in the USSR" in William E. Griffith, ed., *The Soviet Empire: Expansion and Detente* (Lexington, Mass.: Lexington Books, 1976), pp. 25–55.

[9] See, for example, T. H. Rigby, "The Soviet Leadership: Towards a Self-Stabilizing Oligarchy," *Soviet Studies*, 22, no. 2 (October 1970), 167–91.

[10] For the best analysis of the coordinating function of the party apparatus in mediating between the various bureaucracies, see Jerry F. Hough, *The Soviet Prefects: The Local Party Organs in Industrial Decision-making* (Cambridge, Mass.: Harvard University Press, 1969).

[11] For a basic statement on the development of interest-group politics in the Soviet Union, see H. Gordon Skilling and Franklyn Griffiths, eds., *Interest Groups in Soviet Politics* (Princeton, N.J.: Princeton University Press, 1971), especially the chapters by Skilling and Griffiths. For dissenting views, see Andrew C. Janos, "Group Politics in Communist Society: A Second Look at the Pluralistic Model" in Samuel P. Huntington and Clement H. Moore, eds., *Authoritarian Politics in Modern Society* (New York and London: Basic Books, 1970), pp. 437–50, and William E. Odom, "A Dissenting View on the Group Approach to Soviet Politics," *World Politics*, 28, no. 4 (July 1976), 542–67.

Experts and professional groups play an increased and systematic advisory role in the policy-making process;[12]

Mass political terror was abolished, the secret police were largely eliminated from the political process within the elite, the still massive Soviet police state was reduced to the political functions of a traditional authoritarian polity;

The domestic policies of the leadership reflect a growing responsiveness to aspirations of major social groups and to the anticipated, if not openly articulated, popular pressures;[13]

The rural sector in its productive function was transformed from an "inner colony" into a subsidized sector of the economy, the recipient of the single largest investment item of external budgetary resources;[14]

---

[12]For the role of experts in Soviet policy making, see Richard B. Remnek, ed., *Social Scientists and Policy Making in the USSR* (New York: Praeger, 1977), especially the chapter by Linda L. Lubrano, pp. 59–85; David Holloway, "Scientific Truth and Political Authority in the Soviet Union," *Government and Opposition*, 5, no. 3 (Summer 1970), 345–67; and a paper by Peter H. Solomon, Jr., "A New Soviet Administrative Ethos," prepared for the Northeastern Slavic Conference of the AAASS, Montreal, Quebec, 5–8 May 1971.

[13]If the behavior of the leadership can be judged responsive, then to what kind of pressures is it responsive? In part, of course, the responsiveness is connected with changes that have occurred in the distributive sector of the economy, where the population acquired for the first time in Soviet history a limited possibility to express its demands through selective buying. A thousand complaints of irate citizens to local soviets or newspapers will probably have less impact on improving the quality of consumer products than a large inventory of unsold goods. In part, this responsiveness has to do with the importance that the leadership attaches to material incentives in its economic programs. But in large measure, this responsiveness can be described as an anticipatory reaction, that is to say, not a response to actual behavior of workers but to the leadership's fear that if workers' interests are not considered, workers' behavior might become disruptive and dangerous. The dangerous lessons of workers' dissatisfaction in East European countries, and especially the workers' uprising in Poland in December 1970, have not been lost on Soviet leaders. In a situation where such a high premium is placed on stability, where an organized dissident movement is active in the land, where mass terror is absent, where the population's expectations have been encouraged for a long time, and where the opening of Soviet society to foreigners has made material comparisons possible, attention to the material satisfaction of the population is a prime requisite of the party's ability to curtail cultural freedom, withhold political freedom, and preserve the political stability of the system. For a different type of explanation, see Jerry F. Hough, "The Soviet Experience and the Measurement of Power," *Journal of Politics*, 37, no. 3 (August 1975), 685–710.

[14]A leading Western analyst of the Soviet economy has the following to say about the state of the present Soviet agricultural expenditures: "One can now speak of a veritable Soviet 'Project Independence,' a concerted program designed to achieve fairly dependable and steadily rising grain harvests with a view to future self-sufficiency at high per capita levels of consumption of animal products. It is not a cheap program. Whereas in the second half of the 1960's the share of total gross fixed capital investment going to agriculture averaged 23 percent, in 1973 it reached 26.5 percent, and in 1975 it may have attained 27 percent. In fact, during the first half of the 1970's, the value of fixed capital in agriculture

The Soviet state expanded its social services enormously, initiated a virtual income revolution, and became a highly developed welfare state.[15]

It is very common to describe the past and the present Soviet Union as a bureaucratic state. Indeed, some of the key models for the study of Soviet society which have developed as alternatives to the totalitarian model isolate this trait as the determining factor of explanation. They speak about the "mono-organizational society,"[16] the "bureaucracy writ large,"[17] the "monist system,"[18] and so forth. Aside from other reservations which one may have about the utility of those models, one should point out that rarely do they discriminate among the varieties of a key distinguishing factor of macro-bureaucratic behavior: the different political orientations of bureaucracies.

S. N. Eisenstadt, in his magisterial work, *The Political Systems of Empires*, indicates major types of political orientations which a bureaucracy in the historical bureaucratic societies could develop. These include:

1. Maintaining service orientations to both the rulers and the major strata . . .

2. Evolving into a merely passive tool of the rulers, with little internal autonomy or performance of services to the different strata of the population

3. Displacing its goals of serving the various strata and the polity, in favor of goals of self-aggrandizement or usurpation of power exclusively for its own benefit and/or the benefit of a group with which it became closely identified

(exclusive of livestock) grew nearly half again as fast as in industry, though output grew much more slowly in the former sector than in the latter (even if one discounts the effects of adverse weather). For 1976, if one also includes investment going to branches of the economy supportive of agriculture (the tractor and agricultural machinery industries, the fertilizer industry, etc.), agriculture in this sense is to receive over 34 percent of the gross fixed investment in the whole economy for the current year. This is a major dent in the country's resources of investment capital, amounting in fact to over 10 percent of the expected national income (Soviet series) for 1976 (Gregory Grossman, "An Economy at Middle Age," *Problems of Communism*, 25, no. 2 [March-April 1976], 19–20).

[15] On the Soviet welfare state, see especially the imaginative paper by George W. Breslauer, "On the Adaptability of Soviet Welfare-State Authoritarianism" in Karl Ryavec, ed., *Soviet Society and the Communist Party* (Amherst: University of Massachusetts Press, 1978), pp. 3–25, and Robert J. Osborn, *Soviet Social Policies: Welfare, Equality, and Community* (Homewood, Ill.: Dorsey Press, 1970). On changes in income distribution, see Murray Yanowitch, "The Soviet Income Revolution," *Slavic Review*, 22, no. 2 (December 1963), 683–97, and Peter Wiles, "Recent Data on Soviet Income Distribution," *Survey*, 21, no. 3 (Summer 1975), 28–41.

[16] T. H. Rigby, "Politics in the Mono-Organizational Society," in Andrew Janos, ed., *Authoritarian Politics in Communist Europe: Uniformity and Diversity in One-Party States* (Berkeley: University of California Press, 1976), pp. 31–80.

[17] Alfred G. Meyer, *The Soviet Political System: An Interpretation* (New York: Random House, 1965).

[18] George Fischer, *The Soviet System and Modern Society* (New York: Atherton Press, 1968).

4. Replacing its goals of serving the major strata with goals of self-aggrandizement and attainment of political power, while maintaining goals of serving the polity and the rulers

Of course, the bureaucracy in each of the historical bureaucratic polities usually exhibited a mixture or overlapping of all these tendencies or orientations. However, as a rule, a particular tendency preponderated for at least part, if not the whole, of each polity's history.[19]

Soviet bureaucracies under the Stalinist regime fit into the second category, while today they are coming to resemble more and more the fourth type.[20]

One of the most striking aspects of the process of change in post-Stalinist Russia is that the decisive stimuli for their occurrence have come from incumbent leaders and elites. This is not to say that pressures emanating from outside the official framework, especially those originating among the intelligentsia, were not at times an influential factor in policy formation. Some policies, the literary thaws for example, constituted to some degree a reluctant response to demands which the leadership preferred to accommodate, at least in part, rather than to pay the costs of their suppression. Yet, despite the intrusion of external pressures in policy formation, their intensity and their cumulative effect have fallen far short of generating a serious shift in the traditional closed decision-making process.

Moreover, the post-Khrushchev decade has shown not only the narrow base of pressures emanating from outside the official framework, but it has disclosed the determination and the ability of the leadership to resist such pressures. The apposite case concerns the unprecedented appearance on the Soviet political scene of the dissident movement, which is as notable for its ability to establish its presence and to survive as it is for its inability to broaden and to influence official Russia to meet any but some of its most minimal, tactical demands. It would appear that the process of change in post-Stalin Russia, whether liberalizing or restrictive, whether fundamental or mildly reformatory, in its key features can be ascribed to initiative from above or at least to volition of the strongest factions within the Soviet leadership and elites. And the primary pressures inducing institutional and policy innovation in the post-Stalin era have not been the actual pressures of social groups or strata, but those of changing material conditions in society at large and of changing political circumstances within the elite itself. And the men who directed these

[19]S. N. Eisenstadt, *The Political Systems of Empires* (New York: Free Press, 1963), p. 276.
[20]An excellent analysis of different types and functions of Soviet bureaucracies at different periods is contained in Bruce Parrott, "Bureaucracy and Development in the USSR" (unpublished paper, 1978). For an analysis of specific and diverse meanings of the application of the concept of bureaucracy to the Soviet situation, see also Horst Herlemann, "Zur Problem der Bürokratie in der Sowjetunion," *Osteuropa*, 26, no. 12 (December 1976), 1064–78.

changes were reformed Stalinists (or reformist-Stalinists). It is this distinctive feature of the process of post-Stalinist change in the Soviet Union which determines its evolutionary nature, shapes its main characteristics, and conditions its limitations.

Just as the mature Stalinist system, though different from its predecessor, developed from the antecedent Leninist system and from the revolutionary transformations which created its basic shape, so the present Soviet system emerged from mature Stalinism and carries many deep and visible stigmas of its own origin. The evolution of the Soviet system away from Stalinism after 1953 was carried out under the slogan of moving forward, "back to Leninism." In some areas the changes do represent a conscious effort to reestablish the norms that prevailed before the Stalinist revolution was accomplished. This is true in part with regard to the norms established in relations within the political elite, though not within the mass party. It is particularly true with regard to the extent and targets of the coercive aspects of Soviet policies at home which fit into the definition of the newly found, and Leninist post–Civil War, "legality," that is to say, which are directed against real and active adversaries of the state, dissenters against the prevailing orthodoxy.

In many cases, however, the evolution of the Soviet system away from Stalinist extremes has retained many of the values and the norms of Stalinism; and when it moved back, it went farther back than Leninism, to the traditional orthodox values of prerevolutionary Russia. It would be fair to assert that the present system retained especially those norms of Stalinism which Stalin himself restored from the *ancien régime*, on the way from Leninism to the creation of his own order. In this sense it is proper to define this evolution, or at least one of its strong tendencies, in the manner of Brzezinski, whose article carries the most fitting title, "Soviet Politics: From the Future to the Past?"[21]

The crucial characteristic of the Soviet Union today is the deeply conservative and actively nationalistic nature of state and society. The process of the withering away of utopia and utopianism in the thought

[21]In Paul Cocks, Robert V. Daniels, Nancy Whittier Heer, eds., *The Dynamics of Soviet Politics* (Cambridge, Mass.: Harvard University Press, 1976), pp. 337–51. The pursuit of the idea of continuity of the Russian and Soviet tradition has a long history in Western scholarly tradition. One of its latest excellent examples is Tibor Szamuely's *The Russian Tradition* (New York: McGraw-Hill, 1974). It is only recently, however, that this idea finds explicit and developed expression in dissident writings from Russia itself, as for example, in Boris Shragin, *The Challenge of the Spirit* (New York: Knopf, 1978). The more prevalent view of anti-Soviet dissidents is expressed in its most extreme form by Aleksandr Solzhenitsyn, for example in his speech at the Hoover Institute: "The Soviet development is not a continuation of the Russian one but a distortion of it in a completely new, unnatural direction. . . . The terms 'Russian' and 'Soviet' are . . . not part of the same order of ideas: they are irreconcilable opposites, they completely exclude each other. . ." (Aleksandr Solzhenitsyn, "Two Speeches at Stanford," *Vestnik RKhD* [Paris, New York, Moscow], no. 118, p. 170).

and practice of the political elite has been accelerated. This utopianism, the strongest and closest derivative of the doctrinal tradition, still constituted under Khrushchev a component of the vision of the future within which the elite operated.[22] Incorporated in the party program of 1961, the promise of the leader read – "The party solemnly proclaims: The present generation of Soviet people shall live in communism."[23] The present Soviet leadership dislikes and discourages fantasy. *Delovitost'*, businesslike behavior, has become their ubiquitous slogan, the leadership quality most praised in the written and spoken word. The *delovitost'* of the top leaders, however, is that of businessmen concerned with the rationalization of means rather than the definition of ends.

Most significant is the radical decline of the elite impulse to *re*shape society. In the mind of the ruling elite, the Soviet social structure has found its permanent shape – at least for the foreseeable future. What the party proposes to the Soviet population is nothing but the indefinite reproduction of the basic existing social relations and material progress within the framework of these relations. In this respect it resembles the posture and the bias of mature Stalinism. The innovative impulse of the political elite is focused entirely on functioning innovation and not on restructuring innovations.

If nothing else, generations of Soviet leaders have assimilated from the Marxist tradition the dimension it shared with Western rationalism, the belief in Progress. The fundamental decline in the centrality of the affirmative and optimistic idea of progress in the West is not duplicated in the Soviet Union. In some respects one can discern for the first time elements of doubt and a devaluation of expectation. The optimism of the Khrushchev era has been replaced by more somber assessment and much greater realism about what can be achieved in the short and intermediate term. The old attitude, which looked upon nature as a fortress to be conquered, is being complemented by reflections, and fears, about the ecological dilemma. The future looks less like a unilinear, unbridled progression upward. What has changed very little or not at all is the deeply entrenched belief in, and commitment to, continuous economic growth, the all-pervading technological ethos, the faith in science and the lack of recognition of the instrumental nature of scientific knowledge.

The persistent centrality of the belief in Progress and its almost total equation with material growth are associated with and supplemented by a deeply rooted attitude of evaluating one's own performance in "pro-

[22]The term "post-Stalin era" sometimes conceals the real and substantial differences between the periods of Khrushchev's and Brezhnev's leadership. One such difference concerns Khrushchev's genuine attempt to revitalize the party ideologically, an effort which diminished sharply after his ouster. For a reevaluation of the Khrushchev period, see Jeremy Azrael, "Khrushchev Remembered," *Soviet Union*, 2, part 1 (1975), 94–105, and George W. Breslauer, "Khrushchev Reconsidered," *Problems of Communism*, 25, no. 5 (September-October 1976), 18–33.

[23]"Programma Kommunisticheskoi Partii Sovetskogo Soiuza" in *XXII s'ezd KPSS. Stenograficheskii otchet*, 3 (Moscow: Gospolitizdat, 1962), 235.

gressing to Progress" by the standards attained in Western industrial nations. In this basic way alone can the Soviet political elite be said to remain "internationalist." The sources of this "comparative" mentality are manifold: the justification of the past history of sacrifice and denial, the ultimate legitimization of the superiority of the system, the assurance of the security of the system from alien and hostile external forces. The important point is, though, that it is a way of thinking that has taken hold of and pervades all segments of the elite regardless of its specific sources, and that it has acquired an existence of its own. This mentality infuses in the political elite a sense of urgency and a stress on mobilization even in times of notable achievement. Its systemic effects are somewhat contradictory – on the one hand it is conducive to promoting taut planning, mobilizational atmosphere, social discipline, and so forth; on the other hand it is probably the single most important inducement to functional innovations, to performance-oriented reform, once the performance according to old methods becomes unsatisfactory according to standards of Western competitors. The tendency that emerges from this internal contradiction is to opt for reforms which improve performance but preserve the mobilizational atmosphere and social discipline.

The mainstay of the awareness of common purpose within the political elite is provided more than ever by nationalism. Partly in its great-power Soviet variety, partly in its cultural, traditional Russian variety it constitutes the major effective, long-lasting bond within the political elite and between the elite and the masses. The old conservative theme – the cult of national unity – provides the emotional base for a political authoritarian outlook and is in turn reinforced by it. Last, one should mention without any need to elaborate that entire set of beliefs and attitudes dominant within the Soviet political elite which expresses a deep-seated fear and mistrust of spontaneity in political and social behavior, induces an interventionist psychology, and stresses the need for strong central government, organization, and order.

In the post-Stalinist period the Soviet leadership and elites have also developed a set of rules of conduct in their relations with each other by which they abide in their competition and conflict, their bargaining and their compromise. These rules are grounded in the following factors:

> A high valuation placed on the security of the elites themselves, the commonly shared norm that force, that is, physical violence, has no place within the elite itself in resolving political conflicts on policies and power, that such a use of force in internal competition among elites is "improper and unjust";
>
> A high valuation placed on insulating elite decision-making from the direct pressures of outside social strata and a belief in the impropriety of appealing at a time of internal elite conflicts to support from the mass party, let alone from collectivities outside of the elite;
>
> A high valuation placed on the differentiation of rewards and privileges according to social position and to the responsibili-

ties attached to the elite status and the belief in the justness of the security of these privileges when performance standards are met.[24]

To suggest that a core set of beliefs, norms, and values is shared within and among the Soviet elites is not to imply that they are shared by each organizational or functional elite segment to the same extent, with the same intensity. As a matter of fact, the whole notion of institutions and institutionalizations assumes the process of selection and correlation with power of diverse primary values in different functional and organizational segments of the elites. Moreover, it can be taken almost for granted that the underlying principles of order of diverse organizational or functional elite segments will be more particularistic, may not even be included in the commonly shared core norms and beliefs, and therefore may create a potential for conflict among these elite segments which goes beyond the specific utilitarian interest and enters into the symbolic sphere.

What is suggested only is that, first of all, most of the intra-elite conflicts within Soviet society are located within the area of specific interest differentiation, utilitarian concerns, specific policy disagreements, and not within the sphere of norms and values, especially the core values of the political regime. An important example of a mistaken identification of specific interest disagreements with a basic value conflict is committed in my opinion by Roman Kolkowicz when he analyzes party-military relations.[25] I am very much in agreement with William Odom when he questions the political-military value dichotomy alleged by Kolkowicz.[26]

Second, in the post-Stalin and especially the post-Khrushchev era, new norms were established and specific policies were developed which were directed, in my opinion quite successfully, toward reducing the chances of intra-elite conflict over values, so as to keep such conflict out of the symbolic sphere and within the policy interest sphere.

Such policies are reflected especially in two areas: the drawing of a boundary line between science and doctrine and, more ambiguously, the character of professional debates on policy issues. These policies can

[24]The second and third rules were partly broken by Khrushchev, one of the major reasons the opposition among the elites united against him and eventually ousted him. At times, Khrushchev did try to appeal to the mass party and even to outside strata in his conflicts with the Politburocrats (see, for example, Michel Tatu, *Power in the Kremlin* [New York: Viking Press, 1969], pp. 176–207, 244–60, 364–86). With regard to social policy vis-à-vis the elite, both I and Feldmesser have argued that Khrushchev's attitude, while eliminating terror, was to try to prevent the consolidation of the social (and political) status of the elites, to try to prevent their full transformation from a "serving class" to an independent entity (Abraham Brumberg, ed., *Russia under Khrushchev* [New York: Praeger, 1962], chapters by Seweryn Bialer and Robert A. Feldmesser, pp. 223–62).

[25]Roman Kolkowicz, *The Soviet Military and the Communist Party* (Princeton, N.J.: Princeton University Press, 1967), especially pp. 20–7.

[26]William E. Odom, "The Party Connection," *Problems of Communism*, 22, no. 5 (September-October 1973), 12–26.

generally be described as providing a large margin of professional autonomy with regard to the spheres of status, education, and technology (but
not symbols) *within* diverse professions. They thereby limit the area
where the conflicts of interest between professions, functional and organizational elite segments, would be translated into value conflicts. Such
policies can be especially successful with regard to functions whose *internal* principles of legitimization are technocratic, that is, where, as Duncan proposes, "*how* we do something is considered sufficient grounds for
the legitimation of what we are doing."[27]

Third, with regard to the symbolic spheres of all diverse functional
and organizational elite segments, and especially with regard to those
segments whose *primary* functions themselves are in the area of the symbolic integration of elites and of society, the development and expression
of norms and values which would conflict with the core values of the
political regime are forcefully and unhesitatingly counteracted and contained, and the primacy of the latter rigidly preserved. We are speaking
here specifically about the mass media, propaganda, and culture, about
the arts, humanities, and social sciences, where rigidity, dogmatism, and
doctrinal entrenchment in the last decade are so clearly pronounced and
professional autonomy almost nonexistent. All in all, it is as if the present Soviet leadership had assimilated well the Keynesian proposition
that "what one should be afraid of are not vested interests but ideas."

The most striking changes in the post-Stalin era took place in policies;
major changes occurred in the policy-making process, primarily in its
elite dimension; the least profound transformations occurred on the
structural level. Nowhere else is this state of affairs more pronounced
and remarkable than with regard to the Soviet economic system and its
relations with the polity. Despite all the reforms of the Khrushchev and
post-Khrushchev period, all the discussion on improving the planning
and economic mechanism, all the tinkering with indices of success and
performance, all the progress achieved in the level of modernization, the
Soviet economic system today remains virtually unchanged in its basic
characteristics from the model given it by Stalin. The Stalinist supercentralization, the absence of the autonomy of economic subdivisions,
tight and detailed planning, the stress on quantitative output, the lack of
any self-regulating, self-generating mechanism still remain the hall-
marks of the economic system.[28]

To the same extent that the interest of the Soviet leadership and the
various elite coalitions, their need for security, stability, and respectability were the basic contributing factors in effecting changes in the political system, they have constituted the overwhelming obstacle to a major

---

[27]Hugh Dalziel Duncan, *Symbols in Society* (New York: Oxford University Press,
1968), p. 35.

[28]For an excellent discussion of the vicious-circle pattern which prevents the insti-
tutionalization of economic structural reforms in the Soviet Union and Eastern
Europe (except Hungary), see Janusz G. Zielinski, "On System Remodelling in
Poland: A Pragmatic Approach," *Soviet Studies*, 30, no. 1 (January 1978), 3–37.

structural reform in the economy. Such a reform, a governmental research paper concludes,

> would disturb established balances in both political and economic
> power. It would be strongly opposed by the state bureaucracy
> where jobs, careers, and political influence would be at stake, as
> well as by the party bureaucracy, whose control over economic
> decision making and resource allocation would be threatened.
> Faced with uncertain long-run benefits, probably short-run cost,
> and certain strong opposition, a Soviet leadership of any foresee-
> able composition would probably opt against taking such risks.[29]

In some respects the break between mature Stalinism and its Leninist
past was more clear-cut, more profound than between the present system
and its Stalinist past. The Stalinist system was established through a
series of deep revolutionary convulsions and transformations. The present system came into being in a process of incremental, evolutionary
change. The Stalinist system acquired its shape by crushing established
institutions; the present authoritarian system was molded by the process
of their adjustment.

In one respect especially the difference between past and present is
particularly striking and goes far to explain the limitations on the process of post-Stalinist adjustment and its potential reversibility. The last
phase of the Stalinist revolutions from above which engendered the mature Stalinist system – the Great Purge – constituted the equivalent of a
political revolution. This revolution involved the wholesale replacement
of the major societal elites by a new generation of office holders whose
standard of conduct in office was shaped by Stalin, his prescribed rules
of behavior, whose social politicization was accomplished under a Stalinist aegis.

The present Soviet system has not yet evolved, at least in the upper
reaches, its own new generation of elites. It may well be that the retention of the Stalinist generation of elites, their staying power, their longevity in office after Stalin's death, constitute the key Stalinist legacy in
the Soviet Union today. The present Soviet political elite is certainly the
oldest in Soviet history and probably the oldest of any contemporary
industrial nation-state. The sources of this phenomenon go directly and
indirectly back to Stalin: They are on the one hand the delayed results of
the Great Purge itself and on the other hand the reaction against the
Stalinist purges in the quest for elite stability.

The extent and consequences of Stalin's Great Purge of Soviet elites of
the late 1930s and early 1940s are well known. Suffice it to say that the
purge replaced and reshuffled the overwhelming majority of Soviet elites
in all spheres of endeavor. As I indicated before, it can be justifiably

[29]National Foreign Assessment Center, *Organization and Management in the Soviet
Economy: The Search for Panaceas* (Washington, D.C., December 1977,
ER77-10769), p. 21.

considered tantamount to a political revolution.[30] One additional phenomenon which is not usually mentioned in writings on the purge is the
parallel expansion of the network of elite and leadership positions. The
establishment of the victorious Stalinist dictatorship which the Great
Purge signified was accompanied, in the decade which followed the
Great Purge, by rapid growth of the Soviet party-state, a significant
extension of bureaucratic hierarchies and of executive offices.[31] Those
who in the late 1930s and early 1940s filled the vacuum left by the Great
Purge and occupied openings created by the expansion of the network of
elite positions shared two interrelated characteristics: Their advancement in the ranks of bureaucracy was extremely rapid by any standard,
and they were extraordinarily young for the positions to which they
advanced. By 1939–40, the Soviet Union was ruled by the youngest government in the history of contemporary major states.

The survival ratio of the beneficiaries of the Great Purge during the
remainder of the Stalin era was surprisingly high. Nothing even approaching a mass "permanent purge" among the higher echelons took
place in the last decade of Stalin's rule. The purges were narrow and
deliberate in aim. In the Khrushchev period, the beneficiaries of the
Great Purge constituted the basic pool of personnel advancing to leadership positions. Despite the fact that the turnover of personnel under
Khrushchev was considerably higher than under late Stalinism, this
stratum was so broad and so well established on *all* levels of the hierarchies that it constituted by far the largest group from which replacement
came for the personnel dismissed by Khrushchev from positions of influence and power. As a result, on the eve of Khrushchev's ouster, it was
this group which still dominated the top leadership and even middle
levels of the diverse elites. The sudden and almost complete disappearance of the preceding elite generation in the Great Purge, their simultaneous and very rapid advancement to positions of top and middle responsibility, their extremely young age at the midpoint of their careers

---

[30]There are major disagreements about the total number of individuals who perished during the Great Purge. Robert Conquest estimates that the number of
"legal" executions alone approached one million; he quotes a Yugoslav estimate
which suggests three million killed. Conquest and others estimate seven to nine
million arrests in this same period (*The Great Terror* [New York: Macmillan, 1968],
pp. 525–35). Jerry Hough, on the other end, however, considers that a figure for
purge deaths in the low hundreds of thousands is possible and in tens of thousands
conceivable, maybe even probable (*How the Soviet Union Is Governed* [Cambridge,
Mass.: Harvard University Press, 1978], pp. 176–7). For my discussion these differences are not important in themselves because nobody questions the extraordinary extent and thoroughness with which the upper and middle echelons of the
Soviet party-state bureaucracy were purged and decimated.

[31]The expansion of the network of elite positions is partly illustrated by the following data: Between 1935 and 1939 the number of Soviet republics increased from
7 to 11 (and to 16 in 1940), the number of provinces from 70 to 110, and the
number of city and country districts from 2,559 to 3,815. In the same period the
Council of Peoples' Commissars increased from 14 to 34 Commissariats (I.
Stalin, *Voprosy Leninizma*, 11th ed. [Moscow: Gospolitizdat, 1953], p. 634).

made for their inordinate staying power and their tenacity in dominating the Soviet political scene for so long.

However, the Brezhnev period primarily accounts for the fact that the political leadership and elite of mature Stalinism, which passed through middle age in the Khrushchev period, have become the old ones of today. The fifteen-year period of Brezhnev's chairmanship was one of unparalleled bureaucratic stability and, first and foremost, of stability of personnel. Under Brezhnev, turnover on the leadership and elite level was, until recently, lower than in any other period in Soviet history.[32]

It is the stranglehold on the Soviet leadership exercised by the generation which benefited from Stalin's crimes, a generation which was reared, educated, and socialized into politics in the system he created, which is probably the most effective legacy of Stalin and his greatest influence on the Soviet system. It was this generation whose united front cut short Khrushchev's tentative attempt to confront the past and which for the last fifteen years was afraid to permit anything but glorification or silence about the darkest period of Soviet history. Except for a relatively short period during Khrushchev's tenure in office, the Soviet political elite never officially faced its Stalinist past. One may doubt whether without such confrontation Stalin and Stalinism will cease to cast a shadow over the system that his successors have been building.

In the last quarter-century the Soviet system was most often defined as the post-Stalinist system, the post-Stalinist era – that is to say, not by its own intrinsic characteristics but by the fact that it followed the period of Stalin's rule. I cannot stress too strongly that the Soviet Union now faces an inevitable leadership and elite succession, the most important aspect of which will be the changeover in the 1980s from the Stalinist to the post-Stalinist elite generation. In this sense the post-Stalinist era may well be coming to an end. What is most likely to emerge from it is another question.

[32]The stability of personnel under Brezhnev is again a symptom and a reflection of deeper underlying differences between the periods of his and Khrushchev's leadership. As I wrote in another place: "After Stalin's death, his successors saw that the major long-range danger to the efficacy of the regime was stagnation caused by politically redundant and economically counterproductive policies and methods of rule. If the cycle of post-Stalin reforms and revisions was a response to and a reaction against the consolidation, tighter controls, and petrification of the political system in Stalin's postwar Russia, the post-Khrushchev leadership's attempt to stabilize and consolidate the system politically and ideologically has been a response to and a reaction against the cycle of organizational, political, and ideological fluidity in the Khrushchev era, which produced near-chaos" (Seweryn Bialer, "The Soviet Political Elite and Internal Developments in the USSR," in Griffith, ed., *The Soviet Empire*, p. 27).

PART II
SUCCESSION
AND TURNOVER
OF SOVIET ELITES

In its most precise meaning, the term "succession" when applied to modern political phenomena describes the order in which, or the conditions under which, a person or a group succeeds to political office and the effects of this process on the structure and policies of the political system of a nation-state.[1] While the term can be applied broadly to an entire leadership group or even to the top elite stratum, it is characteristically used with regard to the Soviet Union to denote the patterns of political life and their effects on policies during the interval between the death, ouster, or, possibly, retirement of the top leader—usually the first or general secretary of the Central Committee of the Communist party—and the emergence and consolidation of a new leader's position of power.

This statement conveys an assumption that the Soviet system requires and always brings forth such a top leader. It does not imply the extent of power that such a leader is able to amass. Indeed, the very pattern of the succession process itself is one of the key determinants of the extent and type of power and influence which the emerging leader will acquire. Given the centralization of resources in the Soviet Union, the concentration of decision-making power at the center, the highly organized nature of political, economic, and cultural institutions and their enormous size—the fact, in short, that the country is at the same time highly industrialized, bureaucratic, and authoritarian—tends to make the power and influence of the top leader quite considerable and the process of his selection through a succession very significant. The importance of succession is indirectly admitted, if at times exaggerated, by the practice of Western analysts of Soviet affairs to periodize Soviet history according to the tenure in office of its top leaders.

There are a number of reasons why succession is so very important in Soviet political development and at the same time so often difficult for both participants and outside observers to evaluate and analyze.[2] No

[1] For a general discussion of succession in modern nation-states, see Dankwart A. Rustow, "Succession in the Twentieth Century," *Journal of International Affairs*, 18 (1964), no. 1, 104–13.
[2] Indeed, even if our knowledge of the Soviet succession process is quite extensive, it has been codified to a surprisingly small degree. Evidently, only one book-length study goes beyond the analysis of a single succession (Myron Rush, *Political Succession in the USSR*, 2nd ed. [New York: Columbia University Press, 1968]). On political succession in other Communist countries, see Carl Beck,

predetermined tenure of office is ascribed to the position of the top leader. Neither are the terms of the office predetermined to the extent which would make similar from one occupant to another the attributes of rights and obligations, of power and influence. Nor is the manner by which the incumbent of the top leadership position relinquishes his post in any sense standardized. Most importantly, the degree of unpredictability and uncertainty in the procedures for selecting a new leader and in the process of consolidating his position is much higher than in democratic polities or authoritarian military regimes; and this situation injects a more pronounced element of unpredictability and uncertainty into the entire Soviet political process than is characteristic of its operation in "normal" times.

The consequences for the political system are profound. The probabilities of deep personal and policy conflicts within the top leadership structure are increased. The possibilities for resolving these conflicts in more extreme ways are maximized. The tendency toward personnel changes within the leadership itself and among the top elites and bureaucratic hierarchies is heightened. The uncertainties of succession procedures and conflict resolution, the logic of power struggle at various levels of the hierarchy, and the search for support, for allies, and for mass popularity open up the system to initiatives for change in basic policies which would be unthinkable or very difficult to institute in "normal" times. The succession period is conducive to sudden switches in policies. It may influence, and in the past has influenced, long-range changes in the structural and procedural characteristics of the system as a whole.

The period of succession offers a high potential for disrupting the inertia characteristic of the way the business of government was conducted throughout the entire bureaucratic structure by the departed leaders, and for changing the inertial drift of the substance of their policies. It is a period with a high potential for ferment, for greater responsiveness to pressures, real and anticipated, for broadening political participation and opening up the political process. In sum, the succession, aside from its own intrinsic importance, acts as a catalyst for pressures and tendencies which already exist within the polity and society but which previously had limited opportunity for expression and realization.

The Soviet Union has experienced in over sixty years of its history three successions understood in the narrow sense as the change of the top leader. Each of these introduced profound if not equally profound and important changes when compared to the previous period. A new, fourth Soviet succession is rapidly approaching, and in fact may already have started. Many factors argue that the approaching succession is potentially as important as the last one, after Khrushchev's ouster in October 1964, and may even be as important as the one that followed Stalin's death.

William A. Jarzabek, and Paul H. Ernandez, *Political Succession in Eastern Europe: Fourteen Case Studies* (Pittsburgh: University Center for International Studies, University of Pittsburgh, 1976).

Many analysts of Soviet affairs invariably associate the term "succession" with the words "struggle" and "crisis." In the post-Stalin, let alone post-Lenin, successions, both of those associations were without doubt fully justified. Stalin's death introduced a period of debilitating and sharp power and policy divisions and struggles within the Soviet leadership and political elite and created a deep systemic crisis of identity and direction. The pattern of the post-Khrushchev succession, however, differed significantly. No doubt the conspiracy which led to Khrushchev's departure and the very fact of his ouster can be described as a crisis. Yet in the succession which followed, the differences and conflicts over power and policy, while clearly present, did not exceed a "normal" level, easily assimilated by the system; and they did not have visibly and significantly disruptive effects on the working of the system. By no stretch of imagination can they be described as a systemic or deep leadership crisis.

To say it differently, there was a more profound power and policy struggle in the last years of Khrushchev's rule and a greater disruption of the working of the system, that is to say, crisis situation than in the period following his ouster. Nevertheless, it would be erroneous to minimize the importance of the post-Khrushchev succession and its impact on the system just because it lacked drama and appeared relatively smooth. Despite the fact that it did not repeat the kind of "struggle" and "crisis" of previous successions, it did trigger and catalyze profound changes in the working of the system.

That those changes are most often denied suitable recognition and appreciation derives in part from their undramatic, incremental character and the style (so different from Khrushchev's) of the leaders who directed the system and in part from the fact that those changes did not take place in the context of the open, explicit anti-Stalin campaigns of the preceding period. Yet while the reforms of the Brezhnev era were partly restorative in that they undid some of Khrushchev's schemes, in their key aspects they were not restorative in the most important sense, that of a movement back toward Stalinism.

It may well be that the coming succession will again lack the drama of extreme conflict and the elements of a systemic crisis. As a matter of fact, such a pattern is even probable. The Soviet Union, after all, has evolved in the last fifteen years into a highly complex and governable polity, an enormous, routinely functioning bureaucratic edifice with deep social roots and with powerful buffers of established political customs, conflict resolution, and professional administrative expertise to guard it against dangerous fractures and disruptions.[3] Yet one must argue that, whatever characteristics are exhibited, the approaching succession will profoundly

---

[3] For a discussion of the transformation of the Soviet Union into a highly governable and routinely functioning bureaucratic state, see S. Bialer, "The Soviet Political Elite and Internal Developments in the USSR" in William E. Griffith, ed., *The Soviet Empire: Expansion and Detente* (Lexington, Mass.: Lexington Books, 1976), pp. 25–55.

influence the structure and the domestic and foreign policies of the Soviet Union in the crucial decade of the 1980s.

To understand fully the importance of the coming succession, one
must analyze it on three levels. First, one has to inquire into the scope
and type of personnel turnover which the succession will probably entail.
Second, one should examine its policy dimension, that is to say, the
major issues that are most likely to come up during the succession period
for resolution, or at least for consideration. Third, one should analyze the
structural and procedural framework within which the succession will
take place and the tendencies for its change under the impact of succession. The aspect of the coming Soviet succession on which I wish to
concentrate in this part concerns the extent and the nature of personnel
turnover. The other two aspects will be considered in a subordinate manner only when and if necessary.

The trigger and the central fact of any Soviet succession is obviously
the change in the incumbent general secretary of the Communist party,
what we referred to earlier as the fourth in the series of changes of the
top leader in Soviet history. This theme will be developed in the first
section of this part. It is proposed here, however, that the coming succession will most certainly move beyond that phase to effect the replacement in a relatively short span of time of a large part, maybe even the
majority, of the present top Soviet leadership and central elite. This
theme will be developed in Chapter 5. Moreover, the approaching succession period will accelerate for at least part of the leadership level and
certainly for executives of various hierarchies below the leadership level
a process already begun, a process of personnel replacement which can
best be characterized as a generational turnover of elites. And in this
broad and more fundamental sense of a change of the top elite stratum,
it is a central contention of this book that Soviet history has offered only
one true succession – in the late 1930s – and that only now is the second
succession approaching. This theme will be developed in Chapter 6.

4
THE APPROACHING SUCCESSION: THE TOP LEADER

The impact of a change of leader on the system is more pronounced the greater the impact of the leader on the establishment and the society he governed. The latter in turn is a function of such diverse factors as length of tenure in office, the extent and nature of his power, the sources of his influence, the distinctiveness of his style of leadership, the degree of his mass popularity or notoriety, the balance of his achievements and failures, and even the character of the period in which he was active.

Taking these factors into consideration, the era of Brezhnev's leadership presents a mixed picture. On the whole, however, his departure by itself should not constitute a break in any way comparable to the void after Lenin's death, to the trauma of Stalin's death, or even to the drama of Khrushchev's ouster. If one can say that the Brezhnev period represented the maturation of the Soviet system and Brezhnev's leadership embodied its stability, one can argue similarly with good reason that his departure could be handled at least not less routinely than the post-Khrushchev succession.

This is not to minimize the extent of Brezhnev's domination of the Soviet political scene. For sixteen years he occupied the pivotal position in the Soviet political structure. He headed the Politburo, the top party-state decision-making body; he chaired its sessions, decided its agenda, served as spokesman for its resolutions and decisions. As general secretary of the party, he was in title and in fact the head of the Secretariat of the Central Committee, the directing body of the most powerful Soviet bureaucracy, the party apparatus. From at least the early 1970s, he was identified as the commander-in-chief of the Soviet armed forces and as the chairman of the directing body of the Soviet military-industrial complex, the State Defense Council. In 1977 he also became, formally, head of state, by assuming the title of chairman of the Supreme Soviet of the USSR. (He was, of course, accorded the honors of this office during his visits abroad from the early 1970s.)

Brezhnev's dominance of the Soviet political scene, his role as *primus inter pares* of the Soviet leadership, has lasted about twice as long as that of his predecessor Khrushchev. His visibility in Soviet political life is very high, at least not less than that of Khrushchev. His collected speeches and writings appeared in an edition of 500,000 copies (compared to Khrushchev's 75,000), while his total publications have reached the very sizable figure of at least seven million copies and are being studied throughout the party educational system. What can clearly be called a mini-cult of Brezhnev has intensified in the last few years. He receives with increasing frequency and intensity tributes from diverse groups of the population, the highest decorations, and extravagant praise from his colleagues and subordinates.

Starting from the late 1960s, Brezhnev has become the dominant figure in the conduct of Soviet foreign policy, its chief initiator, spokesman, and executor. There are few heads of state whom he has not received; and his trips abroad have been frequent and well advertised. It is most noteworthy that since the time in 1970 when he was able to neutralize Shelepin in the Politburo, he faced a few challenges to some of his policies but no evident challenge to his position. Altogether, Brezhnev is a powerful figure who has dominated the Soviet political scene for over sixteen years (that is to say, longer than Franklin Delano Roosevelt did the American scene). His departure will undoubtedly be of great importance to the political system, as all Soviet successions inevitably have been and will continue to be.[1]

Yet while Brezhnev has shown himself to be quite different from the faceless, dry, dull bureaucrat depicted by Western analysts when he assumed power, his very style of leadership, his very achievements and legacy, would argue that his departure in itself would probably prove less important in terms of ferment, opening for change, and political vacuum than that of his predecessors. His style of leadership was undramatic; its substantive characteristics were orderly procedures, methodicalness, caution, and gradualism. It was a style that stressed the role of institutions and precluded the development of the type of popularity and notoriety possessed by Khrushchev, not to mention Stalin. His imprint on the imagination of elites and population seems to be limited. His demise will be regretted or welcomed but not mourned or celebrated.

In the minds of both Soviet loyalists and dissenters, the successes and failures of his era are associated more with the system than with the person, unlike the cases of Stalin and Khrushchev. But most important of all, some of the very changes in the Soviet social and political structure and process which occurred under his leadership (if not always on his initiative), that is the increase in the complexity of socio-political relations, a higher level of institutionalization of political processes, provide a stabilizing background for the coming succession.

The centralization of the Soviet system of administration, the lack of institutional arrangements concerning tenure and removal from high office, the weakness of legitimate channels of control directed upward from lower elites, let alone from outside the elites, the secrecy affecting decision making and the political process – all have worked in the past and, to the extent they are present today, continue to work to effect a tendency toward concentration of individual power within the top Soviet

---

[1] For an illuminating discussion of Brezhnev's role in the Soviet political system, see Jerry F. Hough, "The Man and the System," *Problems of Communism*, 25, no. 2 (March-April 1976), 1–17.

leadership. It is clear, however, that when compared not only to Stalin's dictatorship but also to Khrushchev's dictatorship, the pattern of distribution of power, of conflict and accommodation, prevalent within the top Soviet leadership in the Brezhnev period is different. If Khrushchev's Presidium could be called "collective leadership" as opposed to Stalin's one-man rule, Brezhnev's Politburo represents this form of leadership in a much more pure and stable edition, and one much less prone to becoming a transitional stage between periods of one-man rule.

The cross pressures which were evident in the Soviet leadership from the beginning of the post-Stalin era, between tendencies toward an oligarchic leadership and toward a dominant leader, became in the Brezhnev period, if not resolved, then at least clearly more pronounced in favor of the oligarchic. The most distinctive and significant traits of this oligarchic pattern are as follows:

1. Brezhnev is undoubtedly the most powerful single member of the Soviet leadership. The most important differences between his and Khrushchev's leadership cannot be expressed very adequately in such terms as "less" or "more." They are concerned rather with the question of "power for what?" The powers of a leader are not a static quality; their limits and scope can be evaluated primarily in their actual use. From this perspective Brezhnev's powers are different from Khrushchev's and differently used.

Khrushchev's power was most notably expended in efforts to change institutions and policies, and its limits were most visibly tested in the tug-of-war with leadership opposition in which he pushed his way through or was forced to retreat from previously stated positions. Brezhnev's power has never really been tested in those terms, and its expenditure has been primarily in serving the continuity of Soviet institutions and in gradual adjustments of policies. Within the scope of these purposes his position is very strong and stable. Khrushchev's leadership was very often directed toward forming a new consensus. Brezhnev's leadership is primarily concerned with maintaining a consensus.

2. There can be identified a core of senior leaders below Brezhnev (somewhat resembling the Standing Committee of the Chinese Communist party's Presidium) who are afforded more respect and exposure and carry more weight in decision making across a broad spectrum of policy issues and have primary responsibility for a number of policy areas. We would include here the following: Kirilenko (party organization, industrial management, Communist bloc economy), Kosygin (economic administration, finance, defense, general foreign relations and trade), Mazurov until 1978 (industrial administration, science, education, economic aid programs), Podgornyi before his ouster (legislative agencies, local economy, defense, general state relations), Suslov (ideology, international communism, China). The length of this group's tenure in the Politburo compares to that of Brezhnev and runs from sixteen to twenty-three years.

3. Conflicts over power and policy, of which there is certainly sub-

stantial evidence, were not accompanied until the last few years by expulsion or disgrace of the losers. (One of the very few exceptions is the case of the first secretary of the Ukraine, Shelest, who was removed from the Politburo in April 1973.)

4. All major specialized hierarchies of the Soviet party-state have their chief executives represented in the Politburo, a situation that existed in Stalin's last Politburo but never in Khrushchev's Presidium. The most notable expansion of the Politburo in this direction occurred in 1973 when the head of the armed forces, Marshal Grechko, Chief of the Secret Police and Intelligence Andropov, and Foreign Minister Gromyko were coopted to full membership.

5. Among the full membership of the Politburo there is a greater representation of leaders who are not associated directly with the central Moscow establishments (for example, Grishin, Kunaev, Shcherbitskii). Previously these were mostly relegated to alternate membership with minimal chances for advancement without transfer to the central bureaucracy. Still, the pattern of the USSR Council of Ministers, where republican heads of government are members ex officio, is far from being implemented here with regard to the republican party secretaries.

6. In the Brezhnev period neither of the other two major institutions of the top leadership, the party's central Secretariat or the Presidium of the Council of Ministers, has placed enough of its members in the Politburo even to approach a majority, as was the case with the central Secretariat in various periods of the Khrushchev leadership and with the Council of Ministers in the late Stalinist period. Without doubt, individuals who were associated with the party bureaucracy in the past constitute an overwhelming majority of the Politburo, but their present institutional power base and interests are diffused. At the same time, one has to note that, without assuming their automatic cohesion, members affiliated at present with the party apparatus constitute the largest single segment of the Politburo – in addition to the general secretary and three central secretaries, they include two republican secretaries, the secretary of Moscow, and the chairman of the Party Control Commission.

Why this leadership pattern has developed and persisted in the last decade, and what some of its consequences are for the system, can be answered in part by looking at the way in which it was established. The present Soviet leaders found an initial unity in dissatisfaction with Khrushchev's behavior and policies; at great risk they formed a broad conspiratorial coalition to overthrow him; they perpetuated a degree of unity after his ouster. The ability of the new leaders to sustain this unity did not rest mainly on a shared positive program, for most certainly they differed both in the depth of their opposition to Khrushchev and in their desired alternatives to his policies. The unity survived initially thanks to a minimum common denominator of political preferences which concentrated their mutual efforts on the negative task of dismantling Khrushchev's so-called "harebrained schemes" (for example, de-Stalinization, the abolition of the regular county party committees, the bifurcation of the party apparatus into industrial and agricultural, the administration of the economy through regional councils, the multiplication of numerous high-level committees and commissions that bypassed the regular party and governmental channels).

The prospects for open splits, factional struggle, and the elimination of the weak at the top with attendant repercussions on the lower strata of leadership, were minimized by the fact that the personal power positions of the probable contenders were at the beginning apparently more evenly balanced than in the past and their personal following much less crystallized. Moreover, the policy stimuli for such splits lacked the urgency of previous periods of succession; the division of opinion among the leaders seemed less polarized and the distance between divergent opinions narrower. In part, this reflected the previously mentioned reaction of the elite to the fluidity of the Khrushchev era and the commonly recognized need to stabilize the regime.

One has also a strong impression that the lessons of Khrushchev's ascent (and descent) have not been lost on the present Soviet leaders, just as the danger of resorting to terrorist methods to settle internal struggle were not lost on Stalin's successors. A leader who would like to imitate Khrushchev's rise to power through the gradual elimination of his opponents would now encounter much less enthusiastic support among his followers and much greater defensive unity among his nonsupporters and outright opponents.

The pattern prevalent in the Soviet leadership emerged from the desire for a "return to normalcy," from the pursuit of policies of institutional continuity, gradualism, accommodation, and reassurance of the elite. In turn, once established and relatively stabilized, the pattern provides a structural base for the continuation of such policies. It puts a premium on compromise and is ill-suited to accommodating innovative ambitions which stray much beyond the existing consensus and to mobilizing support for their fulfillment. The increased security of all leaders, the greater diffusion of their everyday influence, the stability of the position of the top leader himself, are paid for by narrowing the range of accepted alternate solutions in internal policies, by stressing the managerial as opposed to the political dimension of decisions (that is, the question of how rather than what to do), and by increasing the making of "nondecisions."

In the last few years, however, one discerns a deviation from the pattern described above in the direction of greater concentration of power in Brezhnev's hands. The ouster of Shelepin and Polianskii from the Politburo, the dismissal of Podgornyi and Brezhnev's assumption of his position as chairman of the Supreme Soviet, Brezhnev's promotion to marshal of the Soviet Union, the clear increase in the pitch of Brezhnev's mini-cult of personality, the promotion and cooptation of many former associates of Brezhnev, members of the so-called "Dnepropetrovsk group" (for instance, Chernenko, Shchelokov)—all are indications of a shift away from the collective nature of the leadership.

All these changes in the way the top leadership functions would argue for the ability of the Soviet polity to achieve the transfer of the top leadership position without major drama, without undue shock. That is to say, this would be the most probable outcome, were the coming succession in terms of personnel turnover a matter of a change of top leader alone, as was the Khrushchev succession.

With regard to personnel replacement, the Khrushchev succession established a pattern very different from the past. After, and as a result of, Khrushchev's ouster there were none but minor changes instituted within the top leadership or on the elite level. The only punitive personnel changes ordered by the plenary session of the Central Committee which ousted Khrushchev were the removal of his son-in-law A. I. Adzhubei from membership in the Central Committee and the removal of V. I. Poliakov from the Secretariat of the Central Committee. In addition, one alternate member of the Politburo (Shelest) and one secretary of the Central Committee (Shelepin) were coopted to full membership in the Politburo; one secretary of the Central Committee (Demichev) was coopted to alternate membership; and eight alternate members of the Central Committee were promoted to full membership.[2] A year after Khrushchev's ouster, all living members and alternate members of the Khrushchev Politburo and all but one member of the Secretariat (the propaganda secretary, Ilichev, was the exception) still occupied their key positions.

This and the subsequent basic stability of the top party and governmental personnel confirm the overriding impression that Khrushchev's ouster was the work of a unified leadership supported by an overwhelming majority of the elite. Attendant changes of personnel constituted reshuffling *within* the political elite but not *of* the political elite. The likelihood that the Brezhnev succession can repeat this pattern is virtually excluded. I do not mean to say that Brezhnev's death, retirement, or his highly improbable ouster will precipitate a destructive struggle and personnel turnover, because it will occur necessarily with the leadership badly split and with the elite highly divided on which policy courses to pursue. What I am suggesting is that even if the leadership is highly unified, the succession will be attended by major upper- and middle-level personnel changes. To make the situation even more complex, the nature of Brezhnev's policies during the last few years has increased the probability that in the coming succession the Soviet leadership will be divided, that splits and struggle at the top will take place.

We do not know whether the role-set associated with Brezhnev's leadership – not only the traditional one of top policy initiator and administrator but also the newly evolved functions of arbitrating diverse elite interests and reconciling diverse elite pressures – was and is entirely to his liking and chosen by him. In all probability, it was the only role-set which he deemed both possible and safe to aspire to, given the experi-

[2] *Pravda*, 17 November 1964.

ence of Khrushchev's ouster. We do know that it is a role-set best suited, if not the only one suited, to the types of procedural and policy reforms that Brezhnev instituted. Once the oligarchic nature of the leadership and the corporatist nature of Soviet policy making were established, however, it is a type and style of leadership which is prone to take the road of least resistance, one which resists further change and major reform initiatives even in the presence of glaring need. In my opinion, such has been the fate of Brezhnev's leadership.

It is well known to any student of politics that an oligarchical leadership, which by its very nature has to act through bargaining, trade-offs, and compromise, is ill-suited to initiating and executing major reforms of structures, procedures, or even policies. In this sense the future of such reforms in the Soviet Union depends to a large degree on the inclinations of the top Soviet leader and on his ability to pursue and realize those inclinations.

Over long years in office Brezhnev has amassed major influence, built up considerable authority, and concentrated major power resources in his hands. At this stage in his life and career, however, one can dismiss the possibility that he will utilize these resources to initiate major changes, let alone to carry them through. An old man and, according to numerous reliable reports, a very sick man, he has already relinquished major portions of his duties to associates. He works at reduced pace and energy; he exhibits no interest other than to preside over a very stable regime and to try to carry out well-established, if sometimes contradictory, policies. There emerges no long-range plan, no long-range vision in what he is doing. As long as he remains top leader, no major change in the Soviet Union can be expected.

One has the definite impression that Soviet policies in the last five years have been characterized by drift, that the Brezhnev leadership has settled into an ossified mode of continuity, of middle-of-the-road responsiveness to diverse elite pressure, with no major initiatives of its own. Moreover, central from the point of view of my interest, this drift may be discerned in the apparent failure to plan, to prepare, even to think about the forthcoming succession.[3] Evidence for this contention is not difficult to discover.

No heir-apparent to Brezhnev has emerged, and no effort of any kind has been made by Brezhnev to designate a successor. Symbolically, for the Twenty-fifth Party Congress in 1976 Brezhnev could have chosen another party leader to deliver the major report, just as Stalin chose Malenkov at the Nineteenth Party Congress in 1952; or he could have followed Khrushchev, who designated as his heir first Kozlov and then Brezhnev. Brezhnev, furthermore, has made no effort to loosen his hold over the various positions he concentrated in his own person. On the

[3] Of course one may argue, probably with some justification, that the failure to prepare the succession results from Brezhnev's effort to assure that his present power is in no way diminished by arrangements forced upon him. (I am grateful for this insight to Professor Myron Rush.)

contrary, he assumed the post of head of state at the time of the Podgornyi affair in 1977, and he disclosed publicly at the time he became a marshal of the Soviet Union that he was commander-in-chief of Soviet armed forces.[4]

Moreover, there are no public signs that successors are being groomed to replace Brezhnev's old associates who direct the various functional bureaucracies. The party apparatus has yielded no clear second-in-command to the top party organizer, Kirilenko, and no ideologue to succeed Suslov.[5] No prediction can be made with certainty concerning the replacements for Kosygin as prime minister,[6] Gromyko as foreign minister, and Ustinov as defense minister.[7] The cooptation of two additional alternate members to the Politburo in October 1977[8] only reinforces the impression that no thought is being given to the succession: the 77-year-old V. V. Kuznetsov is disqualified by age;[9] the 67-year-old Chernenko was clearly chosen to augment Brezhnev loyalists, since he was associated with Brezhnev throughout his career and served for a prolonged period as his adviser and confidant. The cooptation in 1979 to full membership of the 74-year-old Tikhonov, first deputy prime minister of the USSR, also confirms the pattern. To these indications one should add an event which conspired to exacerbate the situation. The death in 1978 of Kulakov eliminated the only possible successor who combined all characteristics associated with previous succession to leadership: an

[4] Failure to prepare the succession could be construed in part as a defense by Brezhnev, who learned well the lesson of Khrushchev's ouster. This would surely explain his deliberate refusal publicly to designate his heir.

[5] Suslov's replacement could be either Ponomarev (now 74 years old), the party secretary for the international Communist movement, or, less likely, Demichev (now 61 years old), the minister of culture.

[6] The most likely successors to Kosygin would be Tikhonov (now 74 years old), first deputy prime minister, or Solomentsev (now 66 years old), prime minister of the RSFSR.

[7] The question of replacing Ustinov as head of the military establishment presents particular problems. The post-Stalin pattern was broken by appointing a nonprofessional military man following the death of Marshal Grechko in April 1976. Ustinov's appointment can best be understood as Brezhnev's reluctance to appoint to this key position the natural candidate, the 57-year-old Marshal of the Soviet Union Kulikov, second in command to Grechko, who is a man of a different generation and without ties to Brezhnev. It will be very difficult to continue this practice after Ustinov (now 71 years old) and to resist the pressure of the military to place one of their own in the post of defense minister. Initially, Brezhnev's successor will have to court the military and will depend much on its goodwill, as have all successors in Soviet history. If, however, a nonprofessional military man were appointed, the natural candidate would be L. V. Smirnov (now 63 years old), the present deputy prime minister, who rivals Ustinov in the length of his leadership role in the industrial-military complex.

[8] *Pravda*, 4 October 1977.

[9] Kuznetsov's cooptation to the Politburo coincided with and is explained by his relinquishing of the post of first deputy minister of foreign affairs and his appointment as first deputy chairman of the Supreme Soviet, a post created in accordance with the new Soviet constitution.

age over ten years junior to the incumbent, close association with him, and long tenure in both the central party Secretariat and the Politburo.

The uncertainties surrounding the succession to Brezhnev as well as the drift of Soviet policies in the last few years make it extremely difficult but at the same time very important to provide some informed guesses concerning likely successors, their inclinations, and the policy environment in which they will act.[10]

First, the new leader will certainly be selected from the present Politburo and almost certainly from among its core members, those with high seniority and closest association with Brezhnev. He will certainly be a man with considerable experience in the central party administration and almost certainly an ethnic Russian. Circumscribed in this way, the field of likely candidates today is narrower than in any previous succession. If the succession happens soon, almost certain to gain the top leadership post is A. P. Kirilenko, a full Politburo member for eighteen years (plus four years as alternate member), a party Central Committee secretary for fourteen years, a candidate with enormous experience in directing the party bureaucracy and with major expertise in industrial management. Distant second choices are the veteran party leader and ideologue Suslov and the former party secretary and present Minister of Defense Ustinov. An outside and unprecedented choice would be the top Ukrainian leader, Shcherbitskii.[11]

Second, given the required combination of qualifications for the top leadership position and the extraordinary circumstances which currently limit the field of available candidates severely, the man selected for the top post will certainly be an interim leader with a very short tenure in office. Khrushchev, when elected first party secretary, was 59 years old; Brezhnev succeeded Khrushchev at 58. Kirilenko is now 73 years old, exactly the age of Brezhnev. (Suslov and Ustinov are 75 and 69 years old, respectively.) For a consideration of the reformist or conservative inclinations of any future leader, the real question is who will succeed Brezhnev's immediate successor. And here the predictions of today are rendered even more tenuous because of uncertainties over the events and duration of such a period of interim leadership. If one assumes that expectations of an interim leadership by Kirilenko are well founded, that the tenure of his leadership does not exceed five years, one still must look to the present Politburo and Secretariat for the contenders who will follow Kirilenko. Of these, the most probable candidates in order of precedence are Grishin, Kapitonov, Solomentsev, Romanov, Dolgikh,

---

[10]For the most comprehensive treatment of the approaching succession, see Grey Hodnett, "Succession Contingencies in the Soviet Union," *Problems of Communism*, 24, no. 2 (March-April 1975), 1–21.

[11]For a kremlinological discussion of the chances of various candidates to succeed Brezhnev, see Zbigniew Brzezinski, "Who Will Succeed Brezhnev," *The New Leader* (19 March 1973), pp. 6–9.

and Riabov.[12] Without engaging in lengthy speculation about these individuals, one might say that the first three in type of career and generation represent a continuity with Brezhnev and Kirilenko, while the last three would constitute a break from this mold and represent a new generation that only now starts to arrive in the top oligarchy.[13]

Third, as mentioned before, the prerogatives of the top Soviet leader, his power and influence, are only to a small degree established constitutionally. What is ascribed to the office itself is primarily a very significant power base. What the office becomes will depend on the occupant, his inclinations, talents, fortunes, and policy successes and on what his political environment permits him to make of it. Therefore, one may expect very little in terms of major initiatives for change of policies, procedures, not to say structures in the initial consolidating period of a new incumbency, a period which may last for a number of years. Such initiatives to be forthcoming will have to reflect at a minimum the agreement or the pressures of the top oligarchy or even the opinions and inclinations of the dominant elite groups. Only after the position is consolidated can one expect as a possibility those initiatives that will significantly alter the stream of prevalent elite opinions, attitudes, and desires. In other words my argument is that the new top leader, before he can even attempt – should he so wish – to make the elite follow him in his innovative policies, has to follow for a relatively long period the oligarchy and elite consensus.[14] It is hardly to be expected that the length and *terms* of service of an interim top leader will permit him to do anything more than to serve out the consolidation phase (unless, of course, his term of office already coincides with a large turnover of the leadership and elite).

This is especially true at the present time not only because of the pattern and tradition established by Brezhnev's leadership, but also because no contender for the succession disposes of a personal political machine comparable to that of Brezhnev, let alone Khrushchev, a machine which may be presumed to follow the leader for reasons of personal loyalty.[15] The decline of clientelism, of machine politics in the

[12] Of those six only two, Grishin and Romanov, are full members of the Politburo and therefore eligible for the post of general secretary, should a decision be made to dispense with an interim leadership by Kirilenko. In such a case, however, only Grishin can be considered a real candidate; Romanov's experience is so limited that his selection is unthinkable.

[13] For an evaluation of newcomers to the top Soviet leadership following the Twenty-fifth Party Congress, see Borys Lewytzkyj, "Die neuen Gesichter in der sowjetischen Parteiführung," *Osteuropa*, 26, no. 8–9 (August 1976), 651–5.

[14] The terms of his leadership itself, his ability to push through his own preferences and to muster support in the decision-making bodies, will be influenced significantly by the fact that his associates know that he is an interim leader only. His ability to act decisively will depend even more than that of his predecessor on his ability to build alliances within the elite.

[15] The Brezhnev machine is sometimes described as the "Dnepropetrovsk group," taking its name from the city so long associated with Brezhnev. See, for example, "Der Vormarsch der 'Dnepropetrovsk-Faction,'" *Sowjetunion 1967/1977* (Munich: Carl Heuser, 1977), pp. 21–4.

Soviet Union, increases even more the importance of functional group alliances and of institutional arrangements for deciding the degree of flexibility and freedom of action which a new top leader will have in initiating policies and carrying them through.

The questions of central importance, therefore, are: What are the policy preferences of the top oligarchy? What are the yearnings and attitudes toward new policy initiatives on the part of dominant elite groups? How stable, how institutionalized, is the present eminence of those groups in policy making? And, finally, how may they all be influenced by popular pressure and of what kind? These questions will have to be discussed below. An attempt to answer them, however, will be made from only one point of view, namely, how they will be influenced by leadership and elite turnover in the coming succession.

5

THE APPROACHING
SUCCESSION: LEADERSHIP
AND ELITE TURNOVER

The degree to which the political process in a Soviet succession is disrupted directly depends on the extent to which the top leadership stratum immediately below the leader is replaced, the length of the timespan in which such replacement occurs, and the length of time in which the replaced leadership stratum had been in office. The coming succession will inevitably bring about a massive replacement in the top leadership stratum; it will compress the turnover into a relatively short timespan; and it will hit especially hard the inner core of the stratum, those leaders who worked with each other at the top for so long. For the purpose of our analysis, the top leadership is composed of the Politburo, the central party Secretariat, the Presidium of the Council of Ministers, and the upper half of the Presidium of the Supreme Soviet–those collective bodies which administer the Soviet party-state and which include heads of all major bureaucratic hierarchies and most of their key subsections–in all sixty-two positions and fifty-three incumbents. For our interests, the most striking characteristic of this group as a whole is its advanced age, one that is higher than at *any* time in Soviet history and during any of the preceding successions (and, incidentally, higher than the age of the comparable group in any industrial society regardless of its system).[1]

The roles of politicians and administrators in the Soviet Union are fused to a much higher degree than in other societies at comparable levels of development, yet the blend of both roles is not similar in all leadership institutions. In four of five institutions listed in Table 1 the average age exceeds the normal retirement age in most industrial soci-

[1] The aged Soviet political leadership and aging elite reflect a trend which is also visible in the party as a whole, though not, of course, to the same degree. Brezhnev's policy of limiting access to the party when compared to the Khrushchev period has led to what Rigby calls a "maturing membership." At the same time the continuation of recruitment into the party, although at lower rates, has resulted in the situation where at present close to four-fifths of the party consists of post-Stalin recruits (for specific data, see T. H. Rigby, "Soviet Communist Party Membership under Brezhnev," *Soviet Studies*, 28, no. 3 [July 1976], 323–4). One should also not forget that the Soviet Union is a very young country. According to the population census in 1970, almost 50 percent of the population was 25 years old or younger (G. I. Kolosova, "Pol, vozrast i sostoianie v brake naseleniia SSSR," in G. M. Maksimov, ed., *Vsesoiuznaia perepis' naseleniia 1970 goda* [Moscow: Statistika, 1970], p. 168).

Table 1. *Age of the Soviet oligarchy, 1980*[a]

Institution	No.	Average age
Politburo: full members	14	70.1
Politburo: alternate members	9	62.5
Secretariat of the CC	10	67.0
Presidium of the Council of Ministers	14	68.1
Presidium of the Supreme Soviet	15	65.3
All institutions (60 positions)	53	66.2

[a]With a few exceptions, which will be noted in the text, the nature of the data for tables in this book as well as for other information about age, background, and career patterns of Soviet officials makes it highly unwieldy and almost impossible to give specific references for each table or each item. The basic sources of data, aside from files collected from Soviet newspapers by this author for longer than he cares to remember, are: *Ezhegodnik BSE* (Moscow: Izd. Sovetskaia entsiklopediia), 1958–77 (20 vols.); *Deputaty Verkhovnogo soveta* (Moscow: Izd. Izvestiia), 1958, 1962, 1966, 1970, 1974; *Politicheskii slovar'* (Moscow: Gospolitizdat), 1940, 1958.

Table 2. *Age groups of the Soviet oligarchy, 1980*

Institution	70 years old and older (%)	60 years old and younger (%)
Politburo: full members	50.0	7.1
Politburo: alternate members	22.2	33.3
Secretariat of the CC	50.0	20.0
Presidium of the Council of Ministers	35.7	7.1
Presidium of the Supreme Soviet	26.6	33.3
All institutions	28.4	25.5

eties not only for politicians but especially for administrators. All the more striking then is the fact that the age of the Presidium of the Council of Ministers and of the Secretariat of the party where administrative roles are heavily emphasized is almost as high as that of the Politburo.

Average figures, of course, tell only part of the story. First of all, the distribution of age groups within every institution except alternate membership of the Politburo is such that, on the one hand, a large proportion of its members is not simply old but very old and, on the other hand, in the key institutions the proportion of the youngest, though not young, group is relatively small.

As Table 2 shows, a large proportion of members in key institutions is 70 years or older. This group in the Politburo is seven times as large as the "youngsters" of 60 years of age or below, and in the Presidium of the

Table 3. *Age of Politburo members and alternates with responsibility at the center and peripheries*

Responsibilities	Average age
Center	70.9
Peripheries	61.1

Table 4. *Age of the Soviet oligarchy in 1952, 1964, and 1980*

	Average age		
Institution	1952	1964	1980
Politburo: full members	55.4	61.0	70.1
Politburo: alternate members	50.9	52.8	62.5
Secretariat of the CC	52.0	54.1	67.0
Presidium of the Council of Ministers	54.9	55.1	68.1
All institutions	54.1	56.0	66.8

Council of Ministers five times as large. It is within this oldest group, moreover, that one sees individuals who combine membership in the top decision-making bodies with top administrative posts.

Second, it is this oldest group which constitutes the core of each institution, its executive board as it were; that is to say, it encompasses the most important and influential members (Table 3). It is these members (and alternates) in the Politburo whose tenure in the institution and experience of working together average seventeen years. The younger members are either very recent additions without much experience of work within the central apparatus in Moscow or provincial and republican officials whose main responsibilities normally keep them away from Moscow. In the highly centralized Soviet system this fact in itself makes them marginal, second-class members of these institutions.

If, as we mentioned above, the advanced age of this oligarchy has no precedent in Soviet history, there is as well no precedent for the clustering of such a high proportion of this group in the highest age bracket. From the point of view of my inquiry, what is even more important is the lack of precedent for the described type of age configuration on the eve of succession. When Stalin died, he was 73 years old; when Khrushchev was ousted, he was 70. Yet, as Table 4 indicates, the oligarchies which they led were much younger and relatively young. The *youngest* full member of the Politburo today is older than the *average* Politburo member on the eve of Stalin's succession; the *youngest* alternate member of

Table 5. *Age of the central government and party elite, 1978*

Institution	No.	Average age
Council of Ministers	76	65.0
Ministers	59	65.1
Chairmen of state committees	17	64.2
Heads of departments of Central		
Party Secretariat	17	63.6
High command of armed forces	16	65.0
Political directorate of armed		
forces	6	64.0
All institutions	114	64.7
Leadership of Ministry of		
Foreign Affairs	11	64.5
Leadership in fields of		
communication and culture	26	62.1
Trade union leadership	10	58.6

the Politburo today is older than the *average* alternate Politburo member on the eve of Khrushchev's succession.

These combined data strongly support the contention that the approaching succession will not consist simply of the replacement of the top leader, but that during the coming years a massive replacement and reshuffling will take place within the highest echelons of the Soviet hierarchy. Before trying to explain why and how such an extraordinary situation came about and what the probable scenarios of its resolution could be, one should inquire first about the extent to which the described state of affairs is limited to the top oligarchy – that is to say, how far is it also characteristic of the elite directly below this group in the hierarchy of Soviet officialdom.

The evidence which will be presented indicates that one should make a clear distinction among various groups of this elite; the key distinction is that between the central elite in Moscow and the republican and provincial elite groups. The age structure of the top oligarchy, far from being limited to that group, is very nearly mirrored in the case of the central elite, both with regard to its high age characteristics and the clustering of the age group (Table 5).[2]

The Council of Ministers and the departments of the central party Secretariat form the backbone of the Soviet administrative structure, the virtual bureaucratic directorate which under the direction of the top leadership runs the Soviet party-state in all aspects of its activity. It is also

[2] For a thorough discussion of the Politburo and the Council of Ministers under Brezhnev, see two articles by T. H. Rigby: "The Soviet Government since Khrushchev," *Politics*, 12, no. 1 (May 1977), 5–22; "The Soviet Politburo: A Comparative Profile 1951–71," *Soviet Studies*, 24, no. 1 (July 1972), 3–23.

Table 6. *Age clusters of central government and party elite, 1978*

Institution	Under 60	65 and over	70 and over
Council of Ministers	17.1	63.2	26.3
Heads of departments of Central Party Secretariat	23.5	52.9	11.7

this group which provides the base from which the leadership is recruited: In the case of state officials it constitutes the most important source of top leadership cadres and, in the case of the party bureaucracy, the second most important source, almost equal to the traditional recruiting ground of first republican and provincial party secretaries. The high age of the individuals in this group who head major Soviet bureaucracies is quite similar among all types of institutions – all-union ministries, union-republican ministries, state committees. It is equally pronounced in all functional areas, although it is especially high in the industrial-military complex. Owing to the stress on the administrative side of this group's activity and the allegedly compulsory retirement age which applies to it, the age clusters within it, while slightly lower than in the top leadership, are nevertheless very striking and surprising (Table 6).

Somewhat different is the situation of those elites directly below the level of the top leadership which direct the activities of the Soviet party-state in the republics and provinces. It is not a young elite by any standard, including that of the Soviet Union's not-too-distant past. It, too, is certainly older than at any time in Soviet history; but it is not old by the standards of the central elite and leadership, nor can it be described as over-aged considering the level of its responsibilities (Table 7).

The age of the provincial-republican elite today matches that of the *central* Soviet oligarchy on the eve of Khrushchev's ouster and is considerably older than the *central* elite then was. Assuming that the policy applied by the Brezhnev leadership to the central elite will not be pursued with regard to this provincial group – a course that is especially likely in a period of succession – major replacements will soon take place on this elite level. It is not a natural situation to find that over a quarter of the first provincial secretaries have reached or are approaching the age of 65 (Table 8). Yet the average age figures in this case hide a clustering of age groups which is considerably different from the central elite and suggests that a large part of this elite remains far from reaching the upper age limits of replacement, especially if no retirement rules are applied, and that it will occupy a prominent position on the Soviet political scene for a relatively long time to come.

Considering the inevitable massive replacements within the central party-state leadership and elites in the not-too-distant future, and the fact that the provincial and republican elites have traditionally consti-

Table 7. *Age of republican and provincial elites, 1978*

Institution	No.	Average age
Presidium, Council of Ministers, RSFSR	12	59.4
First provincial party secretaries, RSFSR (Russian provinces)	53	57.8
First provincial party secretaries, RSFSR (non-Russian provinces)	17	55.7
First provincial party secretaries, union-republics	33	54.9
First republican party secretaries	15	58.7
Second republican party secretaries	11	54.8
Prime ministers of republics	13	56.8
All institutions	154	56.9
Military elite: commanders of military districts and fleets	23	57.1
Ambassadors	20	59.9

tuted one of the two key reservoirs for such replacements, I shall discuss this group in some greater detail below.[3] (The other personnel source for replacement in the oligarchy and central elite is the group of deputy heads of central institutions. It is my impression that this group is older than the provincial group.)

The extraordinary situation which at present characterizes the Soviet oligarchy and elite with regard to age structure was brought about by a number of factors. It is, however, primarily the product of two processes: one indirect and distant – the delayed and final effects of the great purges of the Stalin era; the other direct and immediate – the stability of personnel during the Brezhnev period and the nature of its turnover on the leadership level.

The extent and consequences of Stalin's Great Purge of the Soviet elites in the late 1930s and early 1940s are well known. Suffice it to say that the purge replaced and reshuffled the overwhelming majority of the

[3] The most notable among a number of studies of regional party leaders are: Jerry F. Hough, *The Soviet Prefects: The Local Party Organs in Industrial Decision Making* (Cambridge, Mass.: Harvard University Press, 1969); David T. Cattell, *Leningrad: A Case Study of Soviet Urban Government* (New York: Praeger, 1968); Ronald J. Hill, *Soviet Political Elites: The Case of Tiraspol* (New York: St. Martin's Press, 1977); Philip D. Stewart, *Political Power in the Soviet Union: A Study of Decision-Making in Stalingrad* (Indianapolis and New York: Bobbs-Merrill, 1968); Joel C. Moses, *Regional Party Leadership and Policy-Making in the USSR* (New York: Praeger, 1974); Peter Frank, "The CPSU *Obkom* First Secretary: A Profile," *British Journal of Political Science*, 1, pt. 2 (April 1971), 173–90; Grey Hodnett, "The *Obkom* First Secretaries," *Slavic Review*, 24, no. 4 (December 1965), 636–52; Robert E. Blackwell, Jr., "Career Development in the Soviet Obkom Elite: A Conservative Trend," *Soviet Studies*, 24, no. 1 (July 1972), 24–40. The most recent and welcome addition to these studies is T. H. Rigby's "The Soviet Regional Leadership: The Brezhnev Generation," *Slavic Review*, 37, no. 1 (March 1978), 1–24.

Table 8. *Age clusters of Soviet provincial and republican elites, 1978 (percent)*

Institution	70 and over	65 and over	Under 55	50 and under
First provincial party secretaries, RSFSR (Russian provinces)	4.0	15.1	33.9	18.7
First provincial party secretaries, RSFSR (non-Russian provinces)	0	5.8	52.9	29.4
First provincial party secretaries, union-republics	0	9.1	54.5	24.2
First republican party secretaries	6.6	20.0	26.6	13.3
Second republican party secretaries	0	0	45.4	27.3
Prime ministers of republics	0	15.4	38.4	38.4
All institutions	2.1	11.9	41.5	23.2

Soviet elites in all spheres of endeavor and can rightly be considered as tantamount to a political revolution. Large parts of the elites disappeared forever, and the remainder of the elites and large parts of the subelites began to advance to higher posts at a breathtaking pace. To provide only a few summary examples: of the 1,966 voting and nonvoting delegates to the Seventeenth Party Congress in 1934, the last pre-purge Congress, 1,108 or 56.3 percent were arrested on charges of treasonable activity in subsequent years, and many others committed suicide or abandoned politics;[4] of the 139 members and candidate members of the Central Committee who were elected at the Seventeenth Party Congress, 98 persons or 70.5 percent were arrested and shot and some others dismissed from their positions. According to my calculation, about 85 percent of the first provincial party secretaries were also purged. In the armed forces no less than one-third of the Red Army officer corps were executed, imprisoned, or dismissed from active service, including three of five Soviet marshals, all eleven deputy people's commissars of defense, and thirteen of fifteen Generals of the Army. According to official Soviet histories, all commanders of military districts, all corps commanders, almost all brigade and division commanders, about one-half of all regiment commanders, and all but one fleet commander were purged, if not shot. At the Eighteenth Party Congress in 1939, the first post-purge Congress, almost 80 percent of the members and candidate members of the Central Committee consisted of newly appointed elite members.

[4] N. S. Khrushchev, "Special Report to the 20th Congress of the Soviet Union," *The New Leader* (1962), pp. 20–1.

An additional phenomenon which is not usually recognized in writings on the purge is the parallel expansion of the network of elite and leadership positions. The establishment of the victorious Stalinist dictatorship, which the Great Purge signified, was accompanied by rapid growth of the Soviet party-state, significant expansion of bureaucratic hierarchies and of offices of executive power in the decade which followed the Great Purge.

The expansion of the network of elite positions is partly illustrated by the following data: between 1935 and 1939 the number of Union republics increased from 7 to 11 (and 16 in 1940), the number of provinces from 70 to 110 (and 141 in 1946), and the number of city and country districts from 2,559 to 3,815 (and 4,285 in 1946). In the same period the Council of People's Commissars increased from 14 to 34 commissariats and by 1946 to 53.[5]

Those who in the later 1930s and early and even mid-1940s filled the vacuum left by the Great Purge and occupied openings created by the expansion of the network of elite positions shared two interrelated characteristics: Their advancement in the ranks of bureaucracy was extremely rapid by any standard; and they were extraordinarily young for the positions to which they advanced. The career patterns of these years are reflected in the biographies of those individuals who at that time were coopted to the top leadership or who achieved high rank:

> N. S. Khrushchev: At the age of 40 became the first party secretary of Moscow and at the age of 44 first secretary of the Ukraine
>
> G. M. Malenkov: At the age of 33 became the head of the organizational department of the Central Committee and at the age of 38 director of personnel of the Central Committee Secretariat
>
> A. A. Zhdanov: At the age of 38 became first secretary of Leningrad and secretary of the Central Committee of the party
>
> L. P. Beria: At the age of 33 became first secretary of the Transcaucasian Region and at the age of 39 head of the Soviet secret police
>
> N. A. Bulganin: At the age of 42 became chairman of the Council of People's Commissars of the Russian Republic
>
> A. S. Shcherbakov: At the age of 38 became secretary of the Central Committee of the party
>
> N. A. Voznesenskii: At the age of 35 became chairman of the Planning Commission of the USSR
>
> M. G. Pervukhin: At the age of 35 became people's commissar of electrical power and industry
>
> M. Z. Saburov: At the age of 41 became deputy chairman of the USSR Council of People's Commissars

[5] I. V. Stalin, *Voprosy Leninizma*, 11th ed. (Moscow: Gospolitizdat, 1953), p. 634; and Barbara Ann Chotiner, "Structural Change and Personnel Circulation in the Bureaucracy of the USSR Council of Ministers, 1938–1969" (1971 seminar paper, Columbia University), p. 23.

Table 9. *Age of Soviet leadership and elite, 1939*

Institution	No.	Average age
Politburo: full members	9	50.3
Politburo: alternate members	2	46.0
Party Secretariat	4	46.0
Presidium of Council of People's Commissars	9	42.2
Council of Ministers (1946) (without Presidium)	32	42.7
Central Committee: full members	71	43.7
(% of those under 40)		(52.1)
Central Committee: alternate members	67	36.8
Military high command	23	41.7

> V. A. Malyshev: At the age of 37 became people's commissar of heavy (then medium) machine building
>
> A. I. Kirichenko: At the age of 33 became secretary of the Ukrainian Communist party

By 1939–40 the Soviet Union was ruled by the youngest government in the history of contemporary major states (Table 9). In 1939–46 the average age of newcomers to the Politburo was 43, to the Central Committee Secretariat 42, and to the Council of People's Commissars 36. Only three members of the Politburo and Secretariat, these key leadership institutions, were 50 years or older. In the armed forces, 35-year-old corps commanders and less than 40-year-old commanders of armies and vast military districts were a rule not an exception. The "old-timer" Timoshenko, when he assumed the post of people's commissar of defense, was 45 years old, as was Chief of the General Staff Zhukov; and Commander-in-Chief of the Soviet Navy Kuznetsov was 39 years old, as was the chief of the Red Air Force.

The survival ratio of the beneficiaries of the Great Purge during the remainder of the Stalinist era was surprisingly high. Nothing ever approaching a mass "permanent purge" among the higher echelons took place in the last decade of Stalin's rule. The purges were narrow and deliberate in aim. In the Khrushchev period the beneficiaries of the Great Purge constituted the basic pool of personnel advancing to leadership positions. Despite the fact that the turnover of personnel under Khrushchev was considerably higher than under late Stalinism, this stratum was so broad and so well established on *all* levels of the hierarchies that it constituted by far the largest group from which replacement came for the personnel dismissed by Khrushchev from positions of influence and power. As a result, on the eve of Khrushchev's ouster, it was this group which still dominated the top leadership and even middle levels of the diverse elites. The sudden and almost complete disappearance of the preceding elite generation in the Great Purge, the simultaneous and very rapid advancement of a new generation to positions of top and middle responsibility, and their extremely young age at the midpoint of their careers made for their inordinate staying power and their tenacity in dominating the Soviet political scene for so long. This can easily be seen by looking at the early careers of some of the men who occupy key or important positions within the present oligarchy and central elite.

The present General Secretary of the party Brezhnev advanced by 1939 at the age of 33 to the post of secretary of one of the major industrial provinces of the Ukraine, having been an engineer in a metallurgical factory in 1936 and director of a vocational school in 1937. The present Soviet Prime Minister Kosygin catapulted from the directorship of a textile factory in 1938 to the post of people's commissar for the textile industry in 1939 and deputy prime minister of the USSR in 1940 at the age of 35. The present Politburo member and second-ranking Central Committee Secretary Suslov achieved in 1939 at the age of 37 the post of first secretary of one of the largest Russian provinces. The present Politburo member and Foreign Minister Gromyko was propelled in 1939 from the editorial staff of an economic journal to become North American Department head in the People's Commissariat of Foreign Affairs and in 1943 at the age of 34 to the post of Soviet ambassador to the United States. The present Politburo member and Minister of Defense Ustinov achieved in 1939 at the age of 33 the position of people's commissar of armaments. Kirilenko, the present Politburo member and heir-apparent to Brezhnev, became in 1939 at the age of 33 secretary of the largest steel-producing province in the Soviet Union.

The present Politburo member Pelshe became in 1940 at the age of 41 secretary of the Latvian Communist party. The present Politburo member and head of the secret police Andropov became in 1938 at the age of 24 first secretary of a provincial Komsomol and at the age of 26 first secretary of the Komsomol of a republic. The present Politburo member Grishin became in 1942 at the age of 28 a secretary of an industrial center. The present Politburo member and First Secretary of the Communist party of Kazakhstan Kunaev became in 1942 at the age of 30 deputy prime minister of Kazakhstan. The present Politburo member and leader of the Ukraine, Shcherbitskii, became in 1948 at the age of 30 second secretary of one of the largest Ukrainian industrial centers. The present alternate Politburo member and Secretary of the Central Committee Ponomarev became in 1937 at the age of 32 a leading official of the Comintern. The present Politburo alternate member and head of the Uzbek Communist party Rashidov became in 1944 at the age of 27 a party secretary of the capital of Uzbekistan and at the age of 33 chairman of the Uzbek Supreme Soviet. The present Politburo alternate member and Minister of Culture of the USSR Demichev became in 1947 at the age of 29 party secretary of a very important district in Moscow, and at the age of 35 he was appointed to a responsible position in the apparatus of the Central Committee Secretariat. The present alternate Politburo member and head of the Belorussian Communist party Masherov became in 1944 at the age of 26 first secretary of a provincial Komsomol, at the age of 30 first secretary of a republican Komsomol, and at the age of 36 party secretary of the capital of Belorussia. The present member of the Presidium of the Council of Ministers Arkhipov became in 1938 at the age of 31 the first party secretary of a key mining center. The present member of the Presidium of the Council of Ministers I. T. Novikov became in 1941 at the age of 35 the secretary of a major provincial party committee. The present member of the Presidium of the Council of Ministers V. N. Novikov became in 1941 at the age of 34 deputy minister of armaments of the USSR. The present member of the Presidium of the Council of Ministers Baibakov became in 1940 at the age of 29 deputy minister of the Soviet oil industry and at the age of 33 the minister. The present First Deputy Chairman of the Supreme Soviet of the USSR V. V. Kuznetsov became in 1940 at the age of 39 deputy head of the Soviet Planning Commission and at the age of 43 the head of the Soviet trade unions.

It is primarily the Brezhnev period, however, which accounts for the fact that the political leadership and elite of mature Stalinism, the youngest in modern history, who passed through middle age in the Khrushchev period, has become the old one of today. The fifteen years of Brezhnev's chairmanship was one of unparalleled bureaucratic stability and, first and foremost, of personnel stability. If Khrushchev brought the Soviet elite the gift of security of life, Brezhnev assured it security of office. Soviet high officials do not fade away; they die in office. Under Brezhnev, turnover on the leadership and elite level was, until recently, lower than in any other period in Soviet history.[6] The exceptional continuity in the selection of the broad leadership strata which rules and administers the Soviet Union under Brezhnev is illustrated by Table 10.

If one excludes from the count those members of the Central Committee who died in the 1971–6 period, then over 90 percent of the key leaders and executives retained their membership in this elite institution at the Twenty-fifth Party Congress. Yet even with the low turnover of personnel, there has certainly been during the Brezhnev period a degree of mobility into and within the top leadership stratum and among the elites. One important case is the accelerated turnover in the last two or three years in the USSR Council of Ministers below the level of its Presidium, where a high proportion of the newcomers are relatively young, that is to say, in their fifties.

The institution where the greatest turnover of personnel, a really massive replacement, has taken place in the 1970s at the upper-middle and

[6] I should like to stress again that the stability of personnel in the Brezhnev period, especially in its first decade, does not indicate the absence of very important changes in the Soviet political system. As Seymour M. Lipset has proposed, "It is possible for the composition of the decision-makers to remain fairly constant, but for the power structure of a society to change when the groups having access to power change" ("Political Sociology" in Robert K. Merton et al., eds., *Sociology Today*, 1 [New York: Harper and Row, 1965], 106).

Table 10. *Survival ratio of members of Central Committee CPSU at consecutive congresses (percent)*

Khrushchev XX: 1956	Khrushchev XXII: 1961	Brezhnev XXIII: 1966	Brezhnev XXIV: 1971	Brezhnev XXV: 1976
62.4	49.6	79.4	76.5	83.4

middle levels of power is the Soviet armed forces. Among the one hundred twenty-six top professional military officials in the Ministry of Defense, 86.5 percent assumed their positions in the 1970s, as did 82.3 percent of the top political personnel (thirty-four positions), 81.2 percent of the commanders of military districts (sixteen positions), 96.2 percent of deputy commanders (seventy-nine positions), all fleet commanders (five positions), and all fleet deputy commanders (twelve positions).

The potential cumulative effect of the turnover on the renewal of the leadership strata was muted, however, by a highly hesitant attitude in the replacement of old cadres with young ones and by the slow advancement of the young elite members to key leadership positions. First of all, the individuals replacing officials in high positions who had died, retired, or been fired are very often in the same age bracket (and sometimes even older) than the individuals they replaced. For example, Minister of Defense Grechko, who died in 1976 at the age of 73, was replaced by Ustinov, who was then 68; the retired head of the Party Control Commission, Shvernik (78 years old), was replaced by the 67-year-old Pelshe (who is now 81); Minister of Transport Construction Kozhevnikov, who died in 1975 at the age of 70, was replaced by 67-year-old Sosnov; Minister of Communications Beshchev, who died in 1978 at the age of 75, was replaced by 69-year-old Pavlovskii; Minister of Shipbuilding Butoma, who died in 1976 at the age of 69, was replaced by the then 69-year-old M. V. Egorov, and so on.[7]

The turnover of the first provincial party secretaries is an interesting case in point (Table 11). As the table shows, about two-thirds of the first provincial secretaries attained their positions under Brezhnev – which indicates a quite considerable turnover. Yet the figures show also that most of the new appointments occurred during the initial period of Brezhnev's tenure in office, while in the last seven years the turnover was quite low. The table shows, moreover, that the seniority of these appointees was very high; that the appointments must have been made in a

---

[7] Despite the tremendous turnover in these cadres, John Erickson has remarked that in the military cadres "as in the political establishment, there are younger men stamping about impatiently and watching for an opportunity to break into the highest echelons, but on the military and political scene it looks as if both are going to have a struggle ahead of them to get just where they want" ("Recruitment Patterns for the Leadership," Briefing for the XX Annual Conference of I.I.S.S., Oxford, England, 7–10 September 1978).

Table 11. *Turnover and career experience of first provincial party secretaries (RSFSR), 1965–78 (percent)*

Experience	Before 1953	Under Khrushchev	Under Brezhnev		Average year for entire group
			1965–71	After 1971	
Appointed to position of first provincial secretary	5.7	28.3	47.2	18.8	1966.5
Achieved position of provincial secretary or equivalent	26.4	62.3	11.3	0	1957.3

very careful, deliberate, and cautious manner, with no mass promotions and advancement of young candidates. (Most striking, of course, is the fact that more than one-quarter of the present first provincial secretaries already occupied high positions in the apparatus under Stalin.)

Second, the staying power of the younger members of the top hierarchy, relative to their representation, is somewhat lower than that of their seniors. As a matter of fact, of the five people who were purged from the Politburo during the entire Brezhnev period, two (Shelepin and Polianskii) were at that time (1975) the youngest members of this body – 58 and 59 years old, respectively.

Third, the advancement of the younger members once they have reached positions in the top leadership is slow and often sidetracked. Of the examples that can be mentioned, two are especially instructive. One concerns Katushev, for whom a great future was predicted when he was coopted in 1968 to the central party Secretariat at the unprecedented age of 41. In 1977 Katushev was removed from the Secretariat and transferred to the post of one of eleven deputy prime ministers, the effective sidetracking of a promising career. The other example concerns the creation in 1976 of a second position of first deputy prime minister (the first was held by Mazurov). The second post was established presumably to reduce the burden on the aged Prime Minister Kosygin and perhaps to prepare a line of succession. The appointee was selected from the group of eleven deputy prime ministers; he is the 74-year-old Tikhonov, the oldest of the entire group.

All this explains why, despite the cooptation of relatively younger people and their mobility to the top leadership, the average age of the incumbents of the most powerful body, the Politburo, is today exactly thirteen years higher than it was thirteen years ago in 1965 at the beginning of the Brezhnev period. That is to say, the end result is the same as if no influx into this body had taken place at all. (The same is also true of the top governmental body, the Presidium of the Council of Ministers.) Most importantly, with the possible exception of the 60-year-old Kulakov, who died in 1978, no younger member of the top hierarchy during the Brezhnev period has penetrated the inner core of the Politburo and Secretariat. And equally important is the fact that the presumed heir-apparent to the 73-year-old Brezhnev is either the 73-year-old Kirilenko or the 76-year-old Suslov.

When on his seventieth birthday Brezhnev's second-in-command, A. P. Kirilenko, received a high state decoration, he made a remark in his acceptance speech which no doubt well reflects the feeling of this generation of leaders: "A 70-year-long life span is not a short one, but at the same time it is not a very long one. It is good that in our country this is only considered middle age."[8] He was not speaking in jest.

The stability of personnel under Brezhnev is a symptom and a reflection of deeper underlying differences between the periods of his and

[8] *Pravda*, 15 October 1976, p. 2.

Khrushchev's leadership. After Stalin's death his successors saw that the major long-range danger to the efficacy of the regime was stagnation caused by politically redundant and economically counterproductive policies and methods of rule. If the cycle of post-Stalin reforms and revisions was a response to and a reaction against the consolidation, tighter controls and petrification of the political system in Stalin's post-war Russia, the post-Khrushchev leadership's attempt to stabilize and consolidate the system politically and ideologically has been a response to and a reaction against the cycle of organizational, political, and ideological fluidity in the Khrushchev era, which produced near-chaos.

Now in the last years of Brezhnev's leadership, ossification seems again to have set in. It is reflected in the lack of any attempt at reforms, especially in the economic structure, despite the major pressure of deteriorating economic performance, and in the inertia and lack of major initiatives in domestic policies. Its key reflection, however, and, one suspects, its major source is the ossification of the leadership structure and personnel, especially at the central level.

The superstability of personnel in the middle and late period of Brezhnev's leadership cannot be comprehended as anything other than a deliberate policy of the top leadership followed by their subordinates. We do not know to what extent it is a policy pursued primarily because the old leaders feel comfortable with the well-known faces around them and, as many old leaders have done throughout history, do not want to think about what comes after them. Considering the homogeneity and closeness of the core leadership group, there is little under Soviet conditions that dissenters from this policy in the Soviet leadership and elite, especially younger dissenters, can do to reverse or revise it.

Initially, however, this policy also reflected an unwritten agreement, a compact, between the top leadership and the elite to provide the security denied to them in the past. It reflected the recognition of the greater role and influence of the elite, and it may still reflect it today. This policy was secured by the preservation of the oligarchical nature of the top Soviet leadership and might have been difficult to change without endangering the balance of power and of policy preferences within this leadership. That this policy is satisfactory to the aged members of the Soviet leadership and elite even today is obvious; that it is not looked at askance by its younger members one may doubt.

The gates of the dam have been closed for very long, and there must be a great deal of pent-up frustration and impatience among the younger members of the elite, a frustration which is mitigated to a large extent by the hopes of advancement which they associate with the expected Brezhnev departure and the passing of the old generation. How quickly, of what scope, and how much compressed in time such a replacement will be depends, of course, partly on the vagaries of nature but largely also on the pattern in which the succession will unfold and the political framework in which the succession will take place – a subject to be discussed in another place.

We do not know how much longer Brezhnev will remain in office. We do expect, however, that as long as he does remain his personnel policy will remain basically intact. From the point of view of the coming succession this continuity is fraught with major dangers. As we stated earlier, Brezhnev's personnel policy seems to give little thought and low priority to a gradual preparation of a leadership changeover, a shortsightedness that may have profound destabilizing repercussions. Very major changes of personnel on the leadership and elite level, especially in the central institutions, cannot be avoided in the coming succession under any circumstances. But every year that the Brezhnev succession is delayed and his policy of personnel stability continued the chance of extraordinarily drastic, massive, and condensed changes within the leadership and elite becomes more and more likely.

Already today there is within the elite a considerable representation of younger members on all levels of power and especially in the middle echelons of the various hierarchies, as well as among the adviser-experts to the leadership. In the highly centralized Soviet system their impact on Soviet policies may well have been circumscribed and dampened by the stability on the top, by the continuing domination of the top places of power on the part of a coterie of old leaders who are afraid of change and actively stifle any initiative for transforming established policies and routines. Assuming that the influx of newcomers to positions of high and intermediate levels of power will accelerate and attain a high level in the coming years, during and partly as a result of the succession, the key question, of course, still remains: How will the newcomers differ from those they replace; how will their style of leadership, their manner of behavior in office, their attitudes, their beliefs, and their actions compare to those of their predecessors?

6

THE APPROACHING
SUCCESSION:
GENERATIONAL CHANGE

Those massive replacements at the levels of the top leadership and central elite that will certainly accompany if not the first then the second stage of the upcoming succession, I would argue, will most probably produce disruptions, political conflicts over policies and procedures, and policy changes regardless of the identities of the newcomers to positions of power. Such a prospect is especially likely because on the one hand the succession follows a period of extraordinary and long-lasting stability during which policy differences were submerged in the name of unity, stability, and compromise while bold initiatives, especially on the domestic scene, were lacking; and on the other hand it comes at a time when the Soviet Union begins to face difficult economic choices, when the possibility of satisfying diverse interests and pressures through compromise solutions will be more difficult than in the Brezhnev period.[1]

It is my argument that a high level of circulation of elites, especially when compressed into a short period of time, can by itself be significant in determining the formation of the styles and behavior of the leadership and elites. By breaking the inculcated official routine in a bureaucratic and centralized structure, by undermining the inertia of a set style of work, by disrupting existing and fixed informal ties, and by weakening the vested interests in long-established substantive policies, it provides a setting that facilitates the elaboration of changed modes of political behavior. Yet the key questions still remain: How disposed will the newcomers be to make use of the opportunity to be different; how much

[1] As I wrote in another place, the situation in the first decade of Brezhnev's leadership can be characterized as follows: A consideration of the changes made in the structure of the Soviet party-state over the last decade, together with the policies pursued by the post-Khrushchev leadership and with the general political mood in the Soviet Union, can support a conclusion which at first glance appears somewhat paradoxical. The establishment of a collective leadership and the policies of this leadership in organizational, political, economic, and ideological matters led in its first few years to an improvement in the power position or in the satisfaction of the group interest of almost all institutional segments of the Soviet political elite, and in the years that followed did not noticeably undermine their positions. While probably no elite group welcomes all changes or all policies, a rare situation has emerged where the fears of almost all elite groups have been to some extent allayed and their desires to some extent satisfied ("The Soviet Political Elite and Internal Developments in the USSR" in W. E. Griffith, ed., *The Soviet Empire: Expansion and Detente* [Lexington, Mass.: Lexington Books, 1976], p. 34).

pressure will they exert and in what direction in order to achieve a change in the policies and processes of the Soviet government? In short, just how different will they be from their predecessors?

For the man who attains the top leadership post, whoever he is, this is largely a question of subjective characteristics, of personality and character. The top leaders of bureaucracies are not restrained by the rules of bureaucratic behavior in the same way as their *apparat*, as students of political behavior have long remarked. Max Weber, for example, states that leaders of organizations occupy their positions of authority by virtue of appropriation or election and "thus at the top of a bureaucratic organization, there is necessarily an element which is at least not purely bureaucratic."[2] And Suzanne Keller has remarked that leaders of major bureaucracies "must be studied both as the heads of large-scale organizations bound by formal rules, and as unpredictable, spontaneous, and potentially creative or destructive leaders who may transcend these rules."[3]

Nobody could and did predict that Khrushchev, such a stellar product of the Stalinist school, would become one of the major reformers in Soviet history. But when a large group of individuals assumes office, especially in a relatively short span of time, their shared objective characteristics may influence in important ways their style of leadership, their attitudes and aspirations, their political behavior.

The question then is: Whether and to what extent does the succession and the replacement of large segments of the elites that will probably accompany it coincide with the distinctive differences of the incoming members as a group when compared to the outgoing as a group – that is, irrespective of inevitably diverse personality characteristics within each group? I should like to suggest that in the approaching succession such coincidence does occur, that in addition to the imminent replacement of the top leader and a large part of the highest leadership stratum, the coming decade will witness simultaneously a generational change among Soviet elites.

"Elite generation" is a simple and viable concept which is difficult, however, to operationalize and apply.[4] Far from being solely an analyti-

---

[2] Max Weber, *The Theory of Social and Economic Organization* (New York: Oxford University Press, 1947), p. 335. See also H. H. Gerth and C. Wright Mills, eds., *From Max Weber: Essays in Sociology* (New York: Oxford University Press, 1958), p. 95.

[3] Suzanne Keller, *Beyond the Ruling Class* (New York: Random House, 1963), p. 74.

[4] If the literature on generations and politics is quite extensive, most of it deals with age groups in the general population; articles and books which deal with elite generations are very few indeed. Among the general books and articles on generations and politics one should mention C. G. Bell, ed., *Growth and Change: A Reader in Political Socialization* (Encino, Calif.: Dickenson, 1973); S. N. Eisenstadt, *From Generation to Generation* (Glencoe, Ill.: Free Press, 1956); Neal E. Cutler, "Generational Approaches to Political Socialization," *Youth and Society*, 8, no. 2 (December 1976), 175–207; Bennett M. Berger, "How Long Is a Generation?" *British Journal of Sociology*, 11, no. 1 (March 1960), 10–23; Gosta Carlsson

cal construct, the concept reflects reality; yet it engenders a number of general and specific questions concerning its explanatory value, its importance, and applications which are difficult to answer. The key general question concerns its importance and weight in determining elite behavior, considering that so many structural and background elements shape the outlook and behavior of elites. That is to say, while there is little doubt that generational differences contribute to shaping elites, how much they contribute is very unclear and difficult to test. Second, unclear is the usefulness of the concept when applied, as it must be in this case, to small groups where rules of statistical averages have little utility, where we deal with small populations rather than random samples, and where extraneous conditions and differences between individuals may have major importance. Finally, its application proves to be imprecise and especially open to misinterpretation in the case of Soviet elites, where objective data are scanty and all tools of the direct study of attitudes and beliefs are excluded. Yet the logic behind the concept is a significant one and without doubt deserves examination in the Soviet case.[5] With all these questions and reservations in mind, therefore, let us look more closely at the concept itself.

"Elite generation" is an age group whose membership is homogeneous with respect to a particular life experience at a similar point of its development. The concept as used here is primarily political, but with an

and Katarina Karlsson, "Age, Cohorts and the Generation of Generations," *American Sociological Review*, 35, no. 4 (August 1970), 710–18; William R. Schonfeld, "The Focus of Political Socialization Research: An Evaluation," *World Politics*, 23, no. 3 (April 1971), 544–78; Matilda White Riley, "Aging and Cohort Succession: Interpretations and Misinterpretations," *Public Opinion Quarterly*, 37, no. 1 (Spring 1973), 35–49; Marvin Rintala, "Political Generations" in International Encyclopedia of the Social Sciences, vol. 6, pp. 92–6; Ted Goertzel, "Generation Conflict and Social Change," *Youth and Society*, 3, no. 3 (March 1972), 327–52; Joseph R. Gusfield, "Problem of Generations in an Organizational Structure," *Social Forces*, 35, no. 4 (May 1957), 323–30; Anne Foner, "Age Stratification and Age Conflict in Political Life," *American Sociological Review*, 39, no. 2 (April 1974), 187–96. The most recent addition to literature dealing at least partly with political elites and generations is Richard J. Samuels, ed., *Political Generations and Political Development* (Lexington, Mass.: D. C. Heath, 1977).

5 Students of the Soviet Union are devoting considerable attention to the question of generations in the broader context of the political attitudes of Soviet youth and its apparent depoliticization. See, for example, Walter D. Connor, "Generations and Politics in the USSR," *Problems of Communism*, 24, no. 5 (September-October 1975), 20–31. With some notable exceptions (e.g., Jerry Hough), however, most students ignore the generational dimension of elite politics. The most comprehensive treatment of Soviet elite generations may be found in the recently published comparative study by John D. Nagle, *System and Succession: The Social Bases of Political Elite Recruitment* (Austin: University of Texas Press, 1977), which applies the generational approach to the elites of the United States, Germany, Mexico, and the Soviet Union. Despite a number of useful insights, the book suffers from a dogmatic Marxist approach with its stress on class origin. The Soviet part suffers from a treatment of the Central Committee en masse, without differentiating between various functional groups; from a lack of attention to detail; and from a general poverty of knowledge of the Soviet system.

important sociological and psychological basis. A number of assumptions underlie the concept of elite generation:

> Life experiences constitute an important factor in social politicization of an elite;
>
> Those life experiences should go beyond the influences of childhood and youth to encompass later periods of life as well;
>
> For politically centered individuals, especially in highly politicized and authoritarian societies, the formative experience of special importance is the introduction into professional-political life;
>
> This formative experience does not provide the prescription or expectation of a detailed role behavior for the individuals in the group, but only general, basic role predispositions which they carry into later life;
>
> These predispositions differ sufficiently from those in other elite age groups so as to consider these individuals a distinct unit;
>
> Political generations, though directly correlated to age, involve discontinuities; a difference of a very few years, therefore, if it occurs at the breaking-off point between political generations, can prove infinitely more important than an age spread of an entire decade located within a single generation;
>
> The differences between elite generations constitute an important milestone in the evolution of the society's elite system in particular and of the political system in general.

While the dominance and acceleration of social and political change in the modern world can hardly be questioned, the student of elites is at least equally struck by the strength of the repetitive, replicating, and regenerating forces at work. Despite the onslaught of momentous internal and international events and the profound transformation of the material environment, some essential characteristics of the societal leadership system in the major countries of the world are being preserved from generation to generation. Among modern societies nowhere is this more true than in the case of the Soviet Union.

There is little doubt that the originating conditions of the Soviet elite system go far to explain some of its most salient traits, such as the high level of bureaucratization and centralization; the fusion of economic and political domains of elite activity; the duality displayed by the official elite ethos, egalitarian and autocratic at the same time; the reflection of this duality in the combination of a basically egalitarian elite recruitment with a pronouncedly autocratic mode of elite behavior; and so on. Obviously, an inquiry which dwells on the *causal conditions of tradition* as a maintaining force of the historically established elite system could be very fruitful. However, we regard the type of explanation that concentrates on the originating traditions as being of secondary importance in explaining long-term institutional continuities in the elite systems, especially when one of the key concerns of the inquiry is the identification of the mechanisms through which the continuity is achieved.

Knowledge of the original causes of a social pattern is necessary to explain why and how it came into being and to understand its *content*. Yet the identification of the original causes of a social pattern may have only a limited relevance to the explanation of its continuity. Such is the case when the basic conditions which initiated the pattern have radically declined in importance or even disappeared. When this happens, the general process by which social patterns reproduce themselves through time is open to another type of explanation, which can be formulated as follows: A social pattern once established becomes a cause of its own replication in succeeding periods, regardless of the fate of the particular causal conditions that generated it at some previous period. As Arthur L. Stinchcombe expressed it: "*Which* of a set of functional alternatives is found in a particular society is generally determined by historical events. But once a functional alternative becomes established, it tends to eliminate the causes of the other alternatives and thus to regenerate itself."[6]

The central aspect of this type of explanation stresses the built-in latent ability of a social institution, in this case the societal leadership system, to preserve its own tradition. We consider this type of explanation of primary importance in the study of elite continuity.

The basic idea behind the self-replicating tendency of elite systems, whether defined as "cultural lag" or "social inertia," is familiar enough. What requires attention is the mechanism by which the process of institutional self-replication is accomplished. That is to say, how does it happen that succeeding generations of elites hold values and display styles and standards of conduct in office that are similar to those of their predecessors?

The self-replication of elites is primarily accomplished through three major processes: (1) Each generation of elites tends to shape directly the styles and standards of conduct of its successors. (2) Each generation of elites tends to codetermine the activities of future elite generations through its control of present-day structures. (3) Each generation of elites tends to utilize its social resources to influence popular values and through this to influence the normative and behavioral profile of its successors.[7]

I do not underestimate the powerful forces at work in the attitudes and behavior of self-replicating elites. But just because these forces are so strong, I see in the combination of a generational gap and succession the rare opportunity for their hold to be weakened if not broken.

In order to apply this concept to the present Soviet elites, one has first to identify those distinctive periods of Soviet history which differ sufficiently from each other as a formative experience to provide a basis for diverse elite generations; and second, to identify the points in an elite member's development which constitute a key formative experience in his political life.

[6] Arthur L. Stinchcombe, *Constructing Social Theories* (New York: Harcourt, Brace and World, 1968), p. 105.

[7] For the most imaginative theoretical discussion of the pattern of self-replication, see Stinchcombe, *Constructing Social Theories*, pp. 107–17.

In the case of the contemporary Soviet political elite, there are three points in a member's life which seem to qualify as his formative introduction into professional-political life. They are, in ascending order of importance, his entrance into the Communist party, his recruitment into a bureaucratic hierarchy, and his assumption of an executive position (or what in the Soviet nomenclature is called "responsible position") within a hierarchy. The study of the post-Great Purge Soviet elites discloses a very high degree of uniformity and continuity of the time-span in the individual's life within which those three events take place – roughly between his early twenties and early thirties. Taking into account the age cohorts represented in the present Soviet elite, one may identify four historical periods which are sufficiently distinctive as a formative political experience to serve to distinguish elite generations. These would be, in consecutive order, the Great Purge generation, the war generation, the late-Stalin generation, and the post-Stalin generation.

There is no need to comment on the Great Purge and late-Stalin generational base. World War II, however, provided a peculiar variation in the Stalinist experience. The formative experience of administrative wartime careers, as Jerry Hough proposes,[8] may well have set many elite members apart from the preceding generation in attitude and outlook by encouraging indifference toward formal "ideological" questions, by placing emphasis on patriotism as a major basis of legitimacy, by stressing considerable freedom of action in daily decision making, by increasing responsiveness to popular aspiration for improved material conditions, and by developing a respect for the need to maintain popular discipline without recourse to terror. Such a suggestive proposition, while of course speculative, has special relevance for the near future when this group will surely enter the central leadership in great numbers and establish its strength at middle levels. The war generation, however, is a relatively small one, spanning five years of recruitment, and therefore has little chance of dominating any elite group, let alone the top leadership. The impact of their different formative experience then would be reduced by virtue of their numbers but also by virtue of the character of the somewhat larger generation which follows them, those who learned their political trade in the 1945–53 period, the most stultifying if not the harshest period of Stalinist rule.

It is also quite possible that the experience of the postwar years eroded for the World War II generation the impact of their war experience and partly resocialized them in the traditional Stalinist mold. It would seem then that, both from the qualitative and, as we shall see, the quantitative points of view, the real turning point may occur only when the post-Stalin political generation enters the elites in large numbers and in high positions.

Our attention then is obviously centered on the post-Stalin generation. It is my contention that some cautious propositions about this gen-

[8] Jerry Hough, "In Whose Hands the Future?" *Problems of Communism*, 16, no. 2 (March–April 1967), 18–25.

eration can be advanced. These will be based not only on the logic of this generation's political socialization, that is to say, on the knowledge of the changed environment in which it occurred, but also on the reading of their writing in the Soviet press[9] and on numerous encounters and conversations with political and academic members of this generation, and the comparison of their attitudes and general behavior with those of representatives of the older generations. Everyone who has met Soviet political figures and academicians cannot but be struck by sharp contrasts for which generational differences can, at least in part, account.

At the outset we must again underscore the tentativeness of this profile of the post-Stalin generation, given the fragmentary evidence at our disposal. This generation entered Soviet politics immediately after Stalin's death.[10] Thus neither did it experience the paralyzing and destructive process of terror which continued to corrode and influence the behavior of the earlier generations despite the renunciation of mass terror as an instrument of rule nor on the other hand does it appreciate from direct involvement—out of its own hide, so to speak—the enormous price paid for the Soviet achievement. There is one thing that seems fairly certain about this new generation. One of its crucial formative political experiences—if not the most crucial one—took place during the protracted ferment and shock of Khrushchev's anti-Stalin campaign, a campaign that frankly admitted the monstrosities no one hitherto had dared to name, a campaign that questioned authority and established truths and thereby stimulated critical thought.[11] Its entrance into Soviet politics coincided as well with open recognition of the gross inadequacies of Soviet development and the backwardness of Soviet technology and at the same time with extravagant predictions of matching Western achievements in the foreseeable future, predictions that collapsed with no little embarrassment.[12]

[9] One member of the new generation whose profile emerges somewhat from his articles in the Soviet press is G. P. Bogomiakov, first secretary of Tiumen'. Unlike the ordinary Soviet fare, his articles are sharp, intelligent, sometimes witty, impatient, and significant. See, for example: *Ekonomika i organizatsiia*, 1976, no. 5, pp. 4–20; *Partiinaia zhizn'*, 1976, no. 23 (December), pp. 43–51; *Leninskoe znamia*, 1 December 1976; *Literaturnaia gazeta*, 2 November, 8 November 1977, 18 January 1978; *Sovetskaia kul'tura*, 20 January, 31 January 1978; *Oktiabr'*, 1978, no. 4 (April), pp. 181–9; *Ekonomicheskaia gazeta*, 1978, no. 25; *Sovetskaia Rossiia*, 16 May 1978, p. 2; *Pravda*, 11 June 1975, p. 3.

[10] The experience of Khrushchev's reforms is only now with some distance being more fully appreciated. See, for example, Jeremy R. Azrael, "Khrushchev Remembered," *Soviet Union*, 2, part 1 (1975), 94–102; and George W. Breslauer, "Khrushchev Reconsidered," *Problems of Communism*, 25, no. 5 (September–October 1976), 18–33.

[11] It is well to remember that the anti-Stalin campaign lasted with fits and starts throughout the Khrushchev period. As a matter of fact, the Twenty-second Party Congress in 1961 was in some respects more sharply anti-Stalinist than was the Twentieth Congress in 1956. Anybody who witnessed this campaign or was in any way associated with it will never underestimate the enormous shock wave it created. That campaign, while formally ended, is never far from the surface of Soviet life.

[12] It is again easy for us to forget the heady days of the first sputniks and of Khrushchev's grandiose plans to catch up with the United States. To the old

The new generation is clearly a Soviet generation in its typical and persistent adherence to the cult of the state. One cannot doubt the sincerity of its members' commitment to the basic forms of Soviet political organization, their belief that the system is right and proper for the Soviet Union. At the same time one is not persuaded that they believe this system is suitable or desirable for developed Western societies. If they share with their predecessors a devoted patriotism, they tend to exhibit little of their predecessors' xenophobia, and much less of their fear and deeply rooted suspicion of the outside world. Rather they display a curiosity that surely reflects intense concern with the patent inadequacies in the working of the Soviet system.

One most striking trait of this group is its skepticism about the grander claims of Soviet propaganda concerning the system's merits. Its members display both a well-developed awareness of the system's functional shortcomings and a restless impatience with them and with Soviet backwardness and provinciality in general. They do not disguise their dislike and lack of respect for the old generation.

This new generation seems scarcely touched by traditions of populism and egalitarianism. Grossly materialistic in wants and expectations, it is characterized by highly developed career orientation, cult of professionalism, and elitism. Condescending in attitude toward compatriots and older colleagues, the members of this generation appear self-confident and less sensitive to real or imagined slights. Just as one postulates for the old elite strong bonds of generational solidarity, one can suppose that the members of the new generation are in the process of forming similar bonds.

Some traits of the new generation may appear contradictory. On the one hand one detects a sense of security that contrasts with the sense of insecurity – one may say inferiority – of the old generation, yet at the same time their attitude toward the Soviet system is defensive. If on the one hand they seem to feel stronger, more self-confident, they are at the same time more conscious than their predecessors of the failures, shortcomings, and backwardness of the Soviet society and polity and less willing to overlook them. Unlike their predecessors, many of them are more ready to engage outsiders in frank and serious exchanges of opinion.

The attempt to ascertain the principal attributes of the new generation bears on the important question of isolating types of official Soviet

generation these were perhaps "harebrained schemes," but to the young people who were then entering politics it was an exhilarating experience. At the Twenty-first Party Congress in 1959 Khrushchev predicted that by the early 1970s the Soviet Union would overtake the USA in industrial production per capita of population (*Vneocherednoi XXI s'ezd KPSS. Stenograficheskii otchet* [Moscow: Gospolitizdat, 1959], p. 65). These predictions were retained intact in the twenty-year program of "socialist construction" (1960–80) conceived later. If one compares these predictions for 1980 with the target figures of the present Soviet five-year plan for 1980, the disparity of key figures is striking. The target for national income will be only 65 percent of the Khrushchev figures, for agricultural production 50 percent, for meat 49 percent, for electricity 48 percent, for labor productivity 71 percent (*Pravda*, 18 October 1961; N. K. Baibakov, *O gosudarstvennom piatiletnem plane razvitiia narodnogo khoziaistva SSSR na 1976–1980 gody* [Moscow: Gospolitizdat, 1976]).

mentality, the variety of which can partly be explained by generational differences. Richard Lowenthal posited for all Communist regimes the dichotomy between a utopian and a modernizing mentality.[13] In my view this dichotomy may have been applicable to the Soviet Union of the 1920s and perhaps the early 1930s, and it certainly fits the Chinese case;[14] but it is not applicable to the Soviet Union today. At the present time the real conflict in the Soviet Union is between different types of modernizing mentality.

One may postulate a number of Soviet types of modernizing mentality. There are two marginal types. The first is a revolutionary mentality that lingers in the regime's rituals and is still probably preserved among the regime's ideologues. It sees modernization as a means to revolutionary goals. The second is the Stalinist type mentality of "barrack-type socialism," a vision of modernization that Robert Tucker so aptly termed "archaic modernity." It is a mentality of regimentation, extreme mobilization, and primitive accumulation at any cost and regardless of social cost.

The present leadership offers another type of modernizing mentality, one that is thoroughly conservative insofar as it seeks to combine incremental material progress and welfare with the total preservation of the existing broad social and political relations and the organizational framework on which the material production is based. It is a mentality which compartmentalizes the process of modernization and tries to insulate each compartment from the others. In its most extreme form I would call it the mentality of modernization on the Saudi Arabian model.

Even with regard to economic development it is a mentality which measures progress by how much things have changed from the past, how much has been accomplished in comparison to what was, rather than by how much still remains to be done in order to achieve a thoroughly modernized society. It is a mentality rooted in the past and in a curious way reconciled to the fact that the Soviet Union is the most developed of underdeveloped countries or the least developed of the developed countries. This would mean, as T. H. Rigby has written, that "Russia's 'second industrial revolution' is presided over by men who may have 'overlearned' the tasks of implementing the first."[15] It is a mentality of progress by small steps without grand vision and grand designs. It is pragmatic in the sense that it has respect for what is possible, but its calculus of what is possible is a petty one.

In 1926 Stalin postulated that what Russia needed was the marriage of the Bolshevik ability for grand design with American practicality.[16]

[13]Richard Lowenthal, "Development vs. Utopia in Communist Policy" in Chalmers Johnson, ed., *Change in Communist Systems* (Stanford, Calif.: Stanford University Press, 1970), pp. 33–116.

[14]For the best discussion of the utopia vs. modernization dichotomy in the Soviet Union of the 1920s, see Zena Sochor, "Modernization and Socialist Transformation: Leninist and Bogdanovite Alternatives of the Cultural Revolution" (Ph.D. dissertation, Columbia University, 1977).

[15]T. H. Rigby, "The Soviet Politbureau: A Comparative Profile 1951–71," *Soviet Studies*, 24, no. 1 (July 1972), p. 23.

[16]I. V. Stalin, *Sochineniia*, 6 (Moscow: Gospolitizdat, 1952), 186–8.

The present generation of Soviet leaders has lost the Bolshevik ability to dream, but it has yet to gain the old American type of practicality which does not shy away from revolutionary transformations of the productive process or organization and from social change. The practicality of the present generation of Soviet leaders is a practicality that is displayed on the micro-level of social organization combined with a highly conservative, traditional view about the macro-level of organization.

The basis for generalizing about the modernizing mentality of the new Soviet elite generation is clearly insufficient. Yet from what we have already said about the generation a limited number of tentative hypotheses can be advanced. It is a generation that perceives the inability of the Brezhnev administration in recent years to lay out a direction for Soviet development. It is a generation that deplores the backwardness of Soviet society, the functional deficiencies of the system, the inability of the present administration to make progress in rectifying the situation, and at the same time it probably stands confident in its own ability to do so. It is a generation that is less likely to accept actual or potential international achievements as substitutes for internal development. It is a generation that may be willing to pay a higher price in terms of political and social change *if* persuaded that such a price would assure substantial improvement in the growth and efficiency of the productive and distributive processes.

It is only with great reluctance that one hazards any statements about the post-Stalin generation in Soviet politics, for our knowledge and understanding of this generation is very limited, our impressions very uncertain. We do not suggest that the new generation is politically homogeneous. That is to say, while we postulate that it will be more than a categorical group, we do not see it as a discrete political group. It can best be described as an experiential group; that is, one which displays a tendency toward a high incidence of similar attitudinal traits yet is composed of individuals who may belong to different political groupings along the liberal-conservative continuum.[17]

[17]Samuel Huntington suggests three theories and approaches which explain generational activity and generational differences. These can be compressed in the accompanying table.

Generational differences

Theory	Differences function of	Compared to predecessor each new cohort is	Change takes place in	Generational conflict	
				Time	Degree
Maturation (life cycle)	Age	Similar	Cohort	Continuous Brief	Moderate
Interaction	Sequence	Different	Society	Recurring Brief	Intense
Experiential	Experience	Similar/ different	Society	Irregular	Intense

Source: Samuel P. Huntington, "Generations, Cycles, and Their Role in Ameri-

Even had our portrait of the new generation of Soviet officials been less provisional and patchy, it would still be presumptuous and unwise to try to deduce any kinds of specific behavior to be expected from them. The formative political experiences to which they were exposed and some of the predilections which they display, and which we tried to identify, suggest only that they might be different as a group from their predecessors in the older generation.

I should like to make one thing clear. I do not suggest the existence of a new generation of Soviet party officials from whom one can expect reformist tendencies similar to those of Dubček in Czechoslovakia. Nor do I expect them to be favorably disposed to the highly ideological, frantic, and campaignlike type of reforms associated with Khrushchev. At the same time I should be surprised if they were not reform minded in the Soviet framework, if they were satisfied with the thoroughly conservative attitudes toward innovation which pervade the present Brezhnev administration.

Neither do I suggest that they will be easier to deal with in the international arena. It may well be that they will be less cautious, more prone to take risks than the present leadership exactly because they have not experienced at first hand the cost of building Soviet might, that they are used to the Soviet great-power status. I am in no way making a judgment here whether the new generation of Soviet officials is better or worse from the standpoint of our value system and our interests. I only suggest that the new generation seems to be different from the old.

Following the elaboration of this profile of the post-Stalin generation, I should like now to examine the representation of all four generations within the various levels of the hierarchy, with particular attention to the placement of members of the fourth, the post-Stalin generation.[18] As Table 12 demonstrates, the Great Purge generation completely dominates the top leadership stratum. Moreover, there is no doubt that third-generation members are not marginal cases who should perhaps be ascribed to the post-Stalin generation, but individuals well rooted in the Stalinist period. (One of them, for example, Aliev, worked in the security apparatus from the age of 18 and has occupied leading positions in this institution during the entire postwar Stalin period.) Indeed, most of these cases are marginal in the reverse sense, namely, they should per-

can Development" in Richard J. Samuels, ed., *Political Generations and Political Development* (Lexington, Mass.: D. C. Heath, 1977), pp. 9–16.

The approach used in this paper is clearly the experiential one. The post-Stalin generation is a group in an experiential sense, the attitudes of whose members is influenced by shared life cycles. It may also be a group in the sense of a developing consciousness of generational separateness. There is no evidence that it is a group in the sense of interaction of its members, a characteristic which, incidentally, we feel is displayed by the Great Purge elite generation.

[18] As the outer parameters of our identification of the post-Stalin elite, no individual who entered the party after Stalin's death was excluded from this group, and no individual who entered a political bureaucracy (Komsomol, party apparatus, or police) under Stalin was included in this group.

Table 12. *Generations in the top Soviet leadership, 1980*

Institution	Generation			
	I	II	III	IV
Politburo: full members	11	1	1	1
Politburo: alternate members	4	1	3	1
Secretariat of the CC	8	0	0	3
Presidium of Council of Ministers	11	2	0	1
All institutions	27	4	4	5
All institutions (percent)	(67.5)	(10.0)	(10.0)	(12.5)

Table 13. *Generations in the Soviet central elite, 1978 (percent)*

Institution	Generation			
	I	II	III	IV
Department heads of CC Secretariat	58.8	23.5	11.7	5.8
Council of Ministers	60.0	17.3	14.6	8.0

haps be assigned to the first generation, since almost all of them entered the party before World War II.

The assignment of certain individuals to the post-Stalin generation should be clarified. Four of them – Romanov, Dolgikh, Gorbachev, and Katushev – entered the party before Stalin's death, the first two during the war, the last two in 1952; but all four remained during the late-Stalin period in low-level professional work and showed no signs of any political activity. The fifth, Riabov, clearly belongs to the post-Stalin generation. A factory technician in the late-Stalin period, he became a party member after Stalin's death and continued his professional work until 1958, when he was recruited into the party apparatus.

The generational profile of the central elite closely parallels that of the top leadership; the post-Stalin generation is scarcely represented (Table 13). As the coming succession and replacement of top personnel in the 1980s will affect not only the top leadership but the central elite as well, it is important to examine the personnel sources for this replacement.

Second-echelon officials in the central hierarchies and the regional party and government officials in the RSFSR are the two key sources for such replacement. We know more about the latter than the former. Limited data at our disposal suggest that about 20–25 percent of the former group – second-echelon central party officials, first deputy and deputy heads of the Central Committee departments – belong to the post-Stalin generation, the majority of them in the ideological field. The proportion of this generation's representatives among second-echelon government officials is roughly the same. To cite typical examples, only one of the

Table 14. *The post-Stalin generation in republican and provincial leadership, 1978 (percent)*

Institution	Post-Stalin generation
Presidium, Council of Ministers (RSFSR)	30.7
First *obkom* secretaries (RSFSR: Russian provinces)	32.0
Second secretaries of republics (Russians)	45.4
Republican and first *obkom* secretaries (Ukrainians and Belorussians)	47.6
Russian first *obkom* secretaries in non-Russian areas of RSFSR and non-Slav republics	38.5
All institutions	36.9
Leading party and Soviet officials of Moscow and Leningrad	75.0

four first deputy chairmen in the Soviet Planning Commission clearly belongs to the post-Stalin generation. Of two first deputy ministers and eight deputy ministers of foreign affairs, not one belongs to the post-Stalin generation.

This situation is not surprising in view of the system of promotion at the center under Brezhnev. For the central government and, to a lesser though still pronounced degree, for the central party apparatus, a system of seniority—what could be called "civil service" rules—has been established and implemented with notably few exceptions. Movement up the ladder was very gradual but, more important, it was systematic and predictable. Ministers of the central government were appointed from among first deputy ministers who in turn had been appointed from deputy minister posts; their advance was slow, and their differences in age were minimized. The same holds true for department heads in the Secretariat who advanced from positions of deputy heads or first *obkom* secretaries. Infrequently were rapid careers and promotions in the central apparatus made in contravention of the seniority rule.

Both the system of advancement within hierarchies and the seniority rule could well break down in a prolonged, two-stage succession, especially should a protracted power struggle develop within the top leadership. If the existing pattern is preserved, however, the pool of the best-known second-echelon officials in the central hierarchies of the party and especially of the government will not offer a large proportion of individuals who belong to the post-Stalin generation. It is our opinion, however, that the major source of replacement, especially in the party, is located not among second-echelon central officials but among the regional personnel of the RSFSR and to some extent of the Ukraine and Belorussia and from Russian secretaries of the non-Russian republics. Table 14 provides the generational profile of this group.

The provincial party first secretaries have been and in all probability will remain the traditional source of renovating the top leadership and the central party establishment. All full members of the Politburo with three exceptions were at one time or another *obkom* or republican secretaries; all but one alternate member of the Politburo and central party Secretariat achieved their positions in this way. (The exception, Ponomarev, made his career almost entirely in the central party apparatus.) The career pattern of top officials in the central government is, of course, quite different, particularly in the highly specialized ministries. Yet even there the leading positions in many functional areas and at the very top belong to individuals who during their career had occupied the post of provincial secretary. In the present Presidium of the Council of Ministers, five out of thirteen top government leaders took this route and in the Council of Ministers, nineteen out of seventy-six, that is 25 percent.[19]

The fact that an overwhelming majority of the provincial first secretaries belong to the Central Committee of the party, it might also be noted, provides them with important advantage and leverage for advancement during the process of succession. As Table 14 shows, a quite considerable proportion of this group – over one-third – belongs to the post-Stalin generation. It should be remarked, moreover, that the secretaries who belong to this generational group are not very recent newcomers to the party apparatus with low seniority in high-level secretarial positions. The RSFSR secretaries of Russian provinces who belong to this generation, for example, occupied on the average of about fifteen years the position of party secretary of a city or province. Furthermore, they do not at present occupy the positions of first secretary in secondary, relatively unimportant areas. Aside from the previously mentioned Romanov, the secretary of Leningrad and one of the newest Politburo members, the areas under their leadership include the key oil-producing region of Tiumen', the key steel- and machine-producing region of Kemerovo, the key textile-producing region of Ivanovo, and the key automobile-producing region of Gorkii; plus three of the largest regions: the Krasnoiarsk, Stavropol, and Far East *krai*. Their advance to such important positions at a time when seniority and age were prized also suggests more than average efficiency, energy, and talent.

If experience suggests that non-Russian personnel of non-Slav republics will not provide a major source of replacement for central officials, it is still useful for a number of reasons to survey this portion of the elite in certain republics. Even more useful, of course, are data for the RSFSR or the Slav republics, the importance of which both intrinsically and as a source of personnel replacement is incomparably greater than for the

---

[19]Some examples of those in the Council of Ministers who took the *obkom* route include such disparate areas of functional responsibilities as those of the ministers of agriculture, internal affairs, trade, industrial construction, procurement, construction of oil and gas industry, food industry, culture, labor and social problems, ferrous metallurgy, and foreign trade.

Table 15. *Average age and representation of the post-Stalin generation among republican elites (7 non-Slav republics[a])*

Position	No.	Average age	Representation of post-Stalin generation (%)
Republican secretaries	37	55.3	27.0
Presidium of Council of Ministers	42	55.7	33.3
Department heads, CC	89	51.1	46.1
Council of Ministers	210	54.2	35.2
First secretaries, *raikom* and *gorkom*	267	47.8	66.6
Chairmen, *raiispolkom* and *gorispolkom*[b]	71	47.2	73.2

[a]Uzbekistan, Tadzhikistan, Kirgizia, Latvia, Lithuania, Estonia, Moldavia. Data sources for these republics are: *Deputaty Verkhovnogo soveta Uzbekskoi SSR* (Tashkent, 1976); *Deputaty Verkhovnogo soveta Moldavskoi SSR* (Kishinev, 1976); *Deputaty Verkhovnogo soveta Latyshskoi SSR* (Riga, 1976); *Deputaty Verkhovnogo soveta Estonskoi SSR* (Tallin, 1976); *Sovetskaia Kirgiziia* (29–30 May 1975); *Kommunist Tadzhikistana* (30 May 1975); *Sovetskaia Litva* (27 May 1975).
[b]Includes also some chairmen of provinces.

seven non-Slav republics on which Table 15 is based. Unfortunately, the data source for these seven republics is not available for the Slav regions.

The importance of analyzing the composition of republican elites, however, goes well beyond their immediate boundaries. The similarities in the age and generational profile among the republics for which we have detailed data together with a comparison of these data with the scanty materials available for the Slav republics would indicate that all republics exhibit a similar pattern. (In addition, one should not forget the appreciable incidence of Russians and other Slavs in non-Russian republican posts. Russians compose a fair proportion of my republican sample.)[20] Furthermore, the age and generational profile of the non-Russian republics provides a basis for reaching conclusions about the possibility that a new type of cleavage is opening between the central Russian authorities in Moscow and the non-Russian authorities in the republics—a generational cleavage—one which may have important political implications.

The data in Table 15 indicate that, while the presence of the post-Stalin generation remains very low on the central level of the Soviet leadership elite, it is already substantial on the top provincial and republican levels, from which many, if not most, of the next members of the

[20]The number of Slavs in my republican sample ranges from 18 percent in Estonia to 21 percent in Tadzhikistan.

central party elite will come.[21] Already massive is the presence of the post-Stalin generation among the second echelon of the provincial party leadership and on the district level, those who in the 1980s will enter the elite in great numbers.

Quite possibly the renovation of the leadership and the elite on the top, central, and middle levels in the first phase of the succession will be very gradual, with strict attention to seniority and with conscious efforts to retain the old generation in office as long as possible. If this proves to be the case, the eventual changeover to the post-Stalin generation, especially in the upper reaches of the elite, will not *cause* policy shifts during the succession period but will rather *result* from such policy shifts. In all probability, the massive transition to the post-Stalin generation can be expected at the earliest during the second stage of the succession – somewhere around the mid-1980s. At the same time the very high generational homogeneity of the elites on all levels and the relatively low level of age differentials among elites of different levels and of different organizational association and functional specialization would argue that once such a replacement starts, it may be very thorough and quick. How suddenly such a replacement starts and how gradual or massive it is will depend in part on actuarial statistics and in part on the pattern which the coming succession follows. Before turning to the factors on which the succession pattern will depend, one should pause to consider another theme related to the generational analysis, namely, the background characteristics of the elites.

The subject of differences between elite generations has to be distinguished from an analysis which stresses differences of background characteristics among elites.[22] As a matter of fact, the generational dimen-

---

[21]Neither have the republican elites escaped the process of aging characteristic of the Brezhnev era. In Latvia and Tadzhikistan, for example, the average age of officials in the various categories of positions represented in our sample has increased in comparison to 1963, the year before Khrushchev's ouster, as follows:

Position	Latvia	Tadzhikistan
Republican secretariat	5.3	10.7
Presidium of Council of Ministers	5.1	0.5
Heads of departments of CC	9.9	12.8
Council of Ministers	4.9	6.6
First secretaries, *gorkom* and *raikom*	6.2	6.4
Chairmen: *gorispolkom* and *raiispolkom*	3.3	7.6

Source: Data for 1963 from *Sovetskaia Latviia* (14 February 1963) and *Kommunist Tadzhikistana* (16 February, 1963).

[22]Studies in background characteristics of political elites are quite popular, although less now than a decade ago. For general reviews which contain useful bibliographies see Lewis J. Edinger, ed., *Political Leadership in Industrialized Societies* (New York: Wiley, 1967); Geraint Parry, *Political Elites* (New York: Praeger, 1969); Urs Jaeggi, *Die gesellschaftliche Elite* (Bern/Stuttgart: Verlag Paul

sions suggest that even groups which share basic formal characteristics, like career patterns, may nevertheless differ markedly in their actual life experience, since identical jobs pursued in periods which differ regarding general political atmosphere, accepted priorities, and prevalent rewards and sanctions can develop different styles and habits, as well as different mentalities, outlooks, and perspectives.

This does not mean, however, that background characteristics may not bear on the impact of a generational turnover among Soviet elites. Let me state at the outset that I do not consider differences in background among elite individuals (such as the ascribed characteristics of social origin or place of birth and upbringing or the achieved characteristics of education or career pattern) to carry *in themselves* much weight for assigning expectations or predicting elite behavior.[23] Yet their importance could be considerable as a reinforcing factor (or their absence a weakening factor) of already existing elite *group* differences when those existing differences overlap with major differences in background characteristics. (This is why, incidentally, the prevalent practice of presenting a background analysis of the Soviet party's Central Committee *as a whole* is in my opinion of very little value.)[24]

Significant differences in elite background characteristics are potentially important when they occur along the lines of organizational associations or functional specializations or levels of leadership. This happens, for example, when the distinctions of organizational associations between the elite of the party and the state bureaucracy overlap with pronounced differences in their respective educational attainment or class origin; or when such pronounced background differences overlap with distinctions which cut across organizational lines (as, let us say, in

Haupt, 1960); Hans P. Dreitzel, *Elitbegriff und Sozialstruktur* (Stuttgart: Ferdinand Enke, 1962). The best examples of country-focused elite background studies are: Frederick W. Frey, *The Turkish Political Elite* (Cambridge, Mass.: MIT Press, 1965); Peter C. Ludz, *The Changing Party Elite in East Germany* (Cambridge, Mass.: MIT Press, 1972); and Wolfgang Zapf, *Wandlungen der deutschen Elite* (Munich: R. Piper, 1965).

[23] A number of empirical inquiries have proved that the link between elite background characteristics and attributes, let alone behavior, is very tenuous and cannot be taken as given. The most important of these inquiries are: Lewis J. Edinger and Donald D. Searing, "Social Background in Elite Analysis: A Methodological Inquiry," *American Political Science Review*, 61, no. 2 (June 1967), 428–45; Allen H. Barton, "Empirical Methods and Elite Theories" (unpublished paper, September 1970); Uwe Schleth, "Once Again: Does It Pay to Study Social Background in Elite Analysis?" (unpublished paper, September 1970). The last two papers were prepared for the Eighth World Congress of the International Political Science Association, Munich, 31 August–5 September 1970.

[24] Studies of the background of Soviet elites include, most notably: George Fischer, *The Soviet System and Modern Society* (New York: Atherton, 1968); Michael P. Gehlen, *The Communist Party of the Soviet Union* (Bloomington: Indiana University Press, 1969); Gerd Meyer, "The Impact of the Political Structure on the Recruitment of the Political Elite in the USSR" in Lenard J. Cohen and Jane P. Shapiro, eds., *Communist Systems in Comparative Perspective* (Garden City, N.Y.: Anchor Press and Doubleday, 1974), pp. 195–221.

the case of party *and* state high officials who specialize in heavy-industry policy problems and those who concentrate on consumer affairs); or when the distinctive lines between central and republican-level leadership groups overlap with clear differences in their respective career patterns; and so on.

Such overlap reinforces already existing elite cleavages and increases their potential impact on attitudes and behavior. The same will also hold true with regard to elite generational distinctions, our present subject. One has, therefore, to ask whether the four elite generations we have been considering differ significantly from each other in background characteristics. This is not the place for an extended analysis of major background characteristics of the elite, understood in the formal and traditional sense of social origin, place of origin, learned skills, education, job experience, and career pattern. Here I should like only to offer an abbreviated profile of each generation and to indicate the conclusions which can be drawn on the basis of their comparison.

The Great Purge generation derives overwhelmingly from lower-class origins, with the sons of peasants a dominant component. Born and raised in a small town or village, they entered the white-collar class very early in life, not later than their mid-twenties. Higher education, which was of a narrow technical nature outside the major educational centers, afforded the initial avenue of social mobility. (It should be clear that while most members of this elite generation were chosen from among graduates of technical institutes, their *general* education falls far short of the standards associated with graduates of institutions of higher learning. Their basic, that is pre-institute, education was in most cases an accelerated version of the three Rs.)[25] While trained as engineers and agronomists for the most part, they spent very little time in these occupations. Their political careers commenced very early, usually away from great metropolitan centers, and their advance was very rapid. They became and remained generalists whose key skill was general organization rather than its application to any particular area.

Examination of the limited sample of the World War II generation suggests to me that in all major respects it shares identical background characteristics with the preceding elite generation.

The late-Stalin generation, however, exhibits interesting variations from its post-purge elite predecessors. While still overwhelmingly of

[25] I am proposing that among the middle and older generations of the elite, a completed higher technical education may go hand in hand with a lack of normal secondary education. According to my research, over one-third of the CC members (elected in 1961) with higher technical education went into the technological institutes from a workers' faculty (*rabfak*) or from a vocational school (*tekhnikum*). In other words, while these elite members may well be regarded as specialists in a particular area, they cannot be regarded as educated people. As an example, one can mention Politburo member A. P. Kirilenko, who at the age of 14 ended his nontechnical education (a village school); but at the age of 24, after a one-year preparation in a *rabfak*, entered an institute of aviation engineering from which he graduated at the age of 30.

lower-class origins, its members are in the main workers. They spent a longer period at their learned occupations in low- or middle-level positions before moving into the bureaucracy. Their career rise was gradual; they received a "responsible position" in the elite at a late age and their advance in the elite was steady.

The formal education of this third elite – overwhelmingly technical and still the principal avenue of mobility – is both more variegated and more haphazard than that of their predecessors. While a sizable minority received excellent training at major educational centers, an even larger group attended correspondence or evening schools. Doubt about the quality of their education is reinforced by the fact that many of them received degrees at a time they already occupied middle-level positions within the bureaucracy. (Indeed, some of them were overseers of the institutions which granted their degrees.) On the other hand, their general basic – that is, pre-institute – education is much more respectable than that of the Great Purge generation. While their generational predecessors received their political training on the job, a large proportion of the late-Stalin generation attended formal indoctrination courses in the higher party school (VPSh).

The background characteristics of the post-Stalin generation will be discussed in greater detail. I have taken as a basis of our profile the group which is by far the most politically significant within this elite generation: the Russian first provincial party secretaries.[26] I should like to signal the fact that, while many background characteristics of this group were expected and predictable, some of our findings are surprising.

To start with, the group as a whole is very homogeneous. Life and career patterns as well as background characteristics are with very few exceptions repeated from individual to individual. As far as it was possible to establish, industrial workers seemed to form the social base of the post-Stalin elite. The peasant base of recruitment shows a clear decline, while the new Soviet middle class for the first time constitutes a sizable and growing minority. One finds also for the first time a dominant proportion of individuals who spent their youth in large cities and a growing number who attended schools in metropolitan areas.

The youth and early working life of this group reflect the normalization of Soviet living conditions and epitomize typical middle-class patterns. The normal route went from high school to an establishment of higher learning; working life started at the age of 22 to 24 in professional or low managerial positions; regardless of social origin, very few of them were at any time workers or peasants.

Education constitutes the dominant avenue of mobility. With but one exception all individuals in our group finished some form of higher education. Moreover, the education of this elite generation on the average

[26]The core of my sample consists of twenty-two Russian first *obkom* secretaries in the RSFSR. For comparative purposes this group is augmented by first secretaries in the Ukraine and Belorussia and Russian secretaries in the non-Slav republics, altogether a group of thirty-seven individuals.

clearly surpasses that of its predecessors in terms of quality. In only two cases were degrees attained through correspondence courses; a sizable minority even acquired graduate degrees. The education of this group still centers almost entirely on technological skills; evenly divided between engineers and agronomists, it also includes for the first time a number of economists.[27] A minority of this group attended the Higher Party School in Moscow at a late point in their party career and in all but one case received important promotions after graduation.[28]

[27]According to summary official Soviet figures, among *all* secretaries (that is, not only first secretaries) of the 170 republics, provinces, and cities with the rights of provinces (Moscow and Kiev), 99.4 percent have completed higher education, 0.1 percent have an incomplete higher education, and 0.5 percent have middle education. Of all these secretaries, about 70 percent are engineers, economists, or agronomists. Among *all* party secretaries of the 4,241 cities and districts, 99.2 percent have completed party education, 0.7 percent have incompleted higher education, and 0.1 percent middle education. Of all those secretaries, about 60 percent are professionals who specialize in industry or agriculture (*Partiinaia zhizn'*, 1976, no. 10 [May], pp. 19, 22). The percentages of engineers, agronomists, economists, etc. are more important than the percentage with higher education. The figures in higher education include graduates of the higher party schools, which by no stretch of imagination can be equated with regular higher education.
   It should be noted that the relatively high percentage of individuals with higher education is characteristic not only of the full-time party apparatus, but of the party cadres as a whole. Among the secretaries of the almost 394,000 primary party organizations, individuals who completed higher education constituted in 1976 49.7 percent, and in addition 4.0 percent had incompleted higher education. Among the 2,221,000 who comprise the cadre of party propagandists, technical specialists (engineers, agronomists, economists, etc.) constituted 62.3 percent and teachers, professors, and "scientific workers" an additional 12.7 percent (*Spravochnik sekretaria pervichnoi partiinoi organizatsii* [Moscow: Gospolitizdat, 1977], p. 355).
   Among the 385,532 members and alternate members of the district and city party committees in 1976, 49.9 percent have completed higher education and an additional 3.0 percent have incompleted higher education; among the 30,201 members and alternate members of the republican central committees, *obkom*s and *kraikom*s, 69.3 percent have completed higher education and an additional 1.4 percent an incompleted higher education (*Spravochnik partiinogo rabotnika*, vyp. 17-yi [Moscow: Gospolitizdat, 1977], pp. 461–2).
[28]The background characteristics of the district and city first party secretaries are very similar to those of the post-Stalin generation of provincial first party secretaries at comparable stages of their careers. An overwhelming majority of them had some experience in managerial or professional work before entering the party apparatus; and, with very few exceptions, almost all of them have higher technical or agricultural education. I am struck by the fact, however, that very few of my sample of provincial first party secretaries have ever occupied the position of first district secretary. Unless the pattern of recruitment changes, therefore, the district party secretaries (as opposed to the city party secretaries) could be considered a source of replenishment of the staff of the *obkom* rather than of the *obkom* secretarial personnel. On the other hand one has no reason to doubt Brezhnev's statement that for all practical purposes *all* secretaries on the republican and provincial levels were at one time or another secretaries of the primary, district, or city party organizations (*XXV s'ezd KPSS. Stenograficheskii otchet* [Moscow: Gospolitizdat, 1976], p. 96).

This group displays three characteristics present to an extent which is surprising and striking.

A. *First, highly pronounced is the decline of what is usually described as cooptation in the career pattern among party secretaries of the post-Stalin generation.* The concept of cooptation, introduced into Soviet studies by Frederic J. Fleron, Jr., indicates the specific career pattern of party officials who start their party careers in relatively high positions following an already lengthy and successful career in management.[29]

Over 50 percent of all newly appointed first provincial party secretaries in the Khrushchev period and about 44 percent in the 1964–8 period achieved their posts via cooptation.[30] Only 20 percent of my sample of the post-Stalin generation can be considered for certain to be coopted officials. The remainder advanced along the regular party route, after having been recruited relatively early into the party apparatus. This is not to say that these secretaries lack managerial or professional experience entirely. It means only that they gained their managerial and professional experience in a relatively short period of time, a little over four years on average for the group, and in relatively low positions, such as factory engineers or state farm agronomists. This trend of the lower incidence of cooptation has been remarked as a characteristic of all newly recruited first provincial party secretaries in the late Brezhnev era;[31] nowhere, however, is it so strongly pronounced as among the group under consideration here.

We should like to suggest a number of possible explanations of this trend. The first, a very important one, would stress what we noted above: the greater ability of diverse elite groups to influence and exert pressure on the Soviet political process and the greater responsiveness of the top leadership to sentiments expressed in bureaucratic structures, first and foremost the party apparatus. In this respect there can be little doubt that the ideal personnel policy preferred by the party apparatus would be one that stresses the advancement, as in any bureaucratic structure, any corporate organization or civil service group, of their "own" cadres, one that gives preference and promotes "insiders" over "outsiders."

Second, the trend also represents the reaction of top party leaders to those tendencies of the late Khrushchev period which obscured the separate identity of the party apparatus, as if to dissolve it within the general party bureaucratic structure.[32] The very high ratio of cooptation under

---

[29]Frederic Fleron, "Representation of Career Types in the Soviet Political Leadership" in R. Barry Farrell, ed., *Political Leadership in Eastern Europe and the Soviet Union* (Chicago: Aldine, 1970), pp. 108–39.

[30]Robert E. Blackwell, Jr., "Elite Recruitment and Functional Change: An Analysis of the Soviet Obkom Elite 1950–1968," *Journal of Politics*, 34, no. 1 (February 1972), 144.

[31]Rigby, "Soviet Regional Leadership," pp. 21–2.

[32]The actual picture of the activities of the professional party functionary differs from most portraits provided by "party-minded" Soviet writers. The major stress in all those accounts is on the fact that the party functionary participates in and affects the administration of state affairs through his "ideological influ-

Khrushchev was only one indication of this tendency. Such was also partly the intention and certainly the result of Khrushchev's reorganization schemes of 1962–4, where he all but merged the party apparatus on the district level with the state's bureaucracies and divided the party on the provincial level into separate industrial and agricultural units.[33] If Khrushchev's policies lowered the esprit de corps of the party apparatus, the policy of the Brezhnev administration was to rebuild morale and to restore the separate identity and the functional distinctness of the party bureaucracy. Decline in the recruitment to high positions in the party apparatus through cooptation is only one element of this policy.

Third, the decline in cooptation among the individuals discussed here and among the provincial first party secretaries in the Brezhnev period in general could be regarded as an expression of the changing nature and functions of the party apparatus itself, a change which began a long time ago but continues still. From this point of view one should look more closely at the concept of cooptation. To depict the career pattern which became very pronounced under Khrushchev the cooptation concept is very useful descriptively, but I would submit that it can be misleading analytically if its importance is exaggerated. The concept implies a basic and, in my opinion, an exaggerated distinction between a party and managerial career which is neither theoretically nor factually justified.[34]

The old party apparatus under Stalin and in Khrushchev's initial period was a political, primarily a mobilizing institution. The new party apparatus toward the end of the Khrushchev era and under Brezhnev engages in the type of decision making which blurs the distinction be-

ence" *(ideinoe vozdeistvie)*. The picture of the party functionary in the Soviet press, especially in professional party journals, provides a more realistic account. One aspect of the party functionary's activities that becomes clear from all these accounts is his direct involvement in daily administration like the so-called state bureaucrat. Of course, this involvement takes different forms, depending on the exact position of the individual in the apparatus and on the level of his activities. A *raikom* secretary will participate in the administration in a manner similar to the *raiispolkom* chairman; the head of an industrial department in the central party *apparat*, in a manner similar to that of an industrial minister.

A district party secretary made the following comment in 1961: "Looking at it from the outside you would never make out what I am – the secretary of the party committee or the chairman of the *ispolkom* or an employee of the *sovnarkhoz*. Really, I am a kind of multiple tool! Of course one has to take part in economic affairs, but surely there ought to be a difference in the approach, in the style of work of a district committee and a factory, or a district committee and a *sovnarkhoz*? But somehow or other, the boundary lines have disappeared" (M. Ivashechkin, *Nash sovremennik* [Moscow: Gosizdat, 1961], p. 136).

[33] See John A. Armstrong, "Party Bifurcation and Elite Interests," *Soviet Studies*, 17, no. 3 (April 1966), 417–30.

[34] Such an exaggeration in my opinion leads Grey Hodnett to propose that "perhaps a qualitative change in the character of the *obkom* leadership depends not so much on how many young men with fresh technical diplomas are drawn into lower Party work as on how many older, experienced non-*apparatchiki* transfer to the Party apparatus well along in their careers, affecting its character rather than vice versa" ("The *Obkom* First Secretaries," *Slavic Review*, 24, no. 4 [December 1965], 652).

tween strict managerial and party secretarial activities and functions. The party secretary is becoming more and more a manager at a different level of decision making.[35] As a matter of fact, underlying the cooptation pattern is the interchangeability of managerial and party secretarial roles, and this interchangeability explains why this pattern could be a functional and successful route of recruitment into the party apparatus. At the same time it suggests the limits of the *necessity* of cooptation into the party apparatus. The key clue to those limits may be found in the career patterns of *all* coopted officials in our sample. They all perform their secretarial functions in highly specialized provinces (that is, provinces where economic life is dominated by one kind of highly specialized activity), and they all have undergone a highly specialized training and were engaged in highly specialized managerial activities before entering the party apparatus. The careers of two such coopted individuals will serve as examples.

G. P. Bogomiakov became an oil engineer at the age of 22. For two years he worked as an engineer with an oil-exploratory expedition in Siberia and then pursued and completed a doctoral program in geological-mineralogical sciences. For the next ten years he served initially in oil-exploration institutions and then became the deputy director of the West Siberian Oil Research Institute. At the age of 37 he was recruited into the party apparatus as head of the Oil Department of the Tiumen' Provincial Party Committee. He then became first secretary of the Tiumen' City Party Committee and second secretary of the Tiumen' Provincial Party Committee; and since December 1973 he has been first secretary of this dynamic and important oil-producing province.

V. G. Kliuev became a textile engineer at the age of 25, and after working in various enterprises in Ivanovo province, he eventually became director of a large factory. He was recruited into the party apparatus at the age of 37 and served first as head of the Textile Industry Department of the Ivanovo Provincial Party Committee. He then became first secretary of the Ivanovo City Party Committee and second secretary of the Ivanovo Provincial Party Committee; and since July 1972 has served as first secretary of this textile-producing province, the largest in the Soviet Union.

What we are saying is that now the *need* of cooptation to the party apparatus is pronounced where highly specialized types of activities are required, whereas the *need* for cooptation to secretarial positions may have sharply declined in nonspecialized provinces of a mixed industrial or agricultural profile because of the basic similarities of general managerial and general party secretarial functions. (What is needed in such provinces is good knowledge and understanding of local conditions, and this, as we shall see later, the noncoopted secretaries do possess.) In fact

[35]One concurs fully with T. H. Rigby's conclusion that "the local party committee exists not just to preach at or jolly along the administration from the outside. . . . The party command-structure is an integral part of the administration" ("Traditional, Market, and Organizational Societies and the USSR," *World Politics*, 16, no. 4 [July 1964], 552).

those individuals in our group who traveled the straight party route in almost all cases occupy secretarial positions in provinces that are either agricultural or of a nonspecialized industrial nature.

B. *The second characteristic of our group of officials of the post-Stalin generation is the total disappearance of party generalists.*[36] The party generalist of the past, a dominant figure in the party apparatus for whom the term *apparatchik* was coined, exhibited a high degree of mobility both in terms of type of job and geographical location.[37] Brezhnev's own career constitutes the epitome of the old-type party generalist.

Brezhnev for the first twenty years of his party career occupied, consecutively, the following positions: deputy chairman of a city soviet, head of the organizational department of a provincial party committee, secretary of the provincial party committee in the Ukrainian industrial center Dnepropetrovsk, deputy head of a political department of an army group, head of a political department of an army, head of a political department of an army group in wartime, head of a political department of a military district in peacetime, first provincial secretary of the party of the Ukrainian industrial centers of Dnepropetrovsk and then Zaporozhe, first secretary of the agricultural Moldavian Republic, secretary of the Central Committee of the party in Moscow, deputy chief of the Main Political Administration of Soviet Armed Forces for Naval Affairs, second secretary and then first secretary of the party of the Kazakh Republic, secretary of the Central Committee of the party in Moscow, and deputy chief of the Bureau of the Central Committee for the RSFSR.[38]

[36]On the general question of generalist versus specialist recruitment and career pattern in the bureaucratic setting, see Michael Cohen, "The Generalist and Organizational Mobility," *Public Administration Review*, 30, no. 5 (September–October 1970), 544–52.

[37]The process of acquiring the "generalist" skill resembles the process of "broadening." One author has described it in the West as consisting of "anticipatory socialization in which executives are prepared for top positions by rotation among various control positions. . . . The purpose of this process is to reduce the specialization of the executive in order to prepare him for the top, highly generalized, command position. Rotation breaks up his narrow outlook and commitment to one subunit; it extends his experience, insight, and information about subunits other than the one from which he is recruited; and it develops in him a broader perspective" (Amitai Etzioni, *A Comparative Analysis of Complex Organizations* [New York: Free Press, 1961], p. 281).

[38]The probable successor to Brezhnev, A. P. Kirilenko, is also a generalist par excellence. He started his party career as a district party secretary and was promoted to secretary of the Zaporozhe province in the Ukraine. During World War II he served as the political commissar of the 18th Army and then became the representative of the State Defense Committee (GKO) at the Moscow Airplane Factory. He was then assigned to the post of second secretary of Zaporozhe province, then moved to become first secretary of Nikolaev province in the Ukraine, moved to become first secretary of Dnepropetrovsk province, and was then transferred to the position of first secretary of Sverdlovsk province in the Urals. While serving in Sverdlovsk, he became a member of the Central Committee Bureau for the RSFSR and alternate member of the Politburo. In 1962 he was transferred to Moscow to become first deputy chairman of the Central Committee Bureau for the RSFSR.

The overwhelming majority of individuals in the post-Stalin generation show a very low degree of mobility with regard to both type of job and geographic location. While they are not specialized in the way of the coopted officials discussed above, they are highly specialized in their generalized areas of responsibility. Almost 70 percent of this group, an astonishing proportion, have been employed throughout their careers in only one province (or, in a very few cases, have moved to an adjacent province) and in only one type of job geared to the profile of their provinces.[39] Those few individuals who circulated in party positions among a number of provinces retained, however, their very specific job specialization; here we speak about party officials who are clearly considered specialists in ethnic minorities.[40]

It is as if the Soviet Union resolved the old dispute in Western literature between those who argue the generalized nature of executive skills and those who argue their specialized character first in favor of the former and now in favor of the latter.[41] The pattern of disappearing

[39]An extreme example is I. A. Bondarenko, whose whole life and career was spent in Rostov province. There he completed the course of an agricultural vocational school. He worked as an agronomist in a local *kolkhoz*, graduated from an agricultural institute located in the province, and continued his graduate studies in the institute where he later became a member of the faculty. After being recruited into the party apparatus, he became first secretary of a district in the province and then head of the agricultural department of the Rostov *obkom*. He then advanced to become secretary for agriculture of the Rostov *obkom*, second secretary of the Rostov agricultural *obkom*, chairman of the Rostov obispolkom, and since November 1966 has served as first secretary of Rostov province.

[40]The examples of V. P. Nikonov and A. V. Vlasov are instructive in this respect. Nikonov, after a brief stint as head of the agricultural department of the Krasnoiarsk *kraikom* and service in the central party apparatus, became second secretary of the Tatar *obkom* of the RSFSR, and has served since 1967 as first secretary of the Marii *obkom* of the RSFSR. Vlasov, after service as secretary and then second secretary of the Iakutsk *obkom* of the RSFSR, served for three years in the central party apparatus and in July 1975 was appointed first secretary of the Checheno-Ingush *obkom* of the RSFSR. Incidentally, in almost all cases I have discovered, the Russian who is appointed to serve as first secretary of an ethnically non-Russian province (or for that matter as second secretary of a non-Russian republic) goes through a preparatory period of service in the central party apparatus, a pattern totally absent in the case of the Russian first secretaries who serve in Russian provinces.

[41]Two different approaches have been advanced in the literature with regard to the occupational division of labor at the executive level. According to the first, technological and administrative peculiarities and requirements of divergent areas of collective social activities determine and limit the scope of the effective interchangeability of occupational executive roles. Executive ability is to be regarded only to a minimal degree as a general skill which can be effectively applied across the technological and administrative boundaries dividing organizations and subsystems of the society. Executive ability consists primarily in a specific type of decision making, in supervision of a particular type of performance, in the management and control of a distinctive organized collectivity. Given the fact that the effectiveness of an executive performance is specified within such narrow limits, the executive horizontal mobility is severely restricted. Beyond the range of similar types of performance which are to be supervised by the executive, the horizontal mobility would require a basic modi-

mobility in job type and geographic location can be explained in part by the factors discussed earlier, especially the changing nature of the party apparatus; it constitutes a functional substitute for coopting outside specialists into the party apparatus.

This present pattern, however, raises a serious problem with regard to future passage of the new generation of provincial party officials into top leadership institutions. These institutions currently employ a large number of generalists among their members and in all probability require a relatively large number of generalists. In the existing situation it is not clear where the new generalists will be found for leadership positions. It is of course possible that for those newly recruited, the "generalization" of their experience will occur after they have become members of the top leadership. Such an eventuality, however, would constitute a very important departure from the past pattern. It would, moreover, strengthen the already existing tendency toward fragmentation which goes hand in hand with specialization and localism, the tendency to represent within the leadership specific interests and areas, and it would increase the difficulties of policy integration by the top leadership.

C. *The third striking and very surprising characteristic of our group of party officials is their almost uniformly rapid advancement to the high positions which they now hold.* The rapidity of their advance can be measured in a number of ways. Surprisingly, in a situation where the Soviet elite is aging rapidly, the average age of their appointment to the position of first *provincial* party secretary is 40, that is to say, considerably younger than the average age of the present first *district* party secretaries in my sample.

An even more striking way of looking at the situation is the fact that on the average only eleven years passed between the points of entrance into the party apparatus and appointment to their high position of first provincial secretary. Such a time span would be normal for coopted

fication of behavior and orientation and would involve a major change in executive effectiveness. Representative of this approach is Peter F. Drucker; see, for example, his *The Practice of Management* (New York: Harper, 1954), pp. 8–9.

The second approach stresses as the dominant characteristic of the executive role the "universal" ability and skill to manage, supervise, control, etc. The exercise of executive authority is a highly general activity; and the skill on which it is based – to manage people and to elicit performance from them – permits a virtually unlimited, effective horizontal mobility across any and all technological and administrative boundaries of specialization. Typical of this approach is the assertion of R. Dubin: "The educated executive is one who can operate effectively in different kinds of organizations having different values and objectives" (*Human Relations in Administration* [New York: Prentice-Hall, 1951], pp. 3–4).

Thus one approach maintains that the executive role of control and supervision is a highly specialized skill; the other, that it is highly general. This author fully concurs with Amitai Etzioni's conclusions about the value of these two approaches: ". . . the executive role should be seen as more specialized than the advocate of universal executive skills would suggest, but much more general than it appears to those who emphasize the specific tasks the executive must direct." See Amitai Etzioni, *A Comparative Analysis of Complex Organizations* (New York: The Free Press, 1961), p. 295.

officials, but it is highly unusual, to say the least, for officials who traveled the regular party career route. (For the other Russian first provincial secretaries in my sample who took the party route in their careers, the average time between the start of party work and assumption of the position of first secretary is close to twenty years.)

I cannot explain this phenomenon. The evidence does not argue that high patronage accounts for the rapid rise of this group of officials. Moreover, one would not expect patronage to have played an important role when the pattern of an entire age group is almost uniform. One would expect that patronage would have played at least as important a role for the remainder of our sample, the older generation of first party secretaries, but the latter exhibit a very different pattern of advancement.

We are left therefore with other possible explanations. One such would require modification with regard to this group of our impressions concerning advancement patterns in the Brezhnev era; it would suggest a deliberate policy of promoting young party officials to positions of high *provincial* influence. Another would lead us to consider that our group is composed of particularly gifted, talented, and ambitious individuals who even under the highly unpropitious conditions for rapid advancement under Brezhnev were able to escape the existing pattern. These tentative explanations are, of course, not mutually exclusive.

Having surveyed the backgrounds of the four Soviet elite generations, one can offer a number of tentative conclusions. The background differences among the three Stalinist generations are marginal. The World War II generation shows a high degree of similarity to the preceding and succeeding elites. This would indicate that background characteristics do not provide reinforcement of suggested generational differences. Moreover, the late-Stalin generation, more important in terms of numbers and weight in the present and future leadership, displays some background characteristics which would seem rather to reinforce the effects of its political socialization in the Stalinist period.

The differences in background characteristics between the post-Stalin generation and its elite predecessors may be more than marginal. This is not at all to say that one should posit here the distinction that is sometimes made between the new "technocrats" and the old or middle-aged *apparatchiki*. With regard to the key characteristics that identify technocrats and *apparatchiki*, the real break between newcomers and the old guard occurred in the late 1930s, during and directly after the Great Purge. This break continued to be accentuated in the subsequent Stalinist and post-Stalinist decades. The distinction in background between the *apparatchik* and the technocrat has by now been blurred to a very large extent. The *apparatchiki* of today are technocrats, regardless of the generation from which they come and, as importantly, regardless of whether they served in the party apparatus or the state bureaucracies. What is important with regard to the new generation, however, is, first, that the "technocratic" elements of its background, such as education, are clearly more pronounced than in the past generation; and, second,

that most of the key social characteristics provide a cumulative reinforcement in a direction away from past generations and are positively
correlated with the changed nature of the political socialization of elites
in the post-Stalin era.

In reviewing the principal findings and propositions of Part II, I am
reminded of the dialogue between the theorist and the empiricist. The
former addresses the latter: "You know that your findings are true, but
how do you know that they are significant?" The empiricist replies to the
theorist: "You know that your findings are significant, but how do you
know that they are true?" The findings of this part, I feel, fall into three
categories. The discussion of the imminent turnover of leadership and
elites during the coming succession is both significant and true. The
discussion of the attitudes of the new elite generation may be significant,
but we are not certain how true it is. The discussion of the background
characteristics of the new elite generation is clearly true, but we are not
certain how significant it is.

I have established that the approaching succession will probably differ in some crucial respects from past successions, as understood both in
the narrow sense of the change of the top leadership and in the broad
sense of the change of the top elite stratum. The succession of the late
1930s, as I wrote, must be seen in the broad sense. A new generation of
elites came to office without the accompaniment of commensurate
change in the composition of the core top leadership. Following both
Stalin and Khrushchev, the succession must be seen in the narrow sense.
In each case the change of top leadership was not accompanied by commensurate change in the generational composition of elite officeholders.
The approaching succession, whatever the form and results of its initial
stage, will eventually involve a replacement in the top leadership and the
central establishment on a scale much greater than the last two successions and will be combined with an increased generational turnover of
the Soviet political elite. This conjunction of successions in both the
broad and narrow senses has no precedent in Soviet history. It will be a
political development of long-term duration and significance.[42]

Some Western students of the Soviet Union have asserted that political developments are no longer central to an understanding of the Soviet
system, that the industrial model with its special set of questions is
assuming the determining role.[43] Without attempting to explore this
problem, one can agree that the post-Stalin era witnessed a decline in

---

[42]The most extreme view on the probability of fundamental changes in the Soviet
Union during the coming succession is expressed by Wolfgang Leonhard in the
very title of his latest book: *Am Vorabend einer neuen Revolution? Die Zukunft des
Sowjetkommunismus* (Munich: C. Bertelsman, 1975).

[43]See, for example, Alex Inkeles, "Models and Issues in the Analysis of Soviet
Society" in *Social Change in Soviet Russia* (Cambridge, Mass.: Harvard University Press, 1968), pp. 419–33.

the role of the political, a decrease in the extent of its relative autonomy from the social environment. At the same time, however, the political factor continues to affect the evolution of Soviet society to a greater extent than it does other societies on a similar level of industrial development. The shaping of the political factor by social influences continues to be low in comparison to the shaping of the social environment by the active, mobilizing, and directing influence of the political factor. Daniel Bell's remark would appear valid still: "The development of Soviet society depends thus on the nature of Soviet political developments."[44]

The pattern of the post-Khrushchev leadership has demonstrated its durability. At the same time it has been able (no small feat) to minimize the danger to the oligarchy "from above" – the accumulation of autocratic power by a leader and his domination – and the danger "from below" – the dispersal of prerogatives to lower and broader segments of the political establishment which goes out of control. The leadership withstood, though with visible strains, the difficult task of dealing with the Czechoslovak crisis; it took the Soviet Union through a major turn in its foreign policy toward detente; it survived three very bad crop years and a decline in the ratio of industrial growth and productivity. Can the existing pattern survive the test of the coming succession?

Were the approaching succession "simply" a question of replacing Brezhnev, one would be strongly inclined to argue that as far as the *internal* factors influencing the dynamics of the Soviet political leadership are concerned, a continuation of the present pattern can be expected despite the disrupting potential of succession. The strong elements of what T. H. Rigby perceptively calls a "self-stabilizing oligarchy,"[45] which developed in the last decade, make the composition of the Politburo more predictable and stable, its politics more balanced, its operation more bureaucratic, and the position of the top leaders less personalized than even before. This provides a base for the succession process which differs significantly from past successions. Of course, the specific circumstances of Brezhnev's departure, whether he retires voluntarily, dies, or is ousted, will make a considerable difference on how orderly the succession will be. Still, whatever the form of Brezhnev's departure, it would seem that the existing arrangements are sufficiently self-regenerating to handle the replacement of the top leader.

The stability and longevity of the existing pattern, however, have been conditional on two internal structural factors: gradualism in major policy changes and gradualism, to say the least, in personnel replacement. We do not know whether the first condition will still obtain in a succession or whether, after the cycle of cautious readjustments and traditionalism of the last decade, the mood of the leadership and the elite will swing toward revitalization and major reforms, just as the frozen conditions of Stalin's Russia were replaced by the flux of the Khrushchev period. Certainly, the

[44]Daniel Bell, *The End of Ideology* (New York: Collier Books, 1961), p. 340.
[45]T. H. Rigby, "The Soviet Leadership: Towards a Self-Stabilizing Oligarchy?" *Soviet Studies*, 22, no. 2 (October 1970), 167–91.

key determinant of what will be the dominant tendency in this respect during the succession will crucially depend on whether there is a major increase in the perception by Soviet leaders and the elite of pressures and frustrations stemming from failures or dangers at home or abroad. What we do know, however, is that the second condition – gradualism in personnel replacement – will most probably not obtain.

Changes in the structure of relations within the Soviet political elite were a more important channel for elite change in the last decade than elite replacement. The greater assertiveness of institutional interests, the increase in the operational autonomy of elite organizations, the diffusion of influence from the top leadership, and the relative stability of the balance of countervailing forces within the top leadership stopped, however, very short of institutionalization. They may therefore be partly reversed, even if with difficulty, in the coming succession.

The post-Khrushchev structural innovations may satisfy the present generation of officeholders. But they may not satisfy the next one, which may want not only to broaden its operational autonomy but also to influence the agenda of decision making. Response to social reality always involves a lag: Not only individuals but also groups respond to new conditions on the basis of attitudes and habits developed under old conditions. The situation which future Soviet leaders will face with regard to their major elite institutions will be very different from the ones faced by Stalin's successors. Stalin did not simply control the party, the military, or the planners – he crushed them. Ironically, only now, when Stalin is again becoming an officially "respectable" figure, is the delayed impact of Stalinism on the character of Soviet bureaucracy dissolving. Soviet administrators display today more self-confidence and professional pride than ever before. These qualities are easily reconcilable with an authoritarian outlook toward the society at large but are difficult to fit into a highly restrictive elite structure without endangering its effectiveness.

PART III
THE NATURE AND EXTENT OF SOVIET POLITICAL STABILITY

7
STABILITY: ANALYTICAL CONSIDERATIONS

If indeed, as our analysis indicates, the imminent succession of leaders and elites over the next decade dramatically increases the potential for change of the Soviet system, whether in the direction of destabilization or orderly development, it is essential to analyze the level of sociopolitical stability with which the Soviet system enters the 1980s and which the coming succession will test. Discussion by Soviet specialists of the nature and conditions of stability in the USSR has suffered from the very same differences, ambiguities, complexities – one might say, at times, the chaos – that permeates the analysis of stability in the general literature of political science. Yet, for all the serious difficulties of working with terms that lack uniform value and perception, we share G. Lowell Field's view of the centrality of the question for political science and especially for comparative politics. He writes: "It is not different forms of system so much as stability and change in systems – what may be expected to last and what may be expected to develop into something else – that constitute the basis of useful knowledge of political systems today."[1] Before turning to our examination of stability in the Soviet context, it would be useful to review certain dominant aspects of the general discussion on political stability, on the one hand, and of the literature relating more specifically to Communist systems, on the other hand, which have contributed to the delineation of my own approach to the subject. I shall then elaborate those criteria on the basis of which I shall argue in subsequent pages the essential stability of the Soviet political system. Stress will fall on the meaning of the concept, leaving aside the even more difficult problem of its operationalization and measurement.

The considerable variety in the definitions of political stability and in the choice of indicators to measure it is less a sign of confusion than an acknowledgment that " 'political stability' must be approached as a multi-faceted societal attribute, composed of the various subindicators, rather than as any one particular monomeasure."[2] Such an approach excludes the possibility that the presence of any single factor could assure a politically stable situation, while the absence of any single factor could serve to indicate an unstable situation. The most commonly used

[1] G. Lowell Field, *Comparative Political Development: The Precedent of the West* (Ithaca, N.Y.: Cornell University Press, 1967), p. 1.
[2] Leon Hurwitz, "Contemporary Approaches to Political Stability," *Comparative Politics*, 5, no. 3 (April 1973), 461.

indicator of political stability, for example, is the absence of violence, a criterion that would surely aid the observer of the last Weimar years but just as surely mislead the student of stability in Germany under the Nazis; and it proves useless in comprehending one of the most significant, recent destabilizing events in a Communist country, the Czechoslovak crisis of 1968. If the presence of violence does not necessarily reflect instability and – even more so – the absence of violence does not necessarily indicate political stability, the same seems true as well for another commonly used indicator of stability, the longevity of government in office.

Those indicators most often selected in analyses of the general concept or in case studies measuring its extent in particular countries or systems are the following: The negative indicators are absence of violence, absence of structural change, and weakness of political movements opposed to the existing system; the positive indicators are governmental longevity, constitutional continuity, effective decision making, and legitimacy, all of which are understood in most cases as positive systemic acceptance and support.[3] To posit that the various dimensions of the concept may be and are in my opinion separate and distinct does not mean that one should eliminate or even discount the importance of single indicators. Rather it serves to underscore how crucial are the overall balance and direction of these single indicators. It is suggested that the direction and intensity of single indicators pointing toward political stability or instability can be counteracted for prolonged periods of time by the direction and intensity of other indicators.

Furthermore, it can be proposed that if one regards political stability as a balanced outcome of numerous, sometimes contradictory forces, at least some of these forces can be different in each specific case being analyzed; that is to say, the positive or negative content of a particular force (from the point of view of stability) can be carried in different situations and systems by functional substitutes (equivalents) or functional alternatives. One can only agree, therefore, with Leon Hurwitz when he concludes: "If emphasis is placed upon isolated monomeasures [of stability], great precision and quantification will result – but to the detriment of theoretical requirements and considerations. If emphasis is placed upon composite societal attributes, which is intuitively more acceptable, one must then forego neat and precise measurement."[4]

Too often the terms "stability" and "instability" are applied indiscriminately and *interchangeably* to different spheres of social endeavor, to different institutional orders of the social system, or to different components within an institutional order. A politically stable country is not necessarily at the same time socially, culturally, or economically stable. The instability of political leadership does not necessarily assume gen-

---

[3] See, for example, Ted Robert Gurr, "Persistence and Change in Political Systems, 1800–1971," *The American Political Science Review*, 68, no. 4 (December 1974), 1482–1504.

[4] Hurwitz, "Contemporary Approaches to Political Stability," pp. 461–3.

eral political instability. (Such confusion in the case of the Soviet Union almost invariably leads to exaggeration of the generalized destabilizing effects of the so-called succession crisis.)

While it is of course an axiom of social science that all institutional orders of any modern society are interconnected and interdependent, the degree of the interdependence may differ significantly in different societies, systems, and countries. Moreover, in every society there is usually a time lag, sometimes very prolonged, before symptoms of instability in one institutional order make themselves felt in other orders. Finally, even in the most tightly integrated societies, each institutional order displays a degree of relative autonomy from the others that can permit the possibility of systemic coexistence of highly stable and highly unstable conditions in separate orders.[5] (The same also seems to hold true with regard to the relation among diverse components *within* an institutional order.)

As distinct from those who concentrate on the definition of stability in terms of its components, its characteristic traits, many analysts take a rather broad and, it appears to me, more dynamic, sophisticated view which stresses the prerequisites of stability, that is, the combination of conditions necessary for the establishment or preservation of political stability. Some authors stress a particular condition, others build a varied structure of necessary conditions; but in all cases the focus is on social, economic, cultural, and political factors that either contribute to or, as some assert, are necessary to the existence of a stable political system.[6]

Often in this kind of approach, however, it is impossible to find in the argument a distinction between the characteristics and causes of the phenomenon, between "what is political stability" and "why is there political stability." The argument appears and often is circular. One particular condition or group of factors is termed necessary for political stability, while the presence of such a condition or factor is described as stability. A second difficulty with this approach has to do with the fact that, if, as we have argued, the concept of stability itself is multivariant and multidimensional, the approach which stresses necessary and contributing conditions of stability has to deal with factors and variables which increase in an almost geometric progression the closer they approach reality. It becomes more and more difficult to distinguish which combination of conditions is necessary and which merely contributes to stability. The mesh of the conceptual net is either so large that comparisons of different periods and systems yield results too general to be of serious value or so small that they are applicable only to special situations, in which case it becomes

---

[5] To give examples, the Great Depression of the 1930s was not accompanied in the United States or Great Britain by political instability, and the "cultural revolution" of the 1960s was not the cause in Western democracies of those political instabilities which some of these countries experienced.

[6] For one such attempt, see Francis G. Castles, "Political Stability and the Dominant Image of Society," *Political Studies*, 22, no. 3 (September 1974), 289–98.

impossible to determine whether the existing associations with stability are correlational, causal, or incidental.

Despite these difficulties, such models and propositions are nevertheless much more important than anything the definitional literature on stability can offer. This is so because if, as Leon Hurwitz writes, "the problem and task still remain to organize and synthesize the concepts [of stability] into a truly cross-national comparative analysis,"[7] the hope that this can be accomplished is better placed in this type of literature than in the definitional literature with its stress on measurements of individual and unweighted characteristics. It is so also because the stress in this type of literature is on relational phenomena, which are the backbone, the prime subject, the real substance of the social sciences.

What is most certain when one considers political stability is that like all social concepts it treats relational phenomena. That is to say, stability is an outcome of relations between social items, groups, and institutions. "The concept of stability implies the idea of a system of recurring or continuing relationships,"[8] both within the political system itself and between the political regimes and other societal institutional orders. One way to categorize these relations is suggested by the distinction between "*intrinsic* factors promoting the stability or instability of the [political] system which stem from the inherent workings of the system itself and *extrinsic* factors promoting the stability or instability of the system which come from outside the system."[9] The extrinsic factors or relations would include social and economic change, communal cleavages, and the international environment; the intrinsic would refer among others to such factors as political leadership, participation, level of political demands, the effectiveness of governmental policies.[10]

---

[7] Hurwitz, "Contemporary Approaches to Political Stability," p. 463.

[8] Samuel P. Huntington, "Remarks on the Meanings of Stability in the Modern Era," in Seweryn Bialer and S. Sluzar, eds., *Radicalism in the Contemporary Age, 3: Strategies and Impact of Contemporary Radicalism* (Boulder, Colo.: Westview Press, 1977), 272.

[9] *Ibid.*

[10] One possible way to categorize these relations is to apply the Weberian distinction between political, politically oriented, and politically significant relations. To judge by the literature which attempts to analyze sources of the stability of diverse contemporary societies or causes of their instability, decay, or breakdown, these relations would include, most importantly, the following:

Political relations: Relations within the political leadership; the relations between the top and lower political elite strata and between the central and peripheral, national and local political elite groups; relations within and between the dominant political organizations, that is, those organizations which perform the major aggregating and integrating functions within the polity; relations between the dominant political organizations and the administrative organizations, that is, those organizations which perform day-to-day executive functions within the society.

Politically oriented relations: Relations between the political elite and other strategic elites, that is, the strata who perform leadership roles in other institutional orders of the society; and relations between the political elite and the politically active publics, that is, the substrata of the population which are most

In delineating an approach to the concept of political stability, the political scientist easily remarks that while the characterization "stable/unstable" is being applied to countries with different political systems, cultures, and levels of economic development, there has evolved within the discipline a strong – one may even say dominant – tendency to associate political stability and instability with stages of one specific process, that of modernization. Samuel Huntington expresses this tendency in the most explicit manner when he states the paradox that "modernity produces stability and modernization instability."[11] The dichotomy "modernity equals stability," "modernization equals instability" is as exaggerated and simplified as the often assumed irreconcilable polarity of traditional versus modern behavior. The a priori assumption of a positive, inherent association between stability and modernity is highly questionable in the light of pre–World War II history and of the present state of many modern societies; and the generalized negative inherent association between instability and modernization is properly questioned by the studies of Robert P. Clark and others.[12] It is especially important to avoid this kind of generalization when studying such countries as the Soviet Union, which is both modern and modernizing and where, we propose, the unevenness of the process of modernization in general and the low level of modernity of some societal sectors in particular may provide an important source of political stability at the present time.[13]

The complex, multivariant nature of the concept of "political stability" makes necessary (and very difficult) its treatment as a dynamic variable, not as an attribute of a particular political regime at a particular time. That is to say, political regimes are not simply stable or unstable; they are or become more or less stable. It would be useless and arbitrary in my opinion to try to define exactly when the "less" becomes "instability" and the "more" becomes "stability." Yet at least one distinction concerning the intensity of the stabilizing or destabilizing process can and should be made. It is the distinction between the reference points to which the "stability" or "instability" of a political regime is being related. The two most general reference points of this nature are survival of the regime and effectiveness. "Survival" in this case obviously refers to the potential for a dramatic transformation of the major

intensely interested in and informed about the political process and which actively participate in it.

Politically significant relations: Mass relations within the society which reflect economic, ethnic, cultural, and generational cleavages and are of potential or actual political relevance through their effect on political order.

[11]Samuel P. Huntington, *Political Order in Changing Societies* (New Haven: Yale University Press, 1968), p. 47.

[12]See Robert P. Clark, Jr., *Development and Instability: Political Change in the Non-Western World* (Hinsdale, Ill.: The Dryden Press, 1974).

[13]To anticipate our later argument: Owing to the past absolute and present relative underdevelopment of the Soviet Union, the growth performance of the Soviet economy provides an important legitimizing rationale in the popular mind, and the high levels of general mobility have constituted for a long time a crucial stabilizing factor.

parameters of the regime; "effectiveness" refers to the extent to which the political elite is able to attain its principal goals.

While there are clearly many interconnections between effectiveness and survivability, one may argue that not only in the short run, but even in the middle run, the two can be largely independent of one another. Such would be the case when a political regime is chronically on the brink of instability with regard to effectiveness but is threatened by no discernible danger to its survival.[14] Such would be the case when a political regime is basically stable with regard to effectiveness, but very often on the brink of severe instability with regard to survival.[15] Most typically, of course, the effectiveness and survival models are positively correlated in both the short and especially the medium run. Aside from situations where this may not be the case, however, there exists also a time lag in the interaction between levels of stability with regard to both reference points; and, anticipating what will be argued later, different political regimes may exhibit different correlations.

It will be noted that very often political regimes and especially Communist regimes are analyzed in terms of "stability" and "change." The formal logical opposite of stability is of course instability not change, and obviously both stable and unstable political regimes undergo political change. To express it differently: Stability does not exclude change within the political regime just as instability does not assume it. This is especially the case with regard to change of a cyclical nature. Moreover, changes that could occur without undermining the stability of a political regime might prove to be not only incremental adjustments (which most social scientists consider rather a condition of stability) but also such changes as transform some very essential characteristics of the regime. Indeed there is just one type of political change which generically refers to political instability alone and can be considered its extreme expression, namely, revolutionary change.[16]

Yet another aspect of the study of political stability, one that is central to the theme of this inquiry, has been seriously neglected in the general literature, and the present level of its discussion provides no well-grounded and tested framework for the forthcoming analysis of the Soviet Union. Is the meaning of "political stability" the same for different types

[14]Such a situation characterizes the entire postwar Italian political system, the condition of which can be considered in a permanent state of "unstable stability."
[15]Such a situation may characterize some East European regimes, particularly the GDR, which despite its highly efficient administration sometimes survives simply because Soviet troops are stationed within its borders.
[16]For a critical review of the very rich literature on revolutionary change, see William H. Overholt, "Sources of Radicalism and Revolution: A Survey of the Literature" in Bialer and Sluzar, eds., *Radicalism in the Contemporary Age, 1: Sources of Contemporary Radicalism* (Boulder, Colo.: Westview Press, 1977), 293–335. Yet precisely because this literature deals with extreme and exceptional situations, it is of very little use in analyzing conditions under which political regimes can and do function from day to day. Unfortunately, too often the discussion of political stability is subtly transformed into an analysis of whether revolutionary conditions do or do not develop in a system.

of political regimes? And, even more important, are the systemic conditions of political stability similar for different political regimes, especially for regimes on comparable levels of socioeconomic development (for example, industrialized democratic and Communist states)? In what important or essential respects do the conditions of political stability in the Soviet Union differ from those in other political regimes?

On this general question it is my view that the sources and parameters of the stability and instability of various regimes do differ from one another, sometimes to a great extent. Of course, all regimes require minimum basic support from their publics and elites for the way they function. What differs rather are the parameters within which such functioning remains undisturbed. What differs is the balance of the specific sources of support. What differs is the capacity of a regime to withstand those conditions which in another system would impair the functioning of the political society. One must thus attempt to ascertain how profound public and elite support must be, in which areas and among which groups it must be most pronounced, and for what reasons and for how long and how efficiently a system can function when even the minimum requirements have not been met.

Our purpose here, however, is not to develop the comparative dimensions of this complex problem in general terms, nor is it to elaborate them with regard to Communist political regimes in general, but rather it is to ascertain those conditions that define political stability with regard to the Soviet Union alone.[17]

---

[17]This question is raised here with specific reference to the Soviet Union in its present, post-Stalinist, "mature" version and not with reference to Communist political regimes in general, for a number of reasons:

Despite great similarities of the structure and process of Soviet and the East European Communist bloc regimes, the crucial, overriding condition of the latter's stability is external to their political regimes, owing to the inauthenticity of their original formation. However much the level of internal compliance and support for these regimes—and their "legitimatization by performance" has advanced in the last decade—it is our judgment that the "original sin" of inauthenticity has not been removed; that is to say, regardless of their level of political stability insofar as effectiveness is concerned, their survival rests primarily on the tested assumption of the fundamental Soviet commitment to the idea of "socialism in one empire" and Soviet readiness to use its overwhelming military power in case of need.

I consider the Yugoslav political regime sufficiently different from the Soviet one in major structural characteristics, not to mention the process of policy making and the policies themselves, to require separate consideration with regard to the *specific* conditions of its political stability.

The case of the other authentic Communist regime, the Chinese, is somewhat similar to that of Yugoslavia. The Chinese political structure and process, and especially its political culture, diverge significantly from the Soviet political regime, past and present. Moreover, in counterdistinction to Yugoslavia, where a definite institutional threshold of system-building and management has been reached, the Chinese situation seems to be, and will probably remain for some time to come, very open-ended and unclear regarding the definite institutional shape of its political regime.

In the last decade the study of Communist societies has swung from one extreme of treating Communist regimes as sui generis, emphasizing their uniqueness and exceptionality, to the other extreme of stressing the applicability of general categories and concepts developed in the study of comparative politics or of democratic political regimes. As is often the case with such swings, the previous lag between the analysis of Communist systems and general comparative politics has been replaced in part by a reverse lag. The general concepts that began to be utilized in studies of Communist societies were increasingly questioned or even discredited in the mainstream studies of comparative politics, for example, the interest-group approach. Moreover, just as studies of Communist regimes began to question the "primacy of politics" in reaction to exaggerations imposed by totalitarian models, the broader general study of politics began its return to the central stage of political science and political sociology, regaining its relative autonomy from the pervasive socioeconomic determinism of the previous period.[18]

In seeking to ascertain conditions of stability, there are quite a few theories of stability that claim general applicability; an even greater number are explicitly designed to apply to the stability of democratic regimes;[19] far fewer theories or models address themselves explicitly to Communist political regimes. The usefulness of some of the latter for our purposes and indeed the most fully developed of them is seriously impaired by the fact that they are relevant primarily to the revolutionary, transformatory stages of Communist regimes. One of them merits special citation because it addresses most directly the case of the Soviet Union.

In April 1962 Professor Alexander Gerschenkron delivered his erudite lecture on "The Stability of Dictatorships," which was later published in a collection of his essays.[20] He enumerated those conditions, the absence of which "creates or is likely to create a situation which threatens a modern dictatorship with the danger of disintegration and possible sudden overthrow":[21]

---

[18]It may be misplaced optimism, but it seems to me that a balance is slowly being restored. In a commonsense way it is well expressed in Joseph LaPalombara's preface to *Politics within Nations* (Englewood Cliffs, N.J.: Prentice-Hall, 1974), which includes not only the study of the American and other democratic regimes but also devotes considerable attention to Communist and other one-party nations, without treating these countries as if they were political freaks or historical aberrations. "However, in thus extending the empirical range of comparative description and analysis," writes LaPalombara, "I have tried to avoid the entrapment of thinking that political systems are in *all* essential and important respects more alike than they are different" (p. ix).

[19]See, for example, Harry Eckstein, *Division and Cohesion in Democracy* (Princeton, N.J.: Princeton University Press, 1966); Ian Budge, *Agreement and the Stability of Democracy* (Chicago: Markham Publishing Company, 1970).

[20]Alexander Gerschenkron, *Continuity in History and Other Essays* (Cambridge, Mass.: Harvard University Press, 1968), pp. 313–43.

[21]*Ibid.*, p. 315.

1. Maintenance of a permanent condition of stress and strain
   a. by the existence or creation of enemies both internal and external, and
   b. by imposing upon the population gigantic tasks that exert strong pressures upon its standards of well-being or, at least, greatly retard improvements in those standards.
2. Incessant exercise of dictatorial power.
3. Creation of an image of the dictator as an incarnation of supreme wisdom and indomitable will power.
4. Reference to an allegedly unchanged and unchangeable value system by which the actions of the dictatorship are justified (including perhaps adherence to an ultimate goal, the attainment of which will render the dictatorship unnecessary but which is steadily kept in an appropriately distant future, although still within sight of the living generation).
5. Proscription of any deviating values and beliefs, coupled with threats and acts of repression, sustained and implemented by appropriate organizational devices.

When Gerschenkron introduced his collection of essays six years later, he returned to his earlier evaluation: "All one can say is that some of the classic stability conditions of dictatorial power have become blurred without visibly placing the dictatorship in any imminent jeopardy."[22] Today, with even greater distance, one can be more certain that either something was wrong with Gerschenkron's "conditions of stability" or that the Soviet political regime has been and is undergoing a process of change which modifies the conditions of its stability. In my opinion the latter is the case. Gerschenkron's conditions of stability describe very well the transformatory (and internationally defensive) stage of Soviet development, but seem much less applicable to its "mature" and "established" stage.[23]

Of the theories or models that concentrate on the conditions of stability of "mature" Communist regimes like the Soviet Union today or from which such conditions can be derived, the most complete, explicit synthesis is that developed by Samuel P. Huntington and Clement H. Moore.[24] Their conclusions may be summarized as follows: The condi-

[22]*Ibid.*, p. 4.

[23]In a curious way the proposition that a forcibly depressed low standard of consumption is a prerequisite of Communist power was recently reintroduced by a Polish economist, Bogdan Mieczkowski ("The Relationship Between Changes in Consumption and Politics in Poland," *Soviet Studies*, 30, no. 2 [April 1978], 262–9). A close reading of his thesis and of the discussion which it evoked shows, however, that what Professor Mieczkowski really suggests is that an increase in Polish consumption is a result of the greater power of the worker-consumer. This proposition differs, first, from Gerschenkron's; and second, its applicability to the Soviet situation where the working class is not "polonized" is doubtful.

[24]Samuel P. Huntington and Clement H. Moore, *Authoritarian Politics in Modern Society: The Dynamics of Established One-Party Systems* (New York: Basic Books, 1970), pp. 3–47, 509–17.

tions of stability of established one-party systems are equated with the party's ability to maintain itself as the sole source of legitimacy. This in turn requires that the political elite is able to assimilate techno-managerial elites, to aggregate and arbitrate group interests, to neutralize the critical intelligentsia, and to mobilize the population toward party goals.

Recently Richard Lowenthal reviewed the various approaches to the study of "established" Communist party regimes in an article which develops and in many important respects supercedes his well-known writing on "Modernization versus Utopia" in Communist societies.[25] He presents, moreover, his own original and comprehensive analysis and reaches a more skeptical verdict concerning the limits of the adaptability of these regimes than any of the works he reviews, and especially that of Huntington and Moore.[26] Lowenthal's conclusions concern primarily the conditions and limits of change, not of stability or instability. Further, they are directed toward the future rather than the present or immediate past. Yet questions of change are closely related to questions of stability, and Lowenthal's conclusions about the future have to be based largely on trends he discovers in the present.

If I understand him correctly, I would derive from his views two conclusions about Soviet political stability. First, the stability of the Soviet political regime at present, while not exactly precarious, displays strong signs of what Huntington would call "decay" and Brzezinski has called "degeneration."[27] Second, the interrelation of the three sets of problems which a "mature" Soviet regime faces – efficiency, interest articulation, and legitimation – constitutes the basic condition of its political stability in the future, with regard to both effectiveness and survival. In the long run the successful resolution of these three sets of problems cannot be achieved. In sharp contrast to Huntington's thesis of the growth of nonideological legitimacy, Lowenthal argues that the chances are low and lowering that the Soviet political regime will "acquire a long-term legitimacy, based not only on a value consensus between rulers and ruled and a doctrinaire self-legitimation of the party that satisfies its own cadres, but on the plausibility of the claim that its procedures of leadership selection and policy decision are likely to meet the needs of a modern society."[28]

With regard to the first conclusion I find myself closer to Huntington's judgment that "bureaucratization, routinization, a decline in ideological commitment, a decline of the attractiveness of political as compared to

[25]Richard Lowenthal, "Development vs. Utopia in Communist Policy," in Chalmers Johnson, ed., *Change in Communist Systems* (Stanford, Calif.: Stanford University Press, 1970), pp. 33–116.

[26]Richard Lowenthal, "On 'Established' Communist Party Regimes," *Studies in Comparative Communism*, 7, no. 4 (Winter 1974), 335–58.

[27]For the view which most strongly suggests progressing decay and degeneration, see Zbigniew Brzezinski, "The Soviet Political System: Transformation or Degeneration?" *Problems of Communism*, 15, no. 1 (January–February 1966), 1–15.

[28]Richard Lowenthal, "On 'Established' Communist Party Regimes," p. 356.

other careers, some dispersion of policy initiative – all these appear more likely to be signs of the institutionalization and consolidation of the system than of its impending downfall."[29] With regard to the second conclusion I share only to a limited degree Lowenthal's skepticism concerning Huntington's expectations for the Soviet future (although for somewhat different reasons). I shall return to these conclusions at a later point.

What is most striking to me in the approach of both Huntington and Lowenthal to the conditions of stability is that the center of gravity of their respective arguments rests on the question of legitimacy. Their different conclusions about the present and future of "mature" Communist regimes derive almost entirely from differences regarding this question. I agree entirely that the question of legitimacy occupies a central place in the discussion of stability and will treat the matter at length following the presentation of my own propositions concerning conditions of stability of the Soviet political regime and following the detailed examination of the sources of stability in the USSR in the present period.

The general propositions concerning conditions of stability that underlie and shape the analysis to which this chapter is devoted may be expressed as follows:

1. The Soviet political order exhibits a high level of ability to prevent the translation of instability conditions in other societal spheres into factors of political instability – which would point toward a greater weight for political factors over social factors as salient conditions of political stability.

2. Soviet experience points to the primacy of relations within the political elite and between the political and other societal elites in influencing the stability of the political regime as compared to the relations between the political and other elites with the political and general publics.

3. In Soviet conditions compliance patterns and levels have a greater importance for stability conditions than patterns and levels of support. To use Amitai Etzioni's expression, Soviet "guidance mechanisms are like jeeps built to drive on rough roads; they are constructed to carry heavier loads with less support."[30]

4. The Soviet political system displays the greater importance for political stability of policy-specific over generalized supports within the public sectors toward which the policies are addressed and are most relevant in their potential effects.

5. In the Soviet system substantive supports are of greater importance for political stability than procedural supports in policy making among the political and other elites and within the general administrative structures.

[29]Samuel Huntington, "Remarks on the Meanings of Stability in the Modern Era" in Bialer and Sluzar, eds., *Radicalism in the Contemporary Age, 3: Strategies and Impact of Contemporary Radicalism,* 277.
[30]Amitai Etzioni, *The Active Society: A Theory of Societal and Political Processes* (New York: Free Press, 1968), p. 524.

6. Consensus mobilization – that is, the process by which society-wide perspectives are transmitted downward from the ruling overlayers to the members in order to reduce the differences among them – have a greater importance for Soviet political stability than consensus formation – that is, the process by which perspectives of the members of a social unit are transmitted upward to the controlling overlayers and the differences among them are reduced.

7. Finally, one should stress the greater importance for Soviet political stability of the community of assumptions among the political and other elites – that is, of the set of assumptions shared by the members of the various elites which provides a context for the view of the world and of themselves – over the reconciliation of different function-based assumptions.

8
SOVIET STABILITY AND ITS SOURCES

The pronounced tendency in journalistic and even academic accounts of the Soviet Union to dwell on difficulties, troubles, and unresolved issues goes far to color and distort our perceptions of conditions within the country. What major aspect of Soviet reality has not been associated with a "problem"? There is the "problem" of the economy, the "problem" of nationalities, the "problem" of technological lag, the "problem" of rising popular expectations. In the last fifteen years more has been written about the "problem" of dissent than about any other single subject. One could only think that dissent is the overwhelming fact of life in the Soviet Union and decisively shapes internal politics and policies. There is, of course, no doubt that all these and other aspects of Soviet life are truly "problem" areas, points of genuine and recognized vulnerability and potential crisis; but what has been most surprising during the Brezhnev era is not the presence of these genuine problems but rather that they did not create any semblance of a systemic crisis whether separately or in combination.

Among more serious observers of the Soviet Union there are some who regard the system as inherently unstable owing to an alleged lack of legitimacy and others who focus on the persistence of crisis situations, some quite profound, which fail to yield durable solutions despite repeated efforts and mobilization of resources. To the former one can for the moment observe that a line of reasoning which admits to no other stability of the regime than its survival over the last quarter-century assigns to stability a very narrow, almost grotesque meaning, while its questioning of Soviet legitimacy is extremely exaggerated and one-sided. It almost equates legitimacy with the existence of constitutional democratic regimes. To the latter one should point out that political stability cannot simply be equated with a lack of crisis situations and challenges to the system but rather with the political regime's ability to resolve these crises, to neutralize or even to ignore them, and to adjust to periods of prolonged coexistence with them.

The overwhelming feature of the Brezhnev era is the sociopolitical stability of the country which has accompanied and sustained the stability we have clearly demonstrated among political leadership and elites. The Soviet political system shows no signs of political fragmentation. The centralization of its administrative structure at the present time is if anything greater than at the beginning of the Brezhnev era. The divisive pull of interest groups, while strong, is manageable for the process of unified policy making; the pressures of participation are containable. The aggregating and coordinating functions of the party apparatus are still pronounced. The centrifugal forces of ethnic self-identification and assertiveness in the multinational Soviet state have not only failed to produce symptoms of political disintegration, but no single situation has developed in the last fifteen years that can be described as a serious challenge to Moscow's ethnic policies.

Alone among the industrially developed states the Soviet Union has avoided the political consequences of a cultural generational chasm. While one can speak of the developing youth culture, especially in large metropolitan centers, one can hardly postulate a politically meaningful youth revolution that actively counters the values of older generations. The Soviet Union has not escaped the wave of rising popular expectations, but these have not evolved into the well-known vicious-circle pattern of exaggerated, unfulfillable, and conflicting hopes which overload and undermine the political process. It is highly significant, moreover, that the rising popular expectations are almost entirely confined to the material sphere and scarcely encroach directly on cultural and political areas.

One feat of the Soviet authoritarian system, so amazing to observers and critics because of its unexpectedness, has been the ability to contain the political consequences of widespread intellectual dissent movements, the first in Soviet history. Surprising was the fact that this containment did not entail resort to mass political terror or to satisfaction of any of the dissenters' demands but the most marginal politically and harmless domestically.[1] The Soviet elite exhibited greater flexibility, self-confidence, and cunning in dealing with dissent than any of its critics had anticipated. Today the international impact and repercussions of dissent far exceed any domestic consequences.

The stability of the Soviet system stands out against the background of events and trends in developed industrial democracies over the last fifteen years. As recently as a decade ago, Samuel Huntington began his major work, *Political Order in Changing Societies*, with the following proposition:

> The most important political distinction among countries concerns not their form of government but their degree of government. The differences between democracy and dictatorship are less than the differences between those countries whose politics embodies consensus, community, legitimacy, organization, effectiveness, stability, and those countries whose politics is deficient in these qualities. . . . The United States, Great Britain, and the Soviet Union

---

[1] The case of the Jewish emigration is truly an exception and, because of its circumstances, has to be treated separately. The key here is Soviet popular anti-Semitism, which makes possible popular mobilization against the Jews who wish to emigrate and prevents the contagion of a successful emigration drive from affecting other, more homogeneous, concentrated, and settled nationality groups.

have different forms of government, but in all three systems the government governs.[2]

Just a few years ago, however, in the superb report to the Trilateral Commission entitled *The Crisis of Democracy* (1975), to which Huntington contributed, the question was posed: Are democracies governable?[3] No such question is being asked about the Soviet system. To be sure a multiplicity of small and large crises afflicts the Soviet Union. As a matter of fact its entire history constitutes an unending chain of crisis situations, primarily in the economic area but also to some extent in social, cultural, and political areas. There is adequate evidence to argue that the dominant style of Communist politics was and remains to a large extent "crisis politics"; the dominant style of its political leadership was and remains largely that of emergency leadership. The increased institutionalization of the Soviet political order was and remains to a large extent the institutionalization of this type of politics and style of leadership. Indeed, far from entering a post-mobilizational state, as some postulate, this leadership is still associated with and committed to high levels of mobilizational effort.[4]

While some serious students have suggested that a process of decay and debilitation is eroding the Soviet political system, even they regard its destructive effects as a long-range potential rather than as a clear and present danger to existence and effectiveness. All would certainly hesitate to proclaim the "crisis of communism in power" or even to raise the question of the "governability" of the Soviet Union. Indeed, the principal author of the Trilateral Commission's report on the "governability of democracies," recently made a strong argument that "to date . . . the Soviet system has certainly demonstrated the ability to contain or protect itself from extrinsic challenges. None of the challenges which are identified for the future, moreover, appear to be qualitatively different from the challenges which the Soviet system has demonstrated the ability to deal with effectively in the past."[5]

[2] Samuel P. Huntington, *Political Order in Changing Societies* (New Haven, Conn.: Yale University Press, 1968), p. 1.
[3] Michel J. Crozier, Samuel P. Huntington, and Joji Watanuki, *The Crisis of Democracy* (New York: New York University Press, 1975).
[4] I find the definition and analysis of the concept of mobilization most fruitfully developed by Amitai Etzioni in *The Active Society*, chaps. 13 and 15, where it refers to the process by which a controlling unit gains significantly in the control of assets it previously did not control. From this point of view, the Soviet regime is still a highly mobilizational regime with an enormous scope of mobilizational activity. What is different from the past is, first, that its mobilization of resources is directed primarily at the creation of new resources rather than the amassing of resources already in existence, and second, that its mobilizational activity is not directed primarily at transforming the society but rather at preserving its present structure.
[5] Samuel P. Huntington, "Remarks on the Meanings of Stability in the Modern Era" in S. Bialer and S. Sluzar, eds., *Radicalism in the Contemporary Age, 3: Strategies and Impact of Contemporary Radicalism* (Boulder, Colo.: Westview Press, 1977), 277. The term "extrinsic" is used here to denote challenges emanating from outside the political system itself.

Whatever the future of the Soviet system may be, it projects internally the image of a society of law and order and externally the image of a growing world power which is just beginning to assert an influence to match its strength. This image contrasts with the realities of an unstable world where an unending stream of coups and rebellions and transitions undermines old and new autocratic regimes and where popular disillusionment, lack of effective leadership, and unprecedented challenges engulf even the most successful industrial democracies.

The purpose here is not to analyze and test the validity of various claims concerning the supposed future of the Soviet system but to examine the almost quarter-century of post-Stalinist development and especially the Brezhnev era. And here, despite wide differences of opinion about the present state of the Soviet system and the even greater disagreement about its possible futures, there does exist a basis for consensus regarding the proposition that the Soviet political system has remained and remains as yet *politically stable* in the Brezhnev era, regardless of disputes concerning the nature and sources of this stability.

By any meaningful standards, the Soviet social and political system during the Brezhnev era has displayed a high level of stability and governability. Surprise has been one ingredient in the reaction to this state of affairs. Not only did such an outcome contradict the expectations of a majority of Western analysts when Brezhnev came to power. Not only did it contrast strikingly with the situation in a majority of Western industrial nations. The element of surprise resulted also from the expectation that certain changes that have occurred in the Soviet system during the post-Stalin period as well as the persistence of certain challenges, some of them clearly unresolved, should normally have yielded destabilizing effects.

Those changes include first and foremost the patent and extensive, if uneven, weakening of mass and elite controls; the acquisition of a relatively higher degree of professional autonomy by the expert and managerial classes; and the greater freedom of access to the decision-making process by elite and subelite groups and institutions. Those past and present challenges that could be expected to undermine the stability of the system include the traumatic shock of the anti-Stalin campaign and the continued questioning of the Soviet past which lingers even after the official closing of the campaign; the novel wave of dissent which seized a small but vocal segment of the intelligentsia; the probably more important newly developing attitude among larger segments of the creative intelligentsia of withdrawal from official life, of internal emigration, at best of neutrality toward the official goals of the regime; the explosion of the massive and unprecedented Jewish emigration drive after decades of assimilation; the shocks in Soviet relations with Eastern Europe which could have brought into question the very principles on which these relations are based; the highly accelerated modernization of many aspects of Soviet life and almost all regions, with the attendant material and spiritual dislocations and displacements – indeed, all the "problems" which commentators have enumerated and which retain their reality and seriousness.

That the extent of systemic stability under Brezhnev has been so unexpected is in part a legacy of the implications of the totalitarian model which for so long governed the study of the nature and future of the Soviet state and in part a consequence of our cumulative experience with modernizing authoritarian regimes. According to the totalitarian model, the abolition of mass terror, personal dictatorship, and the most extreme forms of the transformational-mobilization push of the regime should have weakened the intrinsic ability of the system to survive, should have left it without an internal raison d'être, without a control mechanism to assure its replication. If, on the other hand, the Soviet Union can best be understood as a highly authoritarian but not totalitarian regime, as most students would agree, our experience with the history of such regimes – whether exclusionary, inclusionary, or even Communist – argues for the exceptionality of prolonged and high levels of stability, especially when accompanied by economic growth, social transformation, and particularly political systemic change, the case with the Soviet regime. Our experience with modernizing authoritarian regimes on the contrary calls for recurring crises of legitimacy, participation, and governability. Given the weight of the reasons adduced to anticipate destabilization, it becomes enormously important, for both practical and theoretical considerations, to attempt an explanation of the remarkable stability enjoyed by the Soviet system in the Brezhnev era.

The most general and immediate explanation of Soviet stability is obvious and valid. The Soviet leaders and elites who direct the system work very hard to make the system stable. If there is any single value that dominates the minds and thoughts of the Soviet establishment from the highest to lowest level, it is the value of order; if there is any single fear that outweighs all others, it is the fear of disorder, chaos, fragmentation, loss of control. This fear supports the world's most extensive and methodical police-state machinery which derives its principal strength less from the extent of actual punitive action than from the extraordinary attention paid to preventive action against any form of social deviance, an effort soldiered by untold millions of informers.[6] This enormous coercive effort – potential and actual, preventive and punitive – is augmented by an extensive attempt to inculcate positive socialization through the educational process, massive propaganda efforts, the elimi-

---

[6] In every society the police rely on informers located in criminal circles themselves or on the peripheries of crime as their major, perhaps main instrument of crime detection and prevention. What is different in the Soviet Union is that the society at large is treated by the police as a "criminal circle" and covered by a network of informers placed in factories, collective farms, among journalists, writers, etc. Only the recruitment of party members as informers requires the approval of nonpolice authorities.

nation of competing ideas, and so forth.[7] How is it, though, that these efforts have apparently proved effective for so long?

Part of the reason rests with the fact that fear of disorder and attachment to orderly society are valued not only by political leaders and elites but find strong resonance in the Soviet popular mind. This is to a large extent a historical phenomenon; the mechanism and process of conditioning in this direction are impossible to trace. Undeniably, the Russian people in all walks of life fear the chaos and disorder they sense directly below the surface of their lives; they fear the potential of elemental explosions of violence and rage that mark their historical past and occupy a central place in their history textbooks; they prize and yearn for strong government, the *khoziain* or boss who will ward off the *smuta*, the "time of troubles."

It is noteworthy that this fear pervades the communities of Soviet dissidents, most of whom urge evolutionary, incremental change and have a horror of contributing to the unleashing of spontaneous and destructive forces in Russian society. Pavel Litvinov, the dissident grandson of Stalin's foreign minister Maxim Litvinov, has remarked:

> Under the czars we had an authoritarian state and now we have a totalitarian state but it still comes from the roots of the Russian past. You should understand that the leaders and the ordinary people have the same authoritarian frame of mind. Brezhnev and the simple person both think that might is right. That's all. It is not a question of ideology. It's simply power. Solzhenitsyn acts as if he thinks this has all come down from the sky because of Communism. But he is not so different himself. He does not want democracy. He wants to go from the totalitarian state back to an authoritarian one.[8]

A second ingredient of the explanation for Soviet stability may be found in the largely noncumulative nature of the problems faced by the Soviet leadership. There are very different priorities among the dissatisfactions and demands expressed by Soviet "public opinion." These are not expressed simultaneously; they often contradict rather than reinforce one another. One has only to think of the aspirations of Russians versus those of other minorities (and particularly the large Russian minorities in non-Russian areas); the anti-authoritarianism and desire for creative

---

[7] Our detailed knowledge of Soviet censorship is quite limited. We gained an indirect insight into it, however, through the publication of a unique, original, and authentic series of documents smuggled out to the West from Poland by Tomasz Strzyzewski. When reading them, one has to remember that these instructions limiting freedom of information came from a country where censorship by comparison to Soviet standards may seem very relaxed (see *Czarna Ksiega Cenzury PRL* [London: Anex, 1977]). A partial English translation of this book is contained in "Official Censorship in the Polish People's Republic" (Ann Arbor, Mich.: North American Study Center for Polish Affairs, April 1978).

[8] Quoted from Hedrick Smith, *The Russians* (New York: Ballantine Books, 1976), pp. 332–3.

freedom among intellectuals versus the managers' desire for greater autonomy and for more stringent discipline of workers; and the aspirations of both intellectuals and managers versus the egalitarian goals of workers and their anti-intellectualism.

The multiple cleavages between party and society, with their direct political implications for the present and their disruptive potential for the future, do not overlap. Thus the party can maneuver. It does not confront generalized demands of "society" as a whole but rather specific demands of separate segments of society which can be turned by the party against one another or neutralized in order to keep strong the party's position.

To go to the core of the explanation for Soviet stability, the effectiveness of the regime's massive efforts to maintain order, one must turn to a number of deeper processes and undercurrents in Soviet society. These have frequently been overlooked as a consequence of the coincidence of certain aspects of official Soviet and Western analysis that often leads to a distortion of Soviet reality and inhibits the deeper understanding of the system's social processes and mechanisms of functioning. The Soviet version of this parallel portrayal is best expressed in describing the society as "planned," as evolving in accordance with the law of "planned, proportionate development."[9] The Western version of Soviet society is often not very different. To take but one example, Charles Lindblom makes the following comparison of the polyarchic, market societies of the West with their Communist counterparts:

> In their reach into every aspect of life and in the weakness of major social constraints on their scope and ambition, rulers of these [communist] systems go far to substitute – deliberately – formal organization for the complex social structures found in noncommunist societies. *Formal organization supercedes a variety of other forms of social coordination:* ethnic solidarity, religious belief, market, family, and moral code.[10]

There is undoubtedly a strong element of truth in these parallel images. The issue range of centralized political decision making in the Soviet system is clearly broader, the scope of deliberate decision making consciously directed at managing the society is clearly larger than in Western democratic societies. The role of the "invisible hand" of market and social forces is more dominant in the democratic systems as compared to the

---

[9] According to Soviet political economy, the principal socioeconomic law of Soviet society describes its *goal* as "the securing of the maximum satisfaction of the constantly rising material and cultural requirements of the whole society through the continuous expansion and perfection of socialist production on the basis of higher techniques." But the principal *mechanism* of the society is provided by the law of "planned, proportionate, balanced development." These "laws" were "discovered" by Stalin and were retained virtually unchanged by his successors (I. Stalin, *Ekonomicheskie problemy sotsialisma v SSSR* [Moscow: Gospolitizdat, 1952], pp. 45–6).

[10] Charles E. Lindblom, *Politics and Markets* (New York: Basic Books, 1977), p. 239.

Soviet system where there is a pronounced stress on the "visible hand" of coordinated organizations, regulations, and detailed social policies. Despite the increased complexity of Soviet society on the one hand and the increased role of the state and progressing bureaucratization of Western societies on the other, it would still be correct to argue the unequal weight and significance in both societies of formal organizations as compared to social organization. Relative to one another, the stability and legitimacy of the democratic systems rest and depend much more on the latter and the Soviet system on the former. It is easy to forget, however, that the differences here are only relative, those of degree.

The parallel Western and Soviet images of Soviet society that we have described tend to exaggerate the "visible hand" features of the Soviet system with its stress on formal organizations and to underestimate the "invisible hand" aspects of systemic processes with their stress on social organization. In so doing, they yield a number of consequences which skew our understanding of the Soviet system.

In the first place this picture tends to minimize the elements of spontaneity, the degree of give-and-take in the Soviet political process itself. It exaggerates the planning dimension of Soviet policy making, the phase of adopting decisions and policies, and undervalues the phase of policy implementation in which adopted, "deliberate" policies usually lose their original shape in the cross current of conflicting interests and forces. Second, this picture underestimates the significance and scope of the unintended consequences of Soviet policies. It tends to exaggerate the degree to which Soviet policies even at their inception are deliberate attempts to shape societal environment according to long-range plans rather than continuous reactions to the shape and influence of political and social forces beyond the policy makers' control. Third, and most important for our theme, this picture tends to exaggerate the role of the formalized and guided control mechanism in securing the stability and legitimacy of the regime and to ignore the significant role of social mechanisms and processes in the attainment of these ends.

The analysis of the sources of the stability of the Soviet regime during the Brezhnev era in this chapter will seek therefore to explore some of those processes. It will address four sources of Soviet stability: the performance of the Brezhnev leadership; the nature of rising popular expectations; the relation between the institutionalization of Soviet politics and popular participation; and the effects of social and political mobility.

The performance of the regime

There can be little doubt that a regime's performance in areas which citizens deem important, and especially those which touch on their everyday lives, is directly related to stability. This does not necessarily mean that bad or indifferent performance creates or deepens instability, for the time gap between performance and citizens' response may be quite wide, especially in a society of the Soviet type where social controls are strong and communications are highly managed and manipulated. What it does mean clearly is that good performance contributes to the stability of the regime.

The major question is what one selects to evaluate and how one evaluates the performance. From the vantage point of the Western analyst, the comparison of technological progress in the Soviet Union and the West, for example, may be considered a crucial point of evaluation of Soviet performance over the last fifteen years.[11] Or one can survey the dreary wasteland of Soviet culture in this period and note the forced emigration of some of Russia's most talented and creative writers and artists. By either of these standards one would hardly judge the Brezhnev era a success. I would argue, however, that in order to gauge the regime's stability, the only legitimate vantage point is that of Soviet citizens themselves. And here the crucial sphere is the domestic economy, and the point of reference for judging performance is the comparison with the immediate Soviet past. By this standard the regime's performance in the Brezhnev era can be judged a success.

The aggregate figures of the Soviet economy attest to the impressiveness of the performance. As Table 1 shows, the Soviet Union has solidified and strengthened its position as a great industrial power.

The key successful projects of the Brezhnev era five-year plans – among them the Kama power complex, the Togliatti automobile factory, the Samotlor oil field, the Kama truck plant, the "Friendship" pipeline through the Urals, the chemical fertilizer plants, the Soviet fishing and merchant fleets, the Orenburg natural-gas pipeline, the metallurgical complex at Kursk, the Baikal-Amur Railroad – all are fitting symbols of Soviet economic accomplishments. Yet from the point of view of our interest the most important and impressive change and the most salient characteristic of Soviet economic performance has occurred in the consumer goods sector with the raising of the standard of living. Brezhnev spoke the truth with regard to the raising of Soviet living standards when he proclaimed at the Twenty-fifth Party Congress that "the history of our country has not known such a broad social program as that fulfilled in the period for which I give the report."

Table 2 compares aggregate figures of annual growth of consumption in the decade 1965–75 as compared to the period 1961–5. All major

---

[11]The growth of Soviet industrial might did not lead to any perceptible narrowing of the technological lag behind developed Western societies. In this respect, one very well-researched Western study states: "In most of the technologies we have studied there is no evidence of a substantial diminution of the technological gap between the USSR and the West in the past 15–20 years, either at the prototype/ commercial application stages or in the diffusion of advanced technology" (Ronald Ammann, Julian Cooper, and R. W. Davies, eds. [with the assistance of Hugh Jenkins], *The Technological Level of Soviet Industry* [New Haven, Conn.: Yale University Press, 1977], p. 66). The sources of this lag are to be found in the inflexibility of the Soviet system of management and incentives of the economy, science, and technology (see Bruce Parrott, "Technological Progress and Soviet Politics," *Survey*, 23, no. 2 [Spring 1977–78], 39–60).

Table 1. *Growth of Soviet industrial power, 1965–77 (1965 = 100)*
(percent)

GNP	211
National income	210
Capital funds of the national economy	264
Industrial production	239
Place in world industrial production of:	
Total industrial production	2
Electro-energy	2
Oil	1
Natural gas	2
Coal	1
Pig iron	1
Steel	1
Iron ore	1
Chemical production	2
Chemical fertilizers	1
Machine building	2
Tractors	1
Cement	1
Woolens	1
Shoes	1

Source: Narodnoe khoziaistvo SSSR v 1977 g. (Moscow: Statistika, 1978), pp. 30–1, 51, 56.

Table 2. *Growth of consumption in the Soviet Union, 1961–75 (percent, average annual rates of growth)*

Year	Total	Food	Soft goods	Personal services	Consumer durables	Health and education
1961–5	2.6	2.1	1.5	5.4	8.3	4.2
1966–75	3.9	3.3	4.5	4.7	8.5	4.6

Source: Adapted from Rush Greenslade, "Economic Development and Popular Expectations," paper for the Workshop on Political Stability and Socio-Economic Change in the Soviet Union, Research Institute on International Change, Columbia University, 4–5 May 1976.

categories of consumption are represented in this overall growth. Behind the aggregate figures there is the steady and significant increase in food supplies and a noticeable improvement in the diet of the population. Per capita consumption of high-quality foods rose over 100 percent while consumption of starches dropped by over 30 percent. A significant improvement occurred in the supply of clothing and shoes as well as in styling and quality.

Table 3. *Dynamics of national income and personal services, 1960–76 (1960 = 100)*

Item	1965	1970	1976
Growth of national income	137	199	278
Growth of personal services	176	273	440
Personal services as percent of national income	(26.7)	(28.7)	(32.8)

Source: Narodnoe khoziaistvo SSSR v 1973 g. (Moscow: Statistika, 1974), pp. 603–5; *Narodnoe khoziaistvo SSSR za 60 let* (Moscow: Statistika, 1977), pp. 460, 485.

As Table 3 shows, personal consumer services – commerce, laundries, tailor shops, beauty salons, etc. – have for the first time demonstrated a rapid and visible growth.

Most significantly, however, the government has pursued two consumer-oriented programs with highly visible results: rapid development of the capacity to produce consumer durables, most recently automobiles, and large-scale construction of new housing units. Table 4 illustrates the remarkable progress in the supply of durable consumer goods to the population.

The Soviet housing situation still presents a dismal picture. It will take another fifteen or twenty years to meet even the low standards set by the Soviets themselves. Today about 30 percent of households in urban areas still share apartments. Yet progress over the last fifteen years is very noticeable. In 1961 about two-thirds of all urban families lived communally. The Soviet Union has been building 2.3 million units yearly with 110 square meters of useful space (Table 5). About ten million improve their housing situations every year, a remarkable achievement, even if the quality and size of units are below Western standards.[12]

The scope and extent of the state's welfare function have also been much improved. For the first time, the Soviet peasant has been included in the social security system. In each of the last three five-year plans, the funds of social consumption have increased from 30 to 40 percent. The size of retirement pensions has been increased to include almost three-quarters of the wages and salaries of the retirees.[13] The retirement age was established relatively low: 60 years for men, 55 for women. In 1975

[12]Henry W. Morton, "The Soviet Urban Scene," *Problems of Communism*, 26, no. 1 (January–February 1977), 76. For the Soviet housing situation, see also Henry W. Morton, "Who Gets What, When and How? Housing in the Soviet Union," paper delivered at the Annual Meeting of the American Political Science Association, Washington, D.C., 1–4 September 1977; Alfred John DiMaio, Jr., *Soviet Urban Housing: Problems and Policies* (New York: Praeger, 1974). '
[13]Another step in the same direction was the introduction of stipends for children in families where per capita income is below 50 rubles a month (see G. A. Garibian, *Problemy povysheniia urovnia zhizni naseleniia v razvitom sotsialisticheskom obshchestve* [Erevan: Izd. Erevanskogo universiteta, 1977], p. 245).

Table 4. *Ownership of durable consumer goods by the Soviet population,*
1965–77 (per 100 families)

Goods	1965	1977
Urban population		
Watches	375	533
Radios	67	88
TV sets	32	86
Cameras	36	36
Refrigerators	17	87
Washing machines	29	78
Vacuum cleaners	11	29
Motorcycles and scooters	5	6
Bicycles and motopeds	44	42
Sewing machines	54	61
Rural population		
Watches	245	397
Radios	49	72
TV sets	15	67
Cameras	8	14
Refrigerators	3	45
Washing machines	12	52
Vacuum cleaners	1	10
Motorcycles and scooters	8	16
Bicycles and motopeds	54	70
Sewing machines	50	68

Source: Narodnoe khoziaistvo SSSR v 1977 g. (Moscow: Statistika, 1978), p. 432.

Table 5. *Soviet housing construction*

Year	Units (× 1,000)	Space (× 1,000,000 sq. m.)
1961–5	11,551	490.6
1966–70	11,333	518.5
1971–5	11,224	544.8
1977	2,110	107.8

Source: Narodnoe khoziaistvo SSSR v 1977 g. (Moscow: Statistika, 1978), p. 413.

about 45 million Soviet citizens were receiving pensions in one form or
another.[14]

The visible improvement in the standard of living resulted from major
changes in emphasis in the economic policy of the Brezhnev government.
Two indicators which illustrate this change should be mentioned here:

[14]Iu. Ia. Tsederbaum, *Ischislenie i vyplata pensii* (Moscow: Iurizdat, 1977), pp. 4–5.
See also *Pozhilye liudi v nashei strane* (Moscow: Statistika, 1977).

Table 6. *Dynamics of national income and consumption, 1961–80*

Increase	1961–5	1966–70	1971–5	1976–80[a]
Average yearly increase in national income (percent)	5.7	7.1	5.1	4.7
Average yearly increase in consumption (percent)	5.4	7.0	5.4	5.0
Increase in consumption as percent of increase in national income	94.7	98.6	105.9	106.4

[a] Plan.
Source: Calculated from *Narodnoe khoziaistvo SSSR v 1970 g.* (Moscow: Statistika, 1971), p. 535; *Narodnoe khoziaistvo SSSR za 60 let* (Moscow: Statistika, 1977), pp. 49, 565; *Pravda*, 28 October 1976.

the attitude toward consumption as compared to investment and the attitude toward agriculture. The Brezhnev period saw a significant reduction of the breakneck growth of investment, nowhere so visible as in the latest five-year plan (1976–80) with a decline to 4.5 percent as compared to 6.5 percent during the preceding five years (1970–5). Largely because of this phenomenon, the growth of the consumption fund has been exceeding that of the growth of total national income, increasing therefore the proportion of consumption in the national income to the highest level in Soviet history (75 percent in the plan which ends in 1980).

The situation of Soviet agriculture is much more difficult to judge. From the point of view of efficiency Soviet agriculture is clearly a disaster area. Therefore, when we use the term "performance" here, it is not as an evaluation of the relation of inputs to outputs but only as an indicator of the Soviet leadership's efforts with regard to agriculture and of the achieved output itself. From this point of view the position and achievement of Soviet agriculture have improved substantially in the Brezhnev era.

The single most striking characteristic of Brezhnev's economic policies has been the assignment of top priority to the development of agriculture, including the development of chemical fertilizers, farm machinery, etc. Agriculture constitutes today the single largest item in Soviet budgetary expenditures. For all the years of Soviet power until 1965 capital investments in agriculture amounted to 107 billion rubles; in the years 1965–75 the sum of investments in agriculture totaled 213 billion rubles.[15]

As we mentioned before, due to unbelievable inefficiencies and waste, this massive investment has scarcely produced commensurate agricul-

[15]*XXV s'ezd Kommunisticheskoi Partii Sovetskogo Soiuza. Stenograficheskii otchet*, 1 (Moscow: Gospolitizdat, 1976), 73.

tural growth, but growth there has been. One of the most qualified observers of Soviet agriculture has remarked:

> A series of outrages and disbeliefs prevents many of us from acknowledging and viewing the progress of Soviet agriculture as a process made more difficult and less pliable in its functional performance by existing rigidities. But I would like to submit that this is more our problem as observers than the Soviets. We cannot, or perhaps, should not judge Soviet progress by our criteria or our yardstick of economic efficiency. We should make peace with the reality of differing priorities. The difficulties in producing butter are in part a function of the success in producing guns for a long time.[16]

Most importantly, one should be conscious that if one can speak about Soviet agriculture as a crisis area, it is a different crisis from the past. It is, so to say, a crisis on a higher level of achievement, a crisis of a different qualitative character. In the past, including the Khrushchev era, the crisis was simply that of grain production for direct food consumption and of the pressure on the state's strategic reserves for current food consumption. Today it is a crisis of feed-grain production to meet the rising popular demand for meat and other high-quality foods. As Arcadius Kahan observes, "During the 1970's no one doubted or questioned the availability of a food grain supply even under the most adverse weather conditions."[17] One should not forget, moreover, that the commitment to agriculture includes also the commitment to buy very large quantities of grain abroad for hard currency in years of bad harvests. Those purchases again differ from the Khrushchev era not only in their magnitude, but also in that they are not simply for the purpose of direct food consumption but for the replacement of the feed-grain stock.

The major conclusion that emerges from our presentation of Soviet performance in the Brezhnev era is that the Soviet regime has by and large been able to deliver the goods; it has generally been able to satisfy popular expectations for higher standards of living. The indices which we used to reach this conclusion have been aggregate figures for the entire population. From the point of view of our interest in how the regime's performance influences Soviet stability, it is questionable, however, whether one can draw inferences for political stability from aggregate figures. It can be argued that these figures must be disaggregated to get at the political problems. In other words, what is most important to stability are sudden changes or discontinuous drops in living standards (such as changes in work norms or sudden price increases) and other matters of equity for given groups; because even when aggregate standards rise, the situation of some group or groups may decline. Similarly,

[16]Arcadius Kahan, "Soviet Agriculture: Domestic and Foreign Policy Aspects" in Seweryn Bialer, ed., *Domestic Context of Soviet Foreign Policy* (Boulder, Colo.: Westview Press, forthcoming), p. XV/9–10.
[17]*Ibid.*, p. XV/9.

one should probably make regional breakdowns, since any region which feels disadvantaged by the system may harbor resentments which could erupt into political disturbance. In sum, factors which affect the standards or relative position of specific groups are more important in triggering political disruptions than are slow, continuous changes in the aggregate measures. Moreover, while in decentralized market systems resentment is diffused, in the centralized systems of the USSR and Eastern Europe it is channeled to the center, since economic problems are necessarily blamed on the government and lower authorities usually lack power to act.

The availability of economic data does not permit a detailed disaggregation of the comprehensive indicators by groups and regions. A few well-grounded impressions based on what data do exist, however, would strongly argue that with regard to the main groups of the population and the main regions a disaggregation of indices would not alter the basic conclusion that Soviet performance under Brezhnev in the area of living standards does contribute to the stability of the regime.

First of all, the data indicate that all major groups of Soviet society have participated in the general improvement of living conditions. Although their respective shares were unequal, no group was left out. The improvement affected both the urban and rural populations, the skilled and unskilled workers, the managers and professionals, the students and pensioners. White-collar workers, clerks, typists, etc. probably profited least from the increase in the living standard, but this group from the point of view of political weight in the society, past record of causing trouble, ability to organize, and so forth is the least sensitive for the Soviet regime to deal with.

Second, all major regions, that is, primarily the republics, benefited from the improvement. Regional differences did exist, but they followed the normal, long-standing pattern that the greatest improvement in production and consumption related inversely to the level of the region's development. If differences among regions have therefore somewhat narrowed, the prevailing ranking of the regions has not changed.[18]

[18]The difference in the level of republican development is still considerable, though narrowing. Differentiation in the production of per capita national income in the last year for which official figures are available (1961) was as follows (RSFSR = 100):

Latvia	123.1	Kazakhstan	71.9
Estonia	112.7	Turkmenia	62.9
Lithuania	89.8	Kirgizia	60.7
Ukraine	87.6	Uzbekistan	58.7
Armenia	76.0	Tadzhikistan	51.5
Belorussia	72.5		

Source: Calculated from Iu. F. Vorob'ev, *Vyravnivanie urovnei ekonomicheskogo razvitiia soiuznykh respublik* (Moscow: Gospolitizdat, 1966), p. 192.

Third and most important, by far the greatest improvement in living conditions was felt by the most unprivileged groups in Soviet society, those who were probably most dissatisfied with their lot. Minimum wages rose by about 50 percent; pensions were substantially increased; the peasants were included in the social security system; collective farms were covered by a state insurance system against bad harvests. In the decade 1965–75 the number of people with a monthly income of 100 rubles or more per family member increased eight and one-half times,[19] a virtual income revolution embracing tens of millions of people.[20]

Fourth, the government in this period pursued a very cautious policy with regard to raising norms or increasing prices, that is, the steps which would lead to a drop in the standard of living of specific groups. As a matter of fact, it is the level of prices of basic consumer goods, supported by enormous subsidies and the sometimes absurdly low and unchanging level of industrial norms of production, to mention two of many items, which account to a large extent for the strong inflationary pressures in the Soviet market and for the glaring inefficiencies and low productivity of the Soviet worker. It is virtually certain that this policy of caution betrays exactly the regime's concern over the possible destabilizing effects of any other alternative–a view which the bitter experiences with raising norms and prices in Poland could only have reinforced.

Fifth, the rise in the living standard was achieved in part through a channel which, from the point of view of its contribution to stability, is probably the most advantageous to the regime, namely, through social mobility. Improvement in this area is the most satisfactory, most drastic, and most immediate of all forms of improvement in the standard of living and, incidentally, requires the least investment from the state. I am thinking here not only of the regular channels of mobility through higher education but primarily about mobility from rural to urban occupations and from unskilled to skilled labor.

Between 1965 and 1975 the percentage of the total population employed in agriculture declined by 37 percent, and the absolute number of farmers in the collective farms declined by 20 percent.[21] The change in the structure of the urban working class is indicated in Table 7 by figures concerning requalification of workers.

In our consideration of Soviet performance as a factor contributing to the stability of the regime we have concentrated until now on the eco-

[19]*XXV s'ezd Kommunisticheskoi Partii Sovetskogo Soiuza*, 1, 60.
[20]On the question of wage differentials in the Soviet Union, see Peter Wiles, "Recent Data on Soviet Income Distribution," *Survey*, 21, no. 3 (Summer 1975), 28–41; Janet G. Chapman, "Recent Trends in the Soviet Industrial Wage Structure," paper presented at the Conference on Problems of Industrial Labor in the USSR, Kennan Institute for Advanced Russian Studies, Washington, D.C., 27–29 September 1977.
[21]*Narodnoe khoziaistvo SSSR v 1975 g.* (Moscow: Statistika, 1976), pp. 440, 530.

Table 7. *Upgrading of professional qualifications of workers in the Soviet national economy, 1965–77 (× 1,000,000)*

Professionalization	1965	1970	1977
Workers who received new higher professional specialization	3.4	4.8	5.7
Workers who participated in training for higher qualifications	7.2	9.0	19.9

Source: Narodnoe khoziaistvo SSSR v 1977 g. (Moscow: Statistika, 1978), p. 399.

nomic sphere alone – particularly on the question of the improvement in the Soviet standard of living under Brezhnev. There is, however, another sphere where Soviet performance has been and remains impressive by any standard, one that should be mentioned at least when discussing the stability of the Soviet regime, namely, the international sphere. From the Western point of view, probably the greatest accomplishment of the Brezhnev era has been the achievement by the Soviet Union of global-power status and of strategic parity with the United States.

I do not share the view of those who assign to Soviet foreign policy and international accomplishments an increasingly dominant role in legitimizing the regime and in achieving its stability. In my opinion the dominant sources of both Soviet legitimacy and stability, both for the population and most of the elite, are overwhelmingly domestic in nature. Internal factors are sufficient to explain the regime's legitimacy and stability. Nevertheless, one should not dismiss the contributing influence of international factors.

Ironically, the positive influence of the international factors in this respect acts both through the Soviets' greatest achievements and their greatest failure. The increased recognition accorded abroad to Soviet international achievement, its growing prestige and activization are visibly a source of pride both to the population and especially to the elites – an important factor in their identification with the regime. But the greatest Soviet failure abroad – the unsolved and insoluble conflict with China – acts in the very same direction albeit through a different mechanism. Here the stimulus comes from fear and hatred which unite the population and the elites with one another and with the regime. What is discussed in the Soviet Union is not who "lost" China, but rather what ingrates the Chinese are. One discovers in the Soviet Union that no blame is attached to the leadership for the "loss" of China, but that a palpable sense of unity joins the leadership with the people both with regard to policies toward China and to common apprehensions of a new encirclement.

In sum, the regime's performance in the Brezhnev era goes far to explain Soviet stability. Given the governmental monopoly over the allocation of resources and rewards, economic grievances in the Soviet system inevitably take on a political dimension. On the other side of the coin, however, when things go well, the government tends to get the credit. Since popular demands remain relatively modest and are by and large being met, the strong identification of the government with the state of the economy has enhanced the long-run stability of the system. The government has furthermore been very careful to avoid antagonizing critical groups in the system. These groups are very well treated, and they know that the government is responsible. In all probability, the Brezhnev era will enter Soviet history as a period of the most impressive achievement, a period unequaled in the past and, incidentally, one not likely to be equaled in the foreseeable future. Thus the Soviet government has succeeded fairly well in managing the expectations of the population. It has made a conscious effort to differentiate the expectations of various groups, and it has calibrated its response accordingly. One must now ask: What circumstances account for the ability of the regime to manage them?

The nature of rising popular expectations

Stability of the regime cannot be discussed apart from the question of the nature and level of popular expectations. As we have mentioned, the most important aspect of the rise of popular expectations to date is its confinement largely to the material sphere. No doubt the rise of nonmaterial expectations would present dangers to the system's stability.

It seems clear that the nonmaterial expectations and aspirations of various Soviet groups and the population at large differ today in many respects from what they were twenty or twenty-five years ago. All groups now expect a secure life, free from capricious harassment and from terror. All aspire to live in a state which preserves a respectable level of legality in daily contacts with citizens. The creative intelligentsia—writers, artists, directors—expect greater artistic freedom; they aspire to a state of being where they can, within limits, experiment and err. They expect to continue the often enjoyed advantage to opt out, to engage safely in artistic pursuits which are neutral to the goals of the regime.

The creative and technical intelligentsia as well as the various elites share the expectation and strong desire never again to be isolated from the main streams of non-socialist world culture and progress. Professional groups expect a greater degree of professional autonomy and aspire to extend still further the limits of this autonomy, to gain greater access to information and data about their own and other societies, to be able to address the areas of their expertise more freely if only in closed discussion and publications of limited circulation.

The émigré dissident Valery Chalidze has contended that active dissent in the Soviet Union represents only a tip of the iceberg, that behind each *active* dissenter there are scores of *hidden* dissenters among the intelligentsia and even within the elites who share the ideas but lack the courage or ability or opportunity or desire to act openly.[22] We cannot know whether Chalidze is correct. In all probability he accurately describes those groups of dissenters who hold the most moderate views. Even if Chalidze were right, however, from the point of view of the regime's stability, the point to be made is that the distinction between a small active dissent movement and a large inactive dissent group is a crucial one. The small active dissent movement can be fought with relative ease; it can be fragmented, isolated, neutralized. Where *conditions of stability* already exist, it suffices at most to identify for further reference the larger inactive dissent sympathy mood and then to ignore it. *Inactive dissent does not produce instability: its danger to the regime lies in the possibility of its activation under conditions of instability.*

Yet one may also argue, as this author does, that Chalidze exaggerates the extent of the inactive dissent by identifying it incorrectly as dissent. In light of what has just been said about the raised nonmaterial expectations and aspirations of various groups in Soviet society, it is more probable that what we observe is the partial coincidence of these aspirations and some of the views of the dissenters. What is crucial about the coincidence of shared aspirations, however, is, first, that for the dissenters the aspirations of these strata, especially in scope and intensity, represent only a small part of their program and, second, that for the dissenters their program is to be achieved through systemic change, while the various other groups aspire to realize their goals within the system by means of pressure that results in policy relaxation.

The nondissident groups and strata then do not expect a change of system but seek accommodation within it. Moreover, their expectations and, within limits, their aspirations are not neglected by the system's directors. As a matter of fact, their very expectations are based on changes which have already taken place in the post-Stalin era with the willing or grudging support of the leadership. These changes – toward greater professional autonomy, greater freedom of expression, greater contacts with the non-socialist world – did not endanger the regime's stability. Indeed, their implementation owed perhaps less to pressures from the various groups than to the coincidence of those pressures with some interests of the leadership itself. The leadership slowly became convinced that such changes, when controlled and kept within limits, could serve to enhance the effectiveness and performance of the system or were even necessary to that end. The crux of the matter is to contain the aspirations within limits so as not to impinge on issues which the regime considers crucial to its survival.

It now seems that despite the partial coincidence of the aspirations of these groups and strata with those of active dissidents the former do not pose a threat to the system as long as they do not share the dissidents' broader goals and selection of means for their attainment. In addition, as

---

[22]Valery Chalidze, "How Important Is Soviet Dissent?" *Commentary*, 63, no. 6 (June 1977), 57–62.

long as the regime has the opportunity and these strata show the willingness to trade off nonmaterial aspirations for material demands – and this is what the regime has also been doing throughout the Brezhnev era – the regime is well prepared to cope with those aspirations.

In this connection the following proposition of Walter Connor holds true not only for the relations between the elite and the population at large but for relations between the regime's leadership and all important strata of the Soviet, particularly Russian Soviet, society:

> The political culture links the bureaucratic elite and the "masses" more closely than it links the dissidents to either. The institutional framework that emerged in the Stalin era "fitted" relatively well with the antecedent political culture of tsarist Russia at the most critical points, and to all appearances the *contemporary* Soviet political culture still "fits" this relatively unchanged institutional pattern quite well.[23]

Under Brezhnev the rise in the expectations and aspirations of Soviet citizens of high and low status has been most noticeable in the material sphere. In the last fifteen years a fever of materialism has seized the Soviet population of all classes and stations, a visible and all-pervasive drive to acquire goods, to live better, to enjoy. What is more striking, however, especially when compared to the situation in the West, is first that in absolute terms these expectations are very modest for an industrial nation and second that they are not far removed from what is realistically possible, though often unrealized, in Soviet conditions. To put it differently, although material expectations remain in advance of reality, one doubts whether there is a widening gap between expectations and reality.

The rising material expectations of the Soviet population do not get out of hand. They do not create a vicious circle which narrows restrictively and increasingly the leadership's ability to impose its own set of priorities on the society, which creates unbearable inflationary pressures and, by translating rising expectations into political pressures, overloads the entire system of government. The Soviet situation under Brezhnev, the combination of rising material expectations on the one hand and their limits on the other, has led to a partial reordering of the regime's priorities in the direction of consumerism. At the same time the system's directors have retained enough flexibility to decide the order of priorities, free from society's dictation.

Given that the intensity of popular pressures is very limited, the situation will probably remain stabilized as long as some improvements continue to occur. But however we evaluate the amorphous pressures in Soviet society, the responsiveness by the leadership to certain aspirations is clearly much greater now than in the past. To what kind of

---

[23]Walter D. Connor, "Dissent in a Complex Society: The Soviet Case," *Problems of Communism*, 22, no. 2 (March–April 1973), 50.

pressures do the Soviet leaders respond? In part, of course, the leadership is responsive to changes in the distributive sector of the Soviet economy where the population has acquired for the first time in Soviet history a limited possibility for expressing its demands through selective buying. In part it has to do with the importance attached to material incentives in economic programs. To a much larger extent, however, the responsiveness can be described as an anticipatory reaction with regard to workers, that is to say, a response not to their actual behavior but to the leadership's fear that if the interests of the workers are not sufficiently considered, their behavior might become disruptive and dangerous. The lessons of worker dissatisfaction in East European countries, and especially the workers' uprising in Poland, have not been lost on Soviet leaders. In a country where such a high premium is placed on stability, where organized dissent movements are active, where mass terror is absent, where popular expectations have long been encouraged, where the opening of Soviet society to foreigners has made material comparison more possible than in the past, the party must pay more attention to the material satisfaction of the population. Only at this price can it continue to curtail cultural freedom, withhold much of political freedom, and preserve political stability.

The rise in material expectations of the Soviet public requires no explanation. More problematical is why rising expectations have not developed into a vicious-circle pattern. Of the major reasons for this untypical state of affairs, we should like to introduce four

1. The attitude and behavior of the Soviet population, especially of the middle and older generations, is largely shaped by the past. The restraint in popular expectation is striking in a system which for decades overindulged in utopian promises, but it is exactly the overindulgence which partly explains the restraint. Soviet society was and is a society in which the regime's promises are as quickly devalued as they are issued. Past performance tempers both the expectations for the future and the countervailing influence usually associated with the betterment of the living standard which has occurred recently.

People believe in what they get now and what they can get; they fantasize little about what they will have or may get. A Soviet saying expresses this attitude well: "Please God, may it not get better" – ("Bozhe, chtoby ne bylo luchshe"). This mood is akin, though much stronger, to the feelings of the American generation which experienced the Great Depression and lived long after with the fear that things might again go wrong. The memories and fears act to dampen rising expectations and to keep them from escaping control.

2. By the measuring rod of industrially developed societies, the standard of living in the Soviet Union, even after many years of significant improvements, remains very low.[24] The consequences of this situation

[24]The main reasons for this state of affairs are three. First, even today in the period of the greatest improvements of living standards in Soviet history, consumerism and consumer goals are not at the top of the authorities' list of priorities. The

from the point of view of the level of expectations are significant. In a society where food still constitutes over 50 percent of the family budget, where starches still account for about two-thirds of the food consumed, where fresh vegetables, not to mention fruits, are a rarity in urban areas, where regular meat deliveries to the stores are an exception, where a pair of shoes wears only a few months before disintegrating and a suit of clothes looks as though it was confected at the turn of the century, and where the pattern of building and inhabiting communal apartments with shared kitchens and bathrooms has only recently been abandoned, the "normal" consumer expectations are unimaginative and modest. They are likely to remain so in a society which displays before the public no examples of conspicuous luxury and mounts no advertising campaigns directed to the consumer. The modesty of consumer expectations thus renders them attainable under Soviet conditions long before they become economically and politically difficult to handle. From the existing base any step forward in the quantitative and especially the qualitative indicators of consumer supply will continue to be welcome as a real improvement.

3. An extremely important dimension in evaluating one's standard of living and setting one's expectations concerns the reference point used as the base. It is our contention that for the average Soviet consumer this reference point is neither the West nor even East European Communist countries but his own past.[25] We often exaggerate tremendously the ef-

burdens of militarization, the goals of heavy industrial development, the weight of supporting Eastern Europe, and general foreign policy goals – in brief, the burdens of an aspiring global power without an adequate economic base – weigh heavily on the economy and prevent a fuller satisfaction of consumer demands. Except in wartime, no country of similar productive capacity per capita has failed so pervasively to meet consumer wants as expressed in efforts to spend income.

Second, all other industrial countries have reached the mass consumer stage in an evolutionary and, for the most part, balanced way. Their process of developing consumption was balanced with the progress of their productive capacity, and the development of their productive capacities was balanced with the buildup of their economic infrastructure. In the Soviet Union the shift to mass and relatively high-priority consumption is quite recent; the development of productive capacity has been extremely unbalanced; and the level and shape of the economic infrastructure are more characteristic of an undeveloped than of an industrial country. Much of the delayed consumer demand and much of the reserve of rapid improvement are located in the area of the backward infrastructure. The Soviet Union today still remains the most developed of the developing countries and the least developed of the developed countries.

Third, the low standard of living in the Soviet Union cannot be expressed in quantitative indices alone. It has more and more to do with the low quality and durability, the antiquated styling and design of Soviet products. It is only now that the Soviets are slowly starting to appreciate the centrality of the quality factor in production and consumption. The reserves for improvement here are staggering and any improvement highly visible.

[25]As the accompanying table indicates, the comparable levels of real net average monthly earning in Soviet industry remain below the East European level and much below the West European level as represented by Austria. Moreover, be-

fects that opening the Soviet Union to the West in the last ten to fifteen years has had on the general Soviet public, given both the long history of isolation and the relative narrowness of the present opening. True, many "normal" Soviet citizens in metropolitan areas see foreigners and even have sporadic contacts with them. At the same time they are denied comprehensive and visual information about life in the West and are bombarded, if anything at a greater rate than before, with distorted data and images of life in the West. Travel to the West of course is enjoyed almost entirely by representatives of elites and subelites as a major ingredient of their privileged position.[26]

For the "normal" Soviet citizen who suspects the official version, life in the West has nevertheless no reality of its own. It cannot and does not in my opinion serve as a reference point of his rising expectations. That point is provided by his own and his peer group's past, which, it should be stressed, is very often a peasant past, even in urban areas. Comparison with this past can only heighten approval of ongoing improvements and temper expectations.

The situation differs for elites and subelites and part of the professional classes. Their notion of the Western standard of living acquires plasticity thanks to their access to literature, their contacts with foreigners, their personal travel, or the accounts of friends. To counter potential disaffection the authorities assure these groups a standard of liv-

tween 1960 and 1973 the gap between Eastern Europe and the Soviet Union has somewhat narrowed, but it opens even more in comparison to Western Europe. (Socialist East Europe without USSR = 100.)

Country	1960	1973
Bulgaria	81.5	90.1
Czechoslovakia	106.7	100.1
GDR	112.4	121.5
Hungary	98.3	90.4
Poland	97.9	98.0
Rumania	83.4	92.4
USSR	68.8	79.6
Austria	127.4	160.2

Source: Janet G. Chapman, "Recent Trends in Soviet Industrial Wage Structure," p. 44.

[26]In 1977 about 2.7 million Soviet citizens traveled abroad. Of these, about 1.75 million visited socialist countries while 950,000 went to industrialized and Third World countries. To the six main industrial countries (U.S.A., West Germany, France, Japan, Great Britain, Italy) there were 277,300 Soviet visitors, of whom 16,600 came to the U.S.A. (*Vneshniaia torgovlia*, 1978, no. 9, p. 36). An overwhelming majority of those traveling to capitalist countries were on official business and exchanges of delegations. According to the State Department, fewer than 1,000 of those coming to the United States can be classified as tourists, who incidentally would also come in all probability from the privileged strata of Soviet society.

ing much closer to the West and infinitely higher than the Soviet average. These beneficiaries contrast their superior lot to their less fortunate fellow citizens and enjoy it with some gratitude and even some guilt.

4. The picture we conveyed would not be correct were it to depict simply a harmonious society with modest expectations and high levels of satisfaction. If, as we contend, the basic background is that of modest expectations, the situation is more complex. The level of satisfaction of various Soviet publics is not normally high because the attainment of even modest expectations comes at the cost of constant gripes, dissatisfaction with what is available, and the unceasing competition for it. The point is, however, that the dissatisfaction and unfulfilled expectations with rare exceptions find expression in ways that may be unpleasant and injurious to the system but not dangerous.[27] Discontent is funneled through specifically designated channels which tend to deflect criticism from central authorities to local bureaucracies. (The principal channel for complaints is the local soviet, the authority closest to the citizen.) One senses that expressions of dissatisfaction function for the regime not only as a safety valve but as a pressure on subordinate bureaucracies. Deviant *individual* behavior (alcoholism, absenteeism, and the like) serves as another channel of expression.[28]

Needless to say, dissatisfaction is almost never expressed in more drastic and independent ways through the organization of autonomous groups or actions like strikes, given the stringent controls over nonofficial communication and organization. Restrictions on the articulation of grievances are an essential means by which Soviet authorities manipulate popular expectations. Where they failed to work, as in Poland, the industrial working class achieved a virtual veto over the government's economic policies. The Soviet Union in this regard has very far to go.

Paul Hollander in his excellent comparison of Soviet and American societies has remarked: "The key to the stability of the Soviet system lies in its management of expectations rather than in the powers of the

---

[27]An important safety valve, particularly regarding dissatisfaction with the availability of goods on the official market, is provided by the second market or – to say it simply – by stealing and other illegal transactions, the scale of which we are only now beginning to appreciate (see Dimitri K. Simes, "The Soviet Parallel Market," *Survey*, 21, no. 3 [Summer 1975], 42–52; John M. Kramer, "Political Corruption in the USSR," *Western Political Quarterly*, 30, no. 2 [June 1977], 213–24; Gregory Grossman, "Notes on the Illegal Private Economy and Corruption" in *Soviet Economy in a Time of Change*, U.S. Congress, Joint Economic Committee, 1 [10 October 1979], 834–55).

[28]Absenteeism and especially labor turnover are major and serious problems of Soviet industry which reflect a relatively high level of dissatisfaction with job conditions and pay. While in West Germany about 5 percent of the working force change their work each year (1967–72) and in the U.S.A. 4.8 percent (2.1 percent at their own request [1970]), in the Soviet Union in 1970 the comparable figure was 21 percent. This is especially astonishing when one considers the very close relation in the Soviet Union between income and seniority and job tenure (Anna-Juta Pietsch, "Die Fluktuation der Arbeitskräfte in der UdSSR im Verhältnis zum ökonomisch bedingten Umsetzungsbedarf und in internationalen Vergleich," Working Papers, Osteuropa Institut, Munich).

KGB."[29] As long as Soviet citizens focus their expectations on material achievements, as long as the rising spiral of expectations remains relatively modest and partly satisfied, as long as the articulation of dissatisfaction follows traditional Soviet channels, the Soviet regime will be able to maintain this major pillar of its stability.

Institutionalization and popular participation

The question of stability in the Soviet Union under Brezhnev requires consideration of the interconnections among three processes or characteristics of Soviet society: political apathy, political participation, and professionalization of social and political management. (Only those aspects of these vast topics that relate to stability will be examined here, while the matter of participation will be treated at greater length when I discuss legitimacy.) One of the most accepted and well-tested propositions in the study of political stability concerns the relation between institutionalization and participation. What has been convincingly argued may be summarized as follows: While a modern polity in the process of socioeconomic and political modernization produces and requires an increase in the intensity and scope of political participation, it requires as well a high level of political institutionalization which will keep pace with the increased participation. Political instability inevitably results if the level of political institutionalization is not high enough to absorb the increased pressures of the participation.[30]

Analysts have frequently alleged that in contrast to the Khrushchev period, the succeeding Brezhnev period is characterized by the decline of participatory politics. It is our contention that the level of political participation today seems, if anything, to be higher than in the immediate post-Stalin decade, that what has changed involves some emphases, directions, moods, and forms of political participation but not its level.

The two periods differ most in our opinion in the relation between participation and institutionalization. One may suggest that in the Khrushchev period the levels of participation and institutionalization did not keep step and, indeed, that their respective directions ran counter to one another. Khrushchev, in his attempt to shake up the system, destabilized political institutions. He may be said to have deinstitutionalized Soviet politics somewhat at the very same time that he conducted a partially successful effort to increase popular political participation. In our view participation increased also during the Brezhnev period and went less noticed because the institutionalization of Soviet politics matched its pace of development.

[29]Paul Hollander, *Soviet and American Society: A Comparison* (New York: Oxford University Press, 1973), p. 388.
[30]Huntington writes: "The stability of any given polity depends upon the relationship between the level of political participation and the level of political institutionalization. . . . As political participation increases, the complexity, autonomy, adaptability, and coherence of the society's political institutions must also increase if political stability is to be maintained" (*Political Order in Changing Societies*, p. 79).

Both periods share the un-Stalinist attitude of encouraging criticism, feedback, and initiative, that is, a positive commitment to expanded participation. Yet, while the tendency of the Khrushchev approach was to equalize the political status of full-time officials and the participatory *aktiv*, Brezhnev seeks successfully to reconcile the expanded political participation of nonbureaucrats with a strong commitment to the political and bureaucratic autonomy of Soviet officialdom. (In the apt phrase of George Breslauer, Khrushchev's approaches to achievement, participation, and authority building may be labeled "organizational," "populist," and "confrontational"; Brezhnev's as "financial," "rational-administrative," and "corporate.")[31]

If, as we noted above, expanded participation often produces the danger of destabilization, a degree of political apathy in society, an element of apolitization is not undesirable *from the systemic point of view*, as Huntington suggested. It does, after all, provide a stabilizing cushion, a safety valve. Exactly this is taking place in Soviet society. Contradictory as it may sound, the expanded participation of the Brezhnev era goes hand in hand with the retention of one of the most characteristic features of major Soviet social groups – their high level of apolitization.

In order to understand this apolitization, a major distinction has to be made between "high politics" and "low politics." The former involves the principal political issues of society, the abstract ideas and language of politics, the decisions and actions of the societal leadership. The latter involves the decisions that directly touch the citizen's daily life, the communal matters, and the conditions of the workplace.

The average Soviet citizen is apolitical, indifferent, apathetic with regard to "high politics." Lacking curiosity and interest, he suffers his routine encounters with "high politics," unavoidable in Soviet conditions, but he remains untouched by them. The language is rich in sayings that convey this attitude: for example, "The bosses know best" ("Nachal'stvo luchshe znaet") or "That's none of my business" ("Moia khata s kraiu").[32] The average person considers politics a separate way of life, a profession for which one is trained and paid. He customarily regards dissenters who risk their lives and careers for "high politics" as abnormal and aberrant or simply as trouble-makers. Nowhere is this attitude toward high politics more prevalent than among youth, so often the most politically volatile of all groups, but who in the Soviet Union, according to most competent observers, orient their lives toward careers and leisure.[33] Former Soviet citizens recall from their experience as Komso-

[31]George W. Breslauer, *Dilemmas of Leadership in the Soviet Union since Stalin: 1953–1976* (Berkeley: University of California Press, forthcoming), pp. 14/2–14/3.

[32]Alexander Zinov'ev well expresses, even if he rather exaggerates, the conservative and pessimistic attitude of the Russian worker: "Everything that will be, will happen. Everything that will be, is already here" ("Vse, chto bylo, budet! Vse, chto budet, est' ") (Aleksandr Zinov'ev, *Ziiaiushchie vysoty* [Lausanne: L'Age d'Homme, 1976], p. 221).

[33]Walter D. Connor, "Generations and Politics in the USSR," *Problems of Communism*, 24, no. 5 (September–October 1975), 20–31.

mol members that the organization from the point of view of "high politics" was very nonpolitical.

By contrast, "low politics" regularly involves a very high proportion of Soviet citizenry. As we shall restate later in our discussion of legitimacy, "low politics" constitute the very substance of the Soviet system of political participation. Very seldom under Soviet conditions do the "low" and "high" dimensions of Soviet politics intersect. When they do, it is a matter of the objective *effects* of the "low politics" of mass political participation on "high politics," and not as a consequence of the conscious *actions* of citizens. In all probability only a major shock or a prolonged crisis could provoke such actions.

This form of political apathy, while obviously an important element of political stability in the Brezhnev era, equals or perhaps even yields in significance as a factor of stability to the element of the increased institutionalization of Soviet politics. Increased institutionalization manifests itself in a number of ways – in the stability and streamlining of organizations active in Soviet politics, in the depersonalization of Soviet politics as compared to the Khrushchev period, in the establishment and adherence to long-range procedures in decision making, and so forth. Yet the major and to a large extent the new factor of this institutionalization is the heightened professionalization of all aspects of Soviet politics and administration. Five aspects of this professionalization will be mentioned here.

The first thing to note is the enormous expansion of professions in the Soviet Union. The development of the Soviet educational system has produced in the last twenty-five years a quantitative and qualitative leap in the professional structure of Soviet society. The growth of professional education has achieved the very impressive results indicated in Table 8; and professionals today constitute a weighty segment of society and particularly of the upper strata, dominated by the technical sciences (Table 9).

Today the professionals have reached a critical mass in the Soviet Union, that is to say, their weight has reached a point where their qualifications and typical attitudes exert a considerable influence on the entire administrative structure.[34] The era of the political dilettante lording over an uneducated, developing society and a semiprofessional, self-taught administrative structure is over.

[34]The main point is that the term "intelligentsia" as it was used in prerevolutionary Russian or early Soviet society has largely disappeared. The overwhelming mass of the new intelligentsia consists simply of professionals. The term "intelligentsia" as used with respect to the Soviet Union today, aside from its application to the dissident, has no meaning or connotation other than the educated, professional strata. In this respect the images of some dissidents are perfectly correct. Solzhenitsyn writes: "The modern intelligentsia is in no respect alienated from the modern *state*: those who feel that way, either in their private thoughts or among their immediate circle of friends, with a sense of constriction, depression, doom and resignation, are not only *maintaining* the state by their daily activities as members of the intelligentsia, but are accepting and fulfilling an even more terrible condition laid down by the state: participation *with their*

Table 8. *Professional cadres in the Soviet national economy, 1965–77* (× 1,000)

Cadres	1965	1970	1977
Total number of specialists with higher and special middle education employed in the national economy	12,066	16,841	25,178
Total number of specialists with higher education employed in the national economy	4,891	6,853	10,537
Of those:			
Engineers	1,631	2,486	4,193
Agronomists and veterinarians	303	408	562
Economists	301	493	903
Lawyers	85	106	161
Physicians	501	603	831
Specialists with higher and special middle education as percent of total labor force	(15.7)	(18.7)	(23.7)
Specialists with higher education as percent of white-collar employees	(23.3)	(26.4)	(33.1)

Source: Calculated from *Narodnoe khoziaistvo SSSR v 1977 g.* (Moscow: Statistika, 1978), pp. 380–1, 392–3.

Qualitatively, what is most noteworthy about the new professional strata is either the proliferation of professional associations into which they are organized or the infusion of new life into the existing associations. From an earlier virtually dormant state and a purely marginal role, these associations have become under Brezhnev very active and occupy an important place in the life of their members. One important form of their activity is the organization of major discussions on themes of professional concern. These discussions are characterized by broad, active participation of the membership, by their unideological, technical nature, and by the divergence of views expressed in them. It is as if the professionals engage in a continuous dialogue on matters central to their professional lives.[35]

soul in the common, compulsory lie" (A. Solzhenitsyn et al., *From Under the Rubble* [Boston and Toronto: Little, Brown and Co., 1974], p. 243). Yuri Kuperman writes: "The Soviet *intelligent* is a semi-*intelligent*. He has no intrinsic values; his spiritual culture is popular culture, his spiritual education is popular education. . . . The truth is that the Soviet intelligentsia long ago ceased to exist" (Yuri Kuperman, " 'No Places!': The Jewish Outsider in the Soviet Union," *Soviet Jewish Affairs*, 3, no. 2 [1973], p. 19). For an excellent discussion of the nature of the old Russian intelligentsia, see Martin Malia, "What Is the Intelligentsia?" in Richard Pipes, ed., *The Russian Intelligentsia* (New York: Columbia University Press, 1961), pp. 1–18.

[35] The discussions conducted in the Soviet professional press are characterized by broad thematic scope, extensive participation, and longevity. A very selective list

Table 9. *Distribution and growth of scientific cadres by branches*

Branch	Distribution of Scientific Cadres by Branches, 1974 (%)	Growth of Scientific Cadres, 1974 (1960 = 100)
Physics, mathematics, chemistry, biology, geology	20.6	297
Applied technical	46.8	422
Agricultural	3.6	197
History and philosophy	3.7	221
Economics	6.8	243
Medical	5.0	183

Source: I. S. Puchkov and G. A. Popov, *Sotsial'no-demograficheskaia kharakteristika nauchnykh kadrov* (Moscow: Statistika, 1976), p. 28.

An essential role in all this activity is played by professional journals, of which the increase in the numbers and the size of individual issues and editions is nothing short of amazing. To reword Lenin's remark on the role of the party press, it is the professional Soviet press that produces the spark which feeds the flame of professionalism. From readership questionnaires in the Soviet Union we know that these journals, newspapers, and bulletins constitute the focus of reading interest and the key source of information for Soviet professionals.[36]

Second, for the first time in Soviet postwar history the role of the outsider-professional became in the Brezhnev era a growing and important factor in Soviet decision making.[37] The leap here in comparison with the past is most clearly seen in the "soft" professions of social science, but

from recent years would include the following: the Soviet demographic-ethnic trends, the nature and periodization of feudalism, the nature of managerial labor, the feasibility of the redistribution of wealth between the Third World and industrial nations, the causes of Soviet labor turnover, the ties between Soviet urban and rural populations, the psychology of leadership, the regional differences in style of living, the structure of leisure time, the planning of Soviet cities, the rational norms of consumption, the patterns of scientific discoveries.

[36]It is not only the number and broad readership of professional journals and bulletins that matters. More important is the fact established by readership research in the Soviet Union – that these journals and not political literature provide the basic source of information and the focus of attention of the professional strata.

[37]I am stressing here the professionalization of the Soviet administration and administrative and political elites only from the point of view of its influence on the increased institutionalization of Soviet administrative-political life. I do not claim that Soviet decision making is now based on rational choices rather than on political considerations but only that more rational choices are available and enter political considerations. Least of all do I claim that in the process of decision making professional groups are replacing or will replace politicians. That these groups or their segments try to influence official policies is amply documented. That they are sometimes successful can also be demonstrated.

The question is, however, when are they successful and what policies do they

Table 10. *Professional press in the Soviet Union, 1950–75*

Types of journals and other periodicals	Number of editions				Yearly circulation (× 1,000)				Size of all issues (1960 = 100)			
	1950	1960	1970	1975	1950	1960	1970	1975	1950	1960	1970	1975
Science	222	525	895	974	4,333	12,100	100,951	125,310	28	100	946	1,056
Technology	250	1,034	1,916	2,184	11,671	152,660	335,504	434,389	9	100	352	388
Agriculture	128	378	510	548	7,099	24,594	54,353	64,643	22	100	224	256
Commerce	15	27	71	82	1,859	4,452	17,182	19,876	20	100	367	467
Medicine	103	285	362	340	2,513	21,801	170,093	178,662	9	100	629	659
Culture and education	122	180	202	256	6,757	34,013	90,897	105,945	15	100	300	348

Source: Calculated from *Narodnoe obrazovanie, nauka i kul'tura v SSSR* (Moscow: Statistika, 1977), pp. 416–17. According to another source, in 1976 there appeared in the USSR 3,142 journals and periodicals addressed to professional audiences which published 30,838 issues. This corresponds to 661 periodicals of a mass nature which published 8,947 issues in the same period (calculated from *Pechat' SSSR v 1976 godu* [Moscow: Statistika, 1977], p. 75).

it is evident as well in economics, managerial sciences, communication and information and processing sciences, and, of course, in the applied technological field. The field of economics, for example, has expanded radically and shifted its central focus away from political economy and a pronounced propagandistic function to highly technical macro- and micro-economics and a primary applied function. Sociology and political science have been virtually re-created and now enter areas which were until lately taboo, for example the study of public opinion and attitudes.

try to influence? First, as a rule the closer their profession is to the technological sphere and the more removed from the ideological one, the less ignored are their interests and pressures. Writers on the one extreme and scientists on the other represent the two poles of permissible freedom and influence. (The gravitation of economists from identification with cultural toward scientific spheres is important here.) Second, the main policy pressures emanating from these groups concern the status of their profession, allocation of resources to it, and their right to professional autonomy and integrity. In these concerns the scientific and technological groups have been very successful by and large in the last decade.

Yet one should beware of confusing the importance to the Soviet system and society of science and scientists (let alone other professional groups), their success in developing professional integrity and autonomy in basic research, and their proximity to men of power, with their general political influence. While respecting their expertise and responding to their needs, the Soviet politician is unlikely to attribute to them superior insight and wisdom. Since 1968, under the impact of the Sakharov Manifesto and the subsequent defense of his person and position by a number of scientists, the party has shown increased anxiety about the political and social attitudes of scientists, has considerably tightened supervision over personnel policy in the scientific establishment, and has tried to denigrate by propaganda the expertise of scientists in social and political matters.

The Soviet professional communities are politically fragile groups. Each "group" is not only politically heterogeneous, but it also displays a very broad range of views and opinions concerning matters on which advice is given to political authorities. It is composed of individuals of different generations with different training and diverse institutional associations and career orientations. The choice between conflicting advice and pressures remains the politician's. To what extent his choice will gravitate from those accepted today to those rejected today (e.g., market-oriented economic reform versus mathematization and computerization of centralized planning, civilian versus military stress in scientific research, or restriction or flow of scientific information across institutional and national borders) may have very important systemic consequences. But this choice depends only marginally on what goes on within, or is influenced by, the professional groups. It depends decisively on what goes on within the political elite; and it is influenced by elite goals, by elite perception of internal and international successes and failures, and by the elite's quest for self-preservation. The greatest influence of scientists and science, David Holloway has remarked, "may have been felt in ways that are most difficult to discern: in the changing of social values through technological progress, and in the erosion of the party's legitimacy as a result of the disjunction between political authority and scientific truth" (David Holloway, "Scientific Truth and Political Authority in the Soviet Union," *Government and Opposition*, 5, no. 3 [Summer 1970], 366). But this is a different matter, very long range in its implications, which in our view will have no political effects in the short and intermediate run as long as science advisers are basically the presenters of contingency plans, without the right or the ability to take a stand on the moral and social consequences of proposals under consideration.

Table 11. *Growth of scientific cadres in the Soviet Union*

Item	1950	1960	1970	1974	1977
Scientific institutions	3,447	4,196	5,182	5,275	n. a.
Of those, research institutes and their branches	1,157	1,728	2,525	2,778	n. a.
Number of "scientific workers" (1960 = 100)	45.8	100	261.9	330.2	361.2

Source: Narodnoe khoziaistvo SSSR v 1960 g. (Moscow: Statistika, 1961), p. 784; Narodnoe khoziaistvo SSSR v 1974 g. (Moscow: Statistika, 1975), p. 144; Narodnoe khoziaistvo SSSR v 1977 g. (Moscow: Statistika, 1978), p. 93; Narodnoe khoziaistvo SSSR v 1972 g. (Moscow: Statistika, 1973), p. 129; SSSR v tsifrakh v 1974 g. (Moscow: Statistika, 1975), p. 71.

Most importantly, professionals of all branches who are not a part of the public administration serve as never before the function of consultants and experts in the formulation of the goals and especially the means of Soviet policies in all areas and spheres. This observation holds true not only with regard to the central authorities but also in local administration. The outside professionals perform their role through direct participation in the decision-making bodies, consultative positions with the executive organizations, preparation of position papers, participation in permanent and ad hoc advisory councils, and so forth.[38] One visible expression of their increased role is the major expansion of units which conduct applied research in all branches of science.

Third, the Brezhnev era has witnessed a qualitative expansion of professionalism in the areas of management and administration. Soviet administration has upgraded decisively the place of education and managerial qualifications in recruitment. The promotion system takes into much greater account than ever before the importance of the formal qualifications of the candidate, his specialized experience, and particularly his service in the organization in which he is promoted. There has been a very significant decline in horizontal mobility within the Soviet administration which favors political and generalized nonprofessional personal traits. I can think of only a few examples where individuals promoted to minister and deputy minister of the central government and, increasingly, of the republican governments have not come from within the organization in question or from a post directly below the one to which

[38]For an excellent analysis of the role of scientists and particularly social scientists in Soviet administration and politics, see Richard B. Remnek, ed., *Social Scientists and Policy Making in the USSR* (New York: Praeger, 1977). See also Holloway, "Scientific Truth and Political Authority in the Soviet Union," pp. 345–67; and Erik Hoffman, "Technology, Values, and Political Power in the Soviet Union: Do Computers Matter?" in Frederic J. Fleron, Jr., ed., *Technology and Communist Culture* (New York: Praeger, 1977), pp. 397–436.

they were promoted. This process obviously works to increase the attachment of individuals to their organizations, to strengthen their sense of separateness and of institutional identity.

Even the terminology used in Soviet communications and literature about administration attests to an upgrading of the role of professional management. The difference is stressed between *rukovodstvo* and *upravlenie*, leadership and management, the former being a kind of art which emphasizes personal characteristics, the latter being an impersonal science.[39] More direct steps in the upgrading of management included the reinforcement of the one-man top managerial prerogatives in the enterprises and the abolition in hundreds of key enterprises of the Central Committee's watchdog, the *partorg*, which had shared the top managerial prerogatives and responsibilities. In addition, on the model of the higher party school, there was created with big fanfare and major expenditures the higher managerial school to prepare cadres of qualified and professional top managers for all spheres of administration. Numerous newly created special courses, permanent seminars, and workshops for higher managers have served the function of upgrading the qualifications and developing the managerial ethics and habits of working administrators at all levels.

Fourth, the entire process of professionalization within the Soviet administration is also taking place in that part of it which can be described as political administration proper, that is, the party apparatus. Increasingly, conditions of recruitment and promotion within the party apparatus resemble those in general or specialized administrations. Not only do professional qualifications, education (Table 12), and managerial experience play an increasingly important role in recruitment, but also the promotion to positions of high influence is meant to maximize the professional element.

An overwhelming majority of those promoted during the Brezhnev period to the positions of *obkom* party secretary and first secretary had first served a long apprenticeship in the same region and advanced gradually and regularly through the organization they were then appointed to lead. Horizontal mobility and transfers have declined significantly. Moreover, the advancement of these secretaries has involved more often a pattern where the frequency of crossovers between line and staff positions increased. Most typically, the advancement to line positions, including the most political positions of the first and second secretary, occurred after service in staff positions in spheres which are con-

---

[39]There is a growing Soviet literature on the nature of professionalism and the role of the professional in management and leadership (*upravlenie i rukovodstvo*). Naturally, much of the discussion centers on the role of the engineer, the key professional in Soviet society. For example, one book goes to great lengths to dispel the idea that an engineer is simply an official and tries to establish his professionalism as the main prerequisite of his conduct in office (I. S. Mangutov, *Inzhener—sotsiologo-ekonomicheskii ocherk* [Moscow: Sovetskaia Rossiia, 1973]; see especially chap. 4, "Office or Profession? Technical Specialist or Manager?").

Table 12. *Education of party secretaries on various levels*[a]

Position	Higher education (%)	Middle education (%)
Secretaries of counties, cities, okrugs		
1947	12.7	33.4
1957	28.1	15.3
1967	91.1	2.6
1977	99.3	0.1
Secretaries of provinces, krais, *republics*		
1947	41.3	29.4
1957	86.8	5.6
1967	97.6	1.0
1977	99.5	0.4

[a] The trouble with these figures is that the category "higher education" includes also the Higher Party School and the Academy of Social Sciences. My own estimate is that for higher education proper the figure for the county and city levels is closer to 75 percent and for the provinces and republics closer to 85 percent. The most meaningful official figure is that over 70 percent of the secretaries on provincial and republican levels and 60 percent on county and city levels were specialist-professionals in the national economy. Incidentally, the figures for the leading cadres of the executive committees of the soviets are very similar (for the data, see *Partiinaia zhizn'*, no. 21 [November 1977], p. 40, and *Spravochnik partiinogo rabotnika, 1977* [Moscow: Gospolitizdat, 1977], pp. 463, 469–70). Another noteworthy figure comes from a study of the party apparatus of twenty-seven cities and counties according to which more than 90 percent of the *apparatchiki* worked at their specialties directly in the national economy for at least four years (*Voprosy raboty KPSS s kadrami na sovremennom etape* [Moscow: Mysl', 1976], p. 159).

sidered central to the profile of the organization's specific geographic units.

Training in the higher and regional party schools no longer serves as a substitute for a purely professional education and career.[40] From being virtually the primary channel of recruitment and promotion, they have become avenues of social mobility for the secondary party cadres who

[40]The system of higher party education consists of the Academy of Social Sciences (AON) and the Higher Party School (VPSh) attached to the CC CPSU in Moscow, and fourteen republican and interprovince higher party schools. For the period 1971–5, 1,642 persons graduated from VPSh, 8,506 from the republican and interprovince higher party schools, and 28,400 graduated from the whole system of higher party education including the correspondence VPSh. About half of those admitted to the VPSh are such high-ranking party *apparatchiki* as heads and deputy heads of *obkoms*, secretaries of *gorkoms* and *raikoms*, and chairmen and deputy chairmen of *gorispolkoms* and *raiispolkoms*. Of the graduates of the VPSh, 80 percent are recommended for posts of similar or higher rank (D. M. Kukin, ed., *Voprosy raboty KPSS s kadrami na sovremennom etape* [Moscow: Mysl', 1976], pp. 229–42).

failed to enter normal institutions of higher learning or for late starters who earned a professional degree only at midcareer.[41] If the decline in the role of these party schools has been frequently noted, less seldom has there been remarked another important fact concerning them, namely, the increased professionalization of the party schools themselves. It is my distinct impression that the curriculum, the style and substance of education at the higher party school (VPSh) and the Academy of Social Sciences (AON) attached to the Central Committee have shifted in the Brezhnev era in the direction of more practical, practice-oriented, and "scientific" subjects; they are less doctrinaire and ideological in the strictest sense of the word.[42] The evidence for this is primarily indirect, glimpses from the recent publications for VPSh and AON which are composed for the most part by the faculty and graduate students of these institutions. The themes and substance of these writings exhibit less concern with party history and abstract ideological subjects and more with field studies, "scientific management," practical tasks of the party, and the like.

The altered stress in party apparatus work can be detected even in its most ideological aspect – propaganda. In the past, "scientific" propaganda meant simply the propaganda of Marxism-Leninism. Today it means more often propaganda that is "scientifically" conducted and propaganda of the "scientific" organization of labor. Moreover, continuous efforts are being made to "scienticize" the organizational party work itself, to establish for it some objectivized and modern standards and procedures which can be tested "objectively" and managed "scientifically" and efficiently. However pathetic at times, these efforts are symptomatic of the mood of the party apparatus.[43]

[41]I am far from underestimating the role of VPSh and AON in training party cadres. As of 1977, 46 percent of all party secretaries of counties and cities and 41 percent of provinces and republics were graduates of those schools (*Partiinaia zhizn'*, 1977, no. 21 [November], p. 40). The point is, however, that in a majority of cases the party schools provide the second education for their participants. It is noteworthy that the party schools provide an avenue of mobility into party cadres especially for candidates of worker and peasant origin. In the 1970s, these constituted 75 percent of those sent from Moldavia to the AON and 90 percent of those sent to the VPSh (Kukin, ed., *Voprosy raboty KPSS*, p. 157).

[42]For an evaluation of the changing nature of party education, see William E. Griffith, "Communist Cadre Training: Source, Indication and Reflection of Political Liberalization and Change," Center for International Studies, Massachusetts Institute of Technology, paper no. A/69–14 (1971). For an informative discussion of party education, see *Partiinoe stroitel'stvo*, 4th ed. (Moscow: Gospolitizdat, 1976), chaps. 7 and 8.

[43]Several Soviet authors discussing party activity assert explicitly that the "scientific approach" is a completely new phenomenon in party work. See, for example, G. Shitarev, *Leninskii stil' v rabote i normy partiinoi zhizni* (Moscow: Mysl', 1969), p. 97; V. V. Ostriakov, *Konkretnye sotsiologicheskie issledovaniia v partiinoi rabote* (Khabarovsk, 1969), p. 3. This assertion encountered criticism, of course, because it denigrates the party's past activities and minimizes the implicit "scientism" of Leninism itself. For the criticism, see V. A. Kadeikin, ed., *Voprosy vnutripartiinoi zhizni i rukovodiashchei deiatel'nosti KPSS na sovremennom etape* (Moscow: Mysl',

The party apparatus is *the* political bureaucracy of the Soviet Union, but increasingly it defines its key political role as the direction and coordination of management in all spheres. In so doing, it pays greater attention than ever before to its own professionalism in the field of management.

Fifth, the broader background and underpinning of the evolving professionalization in Soviet society are provided by the theorists and theories of two new concepts in Soviet ideology: the "scientific-technological revolution" (NTR) and the "scientific management of society" (NUO). It goes beyond the scope of this work to discuss these two concepts and their increasing significance for Soviet practice in any detail. We wish only to mention them briefly in the context of our discussion of professionalization.

The concepts NTR and NUO assumed during the Brezhnev period a central place in Soviet ideology. The literature on them is already large and growing by leaps.[44] Far from being confined to a narrow group of specialized and highly esoteric journals, the two concepts appear in popular writings, in party pronouncements, in the speeches of the leaders. The process of mutual adjustment between these two concepts and Marxist-Leninist doctrine affects the latter just as much as the former.

The explanation of the widespread and rapid acceptance of these two concepts is at least partly rooted in Soviet tradition and ideology. The Soviets have always placed extraordinary stress on the leading role of technology in social change and always nurtured a strong cult of technology. Moreover, they have always claimed to possess the key to a scientific management of society and social processes through their adherence to the theory of "scientific socialism." They have always looked askance at "spontaneity." The two concepts reinforce these "natural" tendencies, but in the process they have begun to infuse them with new meaning.

The old cult of technology centered on the means of production, on inanimate objects. The new concepts supplement this focus with a cult of scientism in shaping and managing social-economic and political relations. They proclaim that the optimally effective and profitable ways of managing society should not be equated with the existence of socialist social relations and planning. These are said to provide only propitious conditions for high effectiveness which, however, will not be achieved automatically. The realization of those conditions requires profound understanding, training, and effort which entails the upgrading of the role of science, management of technology and organization; the develop-

1974), p. 82; V. M. Sikorskii, *KPSS na etape razvitogo sotsialisma* (Minsk: Izd. BGU, 1975), p. 145. Yet even those who criticize this assertion make it clear that they consider the "scientific approach" of today to be qualitatively different from the past, particularly in its reliance on empirical social research.

[44]For a review of recent Soviet literature on NTR, see the series of bibliographical essays entitled "Sotsial'no-filosofskie problemy nauchno-tekhnicheskoi revoliutsii (issledovaniia 1971–5 g.,")", *Voprosy filosofii*, 1976, no. 2, 37–53. In the growing Western literature on the Soviet perception of NTR and NUO, I find especially useful the work by Erik Hoffmann and Robbin Laird, *In Quest of Progress: Soviet Perspectives on Advanced Society* (forthcoming).

ment of "scientific methods"; and professionalism in all spheres of leadership and management.

Robbin Laird commented on the functions of the concept of scientific-technological revolution as follows:

> The collective leadership has used the concept of the STR [NTR] as one of the main conceptual modalities for orienting Soviet society towards a developed state of socialism. Domestically, the STR is perceived to be a major component in the transformation of the economic basis of developed socialist society. Internationally, the forces of science and technology (which are universal in character) are becoming a basis both for competition and collaboration with the outside world.
>
> For scientific and technical elites the concept of a STR legitimizes their desire to participate in the direction or guidance of Soviet society in the process of creating a developed socialist society. The concept of the STR increases the salience both of the roles of the scientist, as policy participant and as leading element in initiating technical possibilities, and of the role of the organizational innovator in concretizing technological options.[45]

The Brezhnev era signifies a major step in the transition from the revolutionary ethos of Leninism, from the leadership ethos of Stalinism, from the populist ethos of Khrushchevism to a professional-administrative ethos.[46] The growth of professionalization in the Soviet political process and the institutionalization of Soviet politics and administrations are positively correlated. Increased institutionalization combined with popular apathy in "high politics" and the relatively tempered growth of popular participation in "low politics" provides one of the bases for Soviet stability in the Brezhnev era.

Social and political mobility

Of all the social processes in the Soviet Union there is one that provides the crucial safety valve against discontent and a key basis for the positive identification of various social strata with the regime. It is the process of

[45]Robbin Laird, "The Scientific-Technological Revolution and Soviet Ideology," unpublished paper, pp. 1–2.

[46]On the new administrative-professional ethos, see Peter H. Solomon, Jr., "A New Soviet Administrative Ethos – Examples from Crime Prevention," paper prepared for the Northeastern Slavic Conference of the AAASS, Montreal, Quebec, 5–8 May 1971. For a review of the development of professionalism in the same area, see also Peter H. Juviler, "Crime Prevention: The End of Ideology?" paper for Workshop on Politics and Social Change in the USSR, APSA, Washington, D.C., 7 September 1972. For the same process in the legal profession, see Robert Sharlet, "Soviet Legal Policy Making" in Harry M. Johnson, ed., *Social System and Legal Process* (San Francisco: Jossey-Bass, 1978), pp. 209–29. For an interesting affirmation of professionalism and the administrative ethos among Soviet managers, see the essay by Anatolii Tintenkov, *Delovoi chelovek* (Leningrad: Lenizdat, 1977). The title in English would be "The Businessman."

social mobility in general and, more especially, the process of political mobility. There would appear to be no necessary relation between the degree of democracy within a given political system and the openness of recruitment into its elites and subelites. If one measures the openness of recruitment by the ease of access of diverse social strata to positions of political and administrative power, that is to say, by intra- and intergenerational political and administrative mobility, one must consider a highly democratic society like Great Britain to possess a fairly closed, nondemocratic system of recruitment and, by contrast, a highly authoritarian society such as the Soviet Union to display the most open, democratic system of recruitment of all developed societies.

Soviet society exhibits vast inequalities of class, status, and power. The revolutionary Bolshevik egalitarian ideal is farther from fulfillment today than it was in the first postrevolutionary decade. These inequalities remain firmly embedded in the fabric of Soviet society, despite the appreciable rise in living standards and improvement in the level of political participation during the post-Stalinist and especially the Brezhnev periods.[47] Yet they should not distract attention from the high degree of political mobility within the society, that is to say, from the degree to which the elite system is open, accessible to recruitment from the lower strata of the society.[48]

The original Bolshevik elite came from the intelligentsia or middle class. From the 1930s and especially from the Great Purge until today, however, the overwhelming majority of the national Soviet leadership as well as the leading officials of the various functional bureaucracies are working class in origin. This holds especially true for officials on all levels of the most exclusive and powerful bureaucracy, the party apparatus, as Table 13 illustrates. In this respect the present and the past are differentiated by the type of mobility that has brought individuals of working-class origin into the elites. In the past it was partly intergenerational mobility but to a large extent also intragenerational mobility; today it is primarily or predominantly intergenerational mobility.

To say it differently, those individuals who entered the elite in the late 1930s, 1940s, or even 1950s were very often not only of working-class origin but had actually engaged in physical labor in their youth. Those individuals who entered the elite more recently may still derive predominantly from working-class origins, but their own social position prior to joining the political world was much less frequently that of worker or

[47]A growing number of major studies address the questions of equality and privilege in the Soviet Union. By far the best is Alastair McAuley, *Economic Welfare in the Soviet Union: Poverty, Living Standards, and Inequality* (Madison: University of Wisconsin Press, 1979). Other studies include Mervyn Matthews, *Class and Society in Soviet Russia* (New York: Walker, 1972) and *Privilege in the Soviet Union* (London: George Allen and Unwin, 1978); and Walter D. Connor, *Socialism, Politics, and Equality* (New York: Columbia University Press, 1979).

[48]For a detailed Soviet discussion of this process, see N. M. Katuntseva, *Opyt SSSR po podgotovke intelligentsii iz rabochikh i krest'ian* (Moscow: Mysl', 1977).

Table 13. *Social origin of leading Soviet cadres, 1956–66*

Cadres	No.	% of worker and peasant origin
Top party and state leaders (Politburo, Secretariat, Presidium of Council of Ministers, Presidium of Supreme Soviet)	67	87
Central Committee apparatus	48	73
Council of Ministers	107	76
Provincial and republican party-state leaders	276	82
Key economic managers	185	72
Key military commanders	65	74

Source: Calculated on the basis of the author's personal files. The two major official sources of data on the social origins of Soviet high officials – *Deputaty Verkhovnogo Soveta SSSR, Piatoi sozyv* (Moscow: Izd. Izvestiia, 1958) and *Deputaty Verkhovnogo Soveta SSSR, Shestoi sozyv* (Moscow: Izd. Izvestiia, 1962) – provide the following picture: Of 581 officials listed in those sources, data concerning social origin are provided for 364 individuals (62.6 percent). Of these, 344 officials (94.5 percent) are listed as being of worker or peasant origin.

peasant.[49] The decline in intragenerational mobility reflects the changes which have taken place in the typical lifestyle pattern of educationally mobile working-class youth in Russia in the last few decades, especially with the advent of mass middle education.

The openness of recruitment into Soviet political and administrative elites and subelites results in part from deliberate policies and in part from the functioning of spontaneous social processes. First of all, it can occur only in an ideological atmosphere that encourages the advance-

[49]In his report to the Twenty-fourth Party Congress, Brezhnev declared, "More than 80 percent of the present secretaries of central committees of the union republican parties, of the *kraikom*s and the provincial party committees, of the chairmen of the republican Council of Ministers, of the chairmen of the *krai* and provincial executive committees of the soviets, and about 70 percent of ministers and chairmen of state committees of the USSR Council of Ministers began their active life as workers or peasants" (XXIV s'ezd *Kommunisticheskoi Partii Sovetskogo Soiuza. Stenograficheskii otchet*, 1 [Moscow: Gospolitizdat, 1971], 124). Brezhnev is speaking here about close to one thousand top officials of the party-state. The figures seem somewhat high for the intragenerational mobility suggested by Brezhnev but fit very well my own calculations for intergenerational mobility.
   Other Soviet figures concerning research into the social origin of selected units of the party apparatus seem more realistic. According to a study in 1974–5 of the party apparatus in twenty-nine cities and counties of the RSFSR, Ukraine, Belorussia, Uzbekistan, Moldavia, Latvia, and Tadzhikistan, 82.6 percent of the *apparatchiki* were of worker and peasant origin and, of those, 56.3 percent were at the beginning of their working life workers and peasants themselves (*Voprosy raboty KPSS s kadrami na sovremennom etape* [Moscow: Mysl', 1976], p. 152).

ment of individuals of working-class origin into the elites and subelites. The official Soviet ideology with its symbolic cult of the working classes creates a propitious environment which supports the aspirations of working-class individuals to enter the elite and propitious conditions for their competition with individuals of other social origins.

Second, the dominant working-class origin of the Soviet elites is widely publicized in the Soviet Union precisely because it is ideologically attractive to Soviet rulers and because it confirms the claim that Soviet authority is derived from the people. This too encourages individuals of working-class origin to advance into the elite. Studies of mobility in Western countries have reinforced the axiom that people, as a rule, strive primarily for what they consider attainable and avoid what they consider, rightly or wrongly, unattainable.[50]

Third, the easiest means to recruit individuals of nonworking-class origin into the elites would obviously be to coopt members of the families of the elites and subelites themselves. Such cooptation, however, is officially and strenuously discouraged at all levels of the administrative ladder. Party policy was and remains directed against it for fear of populating the functional bureaucracies and geographical regions with family cliques whose personal loyalties would resist the penetration and supervision of superior authority and create a diffusion of central power. Party policy vigorously encourages recruitment into elites and subelites from families of party members and discourages it from families of elite members.

Fourth, the main precondition of recruitment into elites and subelites is educational achievement, and education constitutes the main channel of entrance. As many studies have shown, the higher educational process in the Soviet Union favors groups of nonworking-class origin, despite official efforts to the contrary. One discerns the discriminatory class element in Soviet higher education, however, only when one examines the relative group representation of various classes in the student body and especially among graduates of the various Soviet institutions of higher learning. But from the point of view of the availability of working-class candidates for recruitment into the elite, the absolute pool of Soviet graduates of working-class origin is so large as to make irrelevant the relative class representation among the graduates.

Fifth and finally, a crucial factor in the advance of working-class individuals into the elites and subelites is on the one hand the attractiveness of this type of career for these individuals and on the other hand the pronounced reluctance of individuals of professional and "upper class"

---

[50]It is known, for example, that for a long time and as recently as the 1960s even such privileged American minority groups as Jews did not apply for some jobs, for example in large Wall Street law firms, because they believed they would have no chance of being accepted. At the same time the study of those firms showed that they were much more ready to accept Jewish lawyers than they themselves believed. If the study is correct, misperceptions of this kind reinforce the exclusion of minorities or disadvantaged from higher status positions through the manipulation of their aspirations.

origin (with the notable exception of the military elite) to embark on a road which would lead them directly to such careers. This is especially true with regard to the political elite in the strict sense of the word, the party apparatus.[51] Were this not the case, one would suspect more obstacles in the path of advancement by working-class individuals.

The degree to which the children of professional and especially elite families are disinclined to choose a political career is striking. A number of reasons may account for such reluctance in addition to the previously mentioned official discouragement of the practice. In the case of individuals from professional families, the attraction of their parents' profession, whether doctor, engineer, or scientist, may be of overwhelming importance. In the case of individuals from elite and subelite families, the force of the negative example of their parents' careers combined with the relative ease of their own advance into the "free" professions or arts or diplomacy thanks to family backing may be crucial.

Parents for their part want their children to have a "better" future than an administrative or political career, the pitfalls and difficulties of which they know so well. They consider it one of the perquisites of office to be able to direct their children along different, attractive, high-status paths. The children, for their part, have an opportunity to observe the tedium, insecurity, and extreme hard work associated with their parents' careers. While taking for granted and even regarding as hereditary the privileges of status, they are at the same time drawn to other high-status careers.[52]

By contrast, ambitious individuals of working-class origin face very stiff competition from better-prepared and better-backed children from professional and elite families in the striving for high-status, nonpolitical, and nonadministrative careers. Moreover, they perhaps idealize the realities of political and administrative careers while coveting the material benefits and power that accompany political elite status.

Whatever accounts for the pattern of recruitment, however, the high level of working-class intergenerational mobility into the political and administrative elites has highly significant consequences for the system. For the working classes, the high levels of social mobility in general and mobility into the elites in particular provide one of the most tangible and visible stakes in the system.

Probably there are few families in the Soviet Union where either the

---

[51]The children of the top leadership can serve as an interesting indicator. I was able to trace the education and/or the type of employment of forty-nine children of post-Stalin Politburo members. Without exception none was or is involved in politics in the strict sense. Science, arts, journalism, and diplomacy are the occupational pursuits of the overwhelming majority.

[52]A career in the political elite proper, in the party apparatus, requires a long period of apprenticeship, years of hard work in low positions before reaching a position of considerable power. Most importantly, it almost inevitably involves service in areas removed from large metropolitan centers. It is interesting to note, therefore, that in an overwhelming majority of known cases, the senior party *apparatchiki* were born or brought up in provincial towns.

nuclear or extended family has no member who can be identified with a ruling group, whether as an officer of the armed forces or the police, a manager of an enterprise, a functionary of the party, or an official of a ministry. There are probably few working-class families where parents fail to hold aspirations for their children's future career and with the reasonable expectation of realization. The Soviets have long provided opportunities of advancement for the working classes, a circumstance which could not fail to influence at least in part a positive identification with the regime and to dilute significantly any feelings of opposition to the regime.

There is yet another important sense in which upward mobility and the predominantly working-class origin of the leadership and elites bear on the legitimacy of the regime. Well before the revolution in Russia and to the present day, society has exhibited a pronounced "we" versus "they" syndrome. Usually we contrast "we," the simple "normal" people, with "they," the power holders on all levels, the *nachal'stvo*. Yet the reality and genuineness of this division may conceal a phenomenon no less real and for questions of stability even more significant. It is the sense of cultural community between "we" and "they," where the "we" represents the workingclasses. After all, they both come from the same social stuff; they share much the same life histories; they resemble one another culturally to an amazing degree, as witness their sentimentalism, basic nationalism, mannerisms, artistic and literary preferences, language, and all the rest. The world of privilege may separate "we" and "they" in Soviet society, but origin and culture unite them. It is in this sense and only in this sense that one should understand the observation of a Russian writer in a conversation with me, "Our power is a genuinely popular power" ("U nas nastoiashchaia narodnaia vlast' ").

To this point the discussion has focused on a number of processes which underlie the stability of the Soviet regime in the Brezhnev era. The argument can be further developed in two directions. First I propose to analyze the question of the legitimacy of the Soviet system, a central ingredient in our understanding of the nature and mechanism of its stability. Then I propose to demonstrate some of my propositions concerning stability by studying in more detail the most serious long-range domestic challenge to Soviet stability at the present time, the national problem.

9
SOVIET POLITICAL STABILITY AND THE QUESTION OF LEGITIMACY

The question of legitimacy lies at the heart of the problem of the stability of political regimes. In the long run it is the legitimacy of the political regime that helps to absorb the tensions and instability which arise from the gap between official and individual interpretations of reality as well as to endure scarcities, deprivations, frustrated aspirations, and short-comings of the political order. As one observer has written:

> The strengths or weaknesses of legitimating beliefs act upon the stability or instability of a political system.... Legitimacy, once established, serves as the most effective justification for the manner in which political power is exercised. It is the most effective argument against attempts to change the structure of the political system. On the other hand, challenges to governmental systems that question their legitimacy are the most damaging.[1]

A concept so central to our understanding of how political regimes survive or become transformed has of course elicited a variety of theoretical attempts to analyze its nature and especially its core meanings and mechanism. Putting aside for the moment reference to certain of these theories, I should like only to suggest that the core meaning of legitimacy at the very least contains the following elements:

It assumes the passive *compliance* and collaboration of the public;

This compliance is at least in part based on *normative* bonds with the political regime, that is, with symbols, values, sentiments of the political elite;

It assumes the active *support* of the basic decision-making groups;

It assumes a *consensus* on the question of the "rules of the game" among the power holders.

If the question of legitimation, its formation, persistence, or possible disintegration is central to the long-run fate of any political regime, it is especially so with regard to the Soviet regime. After all, the regime arose from a revolution guided by a small minority. It developed into a full-fledged dictatorship that for more than a decade waged against society a

[1] Claus Mueller, *The Politics of Communication: A Study in the Political Sociology of Language, Socialization, and Legitimation* (London: Oxford University Press, 1975), pp. 128–9.

183

social, economic, cultural, and political revolution from above. It utilized mass terror as an everyday instrument of societal management until just twenty-five years ago. Napoleon's famous words addressed to Metternich in 1813 sound very relevant in the Soviet context: "Your sovereigns, born to the throne, may suffer twenty defeats and still keep returning to their capitals. I cannot. I am an upstart soldier. My rule will not survive the day on which I have ceased being strong and feared."[2]

But how can one test whether a "revolutionary" regime which virtually abandons the policies of "revolution from above" in favor of "system management," which advances as its major goal the reproduction of existing societal relations, and which renounces mass terror as an instrument of rule has attained the degree of legitimacy denied it previously? Is the internal test of legitimacy discernible only when major challenges to the legitimizing principles surface in violence and explicit systemic opposition? More importantly, can the practical test of modern legitimacy be acquired only in competitive free elections? One author has remarked: "An analysis of society's legitimating principles is similar to a surgical probing for that which is unseen, but nevertheless crucial for survival."[3]

To begin with, a number of general factors work to favor the development of the Soviet political regime's legitimacy or make it possible to evaluate the major tendencies in this respect. First, although conducted by a minority, the Soviet revolution contained the minimal prerequisite for developing a legitimate regime (at least for the Russian majority), that is, *national authenticity*. It was at least possible, therefore, to tap the traditional sources of support and compliance which could have been initially very far removed from the professed goals of the revolutionary elite.

Second, the existence of a political system over a long period of time can, and usually does, contribute to the system's acceptance by the population. Moreover, this acceptance may not be simple habituation; political institutions can come to exert *normative* power merely by their prolonged existence. In this regard the Soviet political regime has obviously passed the point where generational changes of the population have created the aura of the "naturalness" of political institutions.

Third, an important factor in evaluating the development of legitimacy is the regime's survival of major systemic tests, points of crisis which place the question of the regime's legitimacy under enormous stress. Such a critical test for the Soviet Union was World War II. Whatever one thinks about how and why the Soviet Union survived World War II, its survival and victory provide a powerful (probably the most powerful) stimulus for the development of that legitimacy which in many respects came to fruition only after Stalin's death. Another such critical, although incomparably less costly, test was the most dangerous point of transition in any developed dictatorship, the death of the dicta-

---

[2] Quoted from Alexander Gerschenkron, *Continuity in History and Other Essays* (Cambridge, Mass.: Harvard University Press, 1968), p. 332.
[3] Mueller, *Politics of Communication*, p. 128.

tor and the succession. One has only to recall that fear of Soviet leaders about possible reactions to Stalin's death which underlay the notorious public appeal "not to panic." The Soviet political regime also weathered this test; by any standards it survived at a rather low cost. The last decade has marked the emergence of another such test, the first open appearance of dissent in the postwar Soviet Union; and one has to judge that the Soviet political regime has so far shown the ability to repress or neutralize it without major *internal* negative consequences for the stability of the system.

Without any doubt, the factors mentioned above bear witness to the stability of the Soviet political regime with regard to its survival. Yet in what sense do they attest to the manner and degree of legitimation? In what sense, especially, do they affirm the legitimation of the regime not only with regard to key crisis situations but in terms of everyday functioning and "normal," long-range policies. Legitimacy entails a relatively stable margin of operation as well as error, even if particular policies are recognized as contrary to the interests of major groups of citizens.

At this point the concept of legitimacy has to be examined more closely. Most important theories of legitimacy can be differentiated by what they regard as the key legitimizing principles of consent; but, with very few exceptions, they do not ask the question "whose consent," which is crucial for the establishment and especially for the sustenance of the legitimizing principles of a political regime, or they answer it in a nondifferentiated, generalized way, referring to the "population," "subjects," "citizens," and so forth.

Such a generalized understanding of legitimacy seems unsatisfactory, in my view, especially for the most promising level of social studies, the middle-range approaches. Instead, one should distinguish among: (1) *the substance of the legitimizing principles* of a particular political regime or type of regime; (2) *the identity and location* in the social structure of the strata or groups whose acceptance of these principles is crucial to the regime's legitimacy; (3) the *"mechanism"* by which the legitimization among these strata or groups is maintained; (4) *the level and type* of legitimacy attained and sustained by the political regime.

When discussing legitimacy, Huntington, Moore, and Lowenthal concentrate their analysis of the "mature" Soviet system on the first question, that is, on the substance of the legitimizing principles. I should like to start with the second question – "whose consent." The absolutely essential distinction that has to be made with regard to this question concerns the process of formation and sustenance and the extent of legitimization of the political regime among societal elites on the one hand and among large social strata, the "publics," on the other hand. We have already made the argument and will extend it here that the Soviet regime has evolved in the course of its development a base of mass, popular support. This base consists in a combination of the existence of a relatively large stratum which actively identifies with the system together with a public which recognizes as legitimate and "natural" the freedom of the regime to act on its behalf. Both of these elements are evident in the phenomenon of mass political participation in the Soviet Union which is central to an evaluation of the regime's popular legitimacy.

Depending on one's point of view, an analyst could maintain with equal justification that political participation in the Soviet Union is very high indeed or that it is almost nonexistent. The choice would depend first of all on the difference which we previously noted between "high politics" and "low politics"—where something close to popular apathy is the rule in the former and highly developed activity the rule in the latter. The choice would depend even more on how one defines participation itself. If one were to define "real," "authentic" participation as consisting of spontaneous actions alone, fully voluntary and largely uncoordinated from a center, one would describe the Soviet phenomenon as "penetration" of the society by the authorities, "mobilization" of the society by the party, "transmission belts," and other such terms; but one would not use the term participation.

If on the other hand one looked simply at the activities of Soviet citizens which are socially oriented, that is, are neither private nor occur within the family, and define them as participation, one would be struck by their relatively high level. Under Soviet conditions, moreover, where most social activities have political undertones because of the form in which they originate or because of the way in which the authorities view their effects, one would describe this phenomenon as "political participation."

The first way of looking at Soviet popular participation seems too restrictive in the age of mass movements, popular dictatorships, and inclusionary authoritarian regimes. It is also a very ethnocentric point of view which simply defines an idealized Tocquevillian participation which takes place in advanced liberal democracies as the only "real" and "authentic" one.

This is not to say that terms like "penetration," "mobilization," "controlled," and "coordinated" to describe Soviet participation are incorrect. Far from it, by and large they are very true. However, the question is whether, after granting all this, one may not argue that political participation in Soviet society performs for the system functions similar to those performed by the "authentic" participation in democratic societies. The point is that an absolute distinction between "authentic" and "controlled" participation shifts the focus of attention away from the functions and effects it has on the participants and the system to the manner in which it originates. Without being diverted by definitional and terminological distinctions, it is exactly the functions of participation which concern us here. And this, of course, is the most difficult matter. When writing on Soviet political participation, one is in the unenviable position of knowing what the participation is and being able to characterize its manifestations, but one is hard pressed to evaluate its effects on the participants and on the system.

Table 14. *Distribution of primary party organizations, 1976*

Organizations	Absolute numbers	% of Total
Total	390,387	100.0
Industry and construction	101,472	26.0
State and collective farms	48,022	12.3
Commerce	14,488	3.7
Educational institutions	67,446	17.3
Scientific institutions	6,018	1.5
Cultural institutions	5,280	1.4
Medical institutions	16,147	4.1
Administrative institutions (from central to county level)	65,060	16.7
Others	66,454	17.0

Source: Spravochnik partiinogo rabotnika, 1977 (Moscow: Gospolitizdat, 1977), pp. 455–6; *Spravochnik sekretaria pervichnoi partiinoi organizatsii* (Moscow: Gospolitizdat, 1977), pp. 353–4.

It is relatively easy to present a comprehensive balance sheet of the basic forms and manifestations of Soviet popular participation which engage impressive numbers of citizens in various kinds of activities. To begin with party organization, in the year 1978 (the most recent for which we have complete data) the Communist party had in its ranks 16,380,000 regular members of whom 658,000 were candidate members.[4] By way of comparison, in 1964 (July) the party included 11,500,000, that is to say, it grew in the Brezhnev era by 42.4 percent.[5] Russian nationals constitute 60.6 percent of the membership as against 53.3 percent of the population. The number of women in the party has now reached 4,106,000 or 25.1 percent of the membership. In the entire party there are only 489 persons left who entered the party before the revolution and 2,370 who entered during the revolution. If 11.9 percent of the total membership entered the party during World War II, more than one-third has entered in the last ten years.[6]

The party is composed of 390,387 primary party organizations, distributed as indicated in Table 14. It is directed by secretaries, bureaus, committees, and group organizers whose number and distribution according to level of activities are as shown in Table 15, while their profession or social position is shown in Table 16.

In the system of party education in 1976, some 19.6 million people participated on a regular basis, of whom 7.5 million were nonparty

[4] *Ezhegodnik BSE 1978* (Moscow: Sovetskaia Entsiklopediia, 1978), p. 12.
[5] *KPSS: Spravochnik* (Moscow: Gospolitizdat, 1965), p. 5.
[6] *Spravochnik partiinogo rabotnika, 1977* (Moscow: Gospolitizdat, 1977), pp. 449–72.

Table 15. *Membership in leading party organs, 1976*

Secretaries, members of bureaus and committees of	Number (× 1,000)	Workers and peasants (%)
Shop party organizations	1,472.5	43.0
party group leaders	529.7	
Primary party organizations	1,892.7	33.0
County, city, and *okrug* party committees	385.5	41.1
Provincial and republican party committees	30.2	30.2

Source: *Spravochnik partiinogo rabotnika, 1977* (Moscow: Gospolitizdat, 1977), pp. 458–9.

Table 16. *Professional composition of leading party organs, 1976*

Occupation	Members of city, county, and *okrug* committees	Members of provincial and republican committees
Workers and peasants	41.1	30.2
Managers	10.6	7.9
Technical specialists	7.3	2.3
Party *apparatchiki*	15.2	29.9
Soviet administrators	9.7	16.5
Scientific, cultural, educational, and medical personnel	6.6	5.3
Others	9.5	7.9

Source: *Spravochnik partiinogo rabotnika, 1977* (Moscow: Gospolitizdat, 1977), pp. 460–2; *Partiinoe stroitel'stvo* (Moscow: Gospolitizdat, 1976), p. 112.

members. In the system of Komsomol education there participated 6.5 million people and in the system of economic education 36.1 million people.[7] The cadres of propagandists included 2,221,000 persons of whom 4.8 percent were full-time party, trade union, and Komsomol workers, 12.9 percent were leaders of Soviet enterprises, 62.2 percent were specialists-professionals, and 12.7 percent were teachers, scientists, or professors.[8] In addition, there are active in the Soviet Union 3.7 million

[7] *Spravochnik partiinogo rabotnika, 1977*, p. 464; *Spravochnik sekretaria pervichnoi partiinoi organizatsii* (Moscow: Gospolitizdat, 1977), p. 356.
[8] *Spravochnik partiinogo rabotnika, 1977*, p. 465; *Spravochnik sekretaria pervichnoi partiinoi organizatsii*, p. 355.

agitators, 1.8 million of whom engage in regular brief presentations of political information, as well as 300,000 lecturers.[9]

The system of soviets includes 50,561 basic units to which there are elected as deputies 2,210,000 persons, of whom 56.1 percent are not party members. Among the deputies, workers and peasants constitute 67.7 percent of the total.[10] Within the soviets there are organized standing committees which are assigned specialized supervising tasks; over 70 percent of the deputies to the soviets are members of these advisory committees.

Soviet trade unions encompass over 107 million members and are organized into 688,600 primary organizations, 457,800 shop organizations, and 2,433,900 groups. They are led by 25,104 councils and committees.[11] The Communist youth organization, Komsomol, incorporates 34,826,000 members, organized into 1,779,000 primary organizations and 437,000 groups. Working youth constitute 57.3 percent.[12] About 7 million people are employed in the functions of so-called *druzhinniki*, the auxiliary militia. The function of so-called people's inspectors is performed by about 9 million.

In the countryside the most impressive new organization is the system of collective farm councils, which exists from the level of the county to the all-union level. In the 2,417 existing councils there are 125,000 representatives of collective farms, soviet and agricultural organizations, scientific institutes, and so forth; they include about 64,000 rank-and-file members of collective farms.[13] Countless other organizations, such as NOT (Scientific Organization of Labor) and VOIR (All-Union Association of Innovators and Rationalizers), unite virtually tens of millions of members and activate hundreds of thousands of citizens.

What do these figures mean? What can they tell us about the involvement of the citizen with the government? First of all, the figures, high as they are, should not mislead one into thinking that the majority of Soviet citizens participate even in "low politics" with intensity and regularity. In the Soviet Union, as in other countries, such participation is an exception, an occasional and probably a superficial act. Yet one should not ignore the fact that within each participatory category described there exists a stratum which participates regularly and more or less intensively. The active strata within categories partially overlap. Even so, overall, one has the impression that a significant percentage of Soviet citizens are involved more than occasionally in the participatory activities.

Second, the types of involvement or participation are not equally significant. Virtually everybody would agree that the act of running for (and serving in) the office of soviet deputy, especially on the all-union or republican level, has a high significance, a legitimizing and self-justify-

[9] *Spravochnik partiinogo rabotnika, 1977*, p. 465; *Spravochnik sekretaria pervichnoi partiinoi organizatsii*, p. 355.
[10] *Spravochnik partiinogo rabotnika, 1977*, pp. 465–9.
[11] *Ibid.*, pp. 470–1.
[12] *Ibid.*, pp. 471–2.
[13] *Pravda*, 11 March 1975.

Table 17. *Social position of party members, 1976–8*

Occupation	Maximum range	Minimum range
Workers	42.4	42.4
Peasants	13.4	13.4
Employees in nonexecutive or low executive positions	40.2	11.5
Total	96.0	67.3

Source: Ezhegodnik BSE 1978 (Moscow: Sovetskaia Entsiklopediia, 1978), p. 12; *Spravochnik partiinogo rabotnika, 1977* (Moscow: Gospolitizdat, 1977), pp. 451–2. The maximum range is based on the fact that executives proper constitute 8.9 percent of the category of employees who belong to the party, that is, 3.9 percent of the total party membership. The minimum range is based on the fact that about three-quarters of the employees who are members of the party belong to the category of technical and creative intelligentsia and were all counted as executives.

ing meaning. They would also agree that the act of voting is almost meaningless and involves little emotional, normative, or instrumental investment.

Of all forms of popular participation, clearly the most important is that of membership in the Communist party. The strong framework of party activity is the backbone of the entire participatory system and in the final analysis its control. What is involved in party membership from the point of view of participation? We are not speaking here about the party apparatus or the higher and middle levels of the party *aktiv* who form the elites and subelites of society and who are directly and constantly engaged in the business of government. We are referring to the lower *aktiv* and the rank-and-file members who pursue their primarily nonadministrative jobs and who (as Table 17 indicates) constitute the clear majority of the total party membership.[14]

Party membership involves both regular attendance at party unit meetings, where issues of high and low politics are discussed, and regular participation in party education, which has long-range ideological and direct practical purposes. But, most importantly, party membership involves what is called in party language "socio-political duties" ("sotsial'no-politicheskaia nagruzka"), the regular, relatively intensive, and burdensome task of working not only with other party members but

[14]Typical figures on the size of the party *aktiv* are provided for Riazan province by its First Secretary Priezhev. The party organization in the province has about 100,000 members, of whom about 30,000 belong to the "elected" *aktiv* (*vybornyi aktiv*). Of those, 2,289 are secretaries of primary organizations and 1,996 of shop organizations, 3,529 are party group organizers, 2,655 are members of provincial, city, and county committees (among these last, workers and peasants constitute 40 percent) (N. S. Priezhev, *Rabota s vybornym partiinym aktivom* [Moscow: Gospolitizdat, 1976], pp. 12–13).

primarily with nonparty members to whom the party's point of view must be represented. Each party member is given tasks by party unit leaders in accordance with qualifications, talents, and in part inclinations. Such tasks vary widely and may include a party engineer helping in his free time to improve a backward production unit, a party journalist giving a lecture and answering questions in a factory, a worker party member inspecting the local cafeteria and trying to improve the food. Theoretically, there should be no party member exempt from regular performance of such tasks, and in practice few party members fail to participate and remain in the party.

What we are attempting to convey here is that while party membership does not bestow power like an executive position in the administration, it does involve a feeling of belonging to an organization which has power and a feeling that to belong to it is a privilege. In other words, party membership develops a sense of having a stake in the system.

There can be no comparison between the "old" exclusive party and the "new" mass party in the Soviet Union. Yet something of the old party is still left in the new – the feeling of belonging to *the* ruling organization, to the institution which is responsible for the fate of the country. The theme that the CPSU is the ruling organization is so often repeated that some members at least must be persuaded.

If it is true that party membership does create allegiances to the system, it is important to discover what is the relative weight of party membership in Soviet society and its various strata. I will present here only some limited and approximate data which provide the most telling indices.[15] The party stratum constitutes 9.3 percent of the total adult population of the Soviet Union.[16] The figure for adult male population will be closer to 14 percent and for adult male urban population closer to 18 percent, or in Russia proper even somewhat higher. This means that in Soviet cities by the most conservative estimates there is a party member in more than one-quarter of all families.[17] According to one calculation, approximately 27 percent of all Soviet citizens over 30 years of age and with at least ten years of schooling are members of the party, approximately 44 percent of all males with these characteristics.[18] Almost one-third of the population which completed higher education belongs to the party.[19] Over one-third of the specialists

---

[15]The best Soviet source on the social and demographic structure of the Communist party is I. N. Iudin, *Sotsial'naia baza rosta KPSS* (Moscow: Gospolitizdat, 1973).

[16]*Spravochnik partiinogo rabotnika, 1977*, p. 449.

[17]This estimate is based on the most conservative assumption that all party members are married to other party members and that the distribution of party members between unmarried and married is similar to the population at large.

[18]Jerry F. Hough, *The Soviet Union and Social Science Theory* (Cambridge, Mass.: Harvard University Press, 1977), p. 123.

[19]*Narodnoe khoziaistvo SSSR v 1975 g.* (Moscow: Statistika, 1976), p. 36; *Spravochnik partiinogo rabotnika, 1977*, p. 452. Party representation within the scientific establishment (both "hard" and social sciences) is very high. As of 1977, 52.6

employed in the national economy who possess higher or middle education are party members.[20]

The picture that emerges is clearly not that of a miniscule, "elitist"
group lost in the sea of Soviet humanity, an image clearly inherited from
the first two decades of Soviet power and still shared by some observers
today. It is the existence of this strong, politicized, and involved stratum
which provides a buttress of the system's legitimacy within society.[21]

It would serve little purpose to explore in detail the participatory activities of Soviet citizens outside the party in such important areas as the
soviets and its commissions, people's inspection, and the *druzhinniki*.[22]
Without any risk one can assume that the intensity and regularity of the
activity of nonparty members in these spheres of participation are on the
average below those of party members.[23] Still, there are millions and
millions of citizen-activists who participate *nonprofessionally* in the daily
life of their communities and working places and interact with professional administrators, and an even greater number of citizens with whom
they interact and whom they influence.

It is the Soviet participatory system on the one hand and the closed
character of the information system and the massive directed propaganda effort on the other hand which account for the phenomenon of
which we are becoming more and more aware: the pervasiveness of the
official political culture in the civil society. There are not two political
cultures in the Soviet Union, one elite and the other popular. The dominant political culture is accepted by both the elites and a very large part
of the population.

One major confirmation of this tendency comes ironically from the
study and experience of association with those whom one would least
suspect of being influenced by the system: its proclaimed opponents.

percent of all those with a graduate degree belong to the party, among them 51
percent of those with a Candidate of Science degree and 65 percent of those with
a doctoral degree (*Partiinaia zhizn'*, 1977, no. 21 [November], p. 30).

[20]*Narodnoe khoziaistvo SSSR v 1975 g.*, p. 550; *Spravochnik partiinogo rabotnika*,
1977, p. 452. The key personnel of the main branches of industry belong almost
without exception to the party. For example, in the plants, factories, and units
which are subordinated to the Ministry of Instrument-making and Automation,
all the directors and more than 97 percent of the chief engineers are party
members (*Voprosy teorii i praktiki partiinogo stroitel'stva* [Moscow: Mysl', 1974],
p. 244).

[21]For a detailed and imaginative analysis of the role of the Soviet Communist
party in the Soviet social structure, see Jerry F. Hough, "Party Saturation in the
Soviet Union," in *The Soviet Union and Social Science Theory*, pp. 125–39.

[22]The most recent, excellent work on Soviet mass participation is the study by
Theodore H. Friedgut, *Political Participation in the USSR* (Princeton, N.J.: Princeton University Press, 1979).

[23]Aside from social satisfaction and public distinction one should not underestimate the importance of the sense of power which the supervision of other people
in the participatory activity provides. For example, some conversations that I
have had with Soviet students made me aware of the importance of the status
symbol represented by the impressive identity card carried by the members of
the Komsomol's voluntary militia, the *druzhinniki*.

Already several decades ago, Alex Inkeles and Raymond Bauer demonstrated on the basis of interviews with World War II and postwar emigrants from the Soviet Union how deeply these were influenced in basic thought processes by the official political culture.[24] Impressions of more recent observers and my own numerous encounters with the current emigration lead forcefully to similar conclusions. Most interesting is the existence of a strong dividing line between the emigration from East European Communist countries – most notably Poland, Hungary, and Czechoslovakia, the "unauthentic," nonindigenous Communist regimes, where official political culture differs significantly from popular and "highbrow" culture – and the emigration from the Soviet Union, where apparently they largely overlap.

The editor of a Russian émigré journal, Maria V. Rozanova, recently commented that Soviet émigrés find it more difficult to adjust and assimilate than those from other European Communist countries.[25] She proudly explains the phenomenon as a special quality of being Russian. I suspect that a deeper reason lies in the pervasiveness and unconscious acceptance of the official political culture among all strata of Soviet society. This acceptance is weakest among the intelligentsia, from whom most current émigrés come; one can only imagine how much stronger it must be among the working class. This is so not only because the adjustment to and acceptance of this culture have the highest externalized survival value through the lifespan of the individual. I suspect also that in the cumulative process of intergenerational persistence this acceptance has become internalized. It may well be that paternalistic and autocratic Russian traditions reinforce the process, but this theme remains beyond the scope of my discussion.

I have postulated that broad strata of the population exhibit a basic identification with the Soviet system as it is. This identification is to a dominant extent unconscious, amorphous, and unfocused. I am not suggesting, therefore, that it represents a commitment to the system, a readiness to invest in it one's effort. It is for the majority at most an acceptance which goes hand in hand with such actual behavior as mass absenteeism, lack of labor discipline, turnover at the workplace – all of which testify to dissatisfaction with many policies and, most importantly, to the overwhelmingly private concern of the working man with his own well-being. Such self-centered orientation may not be appropriate to collectivistic behavior and to the image which the directors of the system seek for their society. To the extent that it signifies political apathy, however, that it is concerned with the question "what do I get" rather than with abstract questions of justice and equality, and that it goes hand in hand with basic acceptance of the regime's political for-

[24]Alex Inkeles and Raymond A. Bauer, *The Soviet Citizen* (Cambridge, Mass.: Harvard University Press, 1959), p. 179.
[25]Maria V. Rozanova, "V krivom zerkale," *Sintaksis* (Paris), no. 4 (1979), pp. 32–45. Rozanova is the wife of Andrei Siniavskii.

mula, it signifies an acceptable legitimizing base with which the directors of the system have no reason to be dissatisfied.

The existing evidence about all types of regimes demonstrates the direct relationship between the level of legitimization of political regimes among groups and individuals and the degree of their participation in political activities and the management of societal affairs. Most problems of legitimization in modern societies, moreover, concern the legitimacy of some decision-making apparatus (rather than of individuals), that is, the *claims* of collective power centers to have the right to utilize physical resources for specific purposes and to have the right to demand a certain kind of consent behavior from particular individuals, collectivities, groups, and so on. The main question here is what is decisive in making these claims hold. I fully agree here with Arthur L. Stinchcombe's proposition that what is crucial is the legitimacy of these claims in the other centers of power and not their legitimacy among the people who must take the consequences.

> A legitimate right or authority is backed by a *nesting of reserve sources of power* set up in such a fashion that the power can always overcome opposition. The crucial function of *doctrines of legitimacy* and norms derived from them is to create a readiness in other centers of power to back up the actions of a person with a certain right. Doctrines of legitimacy serve the crucial function of setting up that nesting of powers which usually makes appeals to physical force unnecessary. . . . *A power is legitimate to the degree that, by virtue of the doctrines and norms by which it is justified, the power-holder can call upon sufficient other centers of power, as reserves in case of need, to make his power effective.* Some of these reserves may, or may not, be the popularity of a man's powers in public opinion or the acceptance of a doctrine of legitimacy of his powers among subordinates. The doctrine of legitimacy limits a power insofar as the exercise of the power is dependent on its being backed up, for this backing will be available only on terms accepted in other centers of power.[26]

Experience of Communist and authoritarian as well as democratic societies confirms in my opinion the centrality of the *elite dimension* of legitimization of power for the stability of political regimes with regard both to their survival and effectiveness. This is not to say that the "popular" dimension of legitimization is unimportant. What is proposed is merely that it is secondary to the elite dimension in many respects of which two are most important. First, as long as the claims of a particular power center or a particular elite are considered legitimate by other power centers, other elites, the low level of popular legitimacy or its decline do not endanger the stability of the political regime. Second, the decline in popular legitimacy, let alone a vocal or violent expression of

[26]Arthur L. Stinchcombe, *Constructing Social Theories* (New York: Harcourt, Brace and World, 1968), pp. 160–2.

such decline, is in itself more often than not preceded by and associated with the decline of elite legitimacy and very seldom with its increase.[27]

Max Weber, who is the source of much of the current theorizing about the legitimacy of power, seems to be ambivalent on this point. On the one hand, in his general definitions and theory, the legitimacy of power is considered in terms of the acceptance by subordinates of the rights of superiors to control them. But "in his concrete analyses of power phenomena, Weber was very little concerned with any estimations of the state of public opinion or of the ideological enthusiasm of subordinates and subjects. Rather, he analyzed the reactions of other centers of power."[28]

It is the elite dimension of legitimacy that seems to be more crucial from the point of view of the stability of the system and especially its potential for transformation. Most importantly, it is the decline or disintegration of elite legitimacy that either leads to the decline of mass legitimacy or transforms the lack of popular support into an effective popular opposition. The revolutions, revolts, and bloodless "springs" and "Octobers" in Eastern Europe were first and foremost basic crises of legitimacy within the Communist elites. By contrast, the changes in outlook of the Soviet elite that occurred in the post-Stalin era and their internal conflicts did not take the form of a basic crisis of legitimacy among a majority or a crucial segment of the elite.

The Soviet political elite is, of course, not a homogeneous body; it joins varied interests, diverse outlooks and sympathies. During times of internal crisis and severe stress it tends to divide. Yet one may suggest that a core set of attitudes and beliefs which are strong and persistent permeate the elite stratum as a whole. When speaking about groups and interests in Soviet society, there is an understandable tendency to concentrate on the parameters of conflict relationships among different groups. This, after all, is the ingredient of experience which gives groups their uniqueness and variety. But when considering the context of elite group activity in the Soviet Union, it seems important to suggest that it refers to a relationship among groups who fundamentally accept the system but who compete for advantages within it. These groups exist within consensus relationships of a more general and durable kind than their conflict relationships. The difference here between the Soviet politi-

---

[27]Both in Poland and Hungary the crisis of autumn 1956 developed first of all during the period 1953–6, primarily as a basic crisis of belief within the political and other elites. The divisions of views within the elites in that period concerned not simply policies but basic values, the question of justice and equity. Only at a later stage, when the censorship was already weakened and mass communication had become more possible, did the crisis acquire a mass dimension. This is also true about Czechoslovakia in spring 1968. For a good study of this pattern, see Madeleine Albright, "The Role of the Press in Political Change: Czechoslovakia 1968" (Ph.D. dissertation, Columbia University, 1976). The partial exception to this pattern may be found in the summer 1953 events in Germany. But exactly because of the relative unity of the GDR elites, the mass movement of 1953 never did create a full-fledged systemic crisis.
[28]Stinchcombe, *Constructing Social Theories*, p. 161, n. 6.

cal elite and Communist elites of Eastern Europe is as striking as the difference between the Soviet and East European societies.

The most important legitimizing principles and preferences of the Soviet political regime which, it is suggested, are shared by diverse elites include:

> Opposition to a liberal-democratic political organization of society;
>
> The commitment to a one-party state and to the leading role of the party within the state;
>
> A deep-seated fear and mistrust of spontaneity in political and social behavior, which induce an interventionist psychology and stress the need of strong central government, of organization, of hierarchy, and of order;
>
> The cult of national unity and the condemnation of individuals and groups who threaten to impair that unity;
>
> Deep-seated nationalism and a great-power orientation which provides the major effective durable bond among the elites and between the elite and the masses;
>
> The commitment to a Soviet East European empire;
>
> The radical decline of the impulse to reshape society and a commitment to the basic structure which Soviet society has attained;
>
> The withering away of utopianism and a commitment to the rationalization of the system;
>
> The belief in and commitment to progress understood particularly in a highly material and technical way and combined with a technological and scientific ethos.

(All these and other shared beliefs and tendencies were discussed in some detail in Chapter 3 and need not be further elaborated.)

As was stressed before, the responsiveness of other centers of power is crucial for the legitimacy of the claims of power holders. We now turn to the question: What is the "mechanism" by which the legitimizing process is maintained? To express it differently, what are the *modes of integration* of norms and values which sustain the legitimization of claims among diverse functional and organizational segments of the elite, among its diverse institutions? I propose to employ two basic units of analysis: at some points the institutional orders such as the political, economic, military, and cultural in which the decision-making centers are located; and at other points specific organizations such as the party apparatus, economic administration, and so forth, or their functional subunits.

Much useful insight into the modes of integration is provided by Hans Gerth and C. Wright Mills in their *Character and Social Structure*, a work which has not been sufficiently appreciated. The relations of the units is constructed by them in terms of means-ends schemata which involve the dimension of power.[29] They identify four principal modes of integration:

---

[29]Hans Gerth and C. Wright Mills, *Character and Social Structure: The Psychology of Social Institutions* (New York: Harcourt, Brace, 1953), pp. 354–66.

Correspondence. When the integration of legitimizing values is achieved by the working out in several institutional orders of a common structural principle, which thus operates in a parallel way in each;

Coincidence. When different values, different structural principles or developments in various orders result in their combined effects in the same, often unforeseen, outcome of unity for the whole society;

Convergence. When two or more segments or values of diverse institutional orders coincide to the point of fusion, they become one institutional setup;

Coordination. When the integration is achieved by means of one or more institutional orders which become ascendant over other orders and direct them; thus other orders are regulated and managed by the ascendant order or orders.

The authors then add:

It should, of course, be understood that in any concrete social structure, we may well find mixtures of these four types of structural integration or structural change. The task is to search within and between institutional orders for points of correspondence and coincidence, for points of convergence and co-ordination, and to examine them in detail. The presence of one type does not exclude the possibility of others. We do not believe that there is any single or general rule governing the composition and unity of orders and spheres which holds for all societies. Reality is not often neat and orderly; it is the task of analysis to single out what is relevant to neat and orderly understanding.[30]

We propose to apply these four modes of integration to the Soviet Union. The most explicit case of *correspondence* among the diverse institutional orders of Soviet society with regard to legitimizing values is represented by the idea of hierarchy and organization. The basic legitimization of instituted conduct in each of these orders is very much the same—the subordination of the autonomous individual's free initiative for rational and moral self-determination to collective demands expressed by hierarchical structures between and within formal organizations. Thus the symbolic spheres of the various orders run in parallel or corresponding fashion.

The correspondence of the diverse orders, even assuming that they are relatively autonomous (and, as some students of Soviet society argue, they are becoming relatively more autonomous than in the past), is the outcome of processes in which all the significant orders develop in the direction of an integrated principle of planning, hierarchical subordination, and organization. (Another basic legitimation of instituted conduct in each of these orders which leads to a correspondent integrating princi-

---

[30]*Ibid.*, p. 366.

ple is represented by the idea of "mobilization," that is, the disposition of the resources calculated to bring forth the maximum expenditure of efforts and energy.)

In a provocative article, Zbigniew Brzezinski proposes that

> The Bolshevik revolution not only was not a break from the pre-dominant political tradition, but was, in historical perspective, an act of revitalized Restoration. The late Romanov period was a pe-riod of decay, of the gradual weakening of the hold of the state over society . . . and of internal loss of vitality within the top elite, not to speak of the autocrat's own personal weaknesses. The overthrow of that ruling elite brought to power a new group, much more vital, much more assertive, and imbued with a new sense of historical mission. The political result of the Bolshevik revolution was thus revitalized restoration of long dominant patterns.[31]

Brzezinski lists eight central elements of the prerevolutionary tradition which, he argues, are continued in the postrevolutionary Russian experi-ence. It is notable that one element that is not mentioned, and in our opin-ion rightly so, has to do with the question of Great-Russian nationalism.

It is exactly in the interaction between the legitimizing idea of nation-alism on the one hand and the modernizing values propagated by the Soviet party-state on the other hand that the integration of legitimizing values through *coincidence* occurs. Such a legitimization (as Hans Rog-ger argues convincingly) was absent in tsarist Russia, where the forma-tion of a modern political center was already caught up in the contradic-tion between the existing traditional state and modern nationalism.

Speaking about nationalism as a *political phenomenon*, that is, about convictions, attitudes, or movements, Rogger proposes that in sharp con-trast to the West, where in the nineteenth century nationalism became a major factor of political loyalty and social integration, the dilemma of prerevolutionary Russian nationalism consisted in

> that it could only with difficulty, if at all, view the tsarist state as the embodiment of the national purpose, as the necessary instru-ment and expression of national goals and values, while the state, for its part, looked upon every autonomous expression of national-ism with fear and suspicion. . . . This was the case not only when the state was confronted by versions of nationalism formulated by radicals or liberals but even, and here the dilemma is most strik-ingly expressed, when it was defined by those who were most vocal in their support of the established order.[32]

Russia did not experience the Western evolution whereby nationalism transcended vague sentiment and intellectual abstraction, where it came

---

[31]Zbigniew Brzezinski, "Soviet Politics: From the Future to the Past?" in Paul Cocks, Robert V. Daniels, Nancy Whittier Heer, eds., *The Dynamics of Soviet Politics* (Cambridge, Mass.: Harvard University Press, 1976), p. 340.
[32]Hans Rogger, "Nationalism and the State: A Russian Dilemma," *Comparative Studies in Society and History*, 4, no. 3 (April 1962), 253, 256.

to express substantial agreement about societal arrangements and had not only to accept but to affirm the state.

> Modern Russia did not develop a nationalism that was capable of reconciling important segments of Russian society to one another and to the state. In spite of the extraordinary preoccupation of Russian thought with the problem of national identity, culture or mission, nationalism as an ideology or political movement was plagued by contradictions and tensions that kept it from playing a decisive political or social role in the last century of the Empire's existence, that made its relationship with the state one of fateful ambivalence and caused it for the most part to remain a cultural and psychological rather than a political phenomenon.[33]

From the point of view of our discussion of legitimization through coincidental integration of diverse values, the lack of such legitimization in prerevolutionary Russia resulted from the defensive, static, nonmobilizational nature of the legitimizing values of the political (and religious) order, and of the expansive utopian, aspirational nature of the values dominant in the cultural order. The Russian philosopher of history Vladimir Solov'ev formulated the essence of the problem with great clarity: "The national question in Russia was no longer one of national survival or existence; it now concerned the purpose of that existence and its ethical justification."[34]

In the Soviet Union the dynamic, mobilizational, collectivistic, and future-goal-oriented nature of the legitimizing values of the political and economic orders coincided and became integrated with the inherited values of national identity latent in the cultural order and were reinforced by and fused with the new sense of historical mission propagated by the party's doctrine. The stage of Soviet system building coincided with modern nation building; the "mature" stage of Soviet system management coincides with Soviet global-power aspirations.

The integration of legitimizing values through *convergence* occurs, often in unplanned ways, when values of different institutional orders, of diverse organizational or functional segments of elites, coincide to the point of fusion. In my opinion a possible example of such convergence in the Soviet case may be represented by the "defense–heavy industry complex." This complex constitutes above anything else a value, belief, and policy orientation that cuts across the organizational and functional lines of the elite establishment.

Tradition and the present status and ambitions of the Soviet Union in the international arena combine to make the weight of the interests of the defense complex very great. The lingering insecurities of the past and the new insecurities of the present, the commitment to hold at any price

---

[33]*Ibid.*, pp. 253–4.
[34]V. S. Solov'ev, *Sobranie sochinenii*, 5 (St. Petersburg, 1883–97), i, paraphrased in *ibid.*, p. 263.

a potentially explosive empire in Eastern Europe, and the pride of accomplishment in the defense–heavy industry area (by far the single most important area of real attainment by the Soviet regime) guarantees the prominence of the defense sector. The fact that the defense sector is the most modern societal sector, that it concentrates more scientific, technical, and managerial talent and more labor skill than all other sectors combined, adds to its weight. Defense-oriented education is incredibly highly weighted within the general educational establishment. The theme of patriotic nationalism is relatively more effective than the traditional ideological theme in mobilizing support. It exploits the past and present glories of the defense complex. Many former associates or "graduates" of the defense complex, who today retain their association, are present within all segments of the elite and leadership. That is, they are to be found among the generalist politicians and the planners, among the ideologues and leaders of the scientific establishment, among the leading regime writers and famous plant directors. All these factors combine to make the weight of the interests of the defense complex much greater than the weight of the representation of the military–heavy industry elite segments in the leadership institutions and policy-making bodies. Even more important, they also serve to instill the values and beliefs of this "complex" among diverse institutional orders, institutions, and elite segments. The effect is to create a policy orientation, one apparently embedded now in the political culture, which responds almost automatically to the defense–heavy industrial needs on a first-priority basis.

Integration through *coordination* is achieved "by the subordination of several orders to the regulation of direction management of other orders." Integration through coordination by the Soviet political order finds many expressions of which I shall mention two. First, one of its major and most visible expressions is the high level of what Etzioni calls "political intensity,"[35] that is, the ratio of societal activities which are fully or partially controlled politically as compared to those which are not. What probably is the most important dimension of political intensity has to do with the relations between the political and economic spheres, political and economic goals.

A chief goal of the Soviet political regime throughout its history has been economic, especially industrial, growth at the most rapid attainable rate and regardless of the social cost. Lenin's dictum "politics cannot but have primacy over economics" meant initially that economic growth must be correlated with and subordinated to social change, to socialist transformation of society. In Stalinist Russia it came basically to mean that economic growth was too important a goal of the system to be left to managers, technocrats, and economists. Another Soviet slogan which viewed "politics as condensed economics" expressed rather better the dominance of economic growth among the systemic goals of the regime.

[35]Amitai Etzioni, *The Active Society: A Theory of Societal and Political Processes* (New York: Free Press, 1968), p. 670.

The issues of economic growth still permeate the entire Soviet political decision-making process. Economic growth (and the military power that is to proceed from it) constitutes the chief indicator of the political leadership's success and failure. The economic development desired and later achieved has constituted the historical justification of both the social transformation decreed by the leadership and the political order established by it.

Yet while *economic growth* is a decisive systemic goal, *economic criteria* for deciding what, how fast, and at what cost it should develop is not a primary consideration. The key characteristic of the Soviet economic sphere and economic growth is its lack of *economic* self-generating, self-regulating, and adjusting features. To run at all, let alone to perform well, it has required and still requires an enormous political edifice of regulation, supervision, and coordination. In fact, the Soviet political system as we know it was developed largely to run the economy and was shaped by running the economy in line with the chosen growth strategy.

The second and most important expression of the directly coordinative role of the political sphere is the proposition already mentioned: The symbolic sphere of all orders is centrally managed and controlled from the political sphere, and no rival claims to legitimate symbolic communications are recognized. Building on Shils's definition of a societal center, Eisenstadt makes a contrast in this sense, it seems, between the weak and strong societal center: "A 'strong' center is one which enjoys access to other centers and can derive its legitimation from them—either by monopolizing and controlling them or by some more autonomous interdependence with them—and can accordingly command some commitment both within, but also beyond, its own specific sphere."[36]

At this point the discussion will shift from concentration on institutional orders as units of analysis to consideration of the coordinative role of specific political institutions, in this case the Soviet Communist party and especially the party bureaucracy.

The Communist Party of the Soviet Union performs many functions in the system. The party executives, those who act in the name of the party or within the party, play numerous occupational and political roles. In fact one should differentiate among many Communist parties within the Soviet Union. There is the symbolic party, the "ideal-type" image of which serves to legitimize the system and to provide the base of political continuity in a society that changes its social and economic shape. There is the mass party, which unifies in its ranks millions of members in thousands of primary organizations and is a major agency of political socialization in Soviet society. There is the integrative party, which incorporates in its ranks the dominant segments of managers and experts of all spheres of social endeavor and provides a channel of their recruitment into the elite strata. There is the mobilization party, which through the control and

[36]S. N. Eisenstadt, ed., *Political Sociology: A Reader* (New York: Basic Books, 1971), p. 18.

coordination of secondary mass organizations and through the direct activity of its own rank-and-file membership tries through participation to induce mass support for the policies of the regime and seeks to preempt organized and spontaneous expressions of discontent and opposition.

The most important of all the parties, however, and the one that provides the basis for speaking about the party as a ruling party in other than traditional terms, is the party as a public administration. This role of the party is performed by its professional bureaucracy, the "party apparatus." The party apparatus is a public administration in exactly the same sense as are other Soviet bureaucracies. Its core of functionaries performs managerial functions of organization, supervision, coordination, and the like that executives in every Soviet bureaucracy perform. There are, however, three specific attributes of its functioning as a public administration that set the party apparatus apart from the other bureaucracies:

1. The executives in other bureaucracies perform their management functions within and with regard to their own organization and with regard to the resources which their organizations control or are responsible for. In so doing, of course, they enter unavoidably into relations with executives of other hierarchies and organizations and represent their own organizations in those relations; yet this is only a corollary of their basic role. The managerial activities of the executives of the party apparatus are directed not toward their own organization, but outward, toward other Soviet bureaucracies. It is an organization in which each member is an executive whose object of management is located outside his own organization and consists of the managerial strata of other organizations.

2. Each Soviet public administration has a more or less clearly delineated area of activity, sphere of specialization, that is, it participates in what can be described as a managerial division of labor within the society at large. Each segment or unit of the party apparatus too is specialized and oriented toward a specific sphere of activity, be it education, agriculture, finance, or military affairs. But the party apparatus as an administrative organization does not participate in the sphere-focused, overall division of managerial labor. This overall *external* division of labor is replicated in the *internal* division of labor of the party bureaucracy. This unique characteristic of the party apparatus as a whole as compared to other organizations finds an expression below the central level of authority in the offices of the first secretaries, whose responsibilities are, at least nominally, limited only by the territorial boundaries of their respective jurisdictions but not by functional boundaries.

3. The party apparatus is a public administration whose main societal function is political. This is a proposition which is probably more misunderstood and misconstrued than any other proposition about the politics of the Soviet bureaucracy. It is a truism to say that every bureaucracy, not only the Soviet one, is engaged in political activity, and not only within its organizations but also in external relations. Its key societal function, however, is not political; it is to produce or to distribute goods, to defend the country, to combat deviant social behavior, and so

on. It is also true that functionaries of the party apparatus engage extensively in activities that to a large extent duplicate the specific activities of the executives of other bureaucracies with whom they work. What does it mean then when we say that it is a political bureaucracy, that its determining function is political? In whatever way the political function is defined, whether it consists in deciding "who gets what, when, and how," or in coordinating and integrating the specialized activities within society, the essential element is that it deals with the selection among conflicting views in the decision making *for* society.

Jerry Hough has very aptly remarked that in the matter of whose views should prevail, there seldom are rational-technical answers.

> Rather, these are prime examples of "the political question" – the question on which men with different specialized knowledge and different interests come into conflict, the question on which deference to the specialists may have harmful direct or indirect consequences for others in the society. In the Soviet Union as elsewhere, it is conflicts on questions such as these which constitute the essential "political conflicts," and the Party leadership still attempts to ensure that as much as possible they are resolved within the Party organs. . . .
>
> When Party spokesmen insist (as they have with vehemence) that Party officials concentrate their attention on "political questions," they are referring to "political questions" as defined in the last paragraph, not simply to ideological-organizational questions.[37]

The position of the party apparatus in the Soviet power structure has undergone historically a number of changes. From being one of the several channels through which Stalin communicated his commands, the party apparatus achieved in the years following Khrushchev's defeat of the "anti-party group" in 1957 an institutional preeminence greater than ever before or since. In the last years of his rule Khrushchev became increasingly the spokesman not only of the party apparatus but of his own ambition to gain unrestricted leadership. After the ousted leader's efforts to reorganize and reorient the party apparatus were quickly reversed, no significant changes took place in its structure and in its official prerogatives during the entire post-Khrushchev decade. With the restoration of central ministries and the stress on vertical control within the specialized bureaucracies, with the development of new organizational economic structures (associations, for example), with the continuation of an institutional balance within the top leadership, the uniquely favorable conditions for primacy of the party apparatus no more obtain; yet its centrality in the Soviet political process remains in our opinion unquestionable.

[37]Jerry F. Hough, "The Soviet State, Party and Public Administration after Khrushchev," paper prepared for the conference on The Soviet Union after Khrushchev: Implications for Arms Control, 1964–67, Columbia University, 1–5 April 1967, pp. 28–9.

As the power position of the party apparatus underwent a number of historical changes, so also did its major functions within the Soviet administrative structure. As Stinchcombe remarks, functions of specific institutions "may become irrelevant because the tensions to which they respond disappear. Usually they disappear because some other structure is handling or preventing the tensions. . . . But also, many tensions disappear through natural processes. . . . In short, a functional structure may be functional for a function that no longer needs to be served, which no longer operates as a selective force for new structures."[38] From its initial function of "red" versus "expert," the party apparatus switched its major function within the Soviet administrative structure, as Reinhard Bendix suggested, [39] to that of "mobilization" and later to "policy guidance." It is sometimes suggested, however, that the core role of the party organs and party bureaucracy, especially on the territorial level, has switched or is switching from policy guidance to policy brokerage – that is, to the role of an intermediary who brings together, and mediates between, specialized officials in what is basically *their* decision making.

We have too few data and it is too early to say whether in fact such transformation of the core role of the party apparatus from policy guidance to the brokerage role is really taking place. There are a number of qualifications and reservations that come to mind. The broker's image, if at all valid, would refer primarily to the economic field, but in our opinion it is totally unacceptable in other fields, such as culture. The image that the party tries to project to the public and in its own internal communications is exactly that of policy guidance not of brokerage; therefore, the image of brokerage is at most the depiction of a state of affairs that sometimes exists but not of the desired state of affairs. The whole image of the party-broker suggests or implies somehow a condition that is untrue about any bureaucratic hierarchy in the Soviet Union, namely, a neutrality. These reservations and objections notwithstanding, the party apparatus as a broker seems to describe a tendency in Soviet decision making for which examples can be provided. Moreover, it is a tendency which is not inconsistent with the general situation within the Soviet elite and leadership in the post-Khrushchev era.

The main weakness of this image of the party apparatus seems to be of a different nature and lies in its over-concentration on one dimension of the decision-making process and its neglect of a second dimension. The dimension of the decision-making process in which the party apparatus may indeed increasingly perform the broker's role concerns the selection from among conflicting and competing solutions that are defended by the officials of diverse specialized bureaucracies. Here, too, the party functionary's role is not as neutral and his preferences more weighty than the role of broker implies. Yet there seems to be a real decline in the activist role of the party apparatus in this dimension of decision making.

[38]Stinchcombe, *Constructing Social Theories*, pp. 92–3.
[39]Reinhard Bendix, *Work and Authority in Industry* (New York: Harper and Row Torchbook, 1959), pp. 447–8.

The decision-making process has, however, yet another dimension – not the selection from among a range of offered solutions but the delineation of the range, the limits of what are considered acceptable alternative solutions. The power to influence the agenda of decision making and to decide the range of solutions to be considered is a core political function in its broadest sense and with more direct and consequential repercussions for the direction of systemic change than the first dimension. And here, I propose, the role of the party apparatus is still dominant, its prerogative undiminished, its effectiveness not eroded. Indeed, with some hesitation, one may suggest that while in the Khrushchev period Soviet bureaucratic hierarchies had less operational autonomy than they have at present, the range of alternative solutions considered within the party, not only in the ideological and cultural but also in the internal economic spheres, was probably broader than at present.

In sum, the legitimacy of the Soviet system is conditioned by its longevity, by its withstanding the tests of major crises and shocks, by its identification with great-power nationalism which unifies the masses and the elites, by the successful symbiosis of the messianic doctrinal elements of Marxism-Leninism with this nationalism, by the increase in the number and weight of the strata in Soviet society which have a stake in the system and particularly in its activities, by the basic unity of its elites, and by the complex way in which the system is integrated. It is the development of this legitimacy that characterizes the new "mature" phase of Soviet authoritarianism and underlies its basic stability. I shall now turn to examine the question which has the greatest potential for undermining the stability. I shall analyze both why in my opinion the national problem in the Soviet Union has such great destabilizing potential and why until now the Soviet regime has been able to avoid its potentially explosive consequences.

10
SOVIET STABILITY AND
THE NATIONAL PROBLEM

Many contemporary nation-states are faced with the threat of a real or potential crisis of legitimacy and stability owing to the increasingly central problem of ethnic identity. Joseph Rothschild has written, "No society or political system is today immune from the burgeoning pressure of ethnic nationalism, with its possible legitimating or delegitimating effects. Communist and non-Communist, old and new, advanced and developing, centralistic and federalistic states must all respond to the pressures of this ascendant ideology."[1] This issue in the Soviet Union is potentially the most devastating for the state in its possible long-range consequences and presents the deepest challenge to the legitimacy of the regime.

The primary pressures which produced institutional and policy innovation in the post-Stalin era have not been the actual pressures from social groups or strata but changing material conditions in the society and changing political circumstances within the elite. In the future, tensions between political authority and social strata may generate politically significant pressures for change, but this is uncertain. In this respect, the widening cleavage between the two halves of Soviet society – the dominant Great Russians and the other nationalities – is by far the most important tension.[2]

The increasingly assertive and non-Russian ethnic nationalisms are directed not only against specific areas of what they see as discriminatory Soviet political, economic, demographic, and cultural policies, but against the very principle of Soviet federalism: the political and economic centralization of the Soviet party-state which concentrates decision making for the entire Soviet Union in Moscow, while retaining an administrative framework which safeguards the territorial boundaries and formal ethno-cultural institutions of non-Russian nationalities. There are many reasons why the nationality problem should be singled

---

[1] Joseph Rothschild, "Observations on Political Legitimacy in Contemporary Europe," *Political Science Quarterly*, 92, no. 3 (Fall 1977), 495.
[2] The most recent addition to the sparse literature on nationality management in the USSR is Jeremy R. Azrael, ed., *Soviet Nationality Policies and Practices* (New York: Praeger, 1978). See also Azrael, "Emergent Nationality Problems in the USSR," Rand Paper R-2172-AF (September 1977), and Gerhard Simon, "Nationalitätenpolitik: Immobilismus verdeckt ungelöste Konflikte," *Osteuropa*, 26, no. 8–9 (1976), 672–80; B. A. Osadczuk-Korab, "Grundtendenzen im multinationalen Reich," *Osteuropa*, 26, no. 6 (1976), 407–14.

out for attention from the point of view of its potential political significance for the future:

1. Its aggravation threatens the most potent, unifying, and systemic force within the Soviet society – great-power nationalism, which accounts primarily for the political stability of the Soviet state in the last thirty years as opposed to the instability of East European Communist regimes. As we have already mentioned elsewhere, it is the reinforcing combination of the Marxist-Leninist doctrine and great-power nationalism which constitutes the kernel of the Soviet ideology as a legitimizing and motivating force of elite action and popular support. In the case of the Great Russians, this combination is based on the solid foundation of recognition of the *Russian* substance of the *Soviet* great-power nationalism. In the case of other Soviet nations, it is predicated on the submergence, convertibility, or correspondence of their own ethnic identity with *Soviet* nationalism – a condition which is presently tenuous at best and whose further erosion strikes at the heart of the Soviet system.

2. The polarization of the Soviet peoples along ethnic lines is increasing faster than their identification with, and consciousness of, a new Soviet nationhood, and it is nourished both by tradition and by socioeconomic progress. The leadership's earlier hopes that ethnic nationalism would wither away in the "natural" process of Soviet development have not materialized.

It was an axiom of Soviet beliefs – and I am convinced they were genuine – that the process of Soviet socioeconomic development would lead to an accelerated process of the rapprochement of nations (*sblizhenie natsii*) which would in turn result in the harmonious blending (*sliianie natsii*) of all nationalities in a Soviet melting pot.[3] Soviet ideologues were as wrong in these expectations as were Western political scientists in their belief that development would diffuse the sentiment of ethnicity.

To the extent that ethnically non-Russian regions remain undeveloped and culturally peasant in nature, the depth of attachment to the traditional national culture with its religious context remains extraordinarily strong and resists with surprising force the subordination to Russian culture or submersion in the supranational concept and reality of Soviet nationhood (Table 18). To the extent that ethnically non-Russian regions were swept by the tide of modernization, they have developed a new type of intense, urban-centered ethnic identity, the new carriers and main representatives of which are to be located among the newly educated classes, the creative and managerial intelligentsia. The lack of development leads to the cultivation of old types of ethnic identity, therefore, while the process of development results in development of its new strains.[4]

---

[3] For very good expositions of this point of view, see N. Dzhandil'din, *Kommunizm i razvitie natsional'nykh otnoshenii* (Moscow: Mysl', 1964); G. S. Agadzhanian, *K voprosu o prirode i perspektivakh razvitiia sotsialisticheskikh natsii v SSSR* (Erevan: Aiastan, 1972); and G. E. Glezerman, *Klassy i natsii* (Moscow: Gospolitizdat, 1977).

[4] Identification with one's language is one of the most visible, durable, and impor-

Table 18. *Language identification among non-Russians, 1926, 1959, and 1970*

Group	1926 All population	1959 All population	1959 Those living within republican borders	1970 All population	1970 Those living within republican borders
Ukrainians	87.1	87.7	93.5	85.7	91.4
Belorussians	71.8	84.2	93.2	80.6	90.1
Lithuanians	46.9	97.8	99.2	97.9	99.5
Latvians	78.3	95.1	98.4	95.2	98.1
Estonians	88.4	95.2	99.3	95.5	99.2
Moldavians	92.3	95.2	98.2	95.0	97.7
Georgians	96.5	98.6	99.5	98.4	99.4
Armenians	92.4	89.9	99.2	91.4	99.8
Azerbaidzhani	93.8	97.6	98.1	98.2	98.9
Kazakhs	99.6	98.4	99.2	98.0	98.9
Uzbeks	99.1	98.4	98.6	98.6	98.9
Turkmen	97.3	98.9	99.5	98.9	99.3
Tadzhiks	98.3	98.1	99.3	98.5	99.4
Kirgiz	99.0	98.7	99.7	98.8	99.7

Source: V. I. Kozlov, *Natsional'nosti SSSR* (Moscow: Statistika, 1975), pp. 211-12.

3. The nationality problem and the danger of its intensification adds another dimension to, and greatly complicates, many of the administrative and political dilemmas which the party faces. Most important in this respect is the superimposition of the ethnic dimension over the party's dilemma in the field of economic organization. The need for greater economic effectiveness generates pressures for decentralization which in turn excites fears that the party will lose political control. As we shall see below, the need to improve Soviet economic performance, which is becoming a matter of overriding importance for the Soviet leadership, requires at the same time a more efficient and stricter centralization of command and disposition of resources on the macro-level, but especially a greater flexibility, freedom of command, decentralization of initiative, and prerogatives on the intermediate and micro-level of the economy. Even with regard to the Russian regions, this task is far from being easy

tant indices of ethnic identity (Table 18). From this linguistic point of view the ethnic identity of non-Russian Soviet nations which are organized in union republics seems very strong and shows no signs of significant decline. As a matter of fact in some respects it is stronger today than in the first decade of Soviet power. It is even more noteworthy that the identification with one's own language is stronger among the youth than among middle-aged generations.

and raises in its second aspect the specter of the diffusion of political power. But the multinational character of the Soviet state and the nationality problem multiplies the difficulties.

The centralization measures are apt to provoke and irritate the sensitivities of non-Russian ethnic groups, create dissatisfaction and resistance. The decentralizing measures are apt to upset the existing balance, to whet local aspirations and appetites for greater autonomy. The local native elites may use any newly gained prerogatives to circumvent and weaken Moscow's central control. In the case of Russian regions such weakening is considered dangerous enough as the constant struggle against *mestnichestvo* (localism) attests to. In the case of non-Russian regions the localism becomes a much more troublesome national self-assertiveness.

4. The concept and reality of Soviet federalism contains a potentially dangerous dualism: In theory and in practice it denies any but the slimmest margins of autonomy to the federated nationalities, but at the same time its symbolic institutions and administrative framework provide the base from which the struggle for national autonomy can be waged. Soviet nationality policy from its inception was characterized by a duality. On the one hand it granted to formed nations cultural autonomy, territorial integrity, and symbols of nationhood; on the other hand it insisted on the supremacy of the central state and government and strove for a state of affairs where national separateness and ethnic identity would ultimately wither away. One can find sources of this duality in the tension within the Marxist-Leninist ideology, between the accepted idea of the right of self-determination and the principle of equality of nations, and the as strongly embedded idea of the subordination of the national question to the goals of revolutionary development which are best served by supranational organization and centralization.[5]

In the course of Soviet development this dualism was never abandoned, and even at the height of the Stalinist russification effort the forms of autonomous national existence for the basic nations of the Soviet Union were preserved.[6] In the post-Stalin era they were even strengthened. The sensitivity of the issue is underlined by the fact that in the new constitution adopted in 1977 the basic and even secondary structure of

---

[5] This dualism of Soviet nationality policy is very well discussed by M. Dzhunusov in *Dve tendentsii sotsialisma v natsional'nykh otnosheniiakh* (Tashkent: Izd. Uzbekistan, 1975).

[6] The separate national existence of some nationalities, however, was forcibly liquidated. This fate, including deportation of whole nationality groups, befell the Crimean Tatars, the Kalmyks, the Chechens, the Ingush, the Balkars, and the Volga Germans, whose autonomous national organization was destroyed. Khrushchev remarked: "The Ukrainians avoided meeting this fate only because there were too many of them and there was no place to which to deport them" (N. S. Khrushchev, "Special Report to the 20th Congress of the CPSU," *The New Leader*, 1962, pp. 44–45).

Soviet federalism remains unchanged and the dualism of Soviet nationality policy preserved.[7]

The major consequence of this duality is that the russification effort of the central authorities, however strong, remains a hidden and unacknowledged undercurrent, while the symbolism of national autonomy for the basic national groups remains open, fully legal, and praised. The institutions of this autonomy, whatever their actual power (and even in this respect they should not be minimized) are very broad—they replicate almost the entire range of the central cultural and economic institutions. It is these institutions, as I will later show, which are administered by local indigenous elites and which provide a ready-made vehicle for those elites to fight for their autonomous national aspirations.

5. Ethnic identification and aspirations could, and to some extent today already do, bridge the social divisions of occupational interests and class distinctions. Moreover, already today they are the only example where the interests of one segment of the Soviet political elite coincide with a social stratum, and therefore the former may at times represent the latter. This representative function served by segments of the minority political elites for their native social groups is still very limited and tenuous, but in the eyes of the central, primarily Great Russian political elite, it is probably the most dangerous trend because in many respects it repeats the nationalist threats to them in Eastern Europe.

The Soviet Communist elite has so far been unable to design a program to meet the challenge of ethnic nationalism, that is one which could reverse the trend or respond positively to these national aspirations. By all accounts, it is precisely because of the lack of agreement on such a long-range program that the promulgation of the new Soviet constitution to replace the one of 1936 had been so often delayed prior to its final adoption in 1977. In the meantime the party holds the line, fighting against the tolerance often exhibited by native Communist cadres with regard to their own minorities, and hoping that the migration of Russians to minority republics (especially the central Asian and Baltic republics) will achieve what industrialization alone has been unable to do.[8]

The Soviet Union is almost the only state which after World War II has been able to thwart the successful global trend of national and ethnic self-assertiveness against central authority. The growing autonomous as-

---

[7] For a discussion of the nationality question in the new Soviet constitution, see R. G. Abdulatipov, *Konstitutsiia SSSR i natsional'nye otnosheniia na sovremennom etape* (Moscow: Mysl', 1978).

[8] One should note, incidentally, that the pattern of Russian immigration to the cities of Central Asia, which was very pronounced in the 1960s and early 1970s, has been dramatically reversed in two respects: first, the Russian immigration has visibly declined; second, the expansion of these cities now takes place predominantly through the rapid increase of the native population. The cities of Soviet Central Asia which in the 1960s were becoming more and more Russian will probably by the end of the 1980s have a higher percentage of indigenous populations than they had in the 1950s.

pirations of the minority peoples of the Soviet Union and of the minority segments of the political elite, however, may become at some time in the future the major factor contributing to change of the system. In any case, in the foreseeable future, the nationality problem and the attendant fear of the central elite and most other Great Russians for their power is one of the major brakes on the evolution of the Soviet system away from authoritarianism and on the innovative impulses of the Soviet political leadership.

What I have said demonstrates clearly that the multinational character of the Soviet Union poses potentially the most serious threat to the legitimacy of the Soviet state and to the stability of the Soviet regime. The question is why this potential threat has not until now become more of a reality, why the nationality problem has not become a real nationality crisis.

To be frank, we do not have a full answer to this question, and I have not found an answer to it in anything I have read on the subject written in the East or West. (Our detailed knowledge of local politics and local sentiments in the Soviet Union is severely limited.) I can only offer certain key elements of an answer that will explain in part the ability of the Soviet leadership to contain an incipient ethno-political crisis.

As we well know from the experience of many political regimes that have found themselves in a crisis of legitimacy, the worst possible error of their leaderships in meeting the crisis was a combination of bad timing and lack of moderation in reformatory or repressive measures. The political autopsies of such situations are often expressed in the formulas "too little, too late" or "too early, too much," or something similar. One may posit that the absence of acute crises in Soviet multinational relations reflects, first of all, the success of the central Soviet leadership in creating a proper balance, from the point of view of its goals, between repression and tolerance and flexibility as well as the preservation by this leadership of the "nerve," the will to succeed.

The balance of repression with tolerance and flexibility works out according to a quite clear formula: first, no concessions whatsoever where central issues are concerned and decisive and immediate repressive measures against any effort to undermine the system of nationality relations in the USSR; second, a relatively high degree of tolerance and flexibility on those issues contested between the central Russian authorities and the ethnic population or elites which are marginal and do not bear directly on the basic shape of the system.

One should not underestimate the effects of the ruthless and steady application of power on a massive scale, of an enormous and well-functioning repressive apparatus, of the prevention of open communications through strict censorship, especially when these are directed against relatively small nations. Yet when discussing the treatment of non-Russian nations in the Soviet Union we sometimes fall into the same trap which snares the Soviets when they discuss democracy in the West. The official Soviet position holds that Western democracy – which they call "formal," presumably to distinguish it from "real" – provides a number of superficial freedoms and privileges behind which lurks the reality of an absence of real freedom as witnessed by economic exploitation and inequality, racial discrimination, elitism, biased news, and so forth. The trap consists in the fact that they dismiss the "formal" democratic freedoms as without importance, just as if those freedoms provide the conditions of the seamier sides of life in the West and, more importantly, as if despite the reality of those seamier sides the "formal" freedoms do not have a crucial significance of their own.

When discussing the Soviet nationality problem we often argue very similarly. The freedoms afforded to non-Russian nations in the Soviet Union – territory, language, cultural heritage, symbols of statehood, indigenous elites – are clearly circumvented. Moreover, and more importantly, behind those freedoms and privileges lurks the reality of extreme centralization, where key political and economic decisions are being made not in the respective national centers but in faraway Moscow. Ergo, those freedoms are "formal"; they do not have a meaning; they are insignificant in themselves.

But in reality these freedoms, however inadequate and imperfect, are very important to the everyday life of the non-Russian peoples. They are crucial as the safety valve for their rising and unfulfilled national aspirations and as a basis for the containment of the national problem in the Soviet Union. It is those imperfect freedoms and the flexibility shown by the Soviet leadership in granting and administering them which provides the other side of the application of massive power and repressions and is at least of equal importance.

In addition to the combination of a broad application of power with flexibility in administering the national life of ethnically non-Russian regions, the crucial element in the Soviet political process which explains the leadership's ability to contain the nationality problem is the existence and development of indigenous elites in the basic ethnic regions. The Soviet leadership, in contrast to its own prerevolutionary past and to other modern empires, has been willing and able to allow or even foster the development of ethnically indigenous elites who have a stake in the system.

It is sometimes asserted that it is the Russians who rule the Soviet Union. This assertion in itself is not false, but the reality behind it is quite complex. Most importantly, if it is true that the Russians *rule* the Soviet Union, it is equally true that the indigenous ethnic elites to a varying but almost always significant degree *govern* their own regions.[9]

The union republics can be divided basically into three groups from the point of view of the role of ethnically indigenous elites and local leadership and administration. The first group would consist of fully self-administered republics and would include Georgia, Armenia, and

[9] On Russian presence in local elites, see Seweryn Bialer, "How Russians Rule Russia," *Problems of Communism*, 13, no. 5 (September-October 1964), 45–52.

Table 19. *Native cadres in national republics, 1976*

Institution	No.	% of indigenous cadres
Party Central Committee bureaus and Presidium of Council of Ministers of all national republics	252	75.8
Top party-state executive cadres in:		
Uzbekistan	176	76.0
Latvia	112	74.0
Georgia	134	94.0

Azerbaidzhan, and to a large extent also the Ukraine and Belorussia. The second group would be partly but significantly self-administered by ethnically indigenous elites and would include the middle Asian and Baltic republics. Only the third group, consisting of Kazakhstan and Moldavia, can be said to be administered primarily by a nonindigenous elite.[10]

The role of the ethnically indigenous leaders in the top decision-making bodies of all republics and in the key executive positions of a few selected republics is shown in Table 19. In almost every republic regardless of the degree of its self-administration, three top executive positions are almost invariably occupied by Russians. Two of these are so obvious as to require no comment, for they are the basic prerequisites of Russian domination: one is the head of the KGB, the secret police (sometimes also the minister of the interior, who directs the uniformed police);[11] the second is the commander of the military forces stationed within the borders of the republic. The third position, that of second secretary of the republican party organization, requires some clarification.

It is sometimes asserted in an exaggerated way that the second secretary is the Russian viceroy in the republic, the real mover and decision maker among native figureheads. It is asserted, moreover, that this pattern of a behind-the-scenes Russian gray eminence is repeated down the line of executive positions in the ministries and departments of the central committee, in the *obkom*s and *ispolkom*s, including even the *raikom*s and *raiispolkom*s.

Like all exaggerated statements, these assertions contain a solid element of truth: the second secretary is a foreign and artificial element in the republican body politic; his position is that of controller and watchdog. Many other Russian low-level officials in the republics, especially

[10]An exhaustive, encyclopedic study of the leading cadres in the Soviet republics is contained in Grey Hodnett's recent book, *Leadership in the Soviet National Republics: A Quantitative Study of Recruitment Policy* (Oakville, Ont.: Mosaic Press, 1978).

[11]The Ukrainian Republic is here an exception. The Ukrainian KGB chief, while a lifelong policeman (he entered KGB service in 1939), is a Ukrainian by nationality and served for a long period in various posts in the Ukraine.

when they serve as deputies to the native cadres, perform similar roles on their own respective levels of competence. That is to say, native elites are never left entirely on their own with only *outside* supervision; they are to an extent watched also from *inside*, and this watchdog role is performed primarily by Russian appointees. Yet it is wrong to assert that these Russian officials are actually the managers of the republics, behind-the-scenes substitutes for native figureheads. Such a conclusion is supported by a number of indicators, in addition to the impressions derived from an analysis of republican politics.

In the matter of controlling the republican political establishments from within, through Russian emissaries, two tendencies can be discerned. These two tendencies may seem at first to be contradictory, but in fact they condition one another. One tendency works toward a greater independence and influence of the republican leadership and elites, the other toward the increase in the weight assigned by the central leadership to the Russians occupying high offices in the republics.

The first tendency can be illustrated by a number of indicators. One such is the increased visibility and political stature of the indigenous top republican leaders. It is expressed, inter alia, by their increased access to and participation in the top decision-making bodies in Moscow.[12] Another indicator is the lack of growing visibility or the upgrading of the political status of the Russian republican emissaries. The Russian second secretaries of republics retain as in the past only the status of alternate members of the all union central committees, while the relative Russian representation in republican bureaus and central committees has not increased.

First and foremost among these indicators, however, is the upgrading of the quality of the top native personnel in all republics. (One indication of the development of local indigenous cadres is the increase in the percentage of scientific workers of non-Russian nationality in the total of scientific workers in almost every republic [Table 20].) As late as the early 1960s the ethnically indigenous occupants of positions in the republican party and government were people whose education was often limited to the higher or local party school, who offered no extensive managerial experience, and who had to rely on Russian "helpers" to conduct the business of government. Today, for the first time in Soviet history, all republics have at their disposal indigenous top-level personnel whose job qualifications do not differ substantially from their Russian counterparts inside and outside the republics. Today, for the first

---

[12]In the Khrushchev party Presidium of 1961 only one representative of the republics (Ukraine First Secretary Podgornyi) was a full member. Four were alternate members: the first secretaries of Uzbekistan, Belorussia, and Georgia and the prime minister of the Ukraine. In the Politburo of 1979 two are full members (first secretaries of the Ukraine Shcherbitskii and of Kazakhstan Kunaev) and three are alternate members (the first secretaries of Belorussia, Azerbaidzhan, and Uzbekistan). In the Central Committee of the CPSU the representation of the republican elites has increased in that same time by over 20 percent.

Table 20. *Percentage of non-Russian scientific workers in national republics, 1960 and 1973*

Republic	1960	1973
Ukraine	48.3	50.6
Belorussia	46.9	47.6
Latvia	65.4	56.1
Lithuania	83.6	85.9
Estonia	78.9	85.3
Georgia	83.8	83.6
Azerbaidzhan	64.6	72.9
Armenia	93.6	94.8
Kazakhstan	21.4	29.8
Uzbekistan	34.4	46.9
Turkmenistan	36.9	50.8
Tadzhikistan	33.8	39.6
Kirgizia	24.8	32.8

Source: Vysshee obrazovanie v SSSR (Moscow: Statistika, 1961), p. 215; *Vestnik statistiki*, 1974, no. 4, p. 93.

Table 21. *Education and occupation of leadership groups, 1956*

Members, party bureau and Presidium of Council of Ministers	Party education (%)	Professional education (%)	Primary occupation: % employed for any length of time in economic management
Baltic republics	77	23	23
Middle Asian republics	58	42	41
Transcaucasian republics	31	69	62
RSFSR	18	82	73

time, these republics can be administered without Russian participation and extensive help. (While at present the political and professional attributes of Russian and non-Russian leadership groups are very similar, they differed quite considerably in 1956, as Table 21 shows.)

It is the process of the formation of such native elites, of the political and social mobility that it represents, of the opportunity and satisfaction of indigenous cadres that it reflects, which forms the basis of the probably still strong commitment of these cadres to the existing system and a key element of the explanation for the stability of nationality relations in the past decade. At the same time, of course, this situation exacerbates the Soviet di-

Table 22. *Background of second secretaries of union republics, 1964 and 1976*

Experience	1964 (%)	1976 (%)
Higher technical education	21	100
Experience in propaganda work	70	7
Organizational-managerial experience	36	93
Service in Moscow CC apparatus	93	14
Service in high executive provincial posts	42	86

lemma for the future: Once such a plateau of mobility and competence has been achieved, the prospects that indigenous elites will press increasingly for greater autonomy from the central authority may rise sharply.

The second tendency – toward increase in the weight assigned by the central leadership to Russians in high republican office – shows itself primarily in the following indicators. As recently as the 1960s, the Russian personnel assigned to serve in the republican party and government were brought primarily from the outside and came without knowledge of the local language, organization, customs, and problems. At present an increasing and already predominant portion of Russian officials serving in positions *below* the top level are no longer outsiders. They have spent many years of service in the republics; they have advanced up the usual ladder of republican positions to the post they now occupy; they can be expected to be much more effective in both their control and managerial duties in the republican establishment.

But the most interesting permutation in the direction of increased effectiveness has occurred with regard to the top Russian emissary in the republics, the party second secretary. He is still invariably selected from outside the republic in which he is to serve – presumably to forestall the possibility that he will develop ties in the republican establishment which he is called upon to control in the name of the central authorities.[13] For the same reason, he is regularly returned from his republican post to Russia and replaced by a newcomer from Russia so that he has no time to develop such ties. What has changed drastically in comparison to the 1960s is the type of individual who is selected for the post of second secretary. Table 22 contrasts the profile of republican second secretaries in the mid-1960s and the late 1970s. As the table shows, the individual presently selected for the position of second republican secretary is far superior to his counterparts

[13]A rare exception, the present second secretary of the Ukraininan Central Committee, I. Z. Sokolov, while a Russian, is not an outsider. He spent his whole life working in the second largest (and most russified) Ukrainian city, Khar'kov, starting in 1950 as a foreman in its tractor factory and finishing in 1976 as first secretary of its Provincial Party Committee.

in the 1960s with regard to education, managerial experience, organizational background, and so on. His function in the 1960s was primarily that of an *ideological* watchdog for which his past experience prepared him; today he is more a *managerial* watchdog. This contrasting profile is a necessary prerequisite for dealing effectively with the new and altered republican native leadership and elites.

With some partial exceptions, which we shall identify later, the indigenous republican elites are not full partners of the Russians; they are, at most, limited partners. What is their dilemma and the source of the tension between them and the Russian leadership and elites? To the extent that they govern their own republics, their power is limited by the range of decisions left for the republics to make. They can maximize their power in four ways:

> By increasing their influence on central decision making through bargaining with the Russian authorities, that is, by greater and more effective access to the central government;
>
> By altering through implementation the policies adopted by the central authorities, that is, by effective bureaucratic politics;
>
> By increasing the range of decisions which are left to local authorities, that is, by greater republican autonomy;
>
> By advancing from positions of republican leadership to offices within the central leadership and elites, that is, by political mobility.

There is no doubt that the first way, bargaining with the central authorities on specific issues, is at the heart of local politics in the Soviet Union. The key question here, of course, is the availability of funds allocated to the republics from the central budget and the overall size of the republican budget.[14] With regard to such types of issues the republican leadership and elites seem to be fairly united in their pressure on the central authorities and probably enjoy even the backing of the Russian emissaries within the republics. It is difficult to devise a score of battles won and lost in this respect and to design a cumulative index of successes and failures; but one should keep in mind the basic limitations of this road to expansion of republican influence – almost every success by one republic in this respect is bought at the cost of another's failure; and in the all-union scale, therefore, there is probably a draw.

That this key political-economic issue of struggling for central funds and for the size of the local budget is primarily waged not against the central authorities but among the republics themselves points, incidentally, to another strength of the Soviet federal arrangement. As long as a strong central Russian authority exists, there will seldom be a unity of interests and views on economic issues among the republican elites (a unity which is much more likely, for example, in cultural matters).

[14]On the question of formation of the Soviet national and regional budgets, see M. K. Shermenev, ed., *Gosudarstvennyi biudzhet SSSR*, 2nd ed. (Moscow: Finansy, 1978).

There can be little doubt that the ethnically indigenous republican elites are engaged in bureaucratic politics through which they attempt in the process of implementation to change the directives of the central authorities. In so doing, however, they are hampered by the presence in their midst of the local Russian officials whom the central authorities press to oversee the implementation of their directives. Of much more importance, here the republican elites no longer represent a unified front within the republic. They are divided by their subregional and functional interests and points of view. Here the competition for available resources and funds is conducted within each republican elite, with the Russian emissaries and central authorities serving as arbiters. For this reason bureaucratic politics within the republics do not represent a *political* danger to the central authorities and are as manageable as local politics in the Russian region.

It should be clear that the two first ways of maximizing the powers of republican elites are at best very limited, both in what they can and do accomplish. It is the third way which directly addresses the central issue of the degree of national autonomy. And here the record of the Brezhnev period from the point of view of the republican elites is not very promising. In the initial post-Stalin period the rights of republics to organize their own areas had been considerably expanded both in the cultural and economic fields and even in the area of public order. Yet in the last fifteen years what we see is at best a stagnation of the republican prerogatives.[15] It should be stressed that this stagnation does not represent in socioeconomic matters, as counterposed to cultural matters, a discrimination against the ethnically non-Russian areas, but rather a general trend of the Brezhnev period to establish strict central control and to prevent a diffusion of power among all regions whether Russian or non-Russian.

In this situation the fourth way of maximizing the power of ethnically non-Russian elites–through political mobility to the center–becomes even more important. But here the record of the Brezhnev era is dismal. To say it simply, the road to the central establishment, with one exception which I shall discuss later, is closed to non-Russian elites. I do not wish to minimize the importance of coopting a few non-Russian leaders to the central Politburo, but it should be stressed that their executive responsibilities even in the Politburo are basically concerned with their own republics and not with matters of all-union concern or with all-union bureaucracies.

Not one position in the central party secretariat is occupied by a non-Russian. Only three non-Slavs serve within the central party apparatus, among over 150 top officials (department heads, deputy department

---

[15]One example of regress is the case of the Ministry of Internal Affairs. Under Khrushchev this ministry, which controls the uniformed police, was a republican ministry subject to full republican authority. Under Brezhnev it was transformed into a union-republican ministry with the authority concentrated in Moscow.

heads, section chiefs). Only three non-Slavs may be found in the all-union Council of Ministers, with its 97 offices. Less than 5 percent of 400 first deputy and deputy ministers of the central Soviet government are non-Slavs. There are three non-Slavs among the top 150 officials and commanders of the armed forces. There is one non-Slav among the top 20 officials of the Ministry of Foreign Affairs; and so on. The situation in this respect today is even worse than it was at the height of Stalin's rule.[16]

Of all the Soviet nations only the Russians have not been granted separate organizations and institutions to administer their party affairs, a sign, of course, not of discrimination against them but the reverse, of their privileged position. The Russians do not need a separate party organization, as do other Soviet nations, because they run the all-union party and its central establishment as their own fief. The creation by Russians of a separate organization for their own party would be a sign that they were abandoning discriminatory staffing procedures.

To close the road of advancement for non-Slavs into the central party and government elite and to circumvent the prerogatives and local autonomy of the republican elites are policies which guarantee the perpetuation of tension between Russian and non-Slav elites. Yet apparently the limited partnership which exists between Russian and non-Slav elites and the opportunities for mobility within the republics are as yet sufficient to help contain the nationality problem in its present, nonvirulent form.

It is often correctly stated that the Soviet Union is a country of over a hundred nationalities. But from the point of view of political significance and the unraveling ethnic identity problem, it is clear that their respective weights are very unequal. The Soviet Union can tolerate a great deal of resentment in the case of minor nationalities which do not have their own republics (for example, the Crimean Tatars) without major strains on the political system and its stability.

As Tables 23 and 24 suggest, the leadership would be much more sensitive and the repercussions for the system much greater in the case of a mass national movement or the disloyalty of indigenous elites in a union republic or a special group of republics. The Soviet leadership acknowledges the different weight of diverse areas by its differentiated treatment of republics with regard to the degree of direct Russian interference in their respective administrations. One has only to look at the example of the Transcaucasian republics. Their fully self-administered status reflects not only the impossibility of any alternative status given the very high ethnic homogeneity of the republican population and the further circum-

---

[16]Responsibility for the central, that is all-union apparatus, with its subordinate branches is handled in the top institutions in Moscow – the Politburo, the Secretariat, and the Presidium of the Council of Ministers – almost *exclusively* by Russians. With the expulsion in 1977 of Podgornyi, the chairman of the Supreme Soviet, and the retirement in 1978 of Mazurov, first deputy chairman of the Council of Ministers, the last two non-Russians left their positions of responsibility.

Table 23. *Distribution of Soviet population by nationalities, 1970 census (percent)*

Russians	53.4
Nationalities of union-republics	36.6
Other nationalities	10.0

Source: Calculated from *Narodnoe khoziaistvo SSSR v 1970 g.* (Moscow: Statistika, 1971), pp. 15–17.

Table 24. *Weight of non-Russian union republics in total Soviet production, 1972 (percent)*

Annual average of industrial personnel (1974)	36.8
Electro-energy	37.4
Oil	18.7
Natural gas	60.5
Coal	45.2
Iron ore	66.8
Pig iron	51.1
Steel	44.9
Rolled metal	45.4
Cement	39.9
Chemical fertilizers	52.6
Machine tools	50.7
Chemical equipment	49.0
Tractors	51.9
Locomotives	81.4
Agricultural machinery	46.4
Grain	45.6
Cotton	100.0
Potatoes	55.6
Vegetables	59.8
Sugar	77.1
Meat	48.9
Milk	46.7

Source: Calculated from *Narodnoe khoziaistvo SSSR v 1972 g.* (Moscow: Statistika, 1973), pp. 76–83; *Narodnoe khoziaistvo SSSR v 1974 g.* (Moscow: Statistika, 1975), p. 189.

Table 25. *Weight of the Ukraine
among non-Russian union republics,
1972 (percent)*

Population (Ukrainians)	46.1
Party membership (1977)	45.0
Annual average of	
industrial personnel (1974)	52.4
Production of:	
Electro-energy	49.5
Natural gas	50.2
Coal	71.2
Iron ore	85.9
Pig iron	91.4
Steel	87.3
Cement	45.1
Chemical fertilizers	37.4
Tractors	50.7
Locomotives	93.2
Chemical equipment	70.8
Agricultural machinery	53.7
Grain	42.5
Sugar	80.8
Potatoes	50.7
Vegetables	49.8
Meat	48.0
Milk	49.7

Source: Calculated from: *Narodnoe khoziaistvo SSSR v 1972 g.* (Moscow: Statistika,
1973), pp. 76–83; *Narodnoe khoziaistvo
SSSR v 1974 g.* (Moscow: Statistika,
1975), p. 189; *Narodnoe khoziaistvo SSSR
v 1977 g.* (Moscow: Statistika, 1978), p.
18; "KPSS v tsifrakh," *Partiinaia zhizn'*,
1977, no. 21 (November), p. 22.

stance that the local level of education and availability of specialists are
even higher than in Russia itself,[17] but also the appreciation of the political temperament of the local population and elites. Transcaucasia is a
tinderbox which requires special preference and flexibility.

Yet the key to the national question on the all-union scale, though not
the guarantee of its containment, rests with the Slavic republics and

[17]In 1972 the Great Russians constituted only 2.7 percent of the population of
Armenia, 8.5 percent of Georgia, and 10.0 percent of Azerbaidzhan (*Narodnoe
khoziaistvo SSSR v 1972 g.* [Moscow: Statistika, 1973], pp. 9, 18–21). In 1977 the
number of those with higher and middle education per 1,000 people employed in
the national economy of the RSFSR was 771, in Georgia 786, in Armenia 802
(*Narodnoe khoziaistvo SSSR v 1977 g.* [Moscow: Statistika, 1978], pp. 38–9).

particularly with the Ukraine, as Table 25 goes far to indicate. It is not surprising that the treatment of the Ukrainian managerial and technical intelligentsia and especially the political and administrative elite differs from that in all other republics. In one crucial respect it goes beyond that of even the other self-administered republics: Ukrainians are afforded the opportunity to advance in significant numbers into the central elite and to serve in important positions, both as representatives of the central authorities in the non-Slav republics and as officials of all-union central functional bureaucracies.

To demonstrate the presence of Ukrainians in positions of high importance in the central government, KGB, military, and party apparatus, I present the following list, which contains some of the offices occupied by Ukrainians in 1974 outside the borders of their own republic.

> N. V. Podgornyi, chairman, Supreme Soviet, USSR; D. S. Polianskii, first deputy prime minister, USSR; I. T. Novikov, deputy prime minister, USSR; N. A. Tikhonov, deputy prime minister, USSR; M. A. Lesechko, deputy prime minister, USSR; B. P. Bugaev, minister of civil aviation, USSR; I. P. Kazanets, minister of ferrous metallurgy, USSR; B. E. Shcherbina, minister of construction of oil and gas industry, USSR; P. S. Neporozhnii, minister of energy and electrification, USSR; E. S. Novoselov, minister of construction-machine building, USSR; E. P. Slavskii, minister of medium machine building (military equipment), USSR; G. A. Zhukov, chairman, state committee for cultural relations abroad; A. A. Bulgakov, chairman, state committee for professional-technical education; S. A. Skachkov, chairman, state committee for foreign economic relations; R. A. Rudenko, procurator general, USSR; V. N. Titov, first deputy head, Comecon; N. A. Shchelokov, minister of internal affairs, USSR; S. U. Tsvigun, first deputy chairman, KGB; V. I. Konotop, first secretary, Moscow *Obkom;* S. S. Avramenko, first secretary, Amur *Obkom;* I. A. Bondarenko, first secretary, Rostov *Obkom;* A. V. Georgev, first secretary, Altai *Obkom;* V. P. Demidenko, first secretary, North Kazakh *Obkom;* V. G. Kliuev, first secretary, *Ivanovo Obkom;* A. V. Kovalenko, first secretary, Orenburg *Obkom;* M. K. Krakhmalev, first secretary, Briansk *Obkom;* V. A. Liventsov, first secretary, Aktiubinsk *Obkom;* A. K. Chernyi, first secretary, Khabarovsk *Kraikom;* I. Kh. Yunak, first secretary, Tula *Obkom;* N. A. Belukha, second secretary, Latvian CP; A. A. Grechko, minister of defense, USSR; P. F. Batitskii, deputy minister of defense, commander-in-chief of air defense, USSR; K. S. Moskalenko, deputy minister of defense; I. G. Pavlovskii, deputy minister of defense, commander-in-chief, land forces; V. F. Tolubko, deputy minister of defense, commander-in-chief, strategic rocket forces; P. A. Belik, commander, Transbaikal Military District; S. E. Belonozhko, commander, Turkmen Military District; I. M. Voloshin, commander, Odessa Military District; Iu. A. Naumenko, commander, Volga Military District; I. M. Tretiak, commander, Belorussian

Military District; M. G. Khomulo, commander, Siberian Military District; P. N. Lashchenko, first deputy commander-in-chief, land forces.

Of course, this kind of "more equal than others" partnership with Ukrainian elites is facilitated by the racial identity and cultural affinity of Russians and Ukrainians[18] and by the high level of russification among groups of the Ukrainian intelligentsia. Moreover, this Russo-Ukrainian compact, by expanding the opportunities open to Ukrainian elites, enhances the prospects for Ukrainian commitment to the federal system as it exists, the prospect that they will not pursue autonomous aspirations. By so doing, it provides one of the bases for containment of the nationality problem in the Soviet Union.

Soviet leaders managed to contain the genuine problems they faced in the 1970s. While no deep systemic crisis emerged in any area, the very same problems retain their potential to disrupt and undermine the stability of the Soviet Union in the coming decade. The new leadership will face choices that are not only difficult in themselves but in some cases clearly unprecedented in post-Stalinist history. The coming succession, however unpredictable its consequences, will interrupt in all probability what has proved for ten years to be the visible drift and inertia of both internal and external Soviet policies. Disputes over central policy issues, both domestic and international, would already appear to divide the Soviet elite, although their dimensions, outlines, and partisans remain as yet dimly discernible. These disputes will now move to the foreground, and it is precisely around their resolution that the succession struggle will be fought in the 1980s and the new alignment of leadership and elites will emerge.

I now turn to consider these central issues, those of foreign policy in Part IV and those of domestic policy in Part V. My concern in Part IV is not to engage in the hazardous enterprise of identifying specific decisions that will have to be made or specific crises that may have to be addressed, but rather to provide a larger general context in which the specific can be understood. My primary goal is to attempt to elucidate in the case of foreign policy certain key Soviet perspectives on international

---

[18]In the massive propaganda of Slavic unity, and especially the unity of Great Russians and Ukrainians, there is even a strong racial undertone reinforcing the need and sources for such unity. One document proclaims, "The Russian, Ukrainian, and Belorussian peoples trace their origin to a single root – the ancient Rus' people who founded the early Rus' state, Kievan Rus' " (*Tezisy o 300-letiiu vossoedineniia Ukrainy s Rossiei (1654–1954 gg.)* [Moscow: Gospolitizdat, 1954], p. 5). This theme was repeated recently by the Ukrainian first secretary, V. Shcherbitskii (*Kommunist*, 1979, no. 1 [January], 24). The racial undertone is even stronger in the common use of the term "blood-related" (*edinokrovnyi*) with reference to Russian-Ukrainian ties (see, e.g., *Radyanska Ukraina*, 31 January 1979).

relations as they have evolved over the fifteen years of Brezhnev's rule in the writings and conversations of Soviet officials and specialists in international affairs. My concern in Part V is to locate and present the key issues of domestic policy which promise to exert increasingly insistent pressure for change of the system and which, in their interplay with factors of foreign policy, may seriously affect the seemingly durable stability of the last decade.

PART IV
SOVIET PERCEPTIONS
OF INTERNATIONAL AFFAIRS
AND TRENDS IN
SOVIET FOREIGN POLICY

American discourse on Soviet foreign policy more often than not duplicates and exploits the terminology and imagery of Nazi expansion in the period before World War II. Their use on the whole is misleading, for they derive less from a reasoned overview of the last fifteen years of Soviet foreign policy, a serious evaluation of the place of international issues in overall Soviet policy making, than from an emotional and interested response to specific events and aspects of Soviet behavior. In contemplating the prospects for the next decade one cannot exclude major discontinuities in Soviet perspectives with regard to the goals of their foreign policy and the means they are prepared to employ, but a critical review of the priorities on the agenda of the Soviet leadership in the last decade provides limited justification for comparison with Nazi Germany in the 1930s.

In the first place, domestic concerns and internal policy issues—political, economic, and social—have traditionally been a matter of primary concern for Soviet leaders, and in this regard the Brezhnev era is no exception. Second, in the actual determining of foreign policy, considerations of the security of the Soviet state and almost to the same extent the security of its East European sphere of interest, its satellite empire—that is, questions of the defensive posture of the Soviet Union—have remained their greatest concern. Third, in activities and initiatives abroad throughout the Brezhnev era, the managers of Soviet foreign policy have displayed an attitude which assigns the highest value to low-risk and relatively low-cost operations and especially to actions which will have only marginal disruptive influence on the process and plans of maximal domestic development. There is as yet no evidence to indicate that the achievement of strategic parity and the activization of the Soviet Union in the international arena has in any fundamental way altered this state of affairs, although of course the intervention in Afghanistan may well signify such a turning point.

The Soviet Union is obviously not a "sated power." Even when measured only from the viewpoint of great-power competition, it is a new, dynamic great power. Only now attaining global status, it is a great power in a phase of ascendancy which claims a place in the sun commensurate with what it considers its due. This situation in itself would render difficult, highly competitive, complex, and unstable any relations with the Soviet Union now and for the foreseeable future. It would certainly preclude realization of those exaggerated hopes of the early Kissinger detente construed as a long-range balance of power and agreement on spheres of interest.

The Soviet Union is not simply a great and global power, however. Its leadership holds to the view that the world is divided into opposing systems of competing values. Such a view works inherently against the acceptance of any long-range status quo. It is just this combination of the traditional dynamic of an ascending power with the volatile dynamic of a power which postulates a different world outlook and inevitable competition with other powers that undermines the likely success of balance-of-power policies, that limits the scope of bilateral U.S.-Soviet agreements, and that precludes the inherent stability of long-range solutions. Indeed, this is precisely the worst possible situation for American foreign policy, which Richard Lowenthal anticipated when he wrote in 1978: "Possible major Soviet decisions are being prepared in a situation in which the Soviets have the impression that they have nothing to hope and nothing to fear from the United States, and indeed from the West in general."[1]

The difficulties in U.S.-Soviet relations are not rooted in mutual misperceptions. At bottom is the genuine diversity of their interests, a genuine difference in their evaluation and perception of the international situation, a genuine diversity of their priorities in approaching the world system, and a genuine asymmetry in the development of their international appetites and consciousness of what is possible and attainable in the international arena.

Misperceptions, nevertheless, do intrude powerfully into the policy-making process of both countries. The arrangement of relations that would in any case prove difficult is complicated all the more when misunderstanding accompanies disagreement and competition. For this reason it is crucial for us to know what the Soviet perceptions of key issues in the international arena are. Without such understanding, American policies could seriously miscalculate Soviet intentions, unnecessarily aggravate existing tensions, minimize the potential for accommodation and agreement, compromise any steps in the direction of partial solutions, and, most important, simply fail.

In light of these considerations it is the task of this chapter to set aside direct response to the question of American policy toward the Soviet Union during this critical period, a policy which should aim to maximize for Soviet policy makers those options which are least dangerous and most conducive to the promotion of American international interests, in favor of a broader attempt to understand the context in which Soviet policy is formulated, some sources of Soviet conduct in foreign policy, and the contradictory pressures which shape its formation. In other

[1] Richard Lowenthal, "Dealing with Soviet Global Power," *Encounter*, 50, no. 6 (June 1978), 90.

words it is the task of this chapter to elucidate certain key Soviet perceptions of the international environment in the late Brezhnev period. The discussion will concentrate on four of many principal areas where an understanding of Soviet perceptions is crucial to an explanation of Soviet behavior.[2] These areas are: the centrality of U.S.-Soviet relations in the international arena; the arms race and the correlation of forces; the role of the military factor in international relations; and the Third World and the translation of power into influence.

[2] For reasons of space and flow of argument, I very seldom provide direct quotations from Soviet sources on which the analysis of these perceptions is based, although I do provide basic bibliographical information. These sources fall into four categories: (1) Speeches, articles, and interviews by Soviet leaders (Brezhnev, Kirilenko, Suslov, Gromyko, Ustinov, Grechko, Ponomarev). Of special importance are speeches at the Twenty-fifth Party Congress contained in *XXV s'ezd Kommunisticheskoi Partii Sovetskogo Soiuza. Stenograficheskii otchet* (Moscow: Gospolitizdat, 1976), vols. 1–3. (2) Articles in political and specialized Soviet journals: *Kommunist; SShA–ekonomika, politika, ideologiia (SShA); Mirovaia ekonomika i mezhdunarodnye otnosheniia (MEMO); International Affairs; Voprosy filosofii; Partiinaia zhizn'; Voprosy ekonomiki; Voprosy istorii KPSS;* primarily for the years 1977 and 1978. (3) Monographs by G. A. Arbatov, I. P. Beliaev, O. T. Bogomolov, O. N. Bykov, P. N. Fedoseev, B. F. Gafurov, V. I. Gantman, N. N. Iakovlev, N. N. Inozemtsev, A. A. Kokoshkin, A. G. Kovalev, N. I. Lebedev, Iu. M. Mel'nikov, G. I. Mirskii, G. I. Morozov, A. L. Narochnitskii, N. M. Nikol'skii, V. F. Petrovskii, V. I. Popov, E. M. Primakov, V. S. Semenov, A. V. Sergiev, V. G. Shkunaev, A. Iu. Shpirt, Iu. A. Shvedkov, S. L. Tikhvinskii, D. G. Tomashevskii, G. A. Trofimenko, V. G. Trukhanovskii, R. A. Ul'ianovskii, E. M. Zhukov, V. V. Zhurkin, and V. S. Zorin. (4) Talks with Soviet experts on international affairs.

11
THE CENTRALITY
OF U.S.-SOVIET RELATIONS

From the end of World War II, U.S.-Soviet relations have constituted the central axis of international relations in general and of American and Soviet foreign policies in particular. Virtually every major decision, every major turn in American and Soviet foreign policies, has been undertaken primarily with a view to the conduct of the other party and with the intention of influencing the other party's conduct. Three basic circumstances explain the overwhelming centrality of U.S.-Soviet relations in the postwar period. First, the two superpowers have played the dominant roles in the European theater which constituted the main arena of their conflict throughout this period. Second, the United States alone has dominated the global economic and political scene outside Europe, thereby rendering manageable and marginal for American policy makers the conflicts and problems not directly related to the U.S.-Soviet competition. And, third, the two powers have seen in one another mirror images of their greatest danger. For the United States, the Soviet Union and the "Communist menace" represented not only the main obstacle to America's continued dominance in world affairs but also the only long-range military and ideological threat to the survival of "Western civilization." For the Soviet Union, the United States represented the only real danger to Soviet security, the only major obstacle to its domination of the Eurasian theater and to the consummation in terms of political and economic influence of the fruits of victory in World War II.[1]

Under these conditions it is not surprising that for over thirty years Soviet-American relations have monopolized the attention of both great powers to the exclusion of almost all other policy concerns and have colored in a decisive way their policies toward other countries. Modern

[1] The global dominance of the United States and the dominance of the European theater in the Soviet-American conflict has signified a phase in the development of international relations which can best be characterized as the postwar era, a period marked by the lack of a comprehensive settlement of the unfinished business of World War II. The decline of American dominance, the achievement of strategic parity by the Soviet Union, the tacit recognition of the Soviet sphere of influence, the globalization of competition with the Soviet Union, and the sharpening of the Sino-Soviet conflict opened in the 1970s a new phase in international relations and signified an end to the postwar era. For a discussion of this process, see Alastair Buchan, *The End of the Postwar Era: A New Balance of World Power* (New York: Dutton, 1974).

history offers no precedent for this degree of concentration, with the possible exception of relations between Great Britain and France from the French Revolution to the Congress of Vienna. It is our contention that this situation is now finally coming to an end, at least for the American side and perhaps for the Soviet side as well, as the Afghanistan intervention suggests.

Foreign policy analysts and policy makers in the United States, Western Europe, and the Third World (but not the Soviet Union) increasingly suggest that the centrality of the Soviet-American conflict for the two great powers and of U.S.-Soviet relations for international politics is declining and will continue to decline. The end of this bipolarity is sometimes described as a process that is far advanced and proceeding rapidly and sometimes as a desired goal, as a direction in which both U.S.-Soviet foreign policies and international relations should develop.[2] But whether as descriptions of an actual process, predictions of things to come, or prescriptions of desirable developments, these are the first sure signs of the postwar era that U.S.-Soviet relations will not remain the sole dominant axis of international politics and the exclusive preoccupation of the two great superpowers.

In some respects the evolving situation is highly paradoxical. The centrality of Soviet-American relations has coincided with the period when the Soviet Union enjoyed great but not global power and when the United States maintained a degree of strategic superiority over its adversary. Only recently has the Soviet Union made major advances on the way to becoming a global power and has it actually achieved strategic parity with the United States. One would expect, if anything, that this development in itself would only serve to reinforce the centrality of U.S.-Soviet relations for U.S. policy makers and its dominance of international relations generally. This indeed would be the case were it not for a number of other developments and their consequences in the last decades which have worked to erode that centrality. Five of these are most important:

> The postwar economic boom in the West, characterized by relatively low unemployment rates, stable prices, and high ratios of growth, has come to an end. Internal economic problems have become very difficult to resolve and now assume a much greater role in guaranteeing the social and political stability of Western countries.
>
> The international economic order is changing, highly unstable, and even chaotic. Western dominance of world resources of raw materials is declining. The stability of the world monetary system has weakened seriously. The interdependence of economic policies

---

[2] As a prescription, such a view has been advocated by Seyom Brown in "A Cooling-Off Period for U.S.-Soviet Relations," *Foreign Policy*, 28, no. 28 (Fall 1977), 3–21.

among the industrialized countries of the West as well as between the industrialized and developing countries has not only increased radically but is much less tractable than previously to actions and manipulations from one center, whether the United States or the Common Market.

Alongside the two superpowers and the traditional European powers (and China), regional great powers are emerging in different parts of the world. Their growing influence is at times primarily economic (Japan) and at times both political and military (Brazil in Latin America, Iran until recently in the Persian Gulf, Nigeria in sub-Saharan Africa). In all cases their influence competes and to some extent begins to supersede the regional influence of the great powers or at least makes this influence less direct and more dependent on the relation between the great and the regional powers.

The crisis of world communism has entered a new phase where in all probability the very term "world communism" will lose all meaning. The Soviet Union still cannot insure the cohesion and stability of its East European empire by means other than the potential threat of force; it is even less likely to do so in the future. The rapid growth of Eurocommunist tendencies among Communist parties outside the Communist bloc has for all practical purposes destroyed Soviet ability to control the policies of all major Communist parties. Soviet practice as a model for emulation and a symbol of "progressiveness" among the European and non-European left is practically nonexistent. The Sino-Soviet conflict has become for the foreseeable future a permanent fixture in international relations and the most intractable conflict between great powers.[3]

Despite major efforts in the post-Khrushchev era, the Soviet Union remains unable to assure a comparable level of economic development to match the expansion of its military capabilities. Especially pronounced in the crucial areas of technological innovation and labor productivity, the Soviet lag in comparison to industrially developed societies has not been substantially narrowed. The tendencies of Soviet economic development, moreover, show unmistakable signs of the further decline of factor productivity and overall growth, which more than compensate for the West's declining growth and make highly unlikely the prospect that the Soviet Union will catch up in this century with Western societies in per capita production, not to speak of technological level.

---

[3] I am not arguing that Sino-Soviet relations cannot in the foreseeable future assume a more benign form with some relaxation in existing tensions. It does seem, however, that a point of no return has been reached with regard to the possibility of resuming a Sino-Soviet alliance and abandoning a basic competition, the intensity of which may of course differ from one period to another.

Certain key consequences of these five developments account for di-minishing the centrality of American-Soviet relations in international affairs generally and in American policy making particularly. First, the Soviet-American conflict has to a large extent lost its demonic character. It has become less a military, political, and economic struggle rooted in ideology and nourished and reinforced by ideological sources and more a "normal," traditional great-power competition to defend national inter-ests and to extend international influence. Second, the economic aspects of international relations are assuming a significance unprecedented in the past. They are acquiring critical importance in determining the shape of the international order as a whole and of the sociopolitical stability, not to mention the economic development, of major countries in the first and third worlds and, to some extent, the second world. And it is exactly in the international economic arena that Soviet influence is weakest and Soviet policies are largely irrelevant. Third, the erosion of America's dominant role in the international arena is not matched by a parallel extension of Soviet influence approaching anything like a simi-lar order of magnitude. While the Soviet Union is able sometimes to gain influence at American expense, it is not in the process of replacing the United States as a dominant international power.

What is argued here is not at all that Soviet-American relations have ceased to be of crucial importance or will in the foreseeable future disap-pear as one of the decisive factors in international relations. What is proposed is simply that the Soviet-American conflict is ceasing to exert exclusive domination over international relations in general and Ameri-can policy making in particular.

The world order, or rather disorder, presently contains numerous problem areas which are at the same time interconnected and autono-mous. Their influence on one another connects them; the different nature of their component elements as well as the different solutions to which they are amenable afford them autonomy. Each problem area requires policies of a different type. Trilateral relations and problems require economic bargaining and trade-offs, consultations and alliance politics. North-South relations require key attention to regional balances and an effort at maximal disassociation from great-power politics and, above all else, a recognition of the legitimate and overwhelming force of national-ism even when it is not pro-Western. East-West relations require bal-ance-of-power politics adjusted to the realities of the nuclear age, that is, modified in the long range by the combination of conflict, competition, and cooperation subsumed under the term detente.

U.S.-Soviet relations could prove a major obstacle to dealing with other problems in the international arena – without detente for certain and even with a well-developed detente. But U.S.-Soviet relations and the kind of policies applied to these relations are by themselves of lim-ited relevance in dealing with these enormous "other" problems. Stanley Hoffmann underlined both elements of the connection between world problems and U.S.-Soviet relations when he remarked, "What happens on the traditional chessboard of world politics – a metaphor justified, here, by bipolarity – is no longer a cause of all the other processes, but it remains their condition."[4]

It is important to observe, however, that for a number of reasons the decline in the centrality of U.S.-Soviet relations for America was not apparently paralleled until recently by a similar decline in Soviet perceptions. One reason is of prime importance. The Soviets continue to hold that U.S.-Soviet relations are decisive for world peace, that they govern the prospects for a nuclear holocaust. One may observe that fear of such a holocaust among Soviet leaders, elites, and peoples is much more real, much more tangible, than in the United States.

Other important reasons affect the Soviet position as well. First, the United States is perceived as the controlling factor in world affairs, the only state with global interests and global reach, the only power whose policies decide whether, how soon, and at what cost the Soviet quest for international political parity (which in their view should follow their achievement of strategic parity) can be achieved.[5] Second, America is considered a key to the magnitude of the Soviet conflict with China. A hostile China remains for the Soviet Union a long-range political and strategic problem under all circumstances. A hostile China allied with the United States, supported economically and perhaps militarily, could only be termed a hideous nightmare.

There is still another reason why relations with the United States have remained absolutely central for the Soviet Union. Perhaps less direct and immediate than the others, it nevertheless has very deep roots and is psychologically no less important. It is simply the fact that the United States is what the Soviet Union wishes to be. Throughout the postwar period and with particular force during the modernizing drive of the post-Stalin era, Soviet leaders and elites defined as most progressive and most deserving of emulation the example and force of America: America's world position, its wealth, its science and technology, its drive, its imagination, and its economic development. Even when the Soviets were engaged in bitter competition and hostilities with the United States, they most readily and easily identified with this force and wished to be identified with it. It is not enough to say that they regard the United States as the prime and most abundant source of the technological know-

---

[4] Stanley Hoffmann, *Primacy of World Order: American Foreign Policy since the Cold War* (New York: McGraw-Hill, 1978), p. 280. Speaking in the same vein about problems facing U.S. foreign policy, Marshall Shulman remarked that "it is clear that the Soviet Union is a complicating factor rather than a prime cause of the problems we must address" (U.S., Congress, Senate, testimony before the Committee on Foreign Relations, 21 August 1974, p. 102).

[5] Soviet leaders and analysts do not use the term "political parity." But from what they say and write there clearly emerges a picture of their global *political* expectations which should naturally follow their global *military* attainments. Those expectations are succinctly expressed by Gromyko when he says that there should be no international "question of any significance which can be decided without the Soviet Union or in opposition to it."

how and economic imports required for their own modernization, as has been the case most recently. Rather, it is something more fundamental: They see in the United States the prime measuring rod of their own developments and achievements.

This attitude toward the United States has deep historical roots in the Soviet past. Lenin regarded the United States almost obsessively as the model of Soviet economic development; he stressed America's pioneering role in the organization of production and its material achievements.[6] And Stalin can be credited with the following extraordinary statement:

> American business ability [*delovitost'*] constitutes . . . an antitoxin against "revolutionary" Manilov-like behavior and fanciful yarn spinning. American business ability is that unconquerable force, which does not know and does not recognize barriers, which washes away by its business-like stubbornness each and every obstacle, which cannot fail to bring to a conclusion any task once begun, even when it concerns small things, and without which any serious constructive work is unthinkable. [He then concludes:] The union of Russian revolutionary drive with American business ability – this is the essence of Leninism in party and state work.[7]

Under Khrushchev this special attitude toward America became, if anything, even more pronounced. One has only to read Khrushchev's memoirs as he prepared for his first trip to the United States. "After all," he writes, "I'd been to England, Switzerland, France, India, Indonesia, Burma, and so on. These were all foreign countries, but they weren't America. America occupied a special position in our thinking and our view of the world."[8]

This perception of America in my view is absolutely crucial to understanding the psychological sources of the Soviets' overwhelming preoccupation and concern with U.S. relations. In a similar vein it may also be supposed that the centrality of U.S.-Soviet relations in the Soviet mind is further reinforced by the strength and attractiveness to the Soviets of the emulative model represented by the American position of dominance in the international arena after World War II. One has the impression that Soviet expectations concerning the rewards to which their global-power status will entitle them in the long run reflect more the model of the pivotal, many-sided *influence* of the United States in the world of the 1950s and 1960s than the Stalinist model of *power* expressed in an expanded Soviet empire.

Having explored some of the reasons why Soviet-American relations have remained and may still remain central for Soviet policy makers, despite the erosion of this centrality on the American side, I would argue

---

[6] See, for example, V. I. Lenin, *Sochineniia*, 4th ed. (Moscow: Gospolitizdat), 19 (1952), 171–4; 22 (1952), 1–89; 31 (1950), 193–5.

[7] I. V. Stalin, *Sochineniia*, 6 (Moscow: Gospolitizdat, 1952), 187–8.

[8] *Khrushchev Remembers: The Last Testament*, transl. and ed. by Strobe Talbott (Boston: Little, Brown, 1974), p. 369.

that these relations in the last few years have encountered certain difficulties that only an appreciation of this Soviet position can explain. Just as the Soviets have held these relations central, so they have expected America to share their view. Extraordinarily sensitive on this matter, they regard as lack of reciprocity and deliberate slight any indications that American policy makers give precedence and stress to foreign relations other than Soviet. Indeed it is possible, and many Soviets would insist, that the recent activization and attention of Soviet policy makers to axes other than the American, and especially their Third World activity, are intended at least in part to compensate for the paralysis of what they regard as their central axis of international relations.

12
THE ARMS RACE
AND THE CORRELATION
OF FORCES

One of the major points in the American discussion about U.S.-Soviet relations concerns the question of the magnitude of Soviet capabilities or, to say it differently, the question of the relation of U.S.-Soviet forces. An important segment of opinion makers asserts that the Soviet Union has already achieved strategic superiority and an overall military preponderance over the United States.[1] Others speak about an essential equivalence of forces, a relation of overall parity.

Part of the discussion on the relation of forces concerns not so much the existing state of affairs but rather Soviet intentions, the argument being that while the present state is that of essential parity, the Soviets are striving to achieve superiority over the United States. The main evidence for this striving is provided by the unrelenting and unceasing increase in Soviet military expenditures, which shows no sign of abating.

Some participants in the ongoing discussion argue that while the *actual* relation of strategic forces between the United States and the Soviet Union may be that of equivalence, the perception by friends and especially by neutrals is that of growing Soviet superiority. Therefore, their argument goes, the net political-psychological effect is the same as if Soviet superiority were a fact.[2] And it is exactly the political-psychological effects of superiority that they are concerned about. They do not so much fear that in conditions of actual or perceived strategic superiority the Soviet Union will consider a deliberate, planned attack, a first strike against the United States. They rather wonder in such conditions how American policy makers will behave when faced with a Soviet *regional* challenge, political or military, how different will be the reaction of American allies to Soviet pressures, and whether Third World countries will not turn increasingly toward the Soviet Union.[3]

---

[1] See, for example, Fred Charles Iklé, "What It Means To Be Number Two," *Fortune*, 20 November 1978, pp. 72–84.

[2] It seems to me that we are dealing here with a classical case of self-fulfilling prophecy. The Soviet Union does *not* contend that it has achieved military superiority over the United States. If such a perception is being created abroad, it is primarily through the efforts of the domestic critics of the American armament performance. More than anyone else these critics are contributing to American weakness by belittling America's military strength.

[3] See, for example, Walter Laqueur, "Europe: The Specter of Finlandization," *Commentary*, 64, no. 6 (December 1977), 37–41; and Robert W. Tucker, "Beyond Détente," *Commentary*, 63, no. 3 (March 1977), 42–50. See also Robert Conquest

When the focus of the discussion about the U.S.-Soviet relation of forces concerns the perception of this relation and its political-psychological effects, it seems logical and pertinent to inquire, which virtually none of the participants in the discussion does, what is the Soviet perception of the relation of U.S.-Soviet forces. Such an inquiry is not only of great importance for the general current discussions on the U.S.-Soviet relation of forces, and, incidentally, for understanding some of the reasons behind the Soviet arms race, but also central to the understanding of the entire Soviet perception of the international situation.

That the Soviets are engaged in an arms race no one disputes. That their military build-up, strategic and conventional, requires continuous American monitoring and reevaluation and, if necessary, countermeasures to preserve a reasonable balance, is without question.[4] I share, however, Richard Lowenthal's belief that the Soviet build-up

> should be examined not in isolation as a series of "pure" military facts, but in the context of all we know about the nature of Soviet policy. In other words, I do *not* believe that evidence of military capabilities is the *only* clue to an adversary's military intentions: an effort must be made to interpret those capabilities in the context of the policies they are intended to serve.[5]

What emerges by the end of the 1970s from authoritative Soviet writings and talks with Soviet specialists on international affairs concerning the relation of forces in the international arena is the following summary of Soviet perceptions:[6]

et al., *Defending America: Toward a New Role in the Post-Detente World* (New York: Basic Books, 1977) and the articles by Robert Conquest, Colin Gray, and Anthony Harrigan in "U.S. Strategy in the Decade Ahead," *Policy Review*, no. 1 (Summer 1977), 117–28.

[4] It should be stressed, by the way, that the Soviet military build-up, contrary to popular perceptions, did not take the form of a sudden, rapid, and explosive development of strategic and conventional forces. The rate of growth in the Soviet military budget in real terms throughout the Brezhnev era has been a balanced and steady increment of about 3 percent. What we see today, therefore, is a result of two unrelated processes: the cumulative effect of Soviet incremental growth and the delayed effects of the depletion of the American military resources, primarily due to the Vietnam war.

[5] Richard Lowenthal, "Dealing with Soviet Global Power," *Encounter*, 50, no. 6 (June 1978), 90.

[6] Soviet pronouncements with regard to the correlation of forces in the contemporary world and its change are standard in any major Soviet general article on international relations. As good a source as any I can recall for an extensive discussion is the fundamental work on Soviet foreign policy by Sh. P. Sanakoev and N. I. Kapchenko, *O teorii vneshnei politiki sotsializma* (Moscow: Izd. Mezhdunarodnye otnosheniia, 1977), chap. 7. See also N. I. Lebedev, *Novyi etap mezhdunarodnykh otnoshenii* (Moscow: Izd. Mezhdunarodnye otnosheniia, 1976), pp. 41–71; G. Shakhnazarov, "K probleme sootnosheniia sil v mire," *Kommunist*, 1974, no. 3 (February), pp. 77–89; Sh. Sanakoev, "Problema sootnosheniia sil v sovremennom mire," *Mezhdunarodnaia zhizn'*, October 1974, pp. 40–50; V. Zagladin, "Revoliutsionnyi protsess i mezhdunarodnaia politika KPSS," *Kommunist*, 1972, no. 13 (September), pp. 14–26.

The relation of forces in the international arena is still conceived within the framework of the opposing camps of imperialism and socialism. Within this framework two themes emerge as central – that of the advance of the cause and forces of socialism and that of the peaceful coexistence of differing systems. The first theme represents a historical process, the second theme a political strategy of the Soviet Union. The relations between the two are such that it is the first which makes the second possible and fruitful, and the second which reinforces the tendency represented by the first.

The Brezhnev era has seen a basic change in the relation of world forces in favor of socialism. Its crucial expression is the absolute and relative strengthening of the military and economic potential of the socialist bloc. The self-image of the Soviets in their official reports, speeches, and writings as compared to fifteen years ago is that of a newly found self-assurance, confidence, and satisfaction. Its counterpart is the internal weakening of the main imperialist countries and their loss of important positions and influence in the world – an image which in the Soviet rendition is not a little tinged with a note of surprise.

One of the major effects of the change in the relation of forces has been the new success of the strategy of coexistence which led to detente. The process of detente amounts to a growing recognition by the United States of the principle of peaceful coexistence, to the resulting diminution of tensions and a declining chance of direct military clash between the two camps. The best guarantee of the continuation and deepening of detente is the further growth of the might of the socialist camp and decline in the influence of imperialism. In turn, the best guarantor of the further change in the relation of forces in favor of socialism is the progressive development of the process of detente.

The basic discordant note in this picture is provided by the case of China.[7] China has preoccupied the Soviets from the time of the break in the late 1950s, but only in the last decade has it become a virtual obsession that recently has even intensified. Needless to say, there are valid political and military reasons for this obsession. The Chinese treaty with Japan, the normalization of relations with the United States, the weapons purchases in Western Europe, the enormous modernization plan based on the expected influx of Western technology, and the general "opening" of China with its immense activization in the international arena, have created a situation to

---

[7] Another such discordant note is provided by nationalistic tendencies within some East European parties (e.g., Rumania) and revisionistic and anti-Soviet tendencies within the international Communist movement. The speeches of Soviet leaders and the writing of Soviet experts devote to it growing attention and express continuous apprehension. For a Soviet treatment of this subject see V. Zagladin, "Istoricheskaia missiia rabochego klassa i sovremennoe rabochee dvizhenie," *Kommunist*, 1978, no. 11 (July), pp. 67–80.

which the Soviets respond with growing worry, tremendous preoccupation, and with even some notes of hysteria. One has the impression that while the Soviets buried some fifteen years ago the
idea of "capitalist encirclement," the mentality of a besieged fortress, a new specter is raising its head – that of a new encirclement
by a coalition of China and industrialized Western nations – a
specter which revives the old mentality.[8]

However, the importance of China in the Soviet thinking about
the international situation goes much deeper than those immediate
and readily visible reasons. There is an additional dimension which
is psychologically critical and which magnifies the immediate and
long-range preoccupation. It is the association of the Chinese concern in the Soviet mind with the profound question of the fate of the
world Communist revolution. The early Bolshevik hopes of a world
Communist revolution for which the isolated Soviet state would
serve as a base dissipated with relative speed. The belief, however,
that such a revolution when it finally comes would arrive from the
East was more long-lasting. The words of Lenin most often quoted in
this context by Soviet leaders and writers were until recently those
which predicted that "in the final analysis the fate of the world will
be decided by the fact that the majority of the world population –
China, India, and others – will embrace the revolution." Even at the
height of the conflict in the late 1960s the hope still remained with
the Soviets that changes in China would lead to a healing of the
breach. That such hopes are no more entertained is shown by the
fact that the Soviet Union is presently engaged in a major doctrinal
reformulation of its treatment of China, comparable to the reformulation of its position vis-à-vis Yugoslavia in the interval between the
first resolution of the Cominform in 1948 and the second resolution
in 1949.[9] The enunciated goal with regard to China today is for the
first time not the restoration of alliance but the same as that with
regard to imperialist states: peaceful coexistence.[10]

[8] For examples of Soviet writings on China which display strong elements of such
mentality see: Z. Litvin, M. Shmelev, "Riskovannaia igra pekinskoi kartoi,"
MEMO, 1978, no. 10 (October), pp. 39–48; "Chto stoit za maoistskoi 'teoriei
trekh mirov,'" *Kommunist*, 1978, no. 17 (November), pp. 97–121; "Kitai posle
Mao Tse-duna," *Kommunist*, 1977, no. 12 (August), pp. 110–21; B. Pyshkov, B.
Starostin, "Ot 'ul'trarevoliutsionnosti' k soiuzu s imperializmom i reaktsiei,"
Kommunist, 1978, no. 16 (November), pp. 98–109.

[9] The first resolution of the Cominform in 1948 spoke about "The Deviation in the
Policies of the Leadership of the Communist Party of Yugoslavia." The second
resolution adopted in 1949 spoke about "The Communist Party of Yugoslavia in
the Hands of Murderers, Spies, and Saboteurs." The first asked for a change in
Tito's leadership; the second demanded the overthrow of Tito's *regime*. (Incidentally, it is only the second resolution of the Cominform that was annulled when
the reconciliation with Tito took place in 1956. Formally, the first resolution still
stands.)

[10] While the formula of "peaceful coexistence" as applied to China was used occasionally before its official adoption at the Twenty-fifth Party Congress in 1976,

There is no basis for asserting that Soviet policy makers believe, as do many in the West, that the Soviet Union is achieving a position of either military or overall superiority vis-à-vis the Western alliance and, particularly, the United States. The Soviet approach to the measurement of opposing forces in the international arena differs considerably from the one customary in the West. Without minimizing the role of the purely quantitative military factor, the evaluation of the relation of forces in the Soviet view has to include other factors and, most importantly, overall economic power and the level of the technological development of the Soviet Union and its allies and clients as compared with the West, the degree of unity and disunity in the Soviet bloc and the Western "camp," the strength of the "progressive" forces in the Third World, and so forth. The inclusion of these other material and sociopolitical factors is not simply a textbook phrase, but a perception that permeates Soviet thinking, the strength of which is supported by tradition and their general world outlook.

With regard to the strategic balance of power the Soviets see themselves as having achieved parity with the United States. They do not see this parity as being assured once and for all, however, as a stable state of affairs. In the light of American technological superiority and the continuing arms race, especially in the field of new weaponry, it is a parity which the Soviets feel can be secured only by continuous effort.[11] With regard to the general relation of forces they still consider themselves to be weaker than the West, still feel strongly the need for a maximum effort to catch up with the West. This, as a matter of fact, provides one rationale for their purely military build-up effort, an area where they can show the greatest successes and which in their perception at least partly counterweighs their strongly perceived economic and technological inferiority vis-à-vis the West.

when Brezhnev used it in his report, it has remained since then the only formula used with regard to China (see *XXV s'ezd Kommunisticheskoi Partii Sovetskogo Soiuza. Stenograficheskii otchet*, p. 34).

[11]For example, V. M. Kulish makes the following statement in his major work on military force and international relations: "The appearance of new types of weapons could seriously affect the relation of military forces between the two world systems. . . . Far-reaching international consequences could arise in the event that one side possessed qualitatively new strategic weapons which could serve to neutralize the ability of the opposing side to carry out effective retaliatory operations . . .; even a relatively small and brief superiority by the United States over the Soviet Union in the development of certain "old" or "new" types and systems of weapons that significantly increase the strategic effectiveness of American military power could exert a destabilizing influence on the international political situation throughout the entire world and present extremely unfavorable consequences for the cause of peace and socialism" (V. M. Kulish, *Voennaia sila i mezhdunarodnye otnosheniia* [Moscow: Izd. Mezhdunarodnye otnosheniia, 1972], p. 226).

It is legitimate to inquire whether the last assertion does not contradict what was said earlier concerning the fundamental Soviet view about the basic change in the relation of forces in the international arena. In my opinion it does not. When Soviet leaders observe a change in the relation of forces in their own favor, they think primarily in terms of changes in the *correlation of trends*. It is the direction and magnitude of the *trends* in their favor which they have found so satisfying. In their evaluation of the relation of trends they are optimistic; in their assessment of the relation of forces at this particular historical moment they are realistic.

We have now to pass from the more or less firm ground of the Soviet perception of the relation of forces broadly conceived, which, while containing ambiguities and contradictions, provides in my opinion support for the assertion that the Soviet Union does not see itself as superior in strength to the United States, or as achieving superiority, to the question of Soviet intentions and actual policy behavior in the area most sensitive in the discussion raging in the West, namely, the logic of the arms race.

In the military realm the strategic arms race between the superpowers has reached a point of rough parity, with the ability for mutual destruction still assured. At the same time, in the last decade the key dynamic element of the arms race has been provided by the Soviet Union's catching up with the United States and developing its capabilities at a faster rate. The state of rough parity, the preservation of a high-confidence second-strike capability, and the continuing assurance of mutual destruction can continue; and the tilt toward the Soviet Union, introduced by its greater developmental and deployment dynamic, can be slowed or stopped basically in two ways: either through an unrestricted spiraling arms race or through stabilizing strategic arms control agreements that may lead eventually to some arms reductions.

Both superpowers at the end of the 1970s seem to shy away from the prospect of an unrestricted strategic arms race and rather to opt for an arms control agreement that would introduce an element of stability into the strategic power balance. On the American side the incentive is obvious: Soviet strategic build-up is proceeding at a fast pace; improved strategic weapons are introduced into the Soviet arsenal; new, even more dangerous systems are being developed and tested. If present trends continue, there is real danger that a significant strategic imbalance will develop that would favor the Soviet Union.

On the Soviet side the incentives may be less obvious, but they seem to have acquired in the last two years a greater potency. Most important is the frustration of Soviet expectations that the post-Watergate, post-Vietnam trauma in the United States would continue unabated and significantly influence American strategic arms policies. The growing awareness in the United States of the magnitude of the Soviet strategic build-up, the new receptivity of Congress and the public to increased arms expenditures after years of declining appropriations, the vocal determination of the Carter Administration not to permit the Soviet build-up to go unchallenged, backed by plans to deploy such weapons as the Cruise missile and develop less vulnerable ICBMs like the system of mobile land-based missiles, are stimulating a new perception on the Soviet side that unless a new stabilizing agreement is reached, a new uncontrolled arms race with all its inherent unpredictabilities and dangers will start again. I think it highly unlikely in any case that the Soviets expect to sustain the dynamics of the strategic balance of the last five years; they recognize that any alteration of the current balance can only work against the Soviet interest. Despite, therefore, or even perhaps because of the highly publicized cooling of Soviet-American relations under the Carter Administration, the Soviets have made a significant effort to reach agreement on SALT II and are vitally interested in its ratification. SALT II at least promises to reduce uncertainty about the future while at the same time securing American recognition of U.S.-Soviet strategic parity.

Many influential American and European analysts, however, argue that the idea of arms agreements which will stabilize a strategic parity between the two superpowers is an illusion, due to the fact that while American expectations with regard to detente and strategic arms are just such parity, the Soviet aims are different. The Soviets have hoped within the framework of detente to acquire strategic superiority; this is the kind of detente they have supported and why they have supported detente. For example, one highly respected defense expert writes:

> Many in America continue to say that we should settle for parity wherever we had superiorities and tacitly accept inferiorities elsewhere. Yet it is now clear that the Soviet Union will not permanently accept parity in *any* dimension of military power. To its leaders, parity obviously means no more than the transitory moment in which the ascending curve of their strength meets the descending curve of our own.[12]

The easiest answer to this and similar points of view is that of Henry Kissinger, who, when faced with the argument about the Soviet quest for superiority, exclaimed: "In God's name, what does strategic superiority mean?"[13]

This answer is inadequate, however, because most military experts

---

[12]Edward N. Luttwak, "Defense Reconsidered," *Commentary*, 63, no. 3 (March 1977), 58.

[13]Anyway, the Kissinger of 1979 has changed his mind. In an interview in the 3 February 1979 issue of *The Economist* (pp. 17–22), he clearly recognizes strategic *counterforce* superiority. He writes: "I have come to the view, which is different from the view I used to write about in the 1960s, that for one side to have counterforce capability and the other side not to have it (especially if that side is also inferior in forces for local intervention) must tempt a political disaster" (p. 20).

agree that there *can* be strategic superiority (it of course should not be equated with strategic immunity to any retaliation) which would dangerously tilt the balance to one side. More important, even if strategic superiority may not make much sense in purely military terms, it may make sense in political-psychological terms. A belief by the Soviet Union, by the United States, and by other countries that the strategic balance has tilted decisively in Soviet favor may present dangerous temptations to the Soviets and induce equally dangerous timidity on the part of the Western allies in facing Soviet threats. The Soviets will not be tempted to plan ahead a deliberate first-strike attack but rather to take the risk of pushing an unintended confrontation to the point of dangerous miscalculation.

One can, it seems, make the argument that while optimally within the framework of detente the present American administration can hope to assure a stable parity in the strategic balance, the Soviets optimally desire to achieve strategic superiority and favor the kind of detente which would allow them to reach this goal. The Soviets surely know that without detente, in an uncontrolled arms race, they cannot hope to secure such an outcome, owing to the size, strength, and decisive technological superiority of the American and Western economies. (Moreover, an uncontrolled arms race would dramatically maximize all the dangers of escalating confrontations which the Soviet Union wishes to avoid as much as the United States.)

In my opinion one should not confuse these optimal Soviet desires in the strategic realm with reasoned Soviet expectations of what a detente policy will bring them. To do so would entail the assumption that the United States will not respond forcefully in the absence of a new SALT agreement to the dangerous Soviet strategic build-up or that the new SALT agreement will leave the door open for a continued Soviet build-up without an American response, without at least an effort to stabilize the strategic parity relation. There is no evidence whatever in America's behavior of the last two years that would even remotely justify such assumptions.

What we do know is that the Soviet perception concerning strategic superiority and deterrence which emerges in writing after writing, both political *and* military, supports explicitly and unequivocally the idea of balance of power and parity. Already in the late 1960s and especially from the early 1970s, Soviet political and military leaders and commentators uniformly renounced the aim of strategic superiority for either of the superpowers. Despite the view of many American writers and politicians that the Soviet Union does not accept the concept of mutual deterrence, the record, as I see it, does not support their skepticism.[14]

---

[14]Skepticism about Soviet adherence to the concept of deterrence was most forcefully expressed by Richard Pipes in "Why the Soviet Union Thinks It Could Fight and Win a Nuclear War," *Commentary*, 64, no. 1 (July 1977), 21–34, and in his rebuttal to the critics of his article in *Commentary*, 64, no. 3 (September 1977), 20–6.

In refutation of my view, it is often argued that while the United States stresses the "deterrent" role of strategic forces, Soviet thought, and especially military thought, stresses the "war-fighting" and "war-winning" capabilities of the Soviet forces. Such a position seems to me false. It is precisely the development of such capabilities which in the Soviet view represents the best "deterrent." What should rather be remarked is that the American and Soviet concepts of "deterrence" differ. Robert Legvold formulates the key distinction as follows: "the American theory of deterrence is a theory of bargaining; the Soviet notion of deterrence is without a theory and substitutes instead the science of war."[15]

If Americans deeply suspect Soviet attitudes, the Soviets for their part are deeply concerned that once having accepted the idea of balance of strategic power and parity, they will see "influential circles" in the United States aim to achieve strategic superiority. In the Soviet view the recent intensification of an American campaign against the "Soviet menace" serves just this purpose and is to a large extent rooted in just this goal.[16] In an excellent review of Soviet strategic policies and arms control positions Raymond Garthoff reaches the following conclusion:

[15]Robert Legvold, "Strategic 'Doctrine' and Salt: Soviet and American Views," *Survival*, 21, no. 1 (January/February 1979), 8. This asymmetry adds of course to the difficulty of arms negotiations with the Russians and creates additional possibilities of mutual misperception. Pipes, after stating that "the Soviet leadership could not accept the theory of mutual deterrence," adds in a footnote: "I would like to stress the word 'theory,' for the Russians certainly accept the *fact* of deterrence. The difference is that whereas American theorists of mutual deterrence regard this condition as mutually desirable and permanent, Soviet strategists regard it as undesirable and transient: they are entirely disinclined to allow us the capability of deterring them" (*Commentary* [July 1977], p. 29). In response to this, I fully subscribe to the view of Richard L. Garwin, who replies: "The fact of Soviet deterrence is good enough for me; I don't insist that they like being deterred" ("U.S. Strategic National Security Programs" in U.S., Congress, Testimony to the House Armed Services Committee, 31 January 1978, p. 110). For a key article on the role of nuclear weapons and on the fact that in the present age major war cannot be considered any more a "continuation of politics by other means," see A. I. Krylov, "Oktiabr' i strategiia mira," *Voprosy filosofii*, 1968, no. 3, 3–13. See also V. G. Dolgin, "Mirnoe sosushchestvovanie i faktory ego uglubleniia i razvitiia," *Voprosy filosofii*, 1974, no. 1, pp. 57–68; G. A. Arbatov, "The Stalemate of the Policy of Force," *Problems of Peace and Socialism*, 1974, no. 2 (February); M. A. Mil'shtein, L. S. Semeiko, "Problema nedopustimosti iadernogo konflikta," *SShA*, 1974, no. 11 (November), pp. 3–12. For a Soviet military rebuttal of such a view, one that stresses its demobilizing effects on Soviet war preparedness, the basic article is that of General K. Bochkarev, "Problema sotsiologicheskikh aspektov bor'by protiv sil agressii i voiny," *Voennaia mysl'*, 1968, no. 9 (September).

[16]In a most powerful way this view is expressed in the very serious article by M. A. Mil'shtein, "Na opasnom perekrestke," *SShA*, 1978, no. 10 (October), pp. 3–13. See also: V. V. Zhurkin, "Podopleka novoi vspyshki kampanii o 'sovetskoi ugroze,' " *SShA*, 1978, no. 8 (August), pp. 13–22; V. F. Petrovskii, "Evoliutsiia doktriny 'natsional'noi bezopasnosti,' " *SShA*, 1978, no. 11 (November), pp. 12–24; A. Voronov, "Who Needs the Myth of the 'Soviet Menace'?" *International Affairs*, 1978, no. 7 (July), pp. 94–102. A good summary of the Soviet view is contained in the article by Radomir Bogdanov and Lev Semeiko, "Soviet Military Might: A Soviet View," *Fortune*, 26 February 1979, pp. 46–52.

There are, in fact, at this juncture a number of parallel perceptions—and misperceptions—held by both sides. Despite greatly differing ultimate objectives, the principal problems in arms control
accommodations are *not* due to differing operative aims of the two
sides, but to differing perceptions, to suspicions, and to the difficulties of gearing very different military forces and programs into
balanced and mutually acceptable strategic arms limitations.[17]

Constant Soviet denials that they seek strategic superiority and constant assertions that they wish to settle for strategic parity may reflect
less a lack of desire for superiority than a more realistic appraisal of
what they can get from detente, and this they seem to prefer to the
specter of an unbridled new strategic arms race spiral. The key Soviet
expectations associated with detente in the military realm seem to rest
not in the strategic dimension but in the area of conventional power, that
is to say, in the preservation and further expansion of their superiority in
the European theater versus the NATO forces, and, second, in accelerated
development of their global conventional capabilities.

It is with regard to these two goals that Zbigniew Brzezinski's proposition in May 1977 applies most and is most pertinent for evaluating
Soviet expectations from detente: "One could, in the past, see the Soviet
build-up in some measure as a response to the real or perceived asymmetry in the American-Soviet relationship. This no longer prevails. Therefore, the question as to why the Soviets continue their build-up is a very
legitimate one."[18]

There exists a tendency in Western literature to overstate the military-
political implications of the Soviet nonstrategic build-up. Some of its
sources may, and certainly do, reflect conditions which could be less
ominous than they seem and should not be interpreted solely on the
premise of the "worst-case" syndrome. A large number of elements contribute to the Soviet build-up and among those which *may* not properly
fall into the category of "worst-case" explanations, the following are the
most important:

> The long-range threat of China may only increase once China
> begins, as now seems likely, the significant modernization of its
> antiquated military machinery. The Chinese question, a permanent
> ingredient in Soviet military-political thinking, will force on any
> Soviet leadership the necessity to plan for a two-front conflict, a
> necessity spared the United States.[19]

---

[17]Raymond L. Garthoff, "Mutual Deterrence and Strategic Arms Limitation in
Soviet Policy," *International Security*, 3, no. 1 (Summer 1978), 147. See also his
"SALT and the Soviet Military," *Problems of Communism*, 24, no. 1 (January-
February 1975), 21–37.

[18]*U.S. News and World Report*, 30 May 1977, p. 36.

[19]The Soviet Union deploys against China approximately one-third of its active
military units. Moreover, while until a few years ago these divisions were inferior in quality and state of preparedness to those deployed against NATO in
Europe, a major effort to upgrade and modernize them is under way. According

The total Soviet commitment to an East European empire on the one hand and the necessity to rely in the last instance on military forces for the domination of Eastern Europe on the other hand put a double burden on Soviet military deployment in the European theater. First, the Soviet Union commits large forces to the preservation of its empire, that is, to its *internal* security in times of peace and even international relaxation. Second, this situation makes it prudent when planning for times of war or increased tension to assign significant forces to the task of securing rear areas and lines of communications and neutralizing the possible disloyal acts of mistrusted allies. One suspects that the total of Soviet forces committed to secure the loyalty of allies exceeds that of those Warsaw Pact forces on which the Soviet Union feels it can rely with security in times of conflict.[20]

The Soviet concept of national security as shaped by experience, history, and world view tends to exaggerate dramatically the dangers to the homeland and to subscribe to a defensive overkill, to an enormous defensive overcommitment. It leads Soviet decision makers to magnify the requirements of security to a degree unprecedented and unheard of in other modern societies. To describe their concept of national security as oversecurity or total security is to underestimate their position.[21]

The internal dynamics, or rather inertia, of the Soviet military-industrial complex, which is the largest peacetime military enterprise in modern history, an enormous, cumbersome, bureaucratic machinery, has its own momentum. In post-Khrushchev Russia, the growth demands and growth inertia of this machine have been reinforced by a number of factors: for example, by a much greater professional autonomy of the military, that is, their greater influence in deciding the military needs of the Soviet Union; by the oligarchical nature of the leadership, which makes very difficult any major changes in once-established plans and projections; and by the simple but immensely important fact that the leadership takes considerable pride and derives great satisfaction from both

to a CIA research paper, as reported in the *New York Times*, 7 February 1979, p. A11, about 15 percent of the cost of Soviet military activities in the last year has been for forces directed primarily against China.

[20]See, for example, Dale Herspring, "The Reliability of the East European Forces," paper presented at the Columbia University Faculty Seminar on Communism, 12 November 1977.

[21]See, for example, Franklyn Griffiths, "Inner Tensions in the Soviet Approach to 'Disarmament,'" *International Journal*, 22, no. 4 (Autumn 1967), 593–617. Arnold Horelick remarks perceptively on the Soviet military approach to the question of national security: "One looks in vain for evidence in Soviet [military] pronouncements of sensitivity to the insecurity of others that the Soviet Union's own security programs may promote. On the contrary, the USSR's security tends to be viewed as synonymous with the insecurity of the potential enemy; indeed, the latter is expected to behave more 'reasonably' only when the correlation of forces shifts in his disfavor" ("The Strategic Mind-Set of the Soviet Military," *Problems of Communism*, 26, no. 2 [March-April 1977], 85).

the absolute and especially the relative achievements in the military area as compared to other areas of Soviet endeavor.

Another potent factor underlying the Soviet military build-up is the acute perception of their technological lag, their fear that this lag will not perceptively diminish in the near future, and their overwhelming desire to close the gap. First, it creates the tendency to counter the qualitative superiority of the West with Soviet quantitative superiority; second, it makes them feel an urgency to develop new weapons and systems which they hope will narrow the qualitative gap.

Finally, with regard to global capability and the Soviet ability to project their own and their surrogates' military power far from their borders, their asymmetry with the United States is not only perceived; it is very real. With the possible exception of long-range air-lift capabilities, the Soviet Union has taken only the first major steps in acquiring the potential of the United States.

(Incidentally, most of the factors enumerated here could well apply also to the Soviet strategic build-up. They could serve as partial explanations of the intensity of the strategic build-up and the asymmetry in the Soviet and American approach to the *level* at which the arms race should be stabilized.)

Neither the Soviet armament effort nor, least of all, the Soviet view of the changing relation of world forces has been contrary in the Soviet perception to their interest in and commitment to detente. Detente describes a general process which combines conflict, competition, and co-operation at various levels of intensity and in diverse areas. The balance of these diverse elements, not to mention their specific levels, is not preset by the process itself and will never be determined in advance by any particular agreement of the two superpowers. It will be determined rather by the balance of opportunities and risks and the correlation of actual and perceived forces in the world arena. Detente contains elements of symmetry on the part of each superpower, the crucial element of which is that each wishes to avoid both war and the escalation of confrontations which may bring war. But detente is basically an asymmetrical relation.[22] Its actual shape will be decided not by conceptual schemes designed in the Kremlin or the White House, but by the actual policies of the superpowers in various areas and their responses to one another, by the resources brought to bear by the superpowers on this relation, by their ability to mobilize internal support (in the Soviet case primarily economic support and in the American case primarily political support); that is to say, it will depend critically on the nature and success of each superpower's leadership.

[22]On the asymmetrical nature of detente see the stimulating paper by Kenneth Jowitt, "Images of Detente and the Soviet Political Order" (Institute of International Studies, University of California [Berkeley], 1977).

Within the general framework of detente, one can envisage therefore diverse types of detente which may differ significantly in the process by which they are characterized and by their outcomes. To say, as many justifiably do, that detente is probably irreversible is to speak only about the general framework, about the neutralization of the European theater as an area of armed conflict, but not about the specific type of detente which has yet to emerge clearly from this framework, and which even when it assumes a more defined shape may undergo important changes. Present Soviet-American relations concern primarily what kind of detente there should be, what type of detente each superpower would prefer to seek.

This brings us to the two major questions which at present and for a long time to come will critically influence the nature of detente and the optimal and the short-range expectations of each superpower with regard to detente: the question of the role of military force in international relations and the question of the Soviet perception of the Third World, the only arena where in the Soviet view such a force can still be applied, outside their own sphere of influence.

13

THE ROLE OF
THE MILITARY FACTOR IN
INTERNATIONAL RELATIONS

Soviet writings on the role and use of military power in international affairs initially overwhelm the reader with a feeling of unreality, especially when they are compared to Soviet actions. For example, one Soviet writer cites the size of "the colossal American military budget" as proof of the vicious arms race in which the United States is engaged, without mentioning the fact that the Soviet military budget is considerably larger.[1] The arms race seems to be a one-sided affair in which the United States dances alone. In this regard Soviet views provide a much more primitive mirror image of those extremely one-sided views in American writings which depict the Soviet Union as engaged in a vicious arms race, with the United States as the innocent bystander.

The analysis of Soviet views on the role and use of military power in international relations, however, leads one to conclude that they contain an internal logic which cannot be dismissed, one which reflects in part at least the Soviet perception of international reality and which bears on the formulation of policy. The main elements of these views can be presented in a distilled form and logical sequence as follows:[2]

> The United States, the main adversary of the Soviet Union, has traditionally regarded and continues to regard military power as the principal and ultimate means of influencing international relations. Economic actions, diplomacy, political alliances, and other forms of international influence all play supportive roles in American foreign policy. The Vietnam war is only the most extreme if not the last example of general American interventionist policies which move military power to the foreground.

[1] U.S., Central Intelligence Agency, *A Dollar Cost Comparison of Soviet and US Defense Activities, 1968–1978* (SR 79-10004, January 1979). According to this paper, the Soviet Union in 1978 spent about 45 percent more than the United States for military expenditures. For the period 1968–78 the estimated Soviet military spending, measured in constant dollars, exceeded American spending by more than 10 percent (*New York Times*, 7 February 1979). For a comparison of Soviet and American military spending see also Barry M. Blechman et al., *The Soviet Military Buildup and US Defense Spending* (Washington, D.C.: Brookings, 1977).

[2] By far the best source on the Soviet perspective on the use of force in international relations is V. M. Kulish, ed., *Voennaia sila i mezhdunarodnye otnosheniia* (Moscow: Izd. Mezhdunarodnye otnosheniia, 1972). A very valuable source is G. A. Trofimenko, *SShA – politika, voina, ideologiia* (Moscow: Mysl', 1976).

The centrality of military power in American foreign policy is inherent in the nature of the American system. The situation has been aggravated in the post–World War II period because economic, social, and political tendencies of world development have moved in a direction inimical to American interest and ideology and can be counteracted only by direct or indirect use or threatened use of military force.[3]

Due to the growing strength of the socialist camp and progressive forces, the use of military forces becomes more difficult for Americans and the threat of its use less effective. This development contributes to the shaping of two basic tendencies among the groups which formulate and execute American foreign policy: one tendency where relative weakness leads to greater aggressiveness and to policies which attempt to prevent further losses and to recoup lost positions through military pressures and force; the other tendency where relative weakness tends to lead to an acceptance of what was lost, to a decline in aggressiveness, and to attempts to prevent the further decline of American influence primarily by means other than military.[4] The struggle between these two tendencies is constant. While one or the other tendency may be dominant at a particular time, the contest will not be fully resolved as long as the system remains unchanged.[5]

American imperialism exhibits weakness when compared both to its earlier strength and to the shifting relation of forces which favors its opponent. It should be stressed, however, that the Soviets in no way view America as a "paper tiger." America's force is considered enormous, its progress impressive, its accomplishments substantial. In the era of nuclear weapons and new scientific means of destruction, it may no longer be able to dominate the world, but it clearly has the power to lead the world to destruction.

The first-priority policy of the Soviet government is to avoid war

[3] A first-rate recent account of the Soviet image of the United States based on the study of the works of (Arbatov's) SShA Institute is contained in Morton Schwartz, *Soviet Perceptions of the United States* (Berkeley: University of California Press, 1978). It is very instructive to compare it to the earlier view analyzed by Frederick Charles Barghoorn, *The Soviet Image of the United States* (New York: Harcourt Brace, 1950).

[4] For a typical discussion of the two tendencies see for example: G. A. Arbatov, "Amerikanskii imperializm i novaia mirovaia real'nost'," *Pravda*, 4 May 1971, and his "O sovetsko-amerikanskikh otnosheniiakh," *Kommunist*, 1973, no. 3 (February), pp. 101–13; G. A. Trofimenko, "Militarizm i vnutripoliticheskaia bor'ba," *SShA*, 1972, no. 1 (January), pp. 65–72. As a matter of fact, the formulation of the two tendencies is so standard that one can discern the political orientation of the author and ascertain his place on the continuum of the differing views within the Soviet political community by the weights he assigns to each of the two tendencies.

[5] The standard phrase applied to America is that used by Brezhnev in his speech to the Twenty-fourth Party Congress: "the immutability of its reactionary and aggressive nature."

between the two superpowers and the two alliance systems. If Soviet *military* doctrinal writings treat nuclear war in terms of a winning strategy, the authoritative Soviet *political* writings never raise this theme. Quite the opposite, it is clear from these political writings that such a war is viewed as an utter disaster, a total failure of basic Soviet policies, an outcome that has to be avoided at all costs. The increasing military strength of the Soviet Union and its allies is seen as the best deterrent to such a war.

The arms race between the superpowers, the *unrestricted* build-up of nuclear armaments and new weapons, creates, however, a political climate in which the prospects for a nuclear war increase. For this and other mutually reinforcing reasons, the Soviet Union favors arms control which will stabilize or even in the future reduce the mutual level of destructive *strategic* forces.

The Soviet Union regards the areas of conflict between the two superpowers as a series of concentric rings. The closer the ring of conflict is to the center, the more it impinges on the vital interests of the adversaries and the greater is the potential for an allout war. The center ring represents the direct security interests and national integrity of the member nations of NATO and the Warsaw Pact. It is an area where the Soviets denounce the use of military power to support political goals, where they see the need to avoid any direct confrontation and demand the same commitment from the United States. Primarily in this sense one can appreciate that the Soviets perceive their armament policies and their attitude toward the role and use of military force in international relations as defensive in nature.

With regard to the other concentric rings, however – and the farther these are from the center, the more is this feature pronounced – the Soviet view and practice regarding the role of the Soviet or their allied military power and military resources conform astonishingly well and, I suspect, are largely inspired by what I described previously as their view concerning America's perception of the role of military power. There is only one, but fundamental, perceptional difference. American power is being employed against the progressive tendencies of historical development, Soviet power in their service.[6]

The outer rings of conflict are legitimate places for the competition of the superpowers and, by definition, of progress and reaction, as long as no *direct* military confrontation between the superpowers takes place. The Soviet Union in its service of historical progress employs various means of influence. In first place is its strength as a model, as an example of successful socioeconomic development, and the force of its ideological orientation as an ex-

[6] Both the renunciation of force in policies toward the central ring and the applicability of force toward the outer rings are well expressed in an article by V. Fyodorov, "Renunciation of Force in International Relations," *International Affairs*, 1978, no. 7 (July), pp. 32–40.

pression of Soviet experience. Second is the employment of Soviet economic resources. Third is diplomatic action supported by military might which serves as a shield against Western intervention, "the export of counterrevolution." Fourth is the actual deployment of military resources, including in some cases direct armed assistance. The Soviet Union would prefer to secure the success of progressive development and the furthering of Soviet international influence by the first three means alone, but it has no hesitation and no illusion about the importance of the military means.

All of Soviet history, its world outlook, its view of its adversaries prepare the Soviet Union, once it possesses the resources and so long as it does not *intentionally* endanger the cause of peace, still to regard the employment of military resources and power as the central and even the ultimate factor of international relations. Soviet thinking in this respect still depends on the axioms of just wars, of the necessity for violence in revolution, of force as the midwife of history. The slogan "Power grows from the barrel of the gun" was not invented by Mao Tse-tung.

Soviet leaders and writers seem honestly to believe that not only Soviet military assistance but even overt Soviet military action as in Angola do not constitute the export of revolution. The use of Soviet military power did not create a revolutionary situation; it merely altered the balance of forces in favor of revolutionaries against counterrevolutionaries who are actively supported by foreign reactionary interests.

The Soviet definition of what is progressive and, therefore, what Soviet military power may support is almost so elastic as to be circular. Basically, what the Soviet Union supports and what the United States opposes is progressive. This does not mean, however, that distinctions are not made between degrees of progressiveness, as we shall discuss below. Apart from the case of the "inner circle" of progressiveness—those Communist or genuinely left-revolutionary regimes (not movements out of power) which are allied by treaties with or controlled by the Soviet Union—there is no evidence either in Soviet writings or actions that the degree of progressiveness strongly influences the likelihood or magnitude of Soviet military help or intervention. The decision to help or intervene is basically a situational, not a doctrinal one.

We have attempted to depict the internal logic of Soviet views, perceptions, and to some extent actions with regard to the role and use of military power in the international arena. Yet there is an additional logic which is reinforced by those views and perceptions and in turn reinforces them and propels the Soviet leadership's views and actions in the direction of assuming the central importance of military power in international relations. It is the logic of the balance of resources which the Soviet Union has at its disposal in its international activities.

The nature of Soviet power is determined by the character, magnitude, and balance of those resources at its disposal which can be utilized in the international arena. Those resources are ideological, cultural, economic, political, and military. As we shall argue at greater length below, the particular nature of that growing power which the Soviets attempt increasingly to project abroad and on which they try to capitalize in foreign policy defines both the most dangerous and disquieting aspects of the attempted expansion of Soviet influence and the intrinsic weaknesses of this policy.

Soviet ideological resources, at one time among the strongest components of its power, have, with very few exceptions, either been exhausted or are becoming a liability.[7] The Soviet Union has ceased to be the symbol of radical revolution. It has been thoroughly outflanked on the left, partly by the Chinese and more importantly by the new radicals, who reduce it to the position of another great power bent on promoting its own interest and subordinating the revolutionary cause to its own great-power interests. Soviet leadership of the international Communist movement, in the past an important tool of its foreign policy, is at the very least in steep decline and at the very worst in an era of schism and fragmentation of more farreaching ideological consequences than the Sino-Soviet break. As an emulative model and symbol of social progress for the leftist intelligentsia in industrialized societies, the Soviet Union has been irrevocably compromised. In the case of the leftist intelligentsia of the Third World this process is less advanced but tends to develop in the same direction. The revolutionary regimes of the Third World are attracted to the Soviet Union not by Soviet ideology but by expediency and circumstances. Indeed, the revolutionism of these regimes is often no more than superficial by any standards, devoid of radical social and political traditions and roots. In essence, it displays scant affinity for the Soviet ideological mode, let alone the Marxist or even Leninist experience. In the Third World, where the main Soviet effort at expanding its influence takes place, the strongly nationalistic, religious, or socially conservative regimes sometimes ally themselves with the Soviet Union not because of the Soviet official ideology but despite it; very often they do not hide their repugnance for it.[8]

[7] The sources of the radical decline in the attractiveness of the Soviet Union as a revolutionary model of emulation is treated extensively in Seweryn Bialer, "The Resurgence and Changing Nature of the Left in Industrialized Democracies," in S. Bialer and S. Sluzar, eds., *Radicalism in the Contemporary Age, 3: Strategies and Impact of Contemporary Radicalism* (Boulder, Colo.: Westview Press, 1977), 4–13. See also Richard Lowenthal, *Model or Ally? The Communist Powers and the Developing Countries* (New York: Oxford University Press, 1977).

[8] One caveat is in order here. The rapid and almost total decline of the drawing force of Soviet ideology and the Soviet model of development has not been accompanied by a decline of attractiveness of a generalized idea of socialism, which, however, has become as if dissociated from the Soviet experience. The continuous attractiveness of the generalized idea of socialism in the Third World, however, has a number of consequences. First, it reinforces Soviet elite

The cultural assets of a country in the international arena–whether language, educational tradition, mass cultural patterns, or what can generally be described as the attractiveness and impressiveness of a way of life–can be of great importance in furthering its influence. In the American case, the stereotype of the "ugly American" tended to obscure the enormous attractiveness of American mass culture (or in the French case of the high culture) and civilization for widely diverse peoples as well as the importance of cultural assets in the spread of American influence. Soviet cultural patterns are highly formalized, rigid, stolid, intolerant, and strange to an amazing variety of people of various classes and nations who are exposed to them. The Soviet style of life was said maliciously by one foreign leader to combine "the charm and lightness of the Germans, the openness of the Albanians, the humility of the Indians, and the efficiency of the Latins." Far from being the carrier of a culture which would enhance any attempts to gain influence, the Soviet people, including the elite, exhibit in their unofficial behavior tremendous attraction to American style and Western culture. This ambivalence gives to Soviet cultural behavior a poorly concealed feeling of superiority in relations with the poor and "backward" and a feeling of inferiority in their relations with the rich and "developed," that is, the Western. Neither is attractive, and neither serves their foreign policy.

Turning to Soviet economic resources, considerable difficulties in Soviet economic development should not becloud the real achievements of the Brezhnev era. Part of this advance may be seen in the rapid development of Soviet participation in international economic interrelations in general and the expansion of its economic arrangements with and assistance to less developed countries in particular.[9] The sheer size of the economy and especially of the industrial plant and the centralized control over resources provide the Soviet Union with a considerable economic potential in support of its foreign policy. Yet there can be little doubt that for the present and the foreseeable future this potential in its civilian aspect is highly limited. For a number of reasons, the magnitude of Soviet involvement in the world economy is not commensurate with the evolution of the Soviet status as a global power; and, of equal importance, it has not grown perceptibly during the Brezhnev era as compared

belief in their own system, which they regard as socialist; it provides the element of worldwide justification and legitimation for their internal and international efforts. Second, it reinforces the "natural" anti-Western attitude with an anti-capitalist element and in a world of superpowers makes it more difficult to be anti-Soviet. Third, it creates an element of common identification with the Soviet Union, which by tortuous logic, however "falsely socialist," is closer to "socialism" than is the "imperialist West."

[9] For a discussion of Soviet aid to the Third World see U.S., Central Intelligence Agency, *Communist Aid to the Less Developed Countries of the Free World, 1976* (ER 77-10296, August 1977); Orah Cooper, "Soviet Economic Aid to the Third World," in U.S., Congress, Joint Economic Committee (94th Cong., 2d sess., 14 October 1976), *Soviet Economy in a New Perspective*, pp. 189–96.

to that of Western industrial nations. Direct Soviet influence in and on the world economy is minimal.[10]

Soviet economic resources are great. For a number of reasons, however, the availability of these resources for purposes of Soviet foreign policy and the receptivity of foreign recipients to cooperative economic arrangements with the Soviet Union are very limited. Among those reasons one can mention the following:

> The Soviet system of taut economic planning overwhelmed by internal demand, which leaves few reserves for foreign purposes;[11]
>
> The growing pressure of the newly emerged popular consumerism and of ethnic economic assertiveness, which the Soviet leadership may ignore at its own peril;[12]
>
> The marginal character of Soviet agricultural production and its dependence on the vagaries of nature;
>
> The lack of tradition and experience with foreign economic instruments in Soviet planning and managerial organizations;
>
> The nonconvertibility of Soviet currency;
>
> The growing burden of economic relations with Eastern Europe and other socialist states (Cuba, Vietnam), which have become a major prerequisite of the stability of these countries and of Soviet control;[13]

[10]Soviet exports constitute 4.8 percent of the Soviet 1977 GNP as compared to 6.4 percent in the U.S., 11.9 in Japan, and 22.7 in the Common Market (*Indicators of Comparative East-West Economic Strength, 1977* [U.S., State Department, Special Report no. 49, December 1978], p. 2).

[11]The tautness of Soviet economic planning and the extent of internal demands can be seen from the following: For the years 1965–76 the share of fixed investments in the Soviet GNP has fluctuated between 26 and 28 percent without any sign of declining. This figure is almost double that of any major industrial nation with the exception of Japan (Rush V. Greenslade, "The Real Gross National Product of the U.S.S.R., 1950–1975," in U.S., Congress, Joint Economic Committee (94th Cong., 2d sess., 14 October 1976), *Soviet Economy in a New Perspective*, p. 277; U.S., Central Intelligence Agency, *Handbook of Economic Statistics 1977* [Research Aid ER 770-10537, September 1977], p. 49). In the years 1966–70 and 1971–5 the average annual rates of the growth of overall household per capita consumption have been 4.9 and 3.2 percent, respectively, with the consumption of durable goods growing even faster, at 9.7 percent in both periods (Gertrude E. Schroeder and Barbara S. Severin, "Soviet Consumption and Income Policies in Perspective," in U.S., Congress, Joint Economic Committee [94th Cong., 2d sess., 14 October 1976], *Soviet Economy in a New Perspective*, p. 622). One should also mention the significant inflationary pressures in the Soviet economy which are expressed in the increases in savings and the low inventories of *salable* goods.

[12]For the discussion of the pressure of consumerism see Walter D. Connor, "Consumption, Careers and Mass Concerns: Economic Performance and Political Stability in the USSR," and Rush Greenslade, "Economic Development and Popular Expectations," papers for Workshop on Political Stability and Socio-Economic Change in the Soviet Union, Research Institute on International Change, Columbia University, 4–5 May 1976.

[13]On the burden of economic relations with Eastern Europe see Paul Marer, "Has Eastern Europe Become a Liability to the Soviet Union? (III)–The Economic Aspect," in Charles Gati, ed., *The International Politics of Eastern Europe* (New York: Praeger, 1976), pp. 59–81.

The strict compartmentalization of the Soviet economy into
military and civilian sectors and the military burden, which
can be carried only by an overwhelming concentration of advanced technology and cadres in the military sector;

The noncompetitiveness of the quality of Soviet industrial and
agro-technology, medicine, applied science, and so on, in comparison to the everyday standards of Western industrial
nations.[14]

The developing countries of the Third World are obviously the key
target for utilizing such economic resources as technological help and
exports, financial credits and managerial skills in support of Soviet foreign-policy goals. The capacity displayed here by the Soviets has been
primarily or even exclusively for a limited number of show projects, such
as the Aswan Dam or the Indian steel complex, and for highly selective
and limited credit and aid. Moreover, Soviet leaders probably quite correctly show no confidence that their economic efforts will be rewarding
in a political sense, at least within the limits of the resources which they
are willing or able to commit.

The situation differs little regarding Soviet relations with industrialized countries where Soviet foreign-policy assets could consist of providing a significant market and of supplying important raw materials. With
regard to the latter, there is little chance that the Soviet economy can
afford large raw material exports (oil, for instance) without massive technological imports from the West supported by long-range credits, that is
to say, without providing the West with political leverage through economic means rather than gaining leverage over the Western economies.
With regard to the Soviet Union as a market, the present state of Soviet
indebtedness to the West and the 1977–8 decline in total Soviet trade
with the West are only the more recent indications of the limitations of
the Soviet market and its dependence on long-range Western credits and
on political factors.[15]

The political resources at the disposal of Soviet foreign policy are
significant and impressive. The Soviet Union has once and for all ended
its sectarian and isolationist approach to non-Soviet forces abroad. The

[14]The most recent and the most extensive and detailed study of the technological
level of Soviet industrial performance reaches the following conclusion: "In
most of the technologies we have studied there is no evidence of a substantial
diminution of the technological gap between the USSR and the West in the past
15–20 years, either at the prototype/commercial application stages or in the
diffusion of advanced technology" (Ronald Amman, Julian Cooper and R. V.
Davies [with the assistance of Hugh Jenkins], *The Technological Level of Soviet
Industry* [New Haven, Conn.: Yale University Press, 1977], p. 66).

[15]For the discussion of East-West trade see U.S., Central Intelligence Agency,
USSR: Hard Currency Trade and Payments, 1977–78 (ER 77-10035U, March 1977);
Richard Portes, "East Europe's Debt to the West: Interdependence Is a Two-Way
Street," *Foreign Affairs*, 55, no. 4 (July 1977), 751–82.

process of Soviet political activization abroad which started under Khrushchev has been accelerated. Pacts with foreign nations, treaties, diplomatic pressures play an important part in the Soviet foreign-policy arsenal. A major force in the United Nations, the Soviet Union's support and veto are significant instruments of its foreign policy. Through its system of highly controlled alliances with Eastern Europe and other Communist states, the Soviet Union is orchestrating the political activities and considerable foreign-policy resources of those countries in support of Soviet policies and goals.

The political strength and activism of the Soviet Union is especially discernible in the broad range of its mutually supportive relations with non-Communist social and political movements in the Third World, a kind of relations in which it clearly surpasses the other superpower. This brings me to what I would consider the greatest Soviet foreign-policy political resource: the Soviet attitude toward change and toward revolutionary and nationalistic aspirations in the non-Communist world. It is an attitude of almost blank underwriting of any and all change and aspiration which in the Soviet opinion undermines the status quo. It makes of the Soviet Union a natural ally of the nations and movements which harbor such ambitions and aspirations, and by itself, especially in the short run, it has cost the Soviet Union very little.

The Soviet Union, however, displays some very significant weaknesses in its ability to muster political resources for its foreign-policy goals. Most importantly, the expansion of the resources at the peripheries of Soviet foreign activities are accompanied by a pervasive weakness and, to an extent, even constriction of these resources at the center.

Despite all Soviet efforts, its basic alliance system is upheld ultimately by force of arms rather than by political means. Efforts to transform it from the undisguised empire of Stalin's days into a stable commonwealth are counteracted by popular and elite irredentism and by social and economic instability. The Soviet Union is unable to bring Yugoslavia back into the fold, and, for all practical purposes, Rumanian foreign policy is outside the Soviet political line. The centerpiece of its postwar alliance system, China, is shattered beyond redemption. While the interests of the key components of world Communist movements may and do sometimes coincide with short- and medium-range Soviet interests, the control of these movements has irrevocably passed from Soviet hands.

The growth of Soviet great-power status, the development of its global reach, has also brought in addition to greater prestige and influence a growing fear among its non-Communist Third World allies, semi-allies, and partners about Soviet intentions, about the perceived Soviet desire to control their allies. Those fears have led to a number of important setbacks in the Soviet effort to develop alliance systems (Egypt and India, for example) and to a large extent make the strength of newly formed alliances depend on the isolation of the Soviet partners, on their lack of any other choice but to embrace Soviet help.

The situation is quite different with regard to the military assets of Soviet foreign policy. Starting with its ability to offer a vast array of weapons covering the whole range of needs of any nation and fully competitive with what the United States may offer – and in addition to weapons being able to deliver the entire range of aid from large numbers of military advisers through the offensive deployment of the troops of at least one of its client surrogates to the defensive and, in the case of Afghanistan, the massive offensive deployment of its own military forces – the Soviet Union's actions are today a crucial factor in almost every important area of global conflict. The willingness to commit military assets abroad in a growing number of areas strongly suggests a partial redefinition of what constitutes risk. One of the main tendencies and dilemmas of Soviet international behavior is the attempt to translate its military assets into global political influence. The fact that this policy has brought in the past some conspicuous failures and that its present successes are far from being assured should not detract from the fact that the tendency is growing and that this policy carries inherent dangers.

It is primarily with regard to the military resources of its foreign policy that the Soviet Union excels. Starting with the 1955 Arab arms deal, the Soviet Union entered the international weapons and military assistance market in a big way and continues steadily to expand its weight.[16] It is in this area that the Soviet Union is quantitatively and qualitatively competitive with the West. And in all probability, in its *ability* and willingness to deploy direct military force it exceeds the United States in the post-Vietnam era.

The picture that emerges is one of the imbalance of Soviet policy resources, with military resources as the chief asset and all other resources playing at most a supportive role. (This is, of course, exactly the situation that for Soviet analysts distinguishes the American case.) This situation, combined with the expansionist tendency of Soviet foreign policy, is disquieting in its implications. The necessity for the Soviets' inordinate reliance on military assets together with their quest for increased world influence reinforce the already dangerous fact that the Soviet Union is an ascending world power, a power which, while it does not want a war or confrontation with the other superpower, has very limited stakes in the preservation or peaceful reformation of the world order. Given the role of the Soviet Union as an outsider and the limits on its nonmilitary resources, such a peaceful reformation would not in So-

[16]According to one estimate, Soviet arms deliveries to the Third World in the years 1974–7 were of the order of $14,775 million, of which 57.9 percent went directly for weapons and the rest for support and services. In the same period American arms deliveries were $20,101 million, of which 39.1 percent went for weapons. That is to say, while American deliveries in this period were about 36 percent higher than those of the Soviets, Soviet weapons deliveries were about 9 percent higher than those of America (CIA, National Foreign Assessment Center, *Arms Flows to LDC's: US-Soviet Comparisons, 1974–77* [ER 78-10494U, November 1978], p. 10).

viet eyes provide opportunities for the growth of Soviet influence. While it may lead to a further diminution of American power in the world arena or even a decline in the overall influence of the West and a further growth of the influence of regional great powers or blocs of Third World countries, the Soviet Union is primarily interested not in a more equitable economic or political distribution of influence in favor of Third World countries, but in the growth of its own influence. Such a reformation of the world order conducted in a peaceful way holds less attraction and promise from the point of view of the growth of Soviet influence than do conflicts and disorder.

The weakness of other resources and the weight of military assets in the Soviet foreign-policy arsenal means that the Soviet opportunity for spreading its influence can be accomplished primarily where there are conflicts in which the military factor plays an important role and where conflict can be escalated to military solutions. To say it simply, the Soviet Union is interested in fomenting conflicts, escalating conflicts, maintaining them at a high level of intensity, and exploiting them, but not in their peaceful solution, especially in their early stages, when they are most susceptible of solution. One must underline the conclusion that it is in situations where conflicts persist and escalate to military solutions that the translation of the growing Soviet military power into political influence is most probable and where their chief foreign-policy assets can be brought most profitably to bear in the international arena.

As the reader will discover below, I am far from underestimating the weaknesses and the long- or even medium-range costs of the deployment of Soviet military resources in the international arena. Yet their direct and short-term costs are low, their effectiveness high, their returns impressive, and their preponderance in the balance of Soviet foreign policy resources pronounced. It is this logic of the nature of Soviet foreign-policy resources which reinforces the Soviet perception of international reality and provides an additional push for the assumption of the centrality of armed power and resources in international relations.

Two disclaimers are in order here. First, I am not proposing at all that the Soviet Union is a military giant with feet of clay.[17] It is not only that Soviet foreign-policy resources are not confined to the military and that their sheer size and the basic *internal* stability of the Soviet Union pre-

---

[17]Such a view has gained some currency lately. In its most extreme form it is expressed by the late Max Hayward, who states: "Nothing works in the Soviet Union except the armed forces and the KGB." Robert Conquest quotes this approvingly in "A New Russia? A New World?" *Foreign Affairs*, 53, no. 3 (April 1975), 492. It is a view that harbors dangerous illusions and distorts Soviet reality.

[18]For the discussion of internal stability of the Soviet system see Seweryn Bialer, "Stability and Legitimacy of the Soviet System," paper for Workshop on Political Stability and Socio-Economic Change in the Soviet Union, Research Institute on International Change, Columbia University, 4–5 May 1976.

clude any such assessment[18] but also that the Soviet policy makers have displayed an ability to mobilize these resources in times of need and concentrate them on key areas or on key issues. In a curious way, partly because they are not a status quo power and partly due to their world outlook, to their mindset, they have been and are sensitive to the inevitability of change in international relations and therefore even their perceptions provide a better guide for sensing opportunities and too often a better orientation point than our own perceptions.

Yet it seems clear to me that a serious imbalance can be perceived in the nature of their foreign-policy resources and in their perception favoring the military factor (which, it should be stressed, is not the same as favoring war). It is an imbalance in many senses, but primarily in the critical sense of its incongruity with what I perceive as the broadest goals which have evolved in Soviet foreign policy. These are the goals of gaining "a place in the sun," achieving status and influence in world affairs commensurate with the Soviets' own perception of what is due them as a superpower, and achieving international political parity with the United States while at the same time strengthening Soviet security. The imbalance would be even greater if Soviet goals in the 1980s were to go beyond to the highly unrealistic aim of achieving the same degree of dominance enjoyed by the United States in the period after World War II.

I do not wish to dwell on the obvious dangers of such an imbalance. Let me rather stress some of its inherent weaknesses and high long-range costs. First of all, the stress on Soviet military resources and their uses along the peripheries of world power centers does not bear on the central power-balance relation. In this central relation the Soviet Union must resort to detente if it wishes on the one hand to alleviate the pressure of its main fear, direct confrontation with the United States and the danger of war, and on the other hand to satisfy its principal internal economic needs. Moreover, extensive reliance on the military factor produces unintended consequences which endanger the central relation. It has already created a backlash which will grow stronger and which through an unavoidable linkage will affect the priorities of Soviet foreign policy.

Finally, what comes from the barrel of a gun in the world of the 1980s is only short-term power, not long-range influence – unless the gun is used in new areas as directly and mightily as until the Afghanistan crisis it was used only close to Soviet borders in Eastern Europe. When military resources are used to increase Soviet influence with regimes which are ideologically alien to the Soviet Union, the Soviet achievement has already shown itself many times to be rather ephemeral. And in the case of ideologically more friendly regimes, where the Soviet Union hopes to gain a stronger and more permanent foothold through its military resources, they in all probability, after the crisis situation has passed, will find many revolutionary leaders reacting as did Pilsudski, who, when recounting his revolutionary youth, said, "I took the train of socialism and left at the station of independence."

After creating an empire on its own borders and failing to transform it into a commonwealth, the Soviet Union is now in the process of attempting to create a system of client states, some close but most far from its borders. The imbalance of the resources of Soviet foreign policy makes the prospect of success in this endeavor very unlikely aside from exceptional cases like Afghanistan. Even more unlikely is the prospect that they will be able to transform those incipient client states into staunch allies, an attainment that would run counter to their whole tradition and experience.

The second disclaimer has to do with Soviet perceptions themselves. I do not propose that the existing imbalance is perceived as such by the Soviet leadership and elites. I agree to a large extent with Robert Legvold when he writes,

> The Soviet Union does not see itself as only militarily potent and otherwise as economically disadvantaged, technologically deficient, bureaucratically sclerosed and so on. Its leaders admit to a broad range of problems and limitations but, where we constantly view these in terms of fundamental systemic weaknesses, they regard them as normal and corrigible defects. And where we focus on these defects, treating them as a basic disparagement of the Soviet experience, they tend to downplay them, instead emphasizing their accomplishments, and thus retain a genuine faith in the transcendent significance of that experience.[19]

Certainly Soviet writings do not provide any indications that the existing state of affairs is perceived as an imbalance. Nor is there any reason to doubt the deep Soviet belief in the historical validity and viability of their own experience. Indeed, one finds no clear indication that either the relative weaknesses of the Soviet economic position or the backlash consequences of their overreliance on military resources has yet reached the consciousness of Soviet decision makers.[20]

[19]Robert Legvold, "The Nature of Soviet Power," *Foreign Affairs*, 56, no. 1 (October 1977), 65.

[20]Soviet experts are aware, however, of the nature of imbalances in the foreign-policy resources of countries and even speak about the "compensatory" use of one resource in place of another. The following quotation from an authoritative source is clearly meant to include in its description not only the United States but also the Soviet Union: "In accordance with its foreign-policy goals the state puts to the foreground those forms and methods [of activity] which in its view could be the most effective in the existing situation. At the same time the influence of other factors which remain as if in the background does not stop. This should make it clear that with changes in the situation in international relations the forms and the means of foreign policy change also. This as a matter of fact reflects the compensatory nature of foreign-policy resources: they mutually supplement and compensate for each other in accordance with concrete situations. Inevitably there acts also a tendency toward the neutralization of the other side's superiority in one resource with the superiority of one's own side with other resources. . . ." (V. M. Kulish, ed., *Voennaia sila i mezhdunarodnye otnosheniia*, p. 217).

14

THE THIRD WORLD
AND THE TRANSLATION
OF POWER INTO INFLUENCE

Our discussion of the role of military factors in Soviet perception of international relations has already indicated the importance of the Third World in the Soviet scheme of things. As a result of three factors – detente, the growth of Soviet power and its ability to project it far from Soviet borders, and the internal instability and chaotic interstate relations in many regions of the Third World – these regions have become in the 1970s and will certainly remain in the 1980s the center of gravity of the conflict and competition between the Soviet Union and the United States.

The basic Soviet policy in the Third World is two-pronged: an effort to secure and expand what I would call an outer and an inner circle of alliances. The outer circle refers to countries or movements with a system or ideology alien to the Soviet Union where the alliance is based either on a single issue on which they agree (say Iraq and Syria) or on a broad understanding of what they oppose (say India until recently). The inner circle refers to countries or movements either modeled on the Soviet Union or which the Soviet Union considers sociopolitically progressive, revolutionary, and basically appropriate to their existing circumstances. The alliance here is based on a broad range of common interests, ideological proximity, extensive and direct Soviet help; it includes a relatively high degree of dependence on the Soviet Union (Afghanistan and Ethiopia, for example).

Soviet policy is directed at the expansion of both the outer and inner alliance systems. Due partly to the fact that some countries of the inner alliance system were formerly in the outer circle and to the general fear of the countries of the outer circle concerning long-term Soviet intentions vis-à-vis their countries, this policy has a built-in tension which is reflected to some extent in Soviet perceptions of the Third World situation.

Soviet perceptions of this situation are distinguished as much by what they lack as by what they include.[1] They contradict almost completely

---

[1] A representative view of the Soviet perception of the *political* aspects of Third World development is contained in: "Deistvennyi printsip revoliutsionnoi bor'by," *Kommunist*, 1977, no. 7 (May), pp. 3–10; V. Kortunov, "Soiuzniki sotsializma po antiimperialisticheskoi bor'be," *Kommunist*, 1977, no. 6 (April), pp. 107–13; S. L. Agaev and I. M. Tatarovskaia, "Nekotorye problemy razvitiia revoliutsionnogo protsessa v osvobodivshikhsia stranakh," *Rabochii klass*, 1978, no. 5 (September-October), pp. 44–56; A. S. Kaufman, "O roli rabochego klassa i ego partii v

the conceptual framework of the various Western perceptions. They are characterized by fluidity, generality, and an absence of positive, constructive programs for Soviet-Western *coexistence* within the existing framework as well as *cooperative* arrangements for adjusting and changing the framework.

The Soviet Union does not recognize a *general* North-South division in world affairs. It does recognize a specific division between the West and the less developed countries which is seen to constitute a subordinate part of the general relation of forces between West and East. The North-South relation is subordinated to the East-West relation in two respects: in the direct political sense that in the era of detente it has been the key arena of competition for influence between the United States and the Soviet Union; and in the historical sense that in the third stage of the general crisis of capitalism it is the key area of struggle between indigenous forces of socialism, progress, and revolutionary change and reaction.

The Soviet notion of what is positive in the situation and developmental tendencies of the Third World is opposite that of the United States and the West. It welcomes ferment, instability, and revolutionary upheavals not equilibrium, stability, and orderly change. In fact, as long as Third World conditions and regional conflicts do not create the kind of tensions that may lead to a direct confrontation between the superpowers and create a danger of major East-West war, the Soviet notion is not much different from the former Chinese preference for "heavenly disorder."

The basic question concerning Soviet perceptions of the situation and trends in the Third World has to do with the relation between Soviet policies and the internal developments of less-developed countries. During the late Brezhnev era, Soviet perceptions in this regard have shown strong differences in emphasis as compared to earlier periods. In earlier periods Soviet policies depended on their assessment of the genuineness and magnitude of progressive socialist development in Third World countries. In the late Brezhnev era the pendulum has moved toward more open-ended pronouncements, toward more generalized statements which provide much broader definitions of what to regard as "progressive." The Soviet Union is thus given a greater range of options in proferring help. One key manifestation of this attitude has been the abandonment of the formula of the "noncapitalist" path of development as a criterion of Soviet policy.[2]

stranakh sotsialisticheskoi orientatsii," *Narody Azii i Afriki*, 1976, no. 4, pp. 3–17; R. A. Ul'ianovskii, "Ekonomicheskii front bor'by protiv neokolonializma," *Narody Azii i Afriki*, 1978, no. 4, pp. 3–17; V. E. Chirkin, "Idei Velikogo Oktiabria i revoliutsionnoe preobrazovanie politicheskoi sistemy v stranakh sotsialisticheskoi orientatsii," *Narody Azii i Afriki*, 1978, no. 5, pp. 3–16. See also G. B. Starushenko, "Razvitie idei nekapitalisticheskogo puti k sotsializmu," in *Sotsiologicheskie problemy mezhdunarodnykh otnoshenii* (Moscow: Izd. Nauka, 1970), pp. 220–39.

[2] While still figuring prominently in the Reports to the Twenty-third and Twenty-fourth Party Congresses in 1966 and 1971, the theme of the "non-capitalist" path was absent at the Twenty-fifth Party Congress in 1976.

The open-endedness of major Soviet *policy* formulation reflects a mixture of two correlated developments and pressures. First, it reflects the general lowering of expectations when compared to the Khrushchev and early Brezhnev era with regard to the *stability* of Soviet advance and influence building in the Third World and with regard to the progressive (that is, socialist-oriented), revolutionary potential of the Third World countries.[3] Second, it reflects much greater sophistication on the plane of scholarly and policy-oriented discourse below the level of major policy pronouncements where an effort is made to understand the internal dynamics of development in Third World countries. On this level of discourse, Soviet discussions are extraordinarily lively, and the writings display a degree of refinement hitherto absent.[4] Among the major concepts that are being discussed with reference to diverse Third World regions, those of *mnogoskladnost'* and *pererastanie* and to some extent the Chilean experience figure most prominently.

The concept of *mnogoskladnost'*, meaning "multi-dimensionality," refers to the social, cultural, and political structure of less developed countries. It opposes the artificial and forced application of the traditional Marxist concepts of class and social structure derived from industrial and industrializing societies to the analysis of less-developed countries. It stresses the specificity of the social, cultural, and political forces of diverse regions and individual countries. The policy implications of the Soviet work on multi-dimensionality is to advocate a multiplicity of approaches to diverse regions and countries, the abandonment of dogmatism in the classifications of the "progressive" potential of social and political groups in these countries, and the search for political allies and for groups worthy of Soviet support in places untried by Marxist-Leninist doctrine. It suggests the impossibility and counterproductivity of de-

---

[3] The lowering of expectations with regard to "progressive" advancement of the Third World countries, especially perceptible in comparison to the Khrushchev era, leads some analysts to suggest that a sense of frustration has developed in the 1970s among Soviet leaders and experts, a frustration reinforced by their setbacks in Indonesia, Egypt, India, etc. Moreover, it is this sense of frustration, it is sometimes argued, which has led the Soviet Union to its recent application of different forms of struggle for influence, for example in Angola or Ethiopia and, most obviously, Afghanistan. I must stress that I did not detect either in Soviet writings or in discussions with Soviet experts such a sense of frustration with regard to the Third World. Their view is a very long-range one, not visibly affected by what they consider temporary setbacks. Where I do detect a sense of frustration is with regard to U.S.-Soviet relations. The Soviets are apprehensive about the mood of America and have difficulty understanding it. They have difficulty comprehending Carter's policy line. They are baffled by the swings in American policy and the public-opinion pendulum. They are disappointed in the failure to realize early hopes of detente. A rare situation has developed where both sides in the relation have a deep sense of betrayal by their opposite numbers.

[4] One basic recent source for the study of Soviet expert perception of the Third World sociopolitical developmental patterns is P. A. Ul'ianovskii, *Ocherki natsional'no-osvoboditel'noi bor'by: Voprosy teorii i praktiki* (Moscow: Izd. Nauka, 1976), and by the same author, *Sotsializm i osvobodivshiesia strany* (Moscow: Glavnaia redaktsiia vostochnoi literatury, 1972).

vising one general line of Soviet policy toward Third World countries except for the indication of some general preferences.

The concept of *pererastanie*, meaning "growing over," refers to the potentialities for an uninterrupted though gradual transformation of non-socialist revolutionary developments into a socialist revolutionary phase. The writings on this subject are addressed to the question: Under what conditions can the enormous social and political turmoil of Third World regions and countries be channeled into a socialist revolutionary development? The basic consensus in answer to this question stresses the degree and firmness of the development of capitalist social relations as the key orientation point and dividing line between countries and situations where the socialist revolutionary potential is present or absent or doubtful. Once capitalist relations of production are firmly established, the potentialities for socialist transformations "growing over" from revolutionary turmoil decline decisively.

The policy implications of the Soviet writings on growing over are enormous. The concept sensitizes Soviet policy makers to the ultimate potential of movements and regimes whose immediate goals and socioeconomic orientation have little to do with socialist reconstruction but whose political orientation can outpace their socioeconomic environment. It accentuates the proposition that once a radical socialist political orientation is exhibited by a meaningful movement, the course of socialism is better served by trying to skip a stage of socioeconomic development than by waiting for the "natural" maturation of socioeconomic forces. Most importantly, however, it injects into Soviet policy thinking a note of apprehension over lost opportunities once revolutionary turmoil is permitted to yield to a stable pattern, once the opportunity of pushing it to its ultimate socialist end has passed.

The Soviets' own historical experience, the use by the Bolshevik party of the "dialectic of backwardness," is strikingly similar to the entire question of growing over, and one finds numerous allusions and references to the Soviet past in writings on such countries as Angola and Ethiopia.[5]

The theme of the Chilean experience is not often approached directly by Soviet writers, but the lessons of Chile are introduced indirectly in many of the discourses on the Third World situation and trends.[6] Aside from the obvious conclusions on the importance of controlling the army

[5] This point of view on the question of revolutionary developmental patterns in the Third World is elaborated in the materials of an international Communist conference on the theme "Great October and the Contemporary World" (Prague, 1977). A summary of the conference may be found in *Kommunist*, 1977, no. 11 (July), pp. 30–41; the speeches of Suslov and Ponomarev at the conference in *Kommunist*, 1977, no. 17 (November), pp. 18–43. See also Suslov, "Marksizm-Leninizm i revoliutsionnoe obnovlenie mira," *Kommunist*, 1977, no. 14 (September), pp. 13–28.
[6] On lessons of the Chilean experience see K. L. Maidanik, "Vokrug urokov Chili," *Latinskaia Amerika*, 1974, no. 5 (September-October), pp. 112–33. See also the interesting discussion on Chile in *ibid.*, 1978, nos. 4 and 5.

in a revolutionary situation, the Soviets draw three basic lessons with policy implications from the Chilean experience. The first lesson stresses the extreme difficulty of radical revolution in countries of the Third World where capitalist relations are firmly established and a strong middle class exists. Second, while acknowledging the need for a broad alliance to ensure successful revolutionary transformation and solidification, the writings stress the necessity for Communist dominance of the coalition. Third – and from our point of view the lesson with most important political implications – present-day revolutions never occur in an international vacuum and the importation of counterrevolution is an ever-present fact of life of overwhelming importance. For revolutions to succeed, such an importation must be counterbalanced by extensive and timely help offered to the revolutionaries by socialist forces from abroad. If anything, the Chilean experience reinforces on the one hand Soviet skepticism about the potential for revolutions, especially gradual ones, in more developed Third World countries and reinforces the attractiveness and potential of basically antifeudal revolutions, and on the other hand legitimizes in Soviet eyes the need for more active involvement of the socialist camp in supporting fledgling revolutionary regimes.

The attitudes and policies of the Soviet Union toward the Third World are characterized by a combination of two elements. They display above all else a very long-range view. They are dogged, persistent, and perseverant, unswayed by numerous setbacks and zigzags, for basic to them is the expectation that time and history are on their side. At the same time they betray a degree of restlessness and fear over lost opportunities, a sense that now is the right moment to expand their influence else the chance not recur for a long time.

Soviet perception of the economic dimension of Third World problems can be briefly summarized as follows:[7]

> The economic problems of the Third World are basically political in nature; they have to do primarily with relations with the imperialist powers and with internal paths of development.
>
> The Soviet Union welcomes the new self-assertiveness of less-developed countries because it both weakens the imperialist powers and promotes the internal radicalization of forces in the less-developed countries.
>
> The Soviet Union and developed socialist countries are not a part of the problem of the less-developed countries, but a part of the solution. The Soviet Union is the major power whose

---

[7] See for example the following Soviet articles: Y. Ivanov, "The CMEA Countries and World Economic Relations," *International Affairs*, 1978, no. 2 (February), pp. 30–9; E. Obminsky, "Problems of Restructuring Economic Relations," *International Affairs*, 1977, no. 1 (January), pp. 59–67; E. Primakov, "Nekotorye problemy razvivaiushchikhsia stran," *Kommunist*, 1978, no. 11 (July), pp. 81–91; A. Shapiro, "Burzhuaznye proekty perspektiv mirovogo khoziaistva," *MEMO*, 1978, no. 11 (November), pp. 39–55.

support is essential for even partial success of the Third World's demands for redress of their economic grievances.

The hopes and demands for farreaching solutions of the economic problems of Third World countries are utopian illusions. It is not the restructuring of North-South relations within the existing world order but a basic further shift in the East-West relation of forces which is essential (both in the sense of growth of Soviet might and influence and internal "progressive" transformation in the less-developed countries).[8]

The Soviet perception is, of course, ambiguous and vague. On the one hand, it supports the basic Third World position, identifies with its plight, and holds out the prospects for an ultimate solution. On the other hand, in the short and medium run it can offer the Third World very little in terms of actual support. In the down-to-earth question of actual economic help and relations, its position is in fact subordinated to the demands of its own development and not much different from the stance of the capitalist North.[9] This ambiguity comes out clearly in the statement of a leading Soviet expert:

Any restructuring of the world economy cannot be confined to the relations between the industrialized capitalist countries and the

[8] My description of the Soviet position regarding the economic dimension of their relations with Third World countries does not do justice to the complexity of the problem. While the position as described reflects the dominant long-range Soviet view, there are indications that this view may be changing and that at least on the level of expert deliberations some important disputes are taking place. The most important theoretical underpinning of the discussion and of a movement toward the adoption of a new position is the concept of a single world economy which is slowly gaining favor over the hitherto dominant idea of two world economies, socialist and capitalist. For an excellent discussion of the new tendencies in Soviet writings see Elizabeth Kridl Valkenier, "The USSR and the Third World – New Economic Dimensions," background paper no. 4 prepared for the Study Group on the Soviet Union and the World Economy, Council on Foreign Relations, February 1979. See also Toby Trister Gati, "The Soviet Union and the North-South Dialogue over a New International Economic Order," background paper no. 3 prepared for the Study Group on the Soviet Union and the World Economy, Council on Foreign Relations, January 1979; and Robert Legvold, "The Soviet Role in the Restructuring of the International Economic Order," paper prepared for the U.S. State Department, Office of External Research, 1977.
[9] For Soviet views on economic relations with developing countries, see "On Restructuring International Economic Relations: Statement by the Soviet Government," *Pravda*, 5 October 1976; A. Butov, *Na vzaimovygodnykh nachalakh* (Moscow: Moskovskii rabochii, 1978), pp. 87–121; *Vneshne-politicheskaia programma XXV s'ezda KPSS v deistvii* (Kiev: Naukova Dumka, 1978), pp. 174–86, 203–30. An excellent Western analysis may be found in Richard Portes, "East, West and South: The Role of the Centrally Planned Economies in the International Economy" (Cambridge, Mass.: Harvard Institute of Economic Research, discussion paper no. 630, June 1978).

Third World. The democratization of the world economic system also requires complete normalization of East-West relations, and elimination of things like artificial restrictions on economic ties between states with different social systems, discrimination in trade for political and ideological motives, and distortion of the international division of labor under the impact of the policies pursued by the western powers of their economic groupings. Those are the requirements the CMEA countries seek to add to the conceptions of a new international economic order. The unfair international economic order does much to harm the socialist countries. . . .

The CMEA countries support the developing countries on the new world economic order, but emphasize the need for progressive social transformations and the mustering of internal potentialities for economic growth as the chief means for changing their economic condition. The Soviet Union and many other socialist countries resolutely oppose the diverse utopian projects for a worldwide redistribution of wealth. . . . [They] cannot accept similar claims on all industrialized countries, regardless of their social system, and the demand that the socialist countries should accord to the Third World countries unilateral advantages on the nonreciprocity principle.[10]

The biggest ambiguity in the Soviet perception of the Third World political situation and trends has to do with its connection to detente. On the one hand, the Soviet Union looks upon North-South relations, where North is limited to capitalist powers, as subordinate to East-West relations and competition. On the other hand, it denies that there should be any negative effects or linkage on the central East-West relation, the detente, from the course of these subordinate relations.

The Soviet Union has explicitly recognized only two types of linkage between detente and the tendencies of development in the Third World: All countries – East, West, South – are interested in defusing the uncontrolled superpower arms race and limiting the danger of a major war; and detente should encourage "progressive" development in the Third World, that is to say, both indigenous developments and growth of Soviet influence. Detente should perform this function by dissociating the competition in the Third World from the question of war and peace, making the competition more benign, less dangerous, and thereby opening the possibility of its being more extensive; and by recognizing the global *political* parity between the two superpowers and thus the Soviet right not to be excluded from deliberations or decisions on any major questions concerning the Third World. Clearly, the Afghanistan situation suggests that the Soviet Union has found the detente policy wanting in this regard.

[10]Oleg T. Bogomolov, "The CMEA Countries in the Changing International Economic Climate," paper prepared for the conference on The Choice of Partners in East-West Economic Relations, Montebello, Canada, 26–8 April 1978, p. 18.

In the early days of the Carter Administration, Zbigniew Brzezinski made a statement during an interview to which the Soviets objected sharply: "We are trying to stimulate mutual involvement with the Soviet Union in dealing with problems which eventually will confront us with really staggering dilemmas. I can say this: We are challenging the Soviets to cooperate with us or run the risk of becoming historically irrelevant to the great issues of our time."[11] In the short run, Brzezinski's statement was itself entirely irrelevant and did nothing more than provoke Soviet sensitivities and status consciousness. There are probably very few things that can be said to make the Soviets, with their feeling that history is on their side, more angry than to proclaim the possibility of their "historical irrelevance."

It is important to perceive how Soviet thought responds to statements which invite Soviet cooperation in solving the dilemmas of North-South relations on the basis of American perceptions, in the framework of the American concept of "interdependence" or "New Economic World Order" or "Planetary Consciousness."[12] To understand the Soviet response, however, one has to appreciate not only the basic difference of perception but also the differences that stem from the incongruity of the *present* Soviet and American states of mind.

America, in the wake of Watergate and Vietnam, energy crises, and other assorted troubles, has become weary of conflict and competition, has been lowering its activist stance and seeking stability, not an extension of influence. The exaggerated expectations initially attached to detente by U.S. public opinion were precisely a reflection of America's hope to escape cheaply from the most difficult aspects of competition with the Soviet Union, to close neatly a page in America's postwar development. Now, when these expectations have not been met, a reaction has set in because the Soviet Union did not behave according to what was in our mind, and this we consider a breach of faith.

But the Soviet perception has been quite different. There has been much greater continuity in Soviet thinking on world affairs and much greater consistency in Soviet views on detente than in ours. The Soviet Union did not pass through traumatic experiences which would force a reexamination of outlook and a significant lowering of expectations. Whatever difficulties the internal Soviet situation conceals or reveals (and even here, as we mentioned earlier, the Soviet leadership's perceptions may differ very much from ours), in the area of foreign relations the Soviet experience was on the whole a rather exhilarating one. Their perception of what they have achieved, what they wish to achieve, and what is possible to achieve, is rather different from the American experience.

---

[11]*U.S. News and World Report*, 30 May 1977, p. 35.

[12]For Soviet critiques of those American concepts see: V. Petrovskii, "Kontseptsiia vzaimozavisimosti v strategii SShA," *MEMO*, 1977, no. 9 (September), pp. 70–80; V. Smolianskii, "Ot teorii 'konvergentsii' k 'planetarnomu soznaniiu,' " *Kommunist*, 1978, no. 8 (May), pp. 101–10; I. D. Ivanov, "SShA i 'novyi mezhdunarodnyi ekonomicheskii poriadok,' " *SShA*, 1978, no. 9 (September), pp. 3–16.

That is to say, it is not only Soviet and American values and basic perceptions which differ but also our current states of mind. It is as if the United States and the Soviet Union are *out of phase* with regard to one another. It is this incongruity which exacerbates Soviet anger at American accusations and criticisms of Soviet behavior and infuses our views on Soviet international behavior with strong elements of self-righteousness and renewed demonology.

Yet while in the short run the Brzezinski statement is irrelevant, it may be very relevant in the long run with regard to Soviet perceptions and policies concerning the Third World. In light of the disorder and aspirations which are sweeping the Third World and of the interconnectedness of Third World development with that of industrial nations, whatever their systems, the Soviets' present approach may become historically irrelevant.[13]

First, Soviet strength in the Third World is most potent in the presence of internal turmoil or interstate regional conflict. Then Soviet resources, determination, and policies have the greatest weight, bear on the resolution of accumulated grievances, coincide most closely with the interest of the forces which the Soviets support. Once the phase of stabilization sets in, the relevance of Soviet resources declines, the mutuality of common interests subsides, the Soviet hold on allied forces declines.

The Soviet Union is beginning to perceive this conclusion more clearly with regard to the outer circle of alliances. With regard to the inner circle, neither the resources of the Soviet Union and its surrogates nor the geopolitical and socioeconomic situation bodes well for the possibility that the Soviet Union can create a second ring of empire on the East European model, although the world may well experience significant turmoil and grief before this prognosis is fulfilled. I doubt whether the perception of this has yet penetrated the inner circle of Soviet decision makers. It certainly has penetrated the circle of experts and advisers to the leadership on international affairs, who do not hide their skepticism both about the degree of control which the Soviet Union possesses in such countries as Angola or Ethiopia and about the degree to which such control as they possess can endure. The days of the Western empires are over; it is highly unlikely that a Soviet empire can replace them.

Second, to the extent that the United States and democratic industrial nations engage in meaningful dialogue and negotiations with the Third World on the questions of a new economic order, the Soviet Union's position is that of odd man out. This is already observable in the present

---

[13]Soviet writers do not deny the existence of some "planetary" problems and, as a matter of fact, have recently been devoting more attention to them than before. But with the exception of one such problem, nuclear war, they consider them marginal to international intercourse. Moreover, in their view cooperative arrangements that would include all countries and address the alleviation of these global problems do not override the realities of East-West competition and of the struggle between progress and reaction. Finally, they regard as illusory the possibilities for their resolution in an international economy dominated by capitalism.

round of negotiations, where the Soviet Union fails to meet the direct needs and immediate hopes of most Third World countries and intrudes issues of superpower conflict in an atmosphere that is highly charged politically.

Third, Soviet activities in the Third World are to a large extent dictated not simply by aggressive drive but by Soviet fear, by an attempt to build a system of defensive alliances against a new encirclement and perhaps to compensate for its persistent weaknesses at home. The manner in which the Soviet drive is pursued, however, the stress on military factors, exacerbation of conflicts, and resistance to compromise solutions, shape a perception of Soviet intentions and actions in the West that cannot but be detrimental to Soviet interests. An inevitable backlash affects other dimensions of Soviet global relations, the arms race and detente relations. Instead of increasing the security of the Soviet Union, the Soviet position in the long run may lead to even greater insecurity. By increasing the danger in some parts of the world, by refusing to help mute the dangers in others, it makes the world in general a more dangerous place to live, not only for the United States but ultimately for the Soviet Union as well.

Soviet international perceptions and foreign-policy behavior in the period since Stalin's death reflect a mixture of diverse tendencies which Franklyn Griffiths has convincingly demonstrated.[14] He speaks of a sectarian tendency, inward-directed to the socialist camp and isolationist in its effects; a dualistic activist tendency which combines a commitment to pursue peaceful coexistence with the mobilization of external counterforce vis-à-vis the West; and a reformist tendency which in the competition of the contending camps stresses the force of example and political-economic forces over the political utility of military forces and places a premium on the development of stable cooperative arrangements with the West.[15] As I compare the particular blend of Soviet foreign-policy perspectives and behavior between the early and late years of the Brezhnev era, I see the decisive dominance of the activist tendency, the precipitous decline of the sectarian tendency, and the retention of a clear element of the reformist tendency. It is of greatest importance that the

[14]See Franklyn Griffiths, "Images, Politics and Learning in Soviet Behavior towards the United States" (Ph.D. dissertation, Columbia University, 1972); also his "Genoa plus 51: Changing Soviet Objectives in Europe," Wellesley Paper no. 4, 1973 (Toronto: Canadian Institute of International Affairs).

[15]I find Griffiths's differentiation of tendencies within Soviet policy much more convincing than the rather simplified left-versus-right dichotomy. The most persuasive argument against such a dichotomy, especially now, is that it does not account for the activism axis on which to consider Soviet perceptions and behavior. For an able exposition of the left-right view, see Alexander Dallin, "The Domestic Sources of Soviet Foreign Policy," in Seweryn Bialer, ed., *Domestic Context of Soviet Foreign Policy* (Boulder, Colo.: Westview Press, forthcoming).

American side, regardless of provocation however threatening, encourage and strengthen the reformist tendencies in Soviet outlook and behavior during the critical succession period which will determine more than any other single factor the shape of Soviet policies in the 1980s. For these tendencies to advance to a dominant place in Soviet perceptions and behavior, if this is at all possible, will to a considerable extent require the persistent and mature pursuit of a process of learning and adjustment on both sides.

Both the Soviet Union and the United States have yet to learn to live in a world where they share strategic parity. The Soviet Union has to discover above all else that the long-range political costs of using military resources in the international arena may be very high and may ultimately lead to the decline and not the enhancement of Soviet security. The United States has to abandon excessive and at times hysterical preoccupation with the military facet of the competition with the Soviet Union and particularly with the specter, in my opinion largely illusory, of potential Soviet *strategic* superiority.[16] This country has also to learn that while it opposes and it must oppose Soviet use of military force as a means of expansion, it cannot at the same time apply different standards to its own behavior and that of its allies. And, most important, it cannot exclude the Soviets from participating in the solution of international problems. It cannot deny to the Soviet Union the concomitants of the expansion of its influence. I am afraid that the process of learning has not yet advanced very far on either side.

[16]As Raymond Garthoff has remarked, "It is of some interest that those who most firmly assert that a Soviet intention to seek military superiority over us . . . are also those who most strongly call upon the United States to maintain or to reestablish military superiority over the Soviet Union" ("On Estimating and Imputing Intentions," *International Security*, 2, no. 3 [Winter 1978], 28–9).

PART V
PROSPECTS FOR THE 1980s

15
THE POLITICS
OF STRINGENCY

One sometimes has the impression – and it is only a slight exaggeration – that Western sovietologists speak more about the Soviet future than about the present. These futuristic writings construct alternate scenarios with different probability weights attached to them, scenarios that run the entire gamut of logical possibilities. A fairly full list of the alternate futures would read as follows. The Soviet Union will soon experience:[1]

Revolution[2]
Progressive degeneration and decay
Development into an authoritarian Great Russian state
A military coup, a military dictatorship
Neo-Stalinism
Transfer of power to the technocratic-managerial stratum
Convergence with the Western system
Far-reaching liberalization and democratization of the system
Socialist democracy and worker self-management
Liberalization of the system through an ethical-religious rebirth
Limited modernization of the existing system
Continuation of the system unchanged

Needless to say, unless the very different alternatives are to be treated as a logical shell game, there rests behind each of them different sets of assumptions about what the Soviet Union is today, what have been its moving forces in the twenty-five years of post-Stalin development, what are its accomplishments, unresolved issues, and tensions. Some common denominators underlie almost all the widely varied scenarios, however. With the possible exception in some cases of the prediction of limited

[1] All these alternatives are discussed in detail in Wolfgang Leonhard's book, *Am Vorabend einer neuen Revolution? Die Zukunft des Sowjetkommunismus* (Munich: C. Bertelsman Verlag, 1975), pp. 305–403. Another such discussion of alternate futures may be found in Zbigniew K. Brzezinski, *Between Two Ages: America's Role in the Technetronic Age* (New York: Viking, 1970), pp. 154–76.

[2] Aside from the Amalrik version, this alternative is most forcefully presented by Emmanuel Todd, *La Chute Finale* (Paris: Laffont, 1976). The clear possibilities of revolution in the Soviet Union are also stressed by Eugene Lyons in "The Realities of a Vision," in Zbigniew Brzezinski, ed., *Dilemmas of Change in Soviet Politics* (New York: Columbia University Press, 1969), pp. 49–55; and by Robert Conquest, *Russia after Khrushchev* (New York: Praeger, 1965). The Chinese Communists regard a revolution in the Soviet Union as "inevitable," as do the leaders of the Polish dissent movement, Jacek Kuron and Karol Modzelewski.

modernization of the system, they share similar assumptions about the present Soviet regime which explain especially the expectations of the most radical changes, and, curiously enough, also explain the most modest prediction of the continuation of the present system in an unchanged form. I do not subscribe to these assumptions.

First of all, there is the explicit or implicit assumption that the system has not changed significantly in past decades and that, therefore, either the tensions and contradictions are building up to a danger point or the system has demonstrated the staying power to remain unchanged.

Second, one has the impression of a shared disdain for the quality of Soviet leaders. Either they are regarded as a pack of frightened men fighting a rear-guard battle or as a clique of Mafiosi, "mustachioed petes" confident of their ability to keep the lid on and proceeding in their outdated ways. But in all cases the leaders are seen as men who are unable to learn and to make the necessary adjustments to changing reality.

A third assumption is the equation of the undeniable stability of the Soviet regime with simple rigidity. Proper recognition of the probable depth of that stability would make any prediction of radical transformation doubtful. At the same time the depth of stability in my view provides a reserve of self-confidence which makes incremental changes possible.

Fourth, one finds skepticism that the Soviet leaders and elites and the politically active public can actually believe what they profess to believe. In other words, there is accepted a far-reaching "erosion of ideology" thesis which is based on the equation of ideology with doctrine.

Fifth, the most radical expectations, especially those which anticipate a Soviet transition in the direction of liberal democracy or convergence, remain rooted in the view that the Soviet Union is a social experiment associated with the developmental process, and they share a conviction that socioeconomic development proceeds in orderly stages which result in an inevitable affinity of the political-cultural superstructure at similar levels of development.

Whatever the reasons for the preoccupation with predictions about the Soviet future and their radicalism – and I suppose that fear and hope are the strongest motives here – there are also sound rational elements behind the expectations of change in the Soviet Union. First of all, there is the recognition that the Soviet regime is faced with real tensions and unresolved problems with which it will sooner rather than later be forced to deal. Second, there is the sluggishness and half-heartedness of economic reforms in the Brezhnev era which have left the basic economic process to proceed in old, accustomed ways. Third, there is the slowness of changes in the structural features of the Soviet political system and the great difficulties, to use Thane Gustafson's expression, of imposing new priorities on old structures.[3] Finally, there is a strong feeling, difficult to define but pervasive, that one derives from meetings

[3] Thane Gustafson, *Brezhnev's Reform: Political Implications of the New Soviet Agricultural Policy* (Cambridge: Cambridge University Press, forthcoming).

with Soviets: They all expect significant changes to occur after Brezhnev is gone.

In Part II I focused on succession and therefore on the imminence and significance of change in the Soviet Union. In Part III I stressed stability and paid only secondary attention to the tensions and demands placed on the Soviet regime by the requirements of further development. In this closing segment, I should like to concentrate on just those requirements and the pressures for change which they may generate. Without doubt these domestic issues will constitute in my view the most important content of the disputes, conflicts, and realignments that will accompany the succession. (Foreign-policy issues will also figure prominently, however, if for no other reason than their interconnection with domestic problems.)

While stressing the dominance of gradualism, stability, and continuity, we have also identified a number of issues, problems, and structural characteristics which contain great destabilizing potential. They range from the coming succession and the approaching replacement of the entire core leadership group to the potentially explosive national problem which may be contained in the coming decade but seems insoluble within the existing political framework. The failure to deal successfully with any of these problems, and especially their simultaneous aggravation brought about by or combined with an internal economic crisis or external shock, can become a departure point for a profoundly destabilizing chain reaction within the system

In some areas, the stability of the Soviet system is narrowly based. It over-relies on political controls, administrative organization, and conscious manipulation and interventionism; and it is still based too little on socialization, tradition, and internalized controls. One is reminded of Trevelyan's attempt to account for the discrepancy between the fact that the rise of population in England after 1719 was attributed to developments in industry and agriculture while a similar population increase in Ireland in this period occurred without such economic improvements. The decisive factor was apparently the absence of a potato famine in the eighteenth century: "The potato is the easiest method of supporting life at a very low standard–until a year comes when the crop completely fails."[4]

While the failure of will and effectiveness of political elites seems unlikely in the coming decade, what seems even less likely in the foreseeable future is a transformation of the Soviet political system in a democratic direction through a peaceful, "painless" evolution. The nature of the Soviet political elite, the way in which the Soviet system was established, and the way it is now run argue forcefully against the effectiveness of incremental changes in breaking the vicious circle of elite self-replication, bureaucratization, and autocratic societal control. It may

[4] Quoted in Morris Ginsberg, *Essays in Sociology and Social Philosophy* (Baltimore: Peregrine Books, 1968), p. 153.

well be that only a crisis of major proportions, an open struggle within the leadership and the emergence of a dominant leader, can provide conditions under which an initial push of sufficiently high magnitude can occur to precipitate such a change, and that the stimuli for breaking the circle or reversing its direction must appear simultaneously at various points of the system.

To those who think in terms of a historical process which *has* to transform the Communist societies, the confluence of conditions that may be necessary for such a transformation may seem too restricted and exaggerated. Perhaps, as Gregory Grossman has suggested, we fail to appreciate fully the complicated conjuncture of favorable circumstances necessary for a successful transition of the Soviet system beyond its traditional mold.

I will not engage in the game of grand scenarios because my evaluation of the present Soviet system and of the way it has evolved leads me to believe that changes, however significant, will, if they occur, be evolutionary in character. I shall not predict what these changes may be but will rather concentrate on factors which argue for increased pressures to change the system in the post-Brezhnev era.

The Soviet Union faces many difficult problems as it enters the 1980s. Yet these problems have engaged the Soviet regime in the past. It was able to contain them then, and in all probability it would also be able to contain them in the foreseeable future by *old methods*, were it not for one complex of problems, namely, the new economic challenges. *This one set of problems has many new qualitative dimensions* – and this I want to stress very strongly. I shall limit my discussion to this one subject, the complex of economic problems which confronts the Soviet regime and will affect it increasingly in the 1980s, and the political consequences of these problems. To state my argument as succinctly as possible: The era of extensive Soviet economic development, when high rates of growth were assured through growing increments of labor and capital, is ending; and an already poor situation is aggravated tremendously by an impending energy crisis and by demographic trends.[5]

The shape of the forthcoming crisis of the 1980s is already well discernible at present. In the current five-year plan, 1976–80, the yearly growth of capital investments has been set for 4.5 percent, lower than at any other time in Soviet history. The planned yearly growth of man-hours of labor, 1.4 percent, is also set well below the previous ten years (1966–70 = 2.2 percent, 1971–5 = 1.8 percent). The planned yearly growth of

[5] The following discussion of Soviet economic prospects in the 1980s is based on: Testimony of the DCI Adm. Stansfield Turner before the U.S., Congress, Joint Economic Committee, Subcommittee on Priorities and Economy in Government (96th Cong., 26 June 1979); National Foreign Assessment Center, *Simulations of Soviet Growth Options to 1985*, ER 79-10131, March 1979; *idem, SOVSIM: A Model of Soviet Economy*, ER 79-10001, February 1979; *idem, Soviet Economic Problems and Prospects*, ER 77-10436U, July 1977; *idem, Prospects for Soviet Oil Production*, ER 77-10270, April 1977; *idem, USSR: Long-Term Outlook for Grain Imports*, ER 79-10057, January 1979.

consumption set at 4.0 percent is again 20 to 40 percent below that of the last two five-year plans, and the actual growth of consumption is even lower. The factor productivity growth implied by the plan (2 percent) is not only not supported by past trends, but it is now clear that it is totally out of reach and will either be of the order of zero or even a negative growth.

The overall economic performance in 1979 was probably the worst in all the years of Brezhnev's leadership. The weather seriously impeded agricultural performance. Wet weather in autumn reduced the area sown to winter grains by five million hectares compared to the previous year, and the late arrival of spring combined with widespread flooding in parts of the European USSR delayed spring grain planting. Most recently, periods of hot dry winds damaged both winter and spring grains in important grain-producing regions. As a result, 1979 grain production at 179 million tons was 20 percent below the record grain crop of 237.2 million tons in 1978 and below the average of 218.9 million tons for 1976–8. Because of this shortfall in domestic production, one witnessed a large import demand for Western grain.[6]

The severe winter of 1978–9 nearly brought economic growth to a standstill. Demand for energy increased, while at the same time it was more difficult to produce and distribute energy and other raw materials. The resulting disruptions to industrial production in high-priority investment projects were felt throughout the remainder of the year. Coming on the heels of a very poor performance during October-December 1978, industrial production during January-March 1979 increased by less than 1 percent over the first quarter of 1978 and picked up only slightly during April-May. Production of key commodities – including steel, cement, nonferrous metals, mineral fertilizers, and insecticides – dropped *below* the levels achieved in the first six months of last year. *Average daily oil production during this six-month period fell below that of the preceding six months for the first time in Soviet history.* And it exhibited the lowest increase ever in the first nine-month period of 1979.

The first and cumulative fact of the Soviet economic situation in the 1980s will be a radical decline in its overall growth rate.[7] The projections

---

[6] For the moment the Soviet Union should have little trouble paying for the grain it buys from the West. For the time being the Soviet hard-currency balance of payments is fairly satisfactory. Soviet trade and financial behavior over the past two years have reflected a conservative strategy aimed at paring the growth of both imports and hard currency debt – perhaps in anticipation of the drying-up of oil exports in the early 1980s. Unprecedented earnings from gold and arms sales for hard currency have allowed the Soviet Union to achieve a $600 million current account surplus in 1978; the sharp increases of world prices of gold and oil in 1979 should also help the present Soviet balance.

[7] The question of economic growth in the 1980s is of course a major problem as well for the Western democracies. (More correctly, the question is not so much growth itself as the question of inflationary growth.) Yet when comparing Western and Soviet society in this regard, one should stress the questions raised by Ralf Dahrendorf during the discussion concerning the assumptions and conclusions of the Trilateral Commission's study on the governability of democracy:

by the American government and private analysts of Soviet growth rates for the next decade are well known and meet little challenge in the West. Where differences do exist, they concern the *exact* degree of the economic slowdown.[8] Overall there is every reason to believe that the continued decline in the rate of Soviet economic growth is inevitable through most of the 1980s (to what extent the Soviet leadership agrees with this prognosis will remain in part unclear until the new five-year plan is announced, probably by the end of this or the beginning of next year).[9]

In fact, the American government agencies have most recently lowered their forecasts of Soviet GNP growth over both the short and long term. They now expect Soviet GNP to grow at somewhat less than 3 percent annually over the next few years (down from their earlier estimates of about 4 percent) and then to fall gradually. If oil production declines to ten million barrels per day by 1985, growth in GNP would be perhaps 2 percent in the mid-1980s. On the other hand, a sharper fall in oil production, say to eight million barrels per day in 1985, could well push growth in GNP to less than 1 percent in the mid-1980s.

The underlying causes of the growth slowdown remain: a reduction in the growth rate of the labor force, diminishing returns to a more slowly growing capital stock, and projections of little growth in the efficiency of resources used (that is, factor productivity).[10] In addition, the energy

"Why should it be so that democracy is to some extent dependent on economic growth? Is there anything in the concept of democracy that relates it to economic growth? Is democracy unthinkable without it? Is it actually true that those countries in which economic growth was least effective were also the countries in which democratic institutions were least effective? Could it not be said that it is the one-party socialist states above all which are in trouble without economic growth? Is not the link between the assumption of economic growth and political organization in fact much closer in the communist countries, and is that not one of the reasons why they are worried at a time when, for them, too, economic growth is by no means a certainty? Does not perhaps Mr. Brezhnev have much more reason to worry about the future of economic growth than Mr. Ford?" (Michel J. Crozier, Samuel P. Huntington, and Joji Watunaki, *The Crisis of Democracy* [New York: New York University Press, 1975], p. 189).

[8] A representative nongovernmental study of the prospects for the Soviet economy in the 1980s can be found in Holland Hunter, ed., *The Future of the Soviet Economy 1978–1985* (Boulder, Colo.: Westview Press, 1978).

[9] Concern about the difficulties the Soviets are facing in the next five-year plan and their lowered expectations may be found in two articles published recently by Kosygin (*Planovoe khoziaistvo*, 1979, no. 7 [July], pp. 3–17; and *Kommunist*, 1979, no. 12 [August], pp. 16–29). In both articles Kosygin projects a decrease in capital investments and in the growth of national income. Some further decrease in investments may be feasible in the next five-year plan because the energy difficulties will lower the ratio of exploitation of Soviet industrial capacities, thus providing a slack in usable capital resources. Yet the depletion of Soviet capital resources in the 1985–90 plan, which such a course could bring about, may be very detrimental to further Soviet growth.

[10] There are two basic schools of thought among Western economists regarding the slowdown in Soviet economic growth and predictions for its continuation in the future. The first, shared by most economists, including Bergson, Kaplan, and Moorsteen, explains the slowdown by postulating a gradual decline in the rate of technical progress. The second, a minority view best represented by Martin L.

shortage will mean that the Soviets cannot operate all their plant and equipment at full capacity, which in turn will accelerate a downward trend projected for the 1980s.

The Soviet oil industry may have entered a no-growth stage in 1979, to be followed by steady production declines beginning as early as 1980.[11] Especially significant is the drop in production expected by 1980–1 at the giant Samotlor oil field in West Siberia, which currently accounts for more than half of West Siberian oil production and one-fourth of total Soviet output. Production at Samotlor will probably peak this year, after many years of operating above the maximum efficient recovery rate.

The Soviets themselves are aware of the difficulties ahead. An official government decree of June 1979 called for strict conservation and stepped-up production of other forms of energy.[12] The decree reflects the official and popular fears that the severe fuel shortage of the previous winter might be repeated. A major Soviet newspaper reported that oil production was running 140,000 barrels per day behind schedule in 1979.

Exploitation of smaller fields in West Siberia is lagging behind plan because of transportation bottlenecks, soaring drilling requirements, and the failure of the authorities to provide the necessary equipment and infrastructure (roads, pipelines, electrical power, housing). Even a moderate decline in West Siberian production – which makes up half of total Soviet output – would lead to a sharp drop in national production.

Besides the decline in oil production, the Soviet energy picture in the 1980s will be clouded by shortfalls in the coal and nuclear power industries – thereby limiting the possibilities for inter-fuel substitution for oil. Natural-gas production might provide some relief, but as yet the Soviet investment program reveals no major effort to shift the structure of fuel consumption to gas. Moreover, benefits from increased natural-gas pro-

Weitzman, "Soviet Postwar Economic Growth and Capital-Labor Substitution" (*American Economic Review*, 60, no. 4 [September 1970], 676–92), holds that technological progress remains constant; that the rate of growth declines because the input of capital goods is growing faster than input of labor; and that by increasing continuously the capital-labor ratio, the Soviets are experiencing diminishing returns. Both views anticipate the continued decline in growth.

There is yet a third view, however, held by S. Gomulka ("Soviet Post-War Industrial Growth, Capital-Labor Substitution and Technical Changes: A Re-Examination," paper presented to the International Conference of Slavists, Banff, Alberta, September 1974). He casts doubt on the principal hypotheses of both schools and questions as well their basic forecasts. He predicts a continuous Soviet growth at the rate of 6–7 percent per year. The basic test of all these theses will be, of course, whether Soviet industry continues to slow down or retains its ratio of growth.

[11] Recently Marshall I. Goldman took exception in strong words to the CIA forecast about Soviet oil production (*Washington Post*, 20 August 1979, pp. E1, E2). Like many others who question this forecast, however, he does not provide the specific data on which his optimism is based. Most importantly, he seems to be saying that things are not as bad as the *worst* CIA predictions, but that they are bad enough.

[12] See *Pravda*, 16 June 1979.

duction could be limited by a reduction of Iranian gas exports to the USSR. Construction stopped in autumn 1978 on a second trunkline that was to carry increased quantities of gas to the Soviet Union.

Next, as underscored by the performance in 1979, agriculture ranks with energy as a major economic headache for the Soviet leadership. *As economic growth slows, year-to-year swings in farm output will have a greater impact on annual economic performance.* And fluctuations in agriculture may become more pronounced if weather conditions in the 1980s become more normal, that is, harsher. Although farm production has climbed well above the level of a decade ago, severe shortages of meat and quality foods persist.

Meanwhile, the Soviet labor-supply situation is becoming tighter as adverse demographic trends yield steadily declining increments to the labor force. The natural increase in the working-age population will drop off from 2.3 million in 1978 to about 300,000 per year by the mid-1980s. The regional aspects of the labor problem will be particularly critical. During the next decade, increments to the labor force will come almost exclusively from the less skilled and less mobile Turkic population of Central Asia and the Transcaucasian republics.[13]

[13]The differentiated rate of natural reproduction of the population looked in 1973 as follows (per 1,000 population):

RSFSR	5.9	Uzbekistan	27.3
Ukraine	5.6	Turkmenistan	27.1
Georgia	10.8	Tadzhikistan	28.4
Armenia	16.9	Kirgizia	23.0
Azerbaidzhan	19.0	Moldavia	12.2
Kazakhstan	16.7		

Source: Naselenie SSSR (Moscow: Statistika, 1973), pp. 90–5.

Soviet experts are very conscious of the demographic trends. A recent study of M. B. Tatimov, *Razvitie narodonaseleniia i demograficheskaia politika* (Alma-Ata: Nauka, 1978), makes the following prognosis about the ethnic composition of the Soviet population in the year 2000:

Group	Number (× 1,000,000)	Percentage of total
Slavs	195	65
of which Russians		46
Central Asians	51	17
Peoples of the Caucasus	23	8
Peoples of the Volga	14	5
Peoples of the Baltic	6	2
Peoples of Siberia, the North, and Far East	2	0.7
Others	9	2.3

Thus the critical policy issue will be the geographic location of capital investment. Although all areas require investment, the leadership will have to decide whether to put more investment in Central Asia, where most of the labor growth will occur and whence it will not move easily; in the European Soviet Union, which is short of labor and poor in raw materials, but where investment can be carried out more cheaply by modernizing and expanding existing facilities rather than by building plants from the ground up; or in Siberia, where the infrastructure and industrial facilities needed to exploit energy and other raw materials are sorely lacking, and where operating costs are nearly double those in the Western part of the country.

It is highly probable that the labor and resource pressures will lead to preemption by Central Asia and Siberia of an increasing share of total investment, while the growth of total investment continues to decline. Immediate development of Siberian energy and raw material resources is essential because oil, coal, and gas deposits are being depleted elsewhere. Extracting and processing Siberian resources as well as transporting them to urban-industrial regions in the European USSR is costly. In some instances—such as the long-distance transmission of coal-based electric power—reliance on Siberia is still not technically feasible.

What are the most important political consequences of the Soviet economic dilemmas of the 1980s? As I shall mention later, the repercussions of economic dilemmas may be felt in many areas which can be deemed highly political in nature, but by far the central problem, the key to the entire emergency, has to do with the need to reform the entire system of planning and management. At the same time, one should not minimize the enormous costs and difficulties of such reforms, especially, so to say, when conducted under fire.

The Soviet Union has faced other major emergencies in its history on the economic, social, and political "fronts" and was able to solve them or to coexist with them. Yet the most decisive thing to understand is that the post-Stalin leadership is not used to, nor is the Soviet Union as it exists today prepared to deal with, those kinds of emergencies confronting them in the 1980s. Past problems were concentrated either on one area at a time and/or were responsive to a mass mobilization effort, so to say, to the strategy of a hammerblow. The approaching problems of the 1980s are spread across the board to many vital areas and require sophisticated and both micro- and macro-manipulation, the strategy of a scalpel.

It is virtually certain that Soviet leaders cannot prevent or even considerably weaken the reduction in the rates of economic growth by simply exercising the traditional policy levers under its control. What they are facing is an unusual coincidence of restrictive factors—primarily the special conditions in the demographic and energy fields superimposed on the long-range downward trend brought about by the expansion and maturation of the Soviet economy, which less and less responds to the existing old system of organization and stimulation. The future is catching up with the Soviet Union, but it is doing so in the most unpropitious circumstances, with surprisingly little room for economic maneuverability. Depending on whether one agrees with John Kenneth Galbraith or Milton Friedman, the serious economic problems of the West require either strong, imaginative, interventionist governmental leadership in the redirecting and management of the macro-economic problems and resources; or letting the market economy find its own new balance, unhindered by governmental restrictions, expenditures, and taxation. Yet whatever one's point of view, not many seriously doubt the overall, relatively high efficiency and ability to adjust of the West's autonomous, micro-economic structures. In the Soviet Union the necessity of a strong, imaginative, highly interventionist leadership which will redirect and manage macro-resources in the coming squeeze is a sine qua non of any, even partial, success. But by itself, it will not provide any effective answer to the growing problems. The Achilles heel of the Soviet political economy resides in the micro-structures which are highly inefficient and nonautonomous, and which have no self-generating mechanism of innovation, adjustment, and effectiveness in containing waste and increasing productivity.

It is not the lack of proficient cadres that restrains the effectiveness of Soviet enterprises. Soviet industry employs today three times as many engineers as the United States, but its output is less than two-thirds of the American. Soviet agriculture employs five times as many agronomists, but its productivity is less than one-third of the American. It is the system of planning, incentives, and rewards which discourages innovation, encourages waste, and punishes initiative. The decision to change this micro-system must be taken on the macro-level. Without it, other ameliorative measures can only be effective in small part and will fall into a vacuum of the indifference of those whose efforts are decisive for Soviet growth.

The most important macro-economic decisions which the Soviet leadership will be called to make in the 1980s concern the allocation of resources among investment, consumption, and military expenditures. The leadership must take account of the fact that in the future the increments of GNP available to divide among these three areas will be smaller. The low growth rates envisaged for the mid-1980s could squeeze Soviet resources to the point where something has to give.

Reducing growth in investment below current rates seems difficult in view of vast needs for new, more energy-efficient investment goods throughout the country and the already slow pace of investment (3 percent per year). Reducing growth in consumption would have a negative impact on workers' morale and productivity, just when a boost in both is needed most. Reducing growth in defense spending at a time of leadership transition would be equally difficult since those vying for power will probably be reluctant to press for actions that might alienate the military. In the absence of any reduction in the pace of defense expenditures, however, the burden of slowing economic growth would fall squarely on the consumer, whose standard of living would stagnate after more than a decade of continued improvement.

The reordering of priorities, while very difficult, will not have a major effect on the overall growth rate. One governmental study concludes: "Resource reallocations on the scale of the recent past are not likely solutions to the basic problems underlying future Soviet growth." Yet at the same time, if the Soviets move in the direction that tradition dictates – that is, hitting the consumption and the consumer-goods-producing sector, including agriculture – such reallocation may have more far-reaching, unintended effects than the negative influence on workers' productivity, which would be bad enough.

The growth of Soviet consumption in the Brezhnev era, 1965–80, can be evaluated as constituting 4.6 percent yearly and the growth of per capita consumption as being 3.4 percent yearly. The *baseline* projection for the 1981–5 period envisaged a consumption growth of 2.1 percent and per capita consumption growth of 1.2 percent, that is, a growth already less than half of the preceding fifteen years in total consumption and only a little over one-third in the per capita consumption growth. If further inroads were to be made into these very modest projected figures by reallocation away from consumption, then for all practical purposes the standard of living of the Soviet population would freeze at the present level or might even decline.

It was previously proposed that during the Brezhnev era the Soviet performance in raising the living standard of the population has constituted one of the cornerstones of Soviet stability. It was further suggested that for the first time in Soviet history the leaders themselves in all probability regard the increase in consumption level and the satisfaction of the rising expectations of the population as a condition of sociopolitical stability. Their evaluation may be quite right; and the consequences of a prolonged and significant decline in the growth of consumption or, even worse, a virtual stagnation or drop in the living standards may lead to unpredictable consequences.[14]

[14]This will occur also at a time when there will be a perceptible and perceived decline in social mobility and especially educational mobility. As the accompanying table shows, the gap between those who graduate from general middle schools and those who are admitted to full-time higher education is increasing.

Year	Graduates of general middle schools (× 1,000) (1)	Admissions to full-time higher education (× 1,000) (2)	(2) as % of (1)
1960	709	258	36.4
1965	913	378	41.4
1970	1,968	500	25.4
1975	2,716	594	21.9
1977	3,009	613	20.4

Source: Calculated from *Narodnoe khoziaistvo SSSR v 1977 g.* (Moscow: Statistika, 1978), pp. 490, 501; *Narodnoe khoziaistvo SSSR v 1968 g.* (Moscow: Statistika, 1969), p. 687.

The fear of such consequences either may lead to a more restrictive general political climate or, more forcefully than ever before, may present Soviet leaders with the alternative of raising the question of consumption still higher on their list of priorities and, this time, at a clearer and higher cost to the other priorities, especially military. In any case, the squeeze on the allocation of Soviet growth resources is unlikely to be conducive to the conduct of business as usual and to a sociopolitical climate as supportive of stability as during the Brezhnev era.

The estimates of the burden of Soviet military spending fall generally within the range of 11–14 percent of GNP. More telling is the estimate of the CIA, which, using input-output techniques, evaluated that 1975 military requirements, both direct and indirect, accounted for the following shares of output in major branches of Soviet heavy industry: energy—one-sixth of output; chemicals—one-sixth of output; metallurgy—one-fifth of output; machinery and metal-working—one-third of output.[15] In the coming decade it will become more difficult to maintain the policy of guns and butter which remained effective in the 1960s and 1970s.

The levels of Soviet economic development and achievement in the last decade, despite the slowdown, provide a sufficient base for maintaining a strong strategic and conventional military posture, one that is highly competitive with the present level of Western military expenditures. If Soviet economic growth in the 1980s falls in the upper range of the projection of probable development, then for the foreseeable future the Soviet Union can continue to increase the level of its military expenditures at a ratio similar to that of the last decade without incurring additional major difficulties in its economic programs. (The upper-level rate of projected Soviet growth in the 1980s is of the same magnitude as the rate of increase of its military expenditures in the last decade and the projected increase in the coming decade.) In this case, the new Soviet position of strength in the area of military capabilities will persist in the 1980s even if the Western allies increase their military expenditures.

If the revised downward projection is closer to the mark, however, then the ratio of increase of the 1970s military spending will have to go down in order to preserve the existing balance in the economy. In any case, an increase in military expenditures that is rapid or much above the present levels will be very difficult for Soviet leaders to sustain, more than at any time in the past. Assuming that this proposition is correct, there is for the Soviet side a significant disincentive for an unrestricted arms race, apart from (or rather in addition to) the dangers that such a race would entail for the fate of war and peace between the superpowers.

We should have no illusions on this count. If the Soviet leadership concludes that its basic security is endangered, whether by a more rapid military build-up in the West or by a modernizing China, it will take appropriate measures concerning military expenditures regardless of

[15]National Foreign Assessment Center, *Estimated Soviet Defense Spending in Rubles, 1970–1975*, SR 76-101210, May 1976.

their costs. I am arguing simply that, first, the cost will be much higher, the burden much more painful, than at any time in the post-Stalin era; and, second, that under these circumstances the tendency of the Soviet leaders to respond with an almost automatic, conditioned reflex to the demands and requirements of their military establishment may become much more tempered, and the proposed programs of expansion may be exposed to a much closer and critical scrutiny.

The pressure on resources in the 1980s will create a tension within the Soviet decision-making apparatus which will test the ability developed under Brezhnev to preserve collective leadership at the top, to engage in a successful process of bargaining and compromise solution, and to avoid sharp confrontations. The relatively low level of elite-administrative conflict of the Soviet party-state in the 1970s was predicated on the changes in the Soviet system which occurred in the post-Khrushchev era. A consideration of the changes made in the structure of the Soviet party-state over the last decade, together with the policies pursued by the post-Khrushchev leadership and with the general political mood in the Soviet Union, can support a conclusion that at first glance appears somewhat paradoxical. The establishment of collective leadership and the policies of this leadership in organizational, political, economic, and ideological matters led in the first years to improvement in the power position or in the satisfaction of the group interest of almost all institutional segments of the Soviet political elite, and in the years that followed, did not noticeably undermine their positions. While probably no elite group welcomes all changes or all policies, a rare situation has emerged where the fears of almost all elite groups have been to some extent allayed, and their desires to some extent satisfied. This state of affairs was conditioned also by the rate of growth of the Soviet economy, which made possible the partial satisfaction of expectations of all elite groups. The growth rates of the 1980s and the budgetary constraints which they will bring about will lead to a much less benign political climate and will create conditions for a much sharper competition for allocations among interest groups.

No easy choices are available to any set of Soviet leaders in the 1980s. The resource-allocation dilemmas that exist are likely to prove increasingly intractable from a political as well as economic standpoint. There will be strong conflicting pressures from different elements within the Soviet bureaucracy to increase investment and maintain consumption levels and to keep up allocations to agriculture and to avoid cutbacks in military spending also. Whether the post-Brezhnev leadership will be strong enough to impose a coherent and effective strategy for dealing with these demands is uncertain. What is clear is that in the mid-1980s marginal shifts in resource allocations will become more and more contested as energy and labor shortages take their toll.

The coming unavoidable major shortages in labor increments and the increased importance of these labor increments for the Soviet economy, mentioned before, may exacerbate the ethno-national problem in the

Soviet Union, especially with regard to the areas inhabited by Turkic nations. (This, aside from the general impact of a major Soviet slowdown on inter-nation relations within the USSR.) It is from the nationalities of Middle Asia and in part Transcaucasia that the new Soviet labor force in the mid-1980s will come almost exclusively. This presents the Soviet leadership with a choice: either to "convince" the new labor force to move to European Russia or Siberia or to move a major part of the investment activity to the labor source in Middle Asia.

Mass out-migration of Turkic population to the labor-short areas of the European Soviet Union is not likely, and Soviet authorities have not acted as if they believe that such a policy would be successful. Beyond the considerable cultural barriers inhibiting emigration, there are economic factors – such as the relatively high rural living standards – that strengthen the ties of the Central Asians to their native areas. The second possibility could have two consequences. First, it could create a great deal of dissatisfaction among the European republican nationalities by diverting contested capital resources to non-European national areas (and Siberia). Second, it could create unusual social and cultural stresses of the kind inherent in rapid industrialization and could increase the hostility of the native political-administrative structure to encroachment on their autonomy and to the influx of Russian bureaucrats which would certainly accompany the massive influx of Russian capital.

Soviet allocation decisions are further complicated by the future needs and potential of the East European client states, whose dependence on the Soviet Union for energy and other raw materials is likely to increase in the 1980s. Because of resource constraints within both Eastern Europe and the USSR, Moscow cannot do more to help Eastern Europe without seriously injuring its own economy. To do less for Eastern Europe, however, might well endanger political stability in those countries.

The prospects in the 1980s for the East European Communist countries and especially the central two, Poland and the GDR (but also Czechoslovakia), are, if anything, even less promising than for the Soviet Union. In their case, moreover, due to the continuing unauthenticity of their regimes, economic difficulties have a tendency to translate quickly and directly into dangerous sociopolitical instabilities and turmoil. The exposure of these countries to the necessity of finding needed energy resources outside the Soviet Union in their present, persistent, and likely-to-continue condition of major indebtedness to the West would be a blow to their economic well-being of major and unpredictable proportions. Yet at the same time, drastic reductions in oil exports to Eastern Europe may be the only effective way to contain the potential Soviet domestic damages of energy shortages likely to emerge by 1985.

The Soviet Union is running out of incentives for enticing, rather than compelling, allegiance from its East European allied elites. This allegiance is undermined by mounting evidence of the lack of Soviet economic muscle and by the growing certainty that the Soviet Union is no longer able to make good on its economic commitments. Despite its trouble with the East European empire in the past, the Soviet Union has been basically fortunate in being able to confine the most acute troubles to individual countries and to deal with them separately. The economic squeeze of the 1980s lowers somewhat the chances that this good fortune will last.

The continuing economic slowdown, and especially the oil situation, will force adjustment in Soviet foreign trade policy in the 1980s. Moscow will need imports from the West more than ever before, and the leadership may be forced to abandon its current conservative stance toward trade with the West. The Soviets will continue to require substantial imports of grain, steel products (especially large-diameter pipe for oil and gas pipelines), and a wide range of oil and gas technology. As domestic oil production trails off, oil exports for hard currency are likely to fall as Moscow balances the requirements of Eastern Europe against the growing needs of the Soviet economy. This will limit Moscow's capacity to import grain, steel, and Western machinery and equipment. Maintenance and expansion of Soviet trade with the developed West will thus depend increasingly upon Soviet success in negotiating compensation agreements with Western firms so as to ensure an expansion of exports as well as its willingness and ability to increase markedly Soviet medium- and long-term debt to the West.

Already in the 1970s, a basic leadership decision was taken to turn from an autarchic policy toward a greater Soviet dependence on exchange with the West. This policy provided a background and a concomitant of the switch to detente in Soviet foreign policy. The policy of detente did not bring to the Soviet Union all the economic benefits which it hoped for and envisioned at its inception. At the same time, the policy itself became endangered by the Soviet interpretation of its freedom to undertake military and military-oriented activities in the non-European areas of political competition for influence with the United States. Assuming that the American policy toward the Soviet Union will exhibit both a willingness and ability to resist the Soviet interpretation of what detente permits it to do militarily in the Third World, and a greater willingness and ability to assure real prospects of economic cooperation with the Soviet Union, the pressures for restraint in Soviet foreign policy, especially in seizing marginal targets of opportunity, should be much greater in the coming decade.

Today the pressures and dilemmas which were presented above are already objective facts of Soviet socioeconomic and political life as the economic plan for 1981–5 is being formulated and as the measures directed to the 1990s are approved. They are likely to intensify in the coming years. The Soviet leadership must clearly make some very hard decisions in the near future and then be willing and able to adjust them to the evolving reality of the coming decade. The decisions made soon will determine not so much how far the Soviet economic slowdown will proceed in the next five-year plan – this is almost prejudged – but who in the main will pay for it and, as importantly, what steps can still be taken to reverse the trend and salvage as much as possible by the end of the 1980s.

Just how Soviet leaders decide to react to the compounding domestic problems of the 1980s will depend on four major questions: the degree of the expected slowdown in the next decade, the Soviets' own perception of long-range economic prospects, the degree of maneuverability available to the leaders in dealing with economic problems, and finally, the influence of the succession on their economic policies.

With regard to the first, if all Soviet and Western economists agree that the 1980s will see a slowdown in Soviet economic growth, they differ significantly in their evaluations of the likely extent of that slowdown. Most pessimistic is the projection, put forward primarily by a part of the American intelligence community, that Soviet GNP will virtually stagnate. A more optimistic and in my view more realistic prediction from the same source anticipates a yearly growth of GNP on the order of 1–1.5 percent. The most optimistic Western estimates, largely those of nongovernmental economists, hold open the possibility of a growth rate in the range of 2.5–3 percent annually. Soviet economists with whom I discussed the matter in Moscow inclined toward the latter estimates, with some dissent on the downward side. Differences in the prognosis derive in part from evaluations concerning the Soviet leadership's ability to counter the trend with intelligent and reformist policies. More significantly, they emerge as a result of varying opinions concerning the likely magnitude of energy shortages and the options available for minimizing their impact.

For an economist to forecast the annual growth rates of an enormous economy over long periods of time is of course a risky and inexact enterprise. Certain only is the prediction that rates will decline. For the political analyst, however, it is the degree of decline that forms the most crucial element in estimating sociopolitical consequences. In the case of the Soviet Union, realization of the most pessimistic alternative, stagnation or even a growth rate of 1–1.5 percent, would precipitate a sociopolitical crisis of major proportions. The most optimistic alternative of a 3 percent growth rate, while creating serious problems for the system, would nevertheless maintain conditions permitting Soviet leaders to "muddle through," especially in the first years of the decade. Thus these extreme points of the continuum cannot be overlooked in any analysis of sociopolitical implications of slowdown. In my opinion a median position is a more likely outcome in the next decade, since both the most and least pessimistic alternatives would require for their fulfillment a rare confluence of either the most or least favorable passive and active factors, while a random distribution of those factors would appear a more realistic expectation.

With regard to the second question that bears on the possible or probable reaction of the Soviet leadership in the 1980s, the long-range prospects for the Soviet economy, it is instructive, if extremely difficult, to look beyond the difficulties of the 1980s. Especially important here of course is not the Western forecast but rather how Soviet leaders themselves will view the outlook. The trend for a slowdown of economic growth is a secular one brought about by the limits of Soviet extensive growth. Without a major economic reform to stimulate the intensive factors of production, particularly productivity and technological progress, it will persist not only through the 1980s but in the 1990s as well. Moreover, the impact of the next decade's decline in growth is aggravated seriously by the projected situations in energy supply and population distribution. To what extent will these critical complicating factors persist after the 1980s? With regard to the demographic situation, all signs point to a considerable improvement. If the new labor supply is not likely to return to the peak of the early 1970s, it will rise sharply as compared to the mid-1980s. The energy situation is more complicated and unpredictable. As we well know, the Soviet Union possesses the largest known reserves of oil, but these are located in regions of Siberia and the Far East most difficult to reach, explore, and exploit. Without sizable investments of capital, Western technology, and time the areas cannot be developed, thus a major policy decision is required. Unless that decision for an all-out attack on the energy problem from the supply side is made very soon, the present trend would not be reversed by the late 1980s or early 1990s. If it is made, then the specific difficulties of the 1980s may well be alleviated by the start of the next decade.

In this general situation the Soviet leaders of the 1980s may well make the decision that is least difficult politically. They may decide to "tough it through" the next decade and await better times in the 1990s. This would of course again postpone the basic long-range problem of Soviet development, that of adjusting the managerial-planning instruments of the economy to the requirement of intensive growth. Such a policy could be seen as "muddling through" at a lower level of achievement.

The policy of "muddling through" or "business as usual" depends heavily on the margin of maneuverability available in the 1980s for allocating macro-resources. In the long run it seems quite narrow, for the pursuit simultaneously of the pace of increased military spending, growth of consumption, and increasing overall investment—that is, the policy of the Brezhnev era—cannot be harmoniously reconciled. In the short run the Soviet leadership can hope to preserve military and consumer priorities by cutting overall investment sharply. According to a recent estimate, a reduction by one-half in the growth of investment (which would fall most heavily on the capital-goods industries and the long-range agricultural investments) would permit continuation of the growth of military spending at present levels and a rate of increase in consumption in the range of approximately 1.5 percent per year.[16]

[16]See Joseph Licari and F. Douglas Whitehouse, "Soviet Resource Allocation in the 1980's: Some Speculations," paper presented at the USAF Academy–Rand Conference on the Economics of National Security, 15–18 August 1979.

The strategy of drastic cuts in investment growth in the coming five-year plan is a perfectly feasible solution to the question of how best to maneuver the macro-allocation in conditions of increased stringency. It will permit, for a time at least, both guns and butter. But the operative term here is "for a time." We should look at why in the longer run such a policy cannot provide a solution.

First of all, the decision to cut both investment growth and the proportion of investment in the GNP is predicated to a large extent on the assumption that the energy shortages of the early and mid-1980s will leave underutilized larger industrial capacities than is normal under Soviet conditions and that therefore an effort at their greater utilization will produce industrial growth without additional investments. This kind of procedure is a one-time operation only, however. By the mid-1980s, assuming that Soviet calculations are correct, the reserve of underutilized capacities will have been largely exploited once and for all. The investment starvation of the Soviet economy will then begin to be felt very deeply and this time without the possibility of avoiding difficult macro-allocation decisions.

Second and more important, if ever there was a need in Soviet post-Stalin development for large investments, the time is now. To start with, the energy situation itself cannot be ameliorated without gigantic inputs in the development of Siberia and the Far East. One has to assume that this is clear to any configuration of Soviet leaders and that therefore the investment cuts will be made primarily in other economic sectors. But draconic cuts in other economic sectors will frustrate the immediate needs of technological progress and the necessary renovation of the outmoded Soviet industrial plant. Their effect can only deepen the secular trend of decline in Soviet economic growth and produce yet another delay, costly in the long range, in maximizing the intensive factors of Soviet growth. Such a decision may help immediately to postpone hard choices and avoid far-reaching reforms. It solves nothing, as may become painfully evident by the mid-1980s.

Yet the situation is further complicated and its unpredictability further underscored by the fact that the entire political process by which these decisions will be made will coincide with the most thorough and far-reaching change in the top Soviet leadership group and central elites. The process of succession, the crucial and most unusual combination of characteristics which were discussed in Part II, has for all practical purposes already begun. The departure of the Great Purge generation of leaders is in itself an important turning-point in Soviet *political* history. This circumstance, coinciding as it does with another turning-point in Soviet *economic* history, marks a time of unusual opportunities and openings for change.

The politics of stringency in the 1980s, the making of fundamental decisions, requires not only an imaginative leadership but, especially, a strong leadership. But can a strong leadership emerge from the succession process? As I argued at some length in Part II, the most likely prospect after Brezhnev's departure is the selection of an interim leader who during a short term of two to four years in office will fail to achieve a strong position within the oligarchy and yield to a young leader who will require several years to consolidate his power. In this case the earliest that one *may* have a strong leader is the second half of the 1980s.

Other possibilities do exist, of course. For example, an interim leader chosen from the Brezhnev generation could remain in office longer than we foresee. He may hold strong opinions different from those of his colleagues on the desired course of Soviet policies and he may succeed in allying himself with a younger generation of officials whom he will introduce in large numbers to the central hierarchy. It is not excluded, either, that Brezhnev will be followed directly by a younger leader and the entire pattern of interim succession avoided. In these two cases there could emerge a strong and established leadership team before the mid-1980s. What I wish to stress very strongly here is that I attach great importance to the various alternatives because I consider that only a strong and established leadership can take appropriate advantage of the opportunities and openings for change in the coming decade.

The Soviet system in the 1970s has displayed a high level of stability, continuity, and marginality of change. It is my contention that this stability, continuity, and marginality of change may be seriously shaken in the coming decade. It should be clearly stated that the changes which may be expected in the Soviet Union during the 1980s in all probability will *not* constitute a systemic crisis and will *not* lead to a transformation of the Soviet system of government. Nevertheless, they may make the Soviet Union significantly different from the Soviet Union of the 1970s. Of course I am not at all certain that major changes will take place. What I do project is a significant increase in *pressures for change.*

According to information reaching us from Moscow, in 1979 a new major reform of Soviet economic planning and management was under active discussion in central institutions. A major pronouncement in this respect was published in summer 1979.[17] Speaking with Soviet economists and political scientists, one is struck by the extent to which the need for major reform is recognized and the introduction of major reform is expected. What should be the focal point of such a reform is obviously a matter of dispute and major differences of opinion. As far as one can judge, the reform that is being actively discussed or prepared will attempt to reconcile two basic tendencies which clash in their approach to reform.

[17]In July 1979 the Central Committee of the CPSU and the USSR Council of Ministers adopted an extensive and important resolution, "On the Improvement of Planning and the Strengthening of the Influence of the Economic Mechanism on the Increase in the Effectiveness of Production and the Quality of Labor" (*Pravda*, 29 July 1979). The most noteworthy and new part of this resolution deals with a decision to increase the role of the five-year plans as against the one-year plans. If this decision is really put into effect, it would lead to a decline in day-to-day supervision by planning authorities and increase the flexibility of management.

One tendency is to respond to the new difficulties and demands primarily by a greater centralization and discipline, accompanied by a better flow and processing of information between the micro- and the macro-levels. The second tendency is to switch the center of gravity of everyday economic decision making to the direct producer and intermediate links between the producer and the macro-level, which would require a radical shift in the weight of quantitative and qualitative planning indices, the system of incentives and rewards, and the types of association among planning, supplying, and production units. It would seem that the type of reform that is now being discussed in Moscow would go part way to satisfy both these tendencies, thereby assuring the worst possible results and proving as ineffective in its influence on the qualitative indices of economic performance, which are now decisive, as the other reforms which preceded it.

The Soviet Union has many very talented economists and planners. It has major research institutions well suited to the job of remodeling the system of planning and management. Moreover, virtually everyone, not only among experts but among party and government leaders as well, admits the basic proposition that the system as it exists is able to manage economic growth well only when that growth is based on increased *amounts* of the basic factors of production. It is generally accepted that a change of economic system is required in order to generate growth based on increased *efficiency* per factor unit.

Yet while this truth is basically accepted by all, there enters the crucial set of sub-questions which provoke acrimonious disagreement or simply vacillation and paralysis:

> How far-reaching should these changes be to activate "intensive" factors of growth?
> What should these changes consist of?
> How should the transition from the existing to a new economic mechanism be effected?
> Why should the system directors be convinced that the gains of the reforms will be a fair trade-off for its undesirable political side-effects and its interim high costs?

The question of how far-reaching the reforms should be and of what they should consist is probably the most hotly debated between the centralizers and the supporters of a flexible approach.[18] A large group of

---

[18]It is not at all clear whether even a radical reform that will both change the success indicators and dismantle direct planning will largely solve Soviet problems of management flexibility and innovation *as long as the full employment constraint is present*. And to remove or decisively weaken this constraint in the Soviet-type economy is almost impossible, as the experience of the 1968 reform in Hungary has shown. This skepticism about the effectiveness of even radical reforms is most forcefully expressed by David Granick, *Enterprise Guidance in Eastern Europe: A Comparison of Four Socialist Economies* (Princeton, N.J.: Princeton University Press, 1975). See especially his discussion of the Hungarian reform on p. 316.

Soviet economists and virtually all Western specialists would agree that small-scale tinkering can no longer suffice and that the question "What is to be done?" concerns the change from guidance based on *administrative orders* to that based on *economic parameters*.[19] In describing the turning-point in the scope of the needed reform, a Polish economist writes:

> It seems that such a watershed does exist and turns on the abolition (or retention) of direct planning at plan executants level. It is extremely important to notice that abolition of direct planning at plan executants level means also the abolition of the ratchet principle – planning (and rewarding) from the achieved level – with all its far-reaching negative economic consequences both in the sphere of plan construction (bargaining for low/high input/output plans, falsifying information in the planning process) and in its implementation (keeping "reserves" for use in the next planning period, which means keeping actual enterprise productivity permanently below what its managers *know* to be possible).[20]

I have the distinct feeling, however, that the crux of the matter of the difficulties with the reform has to do with the other two questions: the mechanism of its introduction and the probable political-economic trade-offs.[21] There are three clear interconnected sets of contradictions with regard to these two questions which create a vicious-circle pattern in any serious effort to introduce reforms in the Soviet system.

> The initial period of reform is immensely costly, not unlike investment in a plant before it starts to produce. Disorganization is inevitable, temporary decline in productivity most likely. Reserves are required to carry the economy through this difficult initial stage, but at the same time it is precisely the poor shape of the economy and the taut planning that leave few reserves which induce the leadership to introduce the reform in the first place.

> Only a far-reaching reform has a chance to be effective in the long run and is worth trying, and at the same time a far-reaching reform is the most difficult and costly in the intermediate run. It requires the change of deeply ingrained habits, of ways of doing business which have been inculcated through generations. If the need for thorough reform is not generally recognized, it must be forced through by a strong consistent leadership.

[19]The difference between the two types of planning and management systems is well defined by one Hungarian economist: "The difference between the socialist market model according to plan and the model relying on plan directives can be summed up by saying that the planning of the national economy is kept up but obligatory plan indices are omitted" (Béla Csikós-Nagy, *Socialist Economic Policy* [London: Rutledge, 1973], p. 44).

[20]Janusz G. Zielinski, "On System Remodeling in Poland: A Pragmatic Approach," *Soviet Studies*, 30, no. 1 (January 1978), 6.

[21]For differing views on the mechanism of reforms in Communist societies, see the discussion following Zielinski, *ibid.*, pp. 3–37.

The effective introduction of a far-reaching reform has to be done without hesitation across the board, not in a piecemeal way; but until the effects of such a reform are tested and recognized as effective, hesitation is inevitable and the determination and consistency are lacking.

The usual response to these sets of contradictions, which we know from past Soviet experience and particularly from the flirtation with Libermanism, falls precisely into the self-defeating pattern of a vicious circle. Of all the variants of reform, the leadership selects the one that would cause the least disturbance and would require the least cost and effort, that is to say, a compromise solution. Instead of introducing it across the board and with determination, the leadership wants to try it out on an experimental basis and limited scale. Consequently, the results of the reform are far from conclusive and even disappointing, an outcome which in turn fuels the arguments of opponents who prevent its further implementation. The leadership reverts to traditional ways of doing business and further half-hearted tinkering with the system. *This is the political mechanism which explains the inherent stability of the traditional economic system and the inherent instability of reform efforts in the Soviet Union.* Piecemeal and well-intentioned partial reforms, instead of transforming the traditional economic system, are absorbed and changed by this system.

One should not make the mistake of envisaging that the configuration of forces lined up for or against the reform consists of the macro-leaders being pressed to agree to a reform by the micro-managers. The line of divisions is much more blurred and twisted and runs vertically and zig-zaglike through the political managerial establishment. If anything, the inertia at the bottom and middle levels might be even stronger than at the top. As one author has written, "After 60 years of experience with a Socialist economy run by government agencies . . . , nearly everyone seems to have found ways to turn its shortcomings to individual advantage."[22] In this situation, the macro-level leadership has not merely to agree to a reform to make it a reality, it has to push hard to overcome the resistance of habit and interest if it wants to succeed.

It is still too early to conclude, as does one group of analysts, that

a major economic reform would disturb established balances in both political and economic power. It would be strongly opposed by the state bureaucracy where jobs, careers, and political influence would be at stake, as well as by the party bureaucracy, whose control over economic decision-making and resource allocation would be threatened. Faced with uncertain long-run benefits, probably high short-run costs, and certain strong opposition, a Soviet

[22]Gertrude E. Schroeder, "The Soviet Economy on a Treadmill of 'Reforms,' " in *Soviet Economy in a Time of Change*, papers submitted to U.S., Congress, Joint Economic Committee, 2 vols. (96th Cong., 1st sess., 10 October 1979), vol. 1, p. 313.

leadership of any foreseeable composition would probably opt against taking such risks.[23]

Time is not running out on the Soviet system. The regime still possesses enormous reserves of stability, but adjustments have to be made if the system is to remain effective. Yet if the combination of the economic emergencies facing the Soviet Union in the 1980s together with the openings afforded by the approaching succession of leadership and elites do not yield serious efforts to reform the traditional economic system, then I do not know what may and will. Should actual Soviet growth and energy shortages in the 1980s fall within the range of the most pessimistic projections, the Soviet Union, without the reform and a successful one at that, is condemned not simply to a process of "muddling through" but a process of "muddling down."

[23]National Foreign Assessment Center, *Organization and Management in the Soviet Economy: The Search for Panaceas* (ER 77-10769, December 1977), p. 21.

INDEX

Abakumov, V. S., 35n13
Academy of Social Sciences (AON),
    174n40, 175
Adzhubei, A. I., 74
agriculture
    and foreign affairs, 261
    investment in, 51n14, 153–4
    performance of, 26n50, 287, 290
    see also Soviet Union, economy
Aliev, G. A., 107
All-Union Association of Innovators
    and Rationalizers (VOIR),
    189
Andropov, Iu. V., 72, 90
Apter, David E., 17
Arendt, Hannah, 14
Arkhipov, I. V., 91
armed forces
    and Great Purge, 87, 89
    relations with party, 57
    and succession, 76n7, 91–2
Artem'ev, P. A., 13n15
Avramenko, S. S., 222

Baibakov, N. K., 91
Batitskii, P. F., 223
Belik, P. A., 223
Bell, Daniel, 125
Belonozhko, S. E., 223
Belukha, N. A., 223
Bendix, Reinhard, 204
Beria, L. P., 34n11, 88
Beshchev, B. P. 92
Bogomiakov, G. P., 103n9, 119
Bondarenko, I. A., 121n39, 222
Bracher, Karl Dietrich, 17
Breslauer, George, 166
Brezhnev, L. I.
    background, 90, 120
    political role, 69–71, 73–6
    style of leadership, 70
    see also succession, post-Brezhnev
Brus, Wlodzimierz, 26n47
Brzezinski, Zbigniew, 11, 54, 138, 198,
    250, 276

Bugaev, B. P., 222
Bukharin, N. I., 40n21
Bulgakov, A. A., 222
Bulganin, N. A., 88
Butoma, B. E., 92

censorship, 146n7
Central Committee (Party), 32, 87,
    215n12
Central Committee Secretariat (Party),
    33, 72, 81–5, 89, 94, 219
centralization
    as means of Stalinist rule, 21, 32
    and nationality problem, 209–10
Chalidze, Valery, 158–9
change, political, see political change
Character and Social Structure, 196
Chernenko, K. U., 73, 76
Chernyi, A. K., 223
Clark, Robert P., 133
Cohen, Stephen F., 48n2
collective farm councils, 189
collective leadership, 32–3, 70–3,
    97n1, 295
    see also stability, Soviet; succes-
    sion, post-Brezhnev
collectivization, 39
Cominform, 244
Communist Party
    history: collectivization, 39–40;
    and peasantry, 40; and secret
    police, 41; and Stalinism, 14–17,
    20–2
    membership: apparat, 178–9,
    181n52, 219; composition of,
    15n26, 81n1, 178–81, 187–92;
    cooptation, 94, 117–20, 180;
    education, 116n27, 173–5; role
    of generalists, 120–3; see also
    elite, provincial; political par-
    ticipation
    political-administrative role: im-
    portance of apparat, 16, 117–18,
    202–5; and legitimacy, 192; as
    mass party, 190–2; multiplicity

of roles, 201–5; as political broker, 17, 50, 176, 204–5; professionalization, 172–6; propaganda, 175; as a public administration, 202–3; under Stalin, 15–17
Communist Party Congresses
Seventeenth ("Congress of Victors"), 40, 87
Eighteenth, 87
Nineteenth, 26, 75
Twentieth, 103n11
Twenty-first, 103n12
Twenty-second, 103n11
Twenty-third, 270n2
Twenty-fourth, 179n49, 256n5, 270n2
Twenty-fifth, 75, 91, 149, 244n10, 270n2
Connor, Walter D., 160
Conquest, Robert, 60n30, 265n17
Constitution of 1977, 76n9, 210–11
cooptation, *see* Communist Party, membership
Council of Ministers, 60n31, 72, 84–5, 89, 91, 110, 220
see also elite, central
Cult of the Leader, 23, 29–32, 50
culture, political, *see* political culture

Dahrendorf, Ralf, 287n7
Dallin, Alexander and George Breslauer, 11
Darkness at Noon, 42
decision making
post-Stalin, 57–8, 147–8
role of party, 204–5
role of private secretariat, 35
role of professionals, 169, 171–2
and succession, 66
under Stalin, 16–22, 32–8
Dekanozov, V. G., 14n20
delovitost' (businesslike behavior), 55, 238
Demichev, P. N., 74, 76n5, 90
Demidenko, V. P., 222
detente, *see* Soviet Union, international relations entries
Deutscher, Isaac, 23, 48n4
"Dnepropetrovsk group," 73, 78n15
Dolgikh, V. I., 77, 108
druzhinniki, 189, 192
Dubček, Alexander, 107
Dubin, R., 121n41
Duncan, Hugh D., 58
Dunham, Vera, 45n31

Eastern Europe
compared to Soviet Union, 162n25, 195–6, 208, 296
regime legitimacy, 135n17, 193
see also Soviet Union, international relations – Eastern Europe
Economic Problems of Socialism in the USSR, 26, 147n9
egalitarianism, 23–4, 178
Egorov, M. V., 92
Eisenstadt, S. N., 17n31, 52, 201
elite
attitudes, 51, 55–8, 105–6, 195–6
desire for security, 45–6, 56, 95
importance of background differences, 101–4, 112–14, 123–4, 178–9
mobility: under Brezhnev, 91–4, 109, 121–4, 178–81; under Stalin, 44–5, 88–91
nationality: degree of political independence, 213–22; improved training of, 215–18; saturation, 214, 220–2
recruitment, 172–3, 178–81
stability of, 61, 72–4, 86, 91–5
see also political generations; succession
elite, central
age of, 81–5
career patterns, 88–91, 94, 109–10
composition of, 71–2, 81–4
generational representation, 107–8, 111
role of nationalities, 110, 219–20; Ukrainians, 222–4
second-echelon, 108–9
turnover of, 91–4
elite, provincial
age distribution, 85–7, 112n21
generational profile, 109–11
party first secretaries: career patterns, 110, 117–24, 173–5; education, 115–16, 174–5; political status, 110, 117–20; social origins, 115, 179n49; and succession, 110, 122; turnover, 92–4
role in succession, 85–6, 108–12
emigration, 142n1, 193
Erickson, John, 92n7
Etzioni, Amitai, 120n37, 121n41, 139, 143n4, 200
expectations, popular, *see* popular expectations

Fainsod, Merle, 11, 49
federalism, *see* nationality problem

Feldmesser, Robert A., 24n43, 57n24
Field, G. Lowell, 129
Fleron, Frederic, 117

Garthoff, Raymond L., 249, 279n16
Garwin, Richard L., 249n15
generations, political, *see* political
    generations
Georgev, A. V., 222
Gerschenkron, Alexander, 136–7
Gerth, Hans and C. Wright Mills, 41,
    196
Goldman, Marshall I., 289n11
Gomulka, S., 288n10
Gorbachev, M. S., 108
Gouldner, Alvin, 27n51, 39
Great Purge, *see* purges
Grechko, A. A., 72, 76n7, 92, 223
Griffiths, Franklyn, 278
Grishin, V. V., 72, 77, 78n12, 90
Gromyko, A. A., 72, 76, 90, 237n5
Grossman, Gregory, 51n14, 286
Gustafson, Thane, 284

Hayward, Max, 265n17
"high politics," 166–7
    see also political participation
Higher Party School (VPSh), 115–16,
    174–5
Hitler, Adolph, 29, 31, 37
Hodnett, Grey, 118n34
Hoffmann, Stanley, 236
Hollander, Paul, 164–5
Holloway, David, 169n37
Horelick, Arnold, 251n21
Hough, Jerry F., 7, 60n30, 102, 203
Huntington, Samuel P., 106n17, 133,
    142–3, 185
    views on stability, 137–9, 165n30
Hurwitz, Leon, 130, 132

ideology
    current nature of, 176, 208
    erosion of, 284
    and nationalities, 210
    under Stalin, 23, 26, 31
Ignat'ev, S. D., 35n13
Ilichev, L. F., 74
Inkeles, Alex and Raymond Bauer, 193
institutionalization, *see* professional-
    ization; stability, Soviet
intelligentsia, 158, 167n34

Kahan, Arcadius, 154
Kapitonov, I. V., 77
Katushev, K. F., 94, 108
Kazanets, I. P., 222

Keller, Suzanne, 98
Khomulo, M. G., 224
Khrushchev, N. S., 55n22, 57n24, 71–2,
    77, 83, 88, 107, 165–6, 203, 238
Kirichenko, A. I., 89
Kirilenko, A. P., 71, 76–7, 90, 94,
    114n25, 120n38
Kirov, S. N., 40
Kissinger, Henry, 247
Kliuev, V. G., 119, 222
Kolkowicz, Roman, 57
Komsomol, 167, 188–9
Konotop, V. I., 222
Kosygin, A. N., 71, 76, 90, 94
Kovalenko, A. V., 222
Kozhevnikov, V. M., 92
Kozlov, F. R., 75
Krakhmalev, M. K., 222
Kruglov, S. N., 35n13
Kulakov, F. D., 76–7, 94
Kulikov, V. G., 76n7
Kulish, V. M., 245n11
Kunaev, D. A., 72, 90, 215n12
Kuperman, Yuri, 167n34
Kuron, Jacek, 283n2
Kuznetsov, A. A., 34n11
Kuznetsov, N. G., 89
Kuznetsov, V. V., 76, 91

Laird, Robbin, 177
LaPalombara, Joseph, 136n18
Lashchenko, P. N., 224
legitimacy
    centrality of elite dimension, 185,
        194–6
    elements of, 183–6, 194, 205
    importance of, 183–4
    modes of integration, 196–205
    nationality problem, 207–12
    role of ideology, 200, 208
    role of nationalism, 198–200
    role of party, 15, 191–2
    see also political participation; sta-
        bility, Soviet
Legvold, Robert, 249, 267
Lenin, V. I., 26, 38, 238
Leonhard, Wolfgang, 124n42
Lesechko, M. A., 222
Libermanism, 304
Lindblom, Charles, 147
Lipset, Seymour M., 91n6
Litvinov, Pavel, 146
Liventsov, V. A., 223
"low politics," 166–7
    see also political participation
Lowenthal, Richard, 105, 185, 230, 242
    views on stability, 138–9

Malenkov, G. M., 33n8, 75, 88
Malyshev, V. A., 89
Masherov, P. M. 91
Maslennikov, I. I., 13n15
Mazurov, K. T., 71, 94, 220n16
Mekhlis, L. Z., 17
mestnichestvo (localism), 210
Meyer, Alfred, 12
Mieczkowski, Bogdan, 137n23
military-industrial complex, 85, 199–
    200, 251
Mills, C. Wright, 41
mnogoskladnost' (multi-
    dimensionality), 271–2
    see also Soviet Union, international
    relations – Third World
mobility
    and education, 172–5, 180
    of elites, 178–82
    generational, 178–9
    and ideology, 180
    and legitimacy, 181–2
    and nationality problem, 216–17,
        219–20
    sources of, 179–82
    see also stability, Soviet
mobilization, 39n20, 56, 143, 186
Modzelewski, Karol, 283n2
Molotov, V. M., 33n8
Moore, Barrington Jr., 12n12, 48n4
Moore, Clement H., 137–8, 185
Moskalenko, K. S., 223

nationalism
    functions of, 56, 198–9
    and nationality problems, 208, 211
    and Stalinism, 15, 23
nationality problem
    economic competition among re-
        publics, 218–19
    and ethnic identity, 208–11
    and federalism, 207, 210–11, 218
    and indigenous elites, 213–20
    and labor supply, 290, 295–6
    management of, 211–22
    and regional autonomy, 209–10,
        213, 219–24
    and regional economic differentia-
        tion, 155, 221, 291
    role of Great Russians, 121n40, 208,
        211n8, 213–20, 222n17
    role of second secretaries, 214–15,
        217–18
    role of Ukrainians, 222–4
    significance of, 207–12, 220
    Soviet views of, 208
    see also stability, Soviet

Naumenko, Iu. A., 223
Neporozhnii, P. S., 222
Nikonov, V. P. 121n40
Novikov, I. T., 91, 222
Novikov, V. N., 91
Novoselov, E. S., 222

Odom, William E., 57
Orgburo, 33
Ossowski, Stanislaw, 23n40

participation, political, *see* political
    participation
partorg, 17, 173
Party Control Commission, 40
Pavlovskii, I. G., 92, 223
peasantry, 24, 151, 156
Pel'she, A. Ia., 90, 92
pererastanie (growing over), 272
    see also Soviet Union, international
    relations – Third World
Pervukhin, M. G., 88
Peterson, Edward N., 36
Pipes, Richard, 248n14, 249n15
Podgornyi, N. V., 71, 73, 215n12,
    220n16, 222
Poliakov, V. I., 74
Polianskii, D. S., 73, 94, 222
police, *see* secret police
Politburo
    age distribution, 81–4, 89, 94
    under Brezhnev, 71–2, 76, 94,
        215n12
    under Stalin, 33
    see also elite, central
political change
    and economy, 286–99
    and nationality problem, 207, 212
    obstacles to, 58–9, 95–6, 292,
        303–5
    post-Stalin, 50–2
    pressures for, 285–98
    prospects, 75, 284–6, 298–305
    sources of, 53–4
    and stability, 91n6, 285–6
    and succession, 66, 78, 97
political culture
    contemporary, 192–4
    continuities with past, 146, 160,
        198
    Stalinist, 22–3
political generation
    concept of, 98–101
    as experiential groups, 101–3, 106,
        112–13
    importance of background differ-
        ences, 112–24

political generation (*cont.*)
   self-replication, 100–1
   and succession, 61, 78, 124
   see also elite; succession
political generations
   Great Purge, 106n17, 107–8, 114–15
   late Stalinist, 102, 107–8, 114–15,
      123
   post-Stalin: as political group, 106;
      profile of, 102–7, 115–24; repre-
      sentation in elite, 108–12; role
      in succession, 102, 112; *see also*
      elite
   wartime, 102, 108, 114, 123
political participation
   apolitization under Brezhnev, 166–
      7
   Communist Party, 187–8, 190–2
   forms of, 186–9, 192
   and institutionalization, 165, 177
   and legitimacy, 186, 193–4
   post-Stalin, 165–6
   and professionalization, 167–73
   significance of, 189–92
   see also stability, Soviet
Ponomarev, B. N., 76n5, 90, 110
popular expectations
   changes in, 158–60
   management of, 154–8, 164–5
   materialization, 160
   nationality problem, 213
   sources of, 161–4
   see also stability, Soviet
Poskrebyshev, A. N., 35
Presidium (Party), *see* Politburo
Presidium of the Council of Ministers,
      72, 81–3, 91, 94, 110
   see also elite, central
Presidium of the Supreme Soviet, 81–2
   see also elite, central
Priezhev, N. S., 190n14
problem of nationality, *see* nationality
      problem
professionalization
   and administration, 172–3
   and education, 157, 167–8, 174–5
   and institutionalization, 167,
      169n37, 177
   nationalities, 215–16
   and party, 173–6
   patterns of promotion, 172–3
   professional press, 168n35, 169–70
   role of associations, 168
   role of professionals, 51, 57–8, 167–
      9, 171–2
   scientific-technical revolution, 176–
      7

see also political participation
purges
   administrative impact, 60, 88–9
   Doctors' Plot, 34n11, 46n32
   effect on elite, 34, 40–1, 59–61, 86–
      90
   Leningrad Affair, 34n11
   and military, 87, 89
   Mingrelian Affair, 46n32
   and party, 15n26, 39–41
   scope of, 59–60

Rashidov, Sh., 90
"revolution from above," 9, 26
Riabov, Ia. P., 78, 108
Rigby, T. H., 81n1, 105, 119n35, 125
Rodionov, M. I., 34n11
Rogger, Hans, 198
Romanov, A. V., 77, 78n12, 108, 110
Rothschild, Joseph, 207
Rozanova, Maria V., 193
Rudenko, R. A., 222
Rush, Myron, 75n3
russification, 210–11, 224

Saburov, M. Z., 88
Sakharov Manifesto, 169n37
sblizhenie (rapprochement), 208
   see also nationality problem
Schapiro, Leonard, 36
scientific management of society
      (NUO), 176–7
scientific organization of labor (NOT),
      189
scientific-technical revolution (NTR),
      176–7
secret police
   control of, 35–6
   and nationality problem, 214
   and party, 41
   reorganization of, 35–6, 51
   scope of activities under Stalin, 12–
      14
   special departments, 35
   and stability, 145
   see also terror
sharashka, 13
Shchelokov, N. A., 73, 222
Shcherbakov, A. S., 17, 88
Shcherbina, B. E., 222
Shcherbitskii, V. V., 72, 77, 90, 215n12,
      224n18
Shelepin, A. N., 70, 73–4, 94
Shelest, P. Y., 72, 74
Short Biography of Stalin, 30
*Short Course of the History of the All-
      Union Communist Party (B)*, 30

Shulman, Marshall, 237n4
Shvernik, N. M., 92
Skachkov, S. A., 222
Slavskii, E. P., 222
sliianie (harmonious blending), 208
    see also nationality problem
Smirnov, L. V., 76n7
socialization, 15
Sokolov, I. Z., 217n13
Solomentsev, M. S., 76n6, 77
Solov'ev, Vladimir, 199
Solzhenitsyn, Aleksandr, 54n21,
    167n34
Sosnov, I. D., 92
Soviet Union
    economy: agriculture, 153–4, 156,
        287, 290; assessment of Tenth
        Five-Year Plan (1976–80), 286–
        7; balance of payments, 287n6,
        297; consumption, 149–53,
        261n11, 293; demographic fac-
        tors, 290, 296, 299; as a determi-
        nant of foreign policy, 235, 252,
        260–2, 296–7; distribution of
        production in non-Russian re-
        publics, 155, 221; energy prob-
        lems, 287–90, 297; full employ-
        ment, 302n18; GNP growth
        rates, 288, 292, 298; housing,
        151–2; impact of slowdown,
        287–8, 291, 294–300; impor-
        tance of Siberia, 289, 291; in-
        vestment, 153, 261n11, 288n9,
        291–2, 300; labor supply,
        164n28, 290–1, 295–6; loca-
        tional problems, 291; military
        expenditures, 255n1, 294–5; per-
        formance in 1979, 287; priori-
        ties, 152–3, 161n24, 292–5; pro-
        ductivity, 292; prospects for re-
        form, 58–9, 286, 297–305; role
        of planning as restraint, 292,
        301n17, 303; second market,
        164n27; technological lag, 149,
        262n14; welfare services, 151–2
    international relations – China:
        military aspects, 250; prospects,
        235; role of U.S., 237, 243–4;
        status of, 243–4
    international relations – Eastern
        Europe: commitment to empire,
        251; economic aspects, 261,
        296–7; Rumania, 243n7, 263;
        Yugoslavia, 243, 263
    international relations – foreign pol-
        icy: determinants of, 199, 229–30,
        233–5, 238–9, 250–2, 257–9, 265;

    exploitation of conflict, 264–5;
        foreign trade, 262, 297; future pro-
        spects, 277–9; nature of alliances,
        263, 267, 269; purposes of, 243,
        248–50, 256–7, 269; significance
        of Afghanistan invasion, 1–2, 229,
        234, 275; and stability, 157; "ten-
        dencies," 278–9; world commun-
        ism, 235, 244, 259
    international relations – sources of
        power: budgetary limitations,
        294; consequences for detente,
        266; consequent political oppor-
        tunities, 263–7; cultural, 260;
        economic, 260–2; ideology, 259;
        military, 242, 245, 250–2, 264–
        5; political, 262–3
    international relations – Soviet per-
        ceptions: China, 243–4, 250;
        components of power, 245, 267;
        detente, 243, 248, 250, 276; in-
        ternational correlation of forces,
        242–6; international economic
        order, 274–6; national security,
        251; peaceful coexistence, 243;
        prospects for socialism, 243; role
        of military power, 255–8, 265;
        strategic parity and deterrence,
        245–50, 256–7; Third World,
        269–78
    international relations – Third
        World: arms deliveries to, 264;
        and detente, 275; economic rela-
        tions, 262, 273–5; historical
        changes, 270–2; lessons of Chile,
        272–3; prospects, 277–8; Soviet
        intentions, 265, 269–70; Soviet
        Union as model, 259
    international relations – U.S.: and
        arms race, 246–50; and decline
        of bipolarity, 233–8; prospects,
        279; role of detente, 252–3, 276,
        297; role of Europe, 233n1; and
        SALT II, 247; Soviet perceptions
        of, 230, 237–9, 246, 249–50,
        255–6, 271n3
    political system: as bureaucracy, 52–
        3; capacity for reform, 55–6, 58–
        9; essential values of, 200–1; as
        "mature" authoritarianism, 205;
        as oligarchy, 71–3, 75; post-Sta-
        linist, 49–61; scenarios for future,
        283–6; totalitarian model, 10n4,
        145; under Brezhnev, 61, 69–75,
        144, 177; as welfare state, 52; *see
        also* political change; stability,
        Soviet; succession

Soviets, local, 164, 189
stability
  of communist regimes, 135–9
  comparative, 129–35
  and modernization, 133, 165
  and regime survival and effective-
    ness, 133–4
  role of organization, 147–8
  Soviet: challenges to, 144–5; con-
    trast with industrial democra-
    cies, 142–3, 147–8; and dissent,
    53, 141–2, 158–60, 165, 185;
    elite responsiveness, 51n13,
    154–65, 295; and institutional-
    ization, 165–77; and level of
    popular expectations, 146–7,
    149, 158–65; and mobility, 177–
    82; nationality problems, 212,
    216–17, 220; prospects, 293,
    301–5; regulation of conflict,
    56–8, 125–6; role of elites, 145–
    6, 194–6; sources of, 138–42,
    145–8, 165, 183; and system
    performance, 148–58
  see also political change
Stalin, I. V.
  base of support, 32, 38
  and Cult of Leader, 29–31
  as dictator, 8, 36
  perception of U.S., 238
  and political elite, 33–5, 38
  political roles, 9–10
  and private secretariat, 35
  style of leadership, 32–8
Stalinism
  and Bolshevism, 31, 48
  and Communist Party, 14–17
  compared to Nazism, 10n5, 31, 36–7
  core values, 18, 22–7, 37
  elite support, 34, 38–45
  evolution of, 9–10, 38–41, 47–8
  methods of governance, 15–22, 37
  and nationalism, 15, 23
  organizational features, 16–18
  and people's democracies, 26n47
  as personal dictatorship, 27, 29–37
  and political terror, 10–14, 38–41
  social structure of, 23–4
  strategy of economic development,
    18–22, 200
standard of living, 149–56, 161–2
  see also stability, Soviet
State-Party Control Commission, 40
Stinchcombe, Arthur L., 41, 101, 194,
  204
Strachey, John, 43
Strzyzewski, Tomasz, 146n7

succession
  defined, 65
  importance of, 65–9
  post-Brezhnev: contingencies, 74,
    76–9, 96, 125–6, 300–1; economic
    context, 97, 292, 300; lack of prep-
    aration, 75–7; political context,
    70–9, 83–4, 94–8, 122, 125–6;
    probable political impact, 66–70,
    74, 78, 96–7, 109, 124, 224; role of
    nationalities, 110, 224; scope of,
    68, 84, 124; see also political
    change; stability
  post-Khrushchev, 67, 72–5, 95
  post-Stalin, 67
  as source of legitimacy, 184–5
  see also political generations
Suslov, M. A., 71, 76–7, 90, 94

terror
  characteristics of, 10–14, 38–9,
    42n28
  and collectivization, 39
  evolution of, 38–42, 51
  functions of, 12–14, 27
  Lenin's views, 38
The Crisis of Democracy, 143
Tikhonov, N. A., 76, 94, 222
Timoshenko, S. K., 89
Titov, V. N., 222
Tolubko, V. F., 223
trade unions, 189
Tretiak, I. M., 223
Trilateral Commission, 143
Trotsky, L. D., 42n27
Tsvigun, S. U., 222
Tucker, Robert C., 48n4, 105

Ustinov, D. F., 76–7, 90, 92
utopianism, 54–5, 196

Vlasov, A. V., 121n40
Voloshin, I. M., 223
Voznesenskii, N. A., 34n11, 88
Vyshinskii, A. Ia., 11

Weber, Max, 98, 195
Wolfe, Bertram, 49
Workers' and Peasants' Inspection
  (RKI), 40

Yezhov, N. I., 40
Yunak, I. Kh., 223

Zaslavskii, D. I., 11
Zaveniagin, A. P., 13n18
Zhdanov, A. A., 23n39, 33n8, 34n11, 88
Zhukov, G. A., 222
Zhukov, G. K., 89
Zinov'ev, Alexander, 166n32